# Hunter-Gatherer Foraging Strategies

## Ethnographic and Archeological Analyses

Edited by

### Bruce Winterhalder and
### Eric Alden Smith

The University of Chicago Press
Chicago and London

BRUCE WINTERHALDER is assistant professor of anthropology at
the University of North Carolina at Chapel Hill.

ERIC A. SMITH is assistant professor of anthropology at the
University of Washington, Seattle.

The University of Chicago Press, Chicago 60637
The University of Chicago Press, Ltd., London

© 1981 by the University of Chicago
All rights reserved.  Published 1981
Printed in the United States of America
88 87 86 85 84 83 82 81    54321

*Library of Congress Cataloging in Publication Data*

Main entry under title:

Hunter-gatherer foraging strategies.

   (Prehistoric archeology and ecology)
   Bibliography: p.
   Includes index.
   1.  Hunting and gathering societies--Addresses,
essays, lectures.  2.  Indians of North America--
Hunting--Addresses, essays, lectures.  3.  Human
ecology--Addresses, essays, lectures.  I.  Winterhalder,
Bruce.  II.  Smith, Eric Alden.  III.  Title: Foraging
strategies: ethnographic and archaeological analyses.
IV.  Series.
GN388.H86      304.2       81-1366
ISBN 0-226-90216-1         AACR2
ISBN 0-226-90218-8 (pbk.)

Hunter-Gatherer Foraging Strategies

PREHISTORIC ARCHEOLOGY AND ECOLOGY

A Series Edited by Karl W. Butzer and Leslie G. Freeman

# Contents

Series Editors' Foreword      vii

Preface      ix

1. New Perspectives on Hunter-Gatherer Socioecology      1
   Eric Alden Smith and Bruce Winterhalder

2. Optimal Foraging Strategies and Hunter-Gatherer Research in Anthropology: Theory and Models      13
   Bruce Winterhalder

3. The Application of Optimal Foraging Theory to the Analysis of Hunter-Gatherer Group Size      36
   Eric Alden Smith

4. Foraging Strategies in the Boreal Forest: An Analysis of Cree Hunting and Gathering      66
   Bruce Winterhalder

5. Alyawara Plant Use and Optimal Foraging Theory      99
   James F. O'Connell and Kristen Hawkes

6. The Relationship between Northern Athapaskan Settlement Patterns and Resource Distribution: An Application of Horn's Model      126
   Sheri Heffley

7. Archeological Applications of Optimal Foraging Theory: Harvest Strategies of Aleut Hunter-Gatherers      148
   David R. Yesner

8. Optimal Foraging in a Nonmarginal Environment: A Model of Prehistoric Subsistence Strategies in Michigan      171
   Arthur S. Keene

9. The Effects of Information Networks in Hunter-Gatherer Societies      194
   James A. Moore

10. Overview: Optimal Foraging Analysis in Human Ecology      218
    William H. Durham

References                                    233
List of Contributors                          263
Index                                         265

# Series Editors' Foreword

This volume on hunter-gatherer foraging behavior is the third book in the Prehistoric Archeology and Ecology series to deal with theoretical research frontiers, following directly upon Keeley's study of lithic microwear and Behrensmeyer and Hill's symposium on taphonomy. Most of the contributions were originally prepared for a special session, organized by Winterhalder and Smith in late 1978, that one of us (K.W.B.) was privileged to attend. Under the title of hunter-gatherer socioecology, this symposium brought together an exciting range of theoretical, ethnographic, and archeological concepts and applications that had obvious potential for interpretative modeling of evolutionary ecology and the subsistence behavior of prehistoric hunter-gatherers. With our encouragement, Winterhalder and Smith then persuaded most of their colleagues to expand their papers into formal manuscripts. This collaboration centered on a group of innovative young professionals, who have managed to convey their enthusiasm in a coherent and constructive volume that remains low-keyed and nonpolemic. William Durham, who served as discussant at the original symposium, developed his thoughtful evaluation into the concluding chapter.

The individual chapters blend theory with "case studies" in ethnography and archeology, employing specific tests, applications, or inductive exemplifications. The basic strategy is to view hunter-gatherer subsistence, past and present, on its own merits--against a background of ecological theory, microeconomics, and evolutionary biology. The emphasis is not on mean energy flows, but on dynamic interactions and the evaluation of potential strategies in regard to resource concentration, predictability, breadth, time spent, and net energy intake. The groundwork to such an approach had already been laid by ecologists and explored by several archeologists, but this volume makes a quantum jump by systematically interrelating behavioral adaptations, social organization, and environmental space.

It is indeed true that wider application of optimal foraging theory will require types of data not now routinely generated in research on human ecology, ethnographic or prehistoric. But perhaps the primary importance of this approach is that it provides an objective theoretical baseline by which lack of fit can be evaluated and thus better explained. In fact, it will probably not be possible in the near future to gather the hard data from early prehistoric sites that would permit us to "test" models against detailed reconstructions of resource utilization and environmental mosaics. Nevertheless, the authors collectively illustrate the value of such models for a proper perspective on human ecology, as well as showing how they can be used to identify critical research problems for the future.

Karl W. Butzer

Leslie G. Freeman

# Preface

In November 1978 we organized and chaired a symposium on hunter-gatherer socioecology, held at the seventy-seventh annual meeting of the American Anthropological Association (Los Angeles). Several of the papers presented at that symposium form the basis for chapters in this volume. Other chapters were solicited specifically for the book.

The theme of the volume is the relevance of optimal foraging theory--a set of models and explanatory propositions developed originally in evolutionary ecology--to the analysis of human foraging behavior. The emphasis is on systematic explication of the theory and on empirical evaluation of its anthropological utility. We believe that optimal foraging theory has the potential to contribute a great deal to ecological anthropology and to hunter-gatherer studies, and that this potential is illuminated by the work described here.

Although evolutionary ecology covers a variety of topics, the present volume is restricted to the analysis of foraging behavior in hunter-gatherer societies. The focus is deliberate. The ecological theory of foraging strategies is fairly well developed. A cluster of models dealing with various aspects of foraging behavior is available, and most have been subjected to at least preliminary empirical examination. In addition, the topic speaks directly to long-standing interests in anthropology. Many of the phenomena analyzed in the present work (e.g., group size, spatial organization, resource choice, information exchange) historically have interested anthropologists and human ecologists. These subjects, however, have rarely been related to general evolutionary ecology theory.

Another reason for focusing on human foraging behavior is the availability of data. Useful (especially quantitative) data on human foraging are by no means abundant, but they are more common than those on a topic such as life history strategies. Anthropological interest in optimal foraging theory has been developing for several years, and now includes field research explicitly guided by this theory. Attempts to test such a theory solely with data gathered for unrelated purposes can be frustrating because they often produce plausible but less than convincing analyses.

If foraging theory and human ecology data seem ready for this kind of research, it is also true that human foragers provide an excellent subject for socioecological analysis. Hunter-gatherers exhibit a fairly strong degree of interaction with their local environment (as opposed to a regional or global economy), and a limited inclination to modify that environment. These tendencies toward local ecological equilibrium and isolation have probably been exaggerated, but it is evident that analysis of the relations between local resource parameters and social behavior is more feasible and direct with foragers than with many other human populations.  Further, the subsistence patterns of human foragers are fairly analogous to those of other species and are thus more easily studied with ecological models. The generalized nature of optimal foraging theory (chapters 2 and 3, below) usually allows attention to the unique features of human foraging behavior, although human information flow differs from that in other species in ways that can strongly affect interpretation of the theory (cf. chapters 3 and 9, below).

Finally, the very diversity of hunter-gatherer societies, and their wide range of environmental settings, encourage the application of socioecological theory by providing abundant material for comparative hypothesis testing.  In assembling the present collection we have sought a balance between ethnographic and archeological studies, and between presentation of general theory and analysis of specific cases.  There are some omissions of coverage.  These are due largely to the nascent state of this type of research.  In particular, we regret the absence of a chapter treating problems in hominid evolution from the perspective of foraging theory.

Many people have assisted and encouraged us in the process of editing this book.  We are grateful to each.  In particular, we would like to thank Karl W. Butzer and George Armelagos.  Don Grayson and Richard Nelson provided help at several critical points.  The University Research Council (University of North Carolina at Chapel Hill) provided funds for assistance with final proofreading of the camera copy and for preparation of an index. Teresa Smith and Laura Oaks worked with great ability and timeliness on these tasks.  Our spouses, Sara DeGraff and Carol Poliak, supported and in many instances guided our efforts. Finally, we wish to dedicate this volume to R. Brooke Thomas, who over the years has provided an example and inspiration to us both.

Bruce Winterhalder
Eric Alden Smith

# 1

# New Perspectives on Hunter-Gatherer Socioecology

Eric Alden Smith and Bruce Winterhalder

## Introduction

Hunter-gatherer lifestyles have characterized most of hominid history.  The fact that humans evolved in the context of foraging economies is widely recognized, but its implications are only slowly being uncovered.  The broad qualities shared by foraging populations have had a profound influence on the evolution of hominid morphologies, behavioral capacities, and social formations.  As a result, analysis of hunter-gatherer behavior should play a prominent role in the understanding humans assemble about themselves, and particularly in the development of anthropological knowledge.

The goal of this volume is to provide explicit discussions of an innovative perspective on human foraging behavior.  The various chapters express differing viewpoints and cover diverse topics, but exhibit substantial theoretical unity.  In particular, the separate analyses have in common an attention to modeling, an emphasis on hypothesis testing, and a socioecological approach to the subject of hunter-gatherer behavior.

Socioecology is concerned with the application of ecological theory to the analysis of social behavior (Crook 1970b).  To this end, it focuses on the contribution of ecological adaptation processes to the variability observed in foraging or social behavior.  Socioecology relies on sets of theoretically related models which produce fairly explicit hypotheses.  The models are built on optimization assumptions drawn from contemporary evolutionary ecology (Pianka 1978).  The intent is to develop middle-level generalizations about human foraging societies, generalizations that are nonobvious, robust, and capable of being empirically validated.

Throughout the volume, the stress is on adapting, rather than simply adopting, models and approaches developed in evolutionary ecology.  We believe that the studies included here constitute a vigorous demonstration of the possibilities for socioecological analysis of human foraging strategies.  Later sections of this chapter (and chapter 2) provide further discussion of socioecological theory and method, and an introduction to the specific applications described in subsequent chapters.  We will now briefly outline the anthropological context of this work, and discuss how this approach may help to advance ecological anthropology in general, and hunter-gatherer studies in particular.

## Cultural Ecology:  Problems with Functionalism and Empiricism

Attempts by anthropologists to analyze human behavior as ecologically adaptive have had an erratic history (Anderson 1973; Baker 1962; Hatch 1973; Helm 1962; Rappaport 1971a).

Early twentieth-century anthropologists in the United States adopted particularist and historical research approaches (Damas 1969a; Harris 1968; Netting 1971:1-4). Led by Franz
Boas and his students, these anthropologists cultivated an atmosphere of "theoretical aus-
terity" (Hatch 1973:224). They rejected broad materialist or ecological explanations, at
least partly because these approaches were associated with determinism and ethnocentrism.
There were attempts in anthropology to correlate large-scale distribution of cultural patterns with regional features of geography (see Damas 1969a; Helm 1962), work led by Mason
(1905), Wissler (1926), and Kroeber (1939). But while documenting correlation, these anthropologists avoided ecological generalization (Damas 1969a:1; Helm 1962:630; Netting 1971:3).
Instead, they adopted the position of "environmental possibilism"--the view that environment places broad constraining boundaries on sociocultural phenomena, but has little influence on the features that develop within those boundaries.

Dissatisfaction with the particularist orientation produced more general theoretical
approaches to many anthropological subjects during the 1930s and 1940s (Netting 1971:3-4).
One major orientation was functionalism. Functionalism focuses on the role that recurrent
social activities play in maintaining the social structures and viability of the community
(Radcliffe-Brown 1935 1956:180-81). The theory cautiously cites an analogy with the function of structural aspects of living organisms. A second approach, the materialist or
ecological orientation, developed principally in the work of Steward (1955; Steward and
Murphy 1977; Helms 1978; Murphy 1977). Steward sought systematic ways of studying the relationship between sociocultural life and the environment. He emphasized the intervening
variables--technology, material culture, and economic relationships--linking particular aspects of sociocultural life to the local ecology. Thus his analyses avoided the superficial
results of deterministic theories, which linked culture directly to habitat on broad geographic scales, as well as the general poverty of the possibilist approach. Steward paid
careful attention to unique aspects of local habitats, to the distributions of plants and
animals, and to comparative studies of the adaptive histories of local groups, technologies,
and economies. Many of his ideas grew from detailed ethnographic studies of hunter-
gatherers (Steward 1938).

This brief history contributes two points to an understanding of contemporary cultural
ecology (or ecological anthropology). First, Steward's work established that the materialist or cultural ecology perspective could help to explain sociocultural features of human
groups. Although the specifics of his method have been questioned (Vayda and Rappaport
1968), Steward's work chartered ecological anthropology and established its empirical tradition (Helm 1962:638-39). The second point is the pervasive influence of functionalism on
cultural ecology. Practitioners of this subject are consistent in recognizing the functionalist underpinnings of their approach (Netting 1971:4; Damas 1969a:9; Helm 1962:631-32).
Environmental features are used as independent variables in the construction of adaptive or
functional rationales for behavior. Biological adaption concepts or analogies provide the
criteria for the analysis of behavior in an environmental context. Although Vayda and
Rappaport (1968; see also Vayda and McCay 1975) reject the "materialism" of Harris (1968)
and the "cultural ecology" of Steward (1955), their own formulation--"ecological anthropology"--retains a functionalist core (see Rappaport 1971a:243).

Many of the methodological shortcomings of human ecology can be traced to its heritage
of empiricism and functionalism. Internal anthropological critiques have focused on the
latter, stating that cultural ecology is no more than old functionalism revitalized by association with biological concepts (Friedman 1974; Hallpike 1973; Jorgensen 1972; Orans

1975; cf. Rappaport 1977). Some of the problems of functionalism thus continue to dismay the proponents and arm the foes of this approach. These include descriptive research and a strong bias toward inductive argument; normative, case-unique analyses; after-the-fact construction of explanations; a bias toward equilibrium or homeostatic models; and the use of nonrefutable hypotheses. The cultural ecology approach can verge on circularity: extant behaviors are adaptive because they exist in adapted populations. Few criteria have been developed for assessing the degree to which behaviors are adaptive, or perhaps nonadaptive or maladaptive, and almost no attempt is made to examine alternative hypotheses as a basis for judging the adaptiveness of observed behaviors (Alland and McCay 1973:150-51; Alland 1975:65-66). The insights generated by this approach are numerous, but the method leaves some doubts about the behavior-environment articulations identified, and about the reasons given for them. Are the adaptive causes hypothesized only correlations? If causes link the variables, are they the ones identified?

There is no simple way to get around the problems associated with functionalism. Recent fieldwork in cultural ecology has avoided some of them by focusing on a measurable and common attribute of human and nonhuman biotic communities: energy flow. The field studies of Rappaport (1968 1971b), Thomas (1973), Kemp (1971), and Nietschmann (1973) all consider the energy-provisioning aspects of adaptation. In these studies generalizations about adaptations are given definite operational content through the measurement of energy production, consumption, and expenditure (Jamison and Friedman 1974; Montgomery 1978). The results can be compared over a wide range of human communities and evolutionary situations.

## Hunter-Gatherer Studies

### Ethnographic Research

Hunter-gatherer studies reflect the disciplinary history of cultural ecology, some of its problems, and the recent attention to questions of energy flow. Empirical studies of contemporary hunter-gatherers have flourished in the last two decades, strongly influenced by ecological adaptation concepts. The intensive research on San (Bushmen) peoples is well known (Lee 1972a 1979; Lee and DeVore 1976; Marshall 1965; Silberbauer 1972; Wiessner 1977), but foragers in the Arctic and subarctic of North America have also been studied in depth (e.g., Anders 1967; Berkes 1977; Binford 1978; Foote 1968; Foote and Williamson 1966; Freeman 1971 1976; Feit 1973; Kemp 1971, Jarvenpa 1977; Nelson 1969 1973; NHRC 1976; Rogers 1963; Usher 1971). Foraging populations with mixed subsistence systems living in parts of Amazonia (e.g., Siskind 1973; Hames 1979; Vickers 1976), Africa (e.g., Marks 1976 1977b), and Asia (e.g., Gardner 1972; Peterson 1978; Williams 1974) have received attention as well. For the most part these studies adopt ecosystem or energy flow concepts to show how the behavior functions in the particular habitat within which it occurs.

There have been several attempts to construct a general model of band society, timeless and placeless (Service 1962; Williams 1974; Jochim 1976; King 1975). However, these formulations have often been achieved at the expense of ignoring or explaining away diversity. Variability is ascribed to abnormal conditions, extreme or marginal environments, acculturation, or some other factor (Martin 1974). Divergent positions have been taken on issues such as the degree of patrilocality, territoriality, group cohesion, or adherence to formal marriage rules to be expected of "normal," "average," "pristine," or "ideal" hunter-gatherers. For example, the patrilocal-territorial band model of Radcliffe-Brown (1930) and Service (1962) has recently given way to the bilateral, fluid membership model of Lee (1972a). Although these two positions differ, they share the assumption that the hunter-gatherer adaptation is a uniform one. The possibility that diverse behavioral forms characterize hunter-gatherer societies and that *the range of variation* is the correct subject for explanation is generally unrecognized in these typological approaches.

The variability among different hunter-gatherer societies should not be surprising. Populations lumped together by this designation have been drawn from a large number of geographical areas, cultural traditions, and temporal periods, and they have inhabited every environment yet colonized by human beings. Variation within individual societies, or even within local populations of foragers, is equally prevalent, although masked by the common anthropological habit of reporting field research in normative terms (Pelto and Pelto 1975).

General models of hunter-gatherer social organization and behavior are increasingly at odds with evidence of variation among foraging societies (Martin 1974). We thus face an unappealing choice: either to achieve generalizations that fail to explain much of the observed variation, or to give up the task of constructing general models and deal only with specific societies or regions. The first option is normative: diversity is explained away. The second option is particularist: diversity is accounted for in the aggregate but is not explained in a theoretically cohesive fashion.

The shifting anthropological views of hunter-gatherer society illustrate the continuing dominance of typological formulations. The previously accepted view of hunter-gatherer life as nasty, short, and brutish has given way to a new orthodoxy--expounded in the current crop of anthropology textbooks--that foraging represents the original affluent society (Sahlins 1972; Lee 1968). Lee's research on the !Kung San, demonstrating that in this foraging society a relatively small amount of foraging time secured ample food resources, played a major part in fostering the idea of hunter-gatherer affluence (Lee 1968 1969). Lee's analysis was based on a sample quite limited in size and duration, and his ethnographic fieldwork was with only one society. In light of this, the nearly complete reversal in anthropological orthodoxy that followed must have explanations more complex and subtle than Lee's empirical refutation of the earlier view. Not least is the persistent desire to make hunter-gatherers exclusively one thing or another, rather than capable of a range of life styles.

Recent ethnological research has employed statistical summaries to generate typological portraits which ostensibly take account of the diversity of foraging societies. Lee's (1968) statistical review of ethnographic information suggested that the relative affluence of hunter-gatherers was due to their primary reliance on plant foods. At least one "revisionist" interpretation has also used Murdock's *Ethnographic Atlas* (1967) and statistical summaries to question Lee's conclusions, along with other generalities about this form of subsistence (Ember 1978). Martin (1974) has used the same data to raise questions about the usefulness of *any* typological characterization of hunter-gatherer adaptations or lifeways.

In our view the value of typological characterizations or statistical summaries of ethnographic data is quite limited. None of the statistical analyses cited considers the severe problems in sampling methodology associated with the analysis of phylogenetically or historically related taxa or sociocultural groups (see Clutton-Brock and Harvey 1977: 1-8; Naroll 1970). Normative portraits can serve little enduring analytical purpose when-- to our mind--the important questions are ones of ecological causation, diversity, and change. Ember (1978:447) recognizes this in a statement concordant with the goals of a socioecological approach: "We need to discover what predicts variation among recent hunter-gatherers. And then, using archeological indicators, we need to discover the past prevalence of those predictors and their presumed effects."

Along, then, with the difficulties raised by functionalism, we sense a dichotomy in
hunter-gatherer studies between detailed empirical analyses which document variation and
highly generalized models which by their nature must ignore it.  The gap between these endeavors stymies the advance of both.

Archeological Research

Although we are outsiders to the subdiscipline, it is our impression that ecological
approaches in archeology share parts of this twofold dilemma:  (1) Can unsatisfactory aspects of functionalist arguments be mitigated?  (2) Is there a heuristically attractive
approach or perspective which avoids the dichotomizing effects of detailed study and highly
general models?

Exciting recent advances in ethnoarcheology (R. Gould 1978; Binford 1978; Yellen 1977)
and in experimental archeology (Tringham 1978) focus on analyzing how the archeological
record is generated by human behavior, and how it is subsequently modified in its deposi-
tional environment.  Deductive methods applied in this work enhance ability to infer behavior from artifacts and context, but usually with emphasis on how behavior causes the record
rather than on what causes the behavior itself.  This latter question, in our belief, is
largely ecological.  And here archeologists are bound by (and sometimes recreate on their
own) the problematic aspects of ethnographic and ethnological studies of hunter-gatherers.
It is not surprising then that archeologists and paleontologists are unsatisfied with the
interpretive guidance offered by ethnography (Wobst 1978; Schiffer 1975:836-37; Plog 1975:
220-21; Jolly 1973:14) or even cultural ecology (Butzer 1975:108-9 1978a).  The general
state of ecological research in archeology is not well developed (cf. Hardesty 1980; Jochim
1979).

Ethnographic analogs used in archeology unavoidably share limitations of the cultural
ecology approach.  In addition, highly generalized systems models of forager behavior sometimes represent a case of ecological "leapfrogging," to use Tringham's (1978) piquant term.
Fundamental assumptions about ecological relationships are not tested.  Two cases will illustrate.  Williams's (1974:4-17) model of band society incorporates the assumption that
hunter-gatherers are always territorial.  In contrast, Dyson-Hudson and Smith (1978) use
ethnographic evidence and evolutionary ecology models to show that the development of territoriality is contingent on specifiable environmental attributes, which may or may not be
characteristic of particular hunter-gatherer habitats.  In a second instance, Jochim (1976)
has produced an elaborate and intuitively appealing systems model of settlement pattern and
foraging behavior.  His model incorporates optimal foraging concepts and predictions at an
early stage.  In an ethnographic evaluation of the same model, Winterhalder (1977) found
that the relationships are commonly different from those assumed.  For instance, Jochim
assumed that search costs increase with mobility of the prey species.  In fact, the Cree-
Ojibwa hunters he cites often locate animals by tracks, and hence their search time costs
decrease with the mobility of the prey species.

In each of these two cases an untenable assumption about specific socioecological relationships compromised the broader results of the procedure.  Testing of middle-level
socioecological hypotheses is a complementary and indispensible part of such systems-
modeling efforts (Thomas, Winterhalder, and McRae 1979).

Prehistoric archeologists are creating detailed reconstructions of hunter-gatherer
diet and behavior in space and time (Isaac 1976a,b; Walker, et al. 1978).  Paleoecological
studies are generating information about the environmental context of these people with
equal ingenuity and detail (Livingstone 1975; Butzer 1977 1978b).  But there is an essential

socioecological link needed to unite these endeavors:  the detailed and systematic study
of the relationship between behavioral variability and environmental variability (cf.
Wilmsen 1973).  Evolutionary ecology models, ethnographically and archeologically confirmed,
should assist in generating reliable predictions about behaviors not recoverable from or
self-evident in the archeological record.  They should also direct attention to new types
of data, and assist in their interpretation.

In effect, then, we are proposing that socioecological research complements recent
trends in archeological method, and provides a vital framework for analysis of prehistoric
hunter-gatherer ecology.  Heuristic qualities of the approach make ethnographic and archeological study directly relevant to one another.  This should be evident in the mix of
studies that constitute this volume.

## Socioecology as a Field of Inquiry

### History and Scope

The contributions in this volume share a socioecological perspective on human foraging.
Socioecology is not a unified body of theory so much as a topical orientation:  the ecological analysis of social behavior.  Crook (1970b) defines socioecology as "the comparative
study of social structure in relation to ecology," and stresses the focus on "correlations
between social organization and contrasts in ecology."  In biology, socioecology has drawn
on extensive field research and on theory from evolutionary ecology.  To a lesser extent
it has been influenced by evolutionary genetics and classical ethology.

Several other syntheses of evolutionary and ecological theory concerned with animal
behavior have been proposed.  The currently most prominent one has been christened sociobiology (Wilson 1975).  Contemporary sociobiology differs from the present studies, and
from socioecology in general, in its emphasis on the genetics of social interactions in
Mendelian populations.  Some versions give attention to ecology (e.g., Clutton-Brock and
Harvey 1978a), but human applications in particular suffer from an undue emphasis on puta-
tive genetic determinants of behavior (Smith 1979a; Washburn 1978; S. J. Gould 1978).  The
current confusion about the nature of sociobiology and its relationship to other areas of
inquiry requires us to make a disclaimer here that would otherwise be obvious: evolutionary
ecology models and optimization assumptions need not assume genetic causation of behavioral
variation.

Evolutionary ecology had its origins about two decades ago in the work of MacArthur
(1960 1961 1965; see Fretwell 1975), Hutchinson (1959 1965 1975 1978), and other population
ecologists.  This approach marks a self-conscious attempt to make ecology more theoretically
rigorous.  As a consequence it approaches ecological problems with a deductive orientation;
emphasizes mathematical modeling; is often applied to behavioral aspects of ecology; and is
guided always by the basic principles of natural selection.  Brown (1963 1964), Crook
(1965), Orians (1961 1969), and others initiated fieldwork evaluating the concepts and
testing the hypotheses of evolutionary ecology, using models developed by such theorists
as MacArthur (1972) and Levins (1968).  This research, both theoretical and empirical, has
continued and expanded.  Several recent books give excellent overviews of this field (Pianka
1978; Emlen 1973; Cody and Diamond 1975; May 1976; Krebs and Davies 1978).

In contrast to evolutionary genetics, evolutionary ecology is well suited to analysis
of the behavioral variability that is characteristic of hominids.  Emlen (1979; see also
Blurton Jones 1976; Mayr 1974:656) makes it clear that ecological models are of much greater
relevance to behavioral research on vertebrates (especially primates) than are genetic ones,
although the literature on the implications of human sociobiology has proceeded otherwise

(Smith 1979a). Evolutionary ecology combines the deductive features of selection theory and optimization concepts with the operational utility of quantifiable cost-benefit measures (see Winterhalder, chapter 2, below). It does not assume genetic causation of behavioral variability, only a capacity for adaptive decision making. Finally, it emphasizes behavioral plasticity and environmental variability, features crucial to the study of human adaptation.

The third research area, ethology, has recently shifted from phylogenetic studies of stereotypic and species-specific behavior (e.g., Lorenz 1950) to studies assessing the ecological and adaptive significance of the behavior of individuals as members of social groups (Callan 1970; Crook 1970a:xxiii-xxiv 1970b; Orians 1971:513-14). This change was encouraged by the primate field studies following World War II, which indicated that much social behavior was flexible, maintained by learning and tradition in complex groups, and closely related to features of the surrounding habitat (Crook 1970a:xxv 1970b; Clutton-Brock 1974; Eisenberg, et al. 1972; Jay 1968; Jolly 1972; Kummer 1971; Tuttle 1975). This work, and research on mammalian and avian social behavior (e.g., Bertram 1978; Caraco and Wolf 1975; Crook, et al. 1976; Emlen and Oring 1977; Geist and Walther 1974; Krebs 1973; Kruuk 1975), have demonstrated that ecological variables--the spatiotemporal distribution of food, predators, and potential mates and competitors--strongly affect the behavior patterns of species ranging from butterflies to baboons. The influences often operate in ways successfully predicted by optimality models (see reviews in Krebs and Davies 1978; Clutton-Brock and Harvey 1978b; Pyke, Pulliam, and Charnov 1977).

Advantages for Ecological Anthropology

The approach and subject matter of evolutionary ecology and socioecology have specific advantages for anthropological research with respect to difficulties cited earlier.

*Functionalist shortcomings.* Functionalism as practiced in anthropology suffers mainly from ambiguity in its postulates and assumptions. It pays little attention to the formulation of models, the development of realistic alternative hypotheses, or the provision of operational methods for testing hypotheses. These areas are strengths of evolutionary ecology models (see Maynard Smith 1978). Both functionalism and evolutionary ecology assume some kind of goal and optimization, but the latter makes these explicit aspects of the research methodology and considers quite specific topics (e.g., diet breadth). Evolutionary ecology compels detailed attention to the nature of the deductive argument and the testing procedures. Furthermore, it places the optimization assumption within neo-Darwinian theory, and, as a consequence, it generates sets of hypotheses about specific topics that are coherently related to one another and to evolutionary theory in general.

*Middle-level hypotheses.* Demonstrated diversity in foraging societies has left us skeptical about the validity or usefulness of general models of band society. At the same time, pursuit of the scientific goals of ecological anthropology requires that empirical studies not eschew the evaluation of theory. A research strategy emphasizing middle-level theory would seem to be the solution (see Thomas, Winterhalder, and McRae 1979). Middle-level models can be formulated with attention both to diversity and to generalizing goals. They can be applied in analysis of the detailed and varying nature of adaptive behavior without abandoning attempts to reach broader understanding of the process involved in producing that behavior.

Some vital socioecological questions have been little studied owing to the gap between descriptive ethnography or archeology and general models. These include: What resources in an environment should a forager use?  Should the diet be broad or narrow?  How should it change with fluctuations in resource abundance?  If the environment is heterogenous, what parts of the mosaic should be harvested?  How should a forager move among the patches being used?  In what kinds of environment should we expect to find various systems of spatial organization such as territoriality, home ranges, or nomadic behavior?  When should settlement systems be dispersed, and when should they be aggregated?  How does ecological adaptation contribute to the size or composition of foraging groups?  What is the relative importance of energy versus nutrients in foraging decisions?  How does risk affect foraging behavior?  These questions (and others that could be asked) imply that it is possible to specify aspects of foraging behavior based on costs and benefits associated with various alternatives.  We believe that these are all questions amenable to socioecological analysis.

Lacking generalized ecological approaches to such middle-level questions, and faced with the great diversity of hunter-gatherer behaviors, anthropologists have developed few systematic concepts of what constitutes the *effective environment* of a forager--the variables of an ecosystem which the forager or foraging group adapts to or influences.  We know little about how foraging decisions are adjusted to recurrent and nonrecurrent environmental variability to build up patterns or strategies of adaptive responses.  Reconstruction of hominid history, and understanding of foraging adaptations as well as of shifts to alternative subsistence systems, are limited by this deficiency.  The studies in this volume suggest one route to answering these questions.

In effect we are after a set of theoretically coherent but individually simple and topically limited insights.  What, for instance, is the relationship between the population density of a prey species and the likelihood of its being included in an efficient forager's diet?  This type of query is preferable to "What did group X eat?" and to "What is the ecological nature of band society?" because it promises a kind of insight which spans both questions.

*Variability.*  Variation in hunter-gatherer socioecology should be celebrated--as a fact, and as a central preoccupation of theory and explanation.  Generalizations can still be developed and evaluated through the use of models and hypotheses that are comparative and that explicitly allow one to incorporate variance in environmental and behavioral parameters.  Socioecology has these qualities (see Winterhalder, chapter 2, below).  It is not an overstatement to say that variability--its origin, its fate under selection, and its relationship to adaption--is the central concern of evolutionary theory (Lewontin 1974a), a prerequisite to and a fundamental quality of evolutionary change and adaptation.

There is a second reason that ecological anthropologists and prehistorians should make the relationship between behavioral and environmental variability a preeminent concern.  Human behavior is the product of the interaction of jointly interdependent factors--on short- and long-term time scales.  The respective influence of these must be demonstrated through comparative analysis of the contribution each makes to behavioral *variance*.  Without a focus on variability the relative influences of interacting causes cannot be discerned (see Haldane 1936 1947; Hebb 1953; and Lewontin 1974b, for discussion of the analogous problems in developmental and behavioral genetics).

*Mutual relevance to ethnography and prehistory.*  Finally, socioecological analysis is equally at home in ethnographic or prehistoric study.  While the kinds of data available from contemporary or prehistoric studies are different, they are complementary.  Ethnographic study provides direct access to detailed information on socioecological parameters and behavior; prehistoric archeology is limited in this respect but expands the temporal and spatial information to evolutionarily appropriate scales. This gives the two types of study a joint relevance and a mutual need of each other (Terrell and Fagan 1975). We believe that this is demonstrated in the chapters in this volume. As anthropologists we find that kind of interaction a worthwhile result.

## The Studies

The combination of a socioecology subject matter and an evolutionary ecology approach or methodology gives the studies contained here their unique qualities. The optimal foraging models used are derived primarily from evolutionary ecology; complementary economic theory plays a more limited role. Evolutionary genetics scarcely figures, except as background to the predominant focus on individual advantage and in the attempt by the authors of several of the studies to specify how specific cost-benefit functions may ultimately be related to fitness.

The individual studies can be categorized by four attributes: the research problem (e.g., group size or diet choice); the theoretical source (e.g., optimal foraging theory or economic optimization theory); the cost-benefit currency employed (e.g., energy, time, nutrients, or risk); and the modeling techniques (e.g., graphical analysis or linear programming). As such, they exemplify possible combinations of topics and analytic procedures, but only hint at the potential flexibility of socioecology as a research tool.

In chapter 2, Winterhalder summarizes the general framework of optimal foraging theory. He outlines the assumptions and logical format of this research approach, and describes models dealing with optimal patch choice, prey choice, and time allocation. The chapter notes analytic decisions faced by an anthropologist using this theory, and identifies models and hypotheses that are particularly appropriate for anthropological applications. Winterhalder also considers the areas in which significant amounts of empirical information are required to apply foraging strategy models reliably. The chapter considers how this theory can be adapted for research on human behavior. Similar topics have been addressed by Pulliam, writing on the application of optimal foraging theory to humans (1978), and more generally to species in which learning is the basis for strategic adaptive choices (1981).

In chapter 3, Smith reviews evolutionary and ecological theories of group formation and focuses on the diverse, foraging-related determinants of group size. Smith proposes a four-level scheme of group organization in human foragers (foraging, resource-sharing, information-sharing, and coresident groups). The theoretical discussion considers sets of hypotheses relating size variation at each group level to variation in resource harvesting conditions. Smith then tests one of these hypotheses with data on contemporary Eskimo (Inuit) foraging. The hypothesis proposes that foraging group size in this society varies among alternative hunt types so as to maximize the net energy captured per individual per unit foraging time. The test results are positive but indicate that simple models sometimes have to be modified to accommodate the complexities of human foraging behavior. This process itself can provoke insights about human adaptive strategies.

In chapter 4, Winterhalder uses three optimal foraging models to analyze contemporary Cree hunting behavior as a response to resource characteristics of the boreal forest. Detailed description of resource qualities in this patchy environment is combined with quantitative measures of Cree foraging efficiency. Optimal diet and patch choice models, plus Charnov's (1976a) marginal value theorem, are used to predict prey choice, patch utilization, and patterns of time allocation within patches. Historical trends in diet breadth are analyzed, and are shown to be congruent with those predicted on the basis of changing search-time/pursuit-time ratios. Winterhalder notes that ethnographic testing can determine which models are reliable in those circumstances where supporting information is incomplete.

The fifth chapter, by O'Connell and Hawkes, analyzes the foraging behavior of the Alyawara, people living in the central desert of Australia. The study centers on the gathering of plant resources. An energy currency and models of optimal diet and patch choice are applied to explain changes in the exploitation of native vegetable foods, especially seeds, and lizards. Although the models and hypotheses used here are similar to those analyzed by Winterhalder in chapter 4, confirmation and results are reached by a somewhat different approach. In particular, O'Connell and Hawkes make detailed comparisons of within-trip foraging decisions based mainly on the energy costs of harvesting and preparing various species. In doing so they not only confirm the appropriate hypotheses, but highlight the important role that "pursuit and handling" costs have in foraging decisions. Further, although the evidence is limited, hypotheses based on the patch choice model seem to be both more appropriate and more accurate in this environment and population than Smith (chapter 3) or Winterhalder (chapter 4) found in the Arctic and boreal forest, respectively. O'Connell and Hawkes use the results of their analysis to offer tentative explanations for geographic variation in resource use among Australian natives, and for the pattern of prehistoric colonization of Australia.

In chapter 6 Heffley employs a model, first proposed by Horn (1968), to account for the diversity of sociospatial arrangements exhibited by three northern Athapaskan societies. Horn's model is concerned with the adaptive advantage of different forms of social spacing in relation to the predictability and dispersion of key prey species; it predicts maximum aggregation of the foraging population when resources are unpredictable and concentrated, and dispersal when resources are predictable and evenly spaced. Heffley's argument, then, takes Athapaskan prey choices as given, and asks how hunters should disperse or aggregate in order to minimize the time or distance involved in locating these prey. The role of information exchange and food storage is also explored, and related to resource characteristics and variation in coresident group sizes. Heffley's work is a preliminary application of the model (following Wilmsen's [1973] suggestion) to group sizes and settlement patterns, using a comparative (cross-cultural) approach.

In chapter 7 Yesner presents an analysis of Aleut foraging which combines archeological information with an optimal foraging approach. Yesner takes an indirect route to confirmation of an optimal prey choice hypothesis. He observes that those species within the optimal diet breadth (determined by a systematic interaction of resource pursuit and handling times with abundances) should be harvested in proportion to their natural density. Using a careful reconstruction of prey densities in the Aleut ecosystem, and data on the prehistoric diet of the Aleuts, he is able to show that in most instances this is the case. His approach to the confirmation of diet breadth models is well suited to data that are archeologically recoverable. A set of secondary hypotheses is examined to refine the original optimization hypothesis.

The relative merits of an energy/time analysis versus a more complete consideration of hunter-gatherer nutrient and nonfood needs are addressed by Keene (chapter 8). The optimization problem analyzed concerns prey choice by prehistoric temperate forest foragers in the Late Archaic period. Keene shows how foraging strategy models can play an important role in the reconstruction of prehistoric economies in cases where archeological preservation is poor. He predicts an optimal diet for the study population using linear programming

analysis--a tool developed originally by economists but recently employed in several foraging strategy studies (Altmann and Wagner 1978; Pulliam 1975; Belovsky 1978; Reidhead 1976;
Glander, 1981). Keene's analysis highlights how predictions generated by energy efficiency
models may differ from those produced by more complex nutrient models. It also raises the
issue of the modeler's dilemma--how to achieve a balance among realism, precision, and
generality (see Winterhalder, chapter 2, below). In foraging populations relying substantially on vegetable foods, analytical techniques which are capable of simultaneously evaluating the role of multiple nutrient factors are likely to be crucial. Keene's use of linear
programming is exemplary in this regard.

The optimal foraging models developed in biology, and used as the basis for most of
the analyses in this volume, do not explicitly consider regional interactions or information
exchanges between foragers. In chapter 9 Moore analyzes the effects of information gathering and exchange on the spatial distribution of hunter-gatherers, using theory developed
by ecologists and geographers. Moore points out that hexagonal patterning of boundaries
between foraging units does not necessarily indicate efficient use of space. By assuming
that foragers do not have access to the perfect information implied in geographic locational
theory, Moore analyzes the cost of acquiring the information and of arranging nonoverlapping
seasonal movements and settlement patterns. Moore uses optimal foraging models to argue
that groups will attempt to position themselves without overlap in their foraging ranges.
He then uses computer simulation techniques to assess the group-level costs of efficient
spatial organization given various degrees of knowledge about the distribution of resources
and other groups, and various ways of acquiring the relevant information. His analysis
points up the need to consider regional processes affecting the adaptations of individuals
and local groups.

In the final chapter, William Durham places these studies in a general biocultural context, and discusses the rationale for using ecological optimization theory to study the
adaptive significance of cultural behavior. He evaluates the research presented in this
volume in light of four general questions: (1) What are the optima predicted by foraging
strategy models? (2) To what extent do human foragers conform to these predictions? (3) How
and why do hunter-gatherers optimize, if and when they do? and (4) To what extent do these
optimization approaches help us understand hunter-gatherer diversity? Durham concludes
that ecological foraging theory will undoubtedly be modified to take into account more of
the unique properties of human behavior, and he expresses optimism that this approach can
compass the terrain.

Finally, we should note that most of the cases presented here come from arctic, subarctic or temperate North American populations (chapter 5 by O'Connell and Hawkes is the exception). This is a coincidence, unrelated to theory or to guidelines used to choose
authors. Hames (pers. comm.; Hames and Vickers, in preparation) notes that data on diet
breadth and central place foraging behavior gathered in studies of Amazonian Indians support appropriate optimal foraging hypotheses. We expect the theory to be enriched and
changed as it is extended to analyses from this and additional ecozones and populations.

## Conclusion

Evolutionary ecology and socioecological research provide an approach and set of
models which should prove well suited to the investigation of human adaptation--current,
historic, and prehistoric. The models represent heuristic tools for analyzing the evolution
of social behaviors as diverse as mating systems, foraging strategies, predator avoidance,
and demographic (life history) strategies. Some of these models, in particular those

concerned with foraging, are potentially of great usefulness for research on hunter-gatherers. These models are general and realistic, and are designed to predict the behavioral patterns expected to evolve or develop in response to specific patterns and features of the environment. In many instances they generate reliable hypotheses about foraging behavior, some of which are not otherwise evident. They have the further advantage of presenting hypotheses with clear operational significance; that is, the models generate predictions amenable to confirmation or refutation.

If carefully applied, socioecological models may alleviate some shortcomings of the predominantly empirical and functional approaches of anthropological research on foraging. Populations of active hunter-gatherers are rapidly disappearing and with them the basis for ethnographically expanding our knowledge of the major part of human history. As direct fieldwork opportunities dwindle, attention will necessarily shift more to interpretation of historical, prehistoric, and paleontological records. Evolutionary ecology will assist with this interpretation, but to date it has developed almost exclusively from the study of nonhuman species. While ethnographic testing is still possible, it is important for ethnographers and archeologists to work together to determine the applicability of evolutionary ecology theory in studies of human foraging behavior.

# 2

# Optimal Foraging Strategies and Hunter-Gatherer Research in Anthropology: Theory and Models

Bruce Winterhalder

## Introduction

Optimal foraging strategy theory offers a generalized and realistic approach to the analysis of hunter-gatherer behavior. The theory provides a cluster of simple models, partially derived from neo-Darwinian postulates, which produce operational hypotheses about foraging behaviors expected in different environmental circumstances. Some of these hypotheses are nonintuitive. These and other qualities argue for the use of these models in anthropological research. This chapter describes the assumptions and theory of this approach, and outlines models that deal with diet breadth, use of a heterogeneous habitat, patterns of movement in a heterogeneous habitat, and group size and settlement patterns. These models focus on patterns expected if foragers behave so as to obtain a high net rate of energy acquisition while foraging. Because they provide explicit predictions about the behaviors, given energy optimization assumptions, they can be used to disentangle the relative importance of this and other selective influences acting on the formation of behavior. I shall also note points where data and analytic judgment are necessary to adapt this approach reliably to human ecology study.

The potential anthropological importance of this approach rests in its generality. The models seem to provide predictions, based on a limited number of parameters, which identify basic qualities of adaptive solutions to recurrent environmental features. For instance, central place aggregation in species as diverse as fish, birds, and primates appears to be a common foraging adaptation which reduces the costs of finding and successfully recovering foods that are abundant but clumped together and unpredictable in location (Horn 1968; Schoener 1971:395-96). Consequently, when obvious constraints are allowed for, the models are fairly insensitive to phylogenetic context. This generality argues for their use in hunter-gatherer research. Furthermore, the operational qualities of the theory mean that its analytic scope and reliability in anthropological investigation are open to empirical assessment.

Among the people who contributed to the ideas or encouraged the research that led to the writing of this paper I would like especially to acknowledge R. Brooke Thomas, Davydd Greenwood, Ted Steegmann, Stephen Emlen, Eric Smith, Steven McRae, and Sara DeGraff. The manuscript was typed by Sara DeGraff and the figures prepared by Jane Jorgenson. This publication is based on research supported by the National Science Foundation, Grant No. SO 38065 (to Dr. Ted Steegmann; SUNY at Buffalo). The manuscript was completed while the author was a postdoctoral research associate in the Science, Technology, and Society Program, Cornell University. I gratefully acknowledge this support.

The theory discussed here is adapted from ecology. Despite recent applications in ethnographic study (E. A. Smith 1978; Winterhalder 1977 1980a n.d. ab) and in archeology (Jochim 1976; Keene 1979ab 1980; Wilmsen 1973), and considerable promise (Thomas, Winterhalder, and McRae 1979), caution is urged for its use in anthropology. For instance, some of the archeologists cited have assumed a simple interpretation of optimal foraging models to be true for humans, and then elaborated more complex interpretations on this basis, that is, prior to tests of the foraging models themselves. In contrast, Winterhalder (1977) found the optimal foraging approach heuristically very valuable, but noted that assumptions of the theory are not always applicable, and that specific models are sometimes not reliable for predicting human foraging behavior. Consequently, this chapter has as its purpose: (1) identification of the assumptions that lie behind application of evolutionary ecology to anthropological subjects; (2) clear statement of the analytic decisions faced by an anthropologist using this theory; (3) identification of models and hypotheses that are particularly appropriate in human ecology investigation; (4) isolation of points where, despite the semideductive nature of the approach, significant data are required to apply it reliably; and (5) some indication of the analytic shortcomings and promise of these models. Available human ecology analyses using specific models are cited where appropriate.

I hope to establish that the theory provides a theoretically coherent framework for the investigation of the ecology and evolution of hunter-gatherer behavior, generalized with respect to behavioral category and environmental context. As a result the models should perform well in investigating the environmental factors contributing to the behavioral diversity of hunter-gatherers.

## Evolutionary Ecology

The optimal foraging models discussed here are part of evolutionary ecology theory developed over the past fifteen years (see Pianka 1978 for a summary). This theory relies on the observation that neo-Darwinian assumptions (Cody 1974; Pianka 1978:13-14) and simple graphical or algebraic models (Levins 1966 1968:3-9) are often adequate to predict selected aspects of an organism's behavior.

Evolutionary ecology deals with a broad array of topics, including resource procurement (Krebs and Cowie 1976; Pyke, Pulliam, and Charnov 1977; Schoener 1971); life history and mating (Brown 1975:166-75; Orians 1971:536-38; Stearns 1976); and avoiding predators (W. D. Hamilton 1971; Orians 1971:540-41; Pulliam 1973). Each area is broken into more specific behavioral categories for analysis. For instance, foraging is usually considered in terms of four overlapping sets of questions: diet breadth and choice of items, foraging space, feeding period, and foraging group size. These sets of questions focus on individuals or groups of individuals of a single species, but analysis at this scale can be considered the "microecological theory" (Pyke, Pulliam, and Charnov 1977:140) of behavior producing population phenomena such as interspecific competition, predation, and trophic relationships (e.g., Orians 1975). The division of behavior into these four categories rests on analytic convenience; it does not necessarily mirror a similar partitioning of life processes by the organism.

An important facet of the development of ecological research since 1960 lies in the type of questions asked. Orians (1971:529-30) has discussed this shift of perspective with respect to analysis of territoriality. Prior to 1960 the major research question was, What is the function of territoriality? Investigations centered on behaviors occurring in territories and produced a list of activities associated with defended space. The functional orientation did not, however, yield results which could be generalized or which, in the case of birds, for example, directed attention to data "that could explain the diversity of avian territorial systems rather than just describe them" (Orians 1971:530).  In 1964 Brown reformulated the question, and significantly altered the success of the inquiry: "Brown's major contribution was to point out that the way to explain the diversity of territorial systems was to ask the question in the form, What factors select for increased aggressiveness with respect to space?" (Orians 1971:530; see also Brown and Orians 1970: 246-54).  It emerged that a major variable--the density and predictability of resources-- accounts for much of the behavioral variability of avian species with respect to territoriality (Brown 1964).  Resource-based hypotheses were promulgated prior to Brown's analysis, but, stated in the functional form, they did not suitably link observations with theory.

Two shifts in the rephrasing of this question underlie the microecological elements of evolutionary ecology.  First, there is an emphasis on individual-level selection and adaptation (Lewontin 1970; Williams 1966).  Second, there is a shift to analysis of the mechanisms and conditions which interact to produce adaptive processes.  Less attention is given to classification of the functional results of evolution or to correlation of these with environmental features.

It is possible that the tendency in human ecology research to state questions in functional terms similarly impedes the identification of environmental variables useful for analyzing the evolution of behavior.  This chapter describes models which pose questions about foraging in the form suggested by Brown--in terms of selection and individual-level adaptive behavior.  Explicit attention is given to procedures for testing sets of alternative hypotheses.  The focus here is on foraging, but the approach parallels that of Durham (1976b) on warfare.

## Assumptions and Concepts of Optimal Foraging Theory

### Adaptation and Optimization

The optimization concept derives from the postulates of synthetic evolutionary theory. Pianka (1978:12) states, *"Natural selection and competition are inevitable outgrowths of heritable reproduction in a finite environment"* (italics in original).  Direct and indirect competition for resources gives advantages to organisms that have efficient techniques of acquiring energy and nutrients which can be turned into offspring or used to avoid predators (Pianka 1978:12).  Pianka's statement identifies the "source" of optimal phenotypes and the three arenas of behavior usually considered:  resource acquisition, reproduction, and predator avoidance (see Crook, Ellis, and Goss-Custard 1976:262).  Optimization pertains to the efficiency, relative to time or energy costs, with which these activities are performed, with the assumption that increased efficiency relative to a standard of performance leads to a relative increase in fitness.

The extensive use of optimization or maximization principles in ecology has led to a serious debate about their merits (Maynard Smith 1978; Lewontin 1979a 1979b).  Here it is assumed that an optimality principle provides a structured and contingent guide to the expected direction of evolution by selection.  It is structured because, with specification of auxiliary conditions and parameter values, hypotheses about the development of particular behaviors can be devised; contingent, because no set of conditions or derived hypotheses can be stated which have theoretical generality sufficient to qualify as evolutionary universals. Further, optimality analysis assists in identifying the products of selection at the expense of attention to other evolutionary processes.

It is assumed in the biological literature that adaptive phenotypes result from natural selection acting over time to produce changes in the gene pool of a population.  Selection acts through its effects on the reproductive fitness of individuals. The focus on genetic adaptation is, however, an unnecessary restriction. The evolution of foraging strategies can reside in the realm of sociocultural behaviors and yet be analyzed by evolutionary ecology models (Campbell 1965; Durham 1976a; Pyke, Pulliam, and Charnov 1977:138). Genetic differences among individuals presumably have no significant effect on the behavioral variability relevant in ethnographic studies of human foraging behavior. Consequently, it is necessary to assume only that foraging is characterized by recurring variability; that the "successful" variations are consciously or unconsciously adopted by individuals; and that the "selected" behavioral variants are passed from parent to offspring or between generations by other persons (cf. Lewontin 1970:1).

As Cody (1974:1156) states, it is somewhat tautologous to invoke optimization in an evolutionary context. Selection is sometimes defined as producing the optimal or best-adapted phenotype. Nonetheless, optimum phenotypes hypothesized by ideal models ignore a variety of effects manifest in the real world. It is possible, for instance, that the constraints of history, chance, or competing goals (Cody 1974:1156) prevent the evolution of phenotypes that are ideal relative to certain goals of behavior. Selection or adaptation may more or less adroitly track but not approach conceivable optima. Appropriate preadaptations may not be available; conditions in the environment can change; or conflicting adaptive goals may be set up by alternating environmental states, or by the necessity to harvest two resources for which the "optimal" strategies are mutually exclusive. Evolutionary ecology analysis becomes interesting when it attempts to specify the optimal pattern of behavior in a particular situation, or when it attempts to assess the constraints that multiple goals or historical circumstances place on an organism's ability to achieve a particular optimum.

In the human case two points arise concerning the possible disjunction between modeled optima and observed behaviors. First, much of the historical constraint on nonhuman organisms stems from the fortuitous nature of mutations and preadaptations, and from relatively inflexible behavioral abilities. Genetic evolutionary change can be slow relative to change in environmental features. This constraint is partially relaxed in the human case owing to behavioral flexibility and to the possibility of rapid cultural innovation in response to particular ecological circumstances. Second, humans have cultural goals which take on the status of social imperatives by virtue of their residence in the coherent systems of belief and meaning which pervade and structure much behavior (Geertz 1973; Slobodkin 1977). It is possible that constraints on optimal (as opposed to biologically minimal) solutions to particular adaptive problems from this cultural source are significant. The balance of the two influences--biological flexibility and cultural constraints--on the realization of optimal behaviors is not easily determined. Little empirical information and few theoretical guidelines are available (cf. Durham 1976a).

## Foraging

Foraging refers inclusively to tactics used to obtain nonproduced foodstuffs or other resources, those not directly cultivated or husbanded by the human population, although they may in some senses be conserved or managed (Feit 1973). Foraging may involve hunting, trapping, netting, snaring, gathering, or other techniques. The word hunting implies that the forager is directly and immediately involved in the capturing or killing of animal prey.

The focus here on the foraging practices of hunter-gatherers is not based on recognition of a traditional category or the desire to isolate a manageable set of examples. These criteria would imply the misapprehension that hunting and gathering behavior represents a uniform or simple class of subsistence adaptations (Martin 1974). Rather the restriction identifies a set of behaviors amenable to analysis using evolutionary ecology concepts much as they would be used by biologists. Two criteria bound this class, aside from the previously stated condition that the resources be nonproduced. First, the choice of foraging largely obviates the need to consider money. This circumvents the problem of mixing "currencies" (see below) of different conceptual status. The second criterion is the restriction to subsistence. The models described here can thus employ a limited form of cost-benefit comparison, evaluating both the costs and benefits associated with particular activities in commensurate ecological units (primarily calories).

## Strategy Analysis and Temporal Scales of Assessment

Strategy analysis links a certain kind of explanation to an evolutionary time scale (Pianka 1978:15; Mayr 1976b:360-63). It looks for the origins of complex behaviors in the effects of selection in patterned environments (Levins 1968). Despite emphasis on long-term adaptation, strategies are not fixed. Considering a series of intervals in which an organism must make decisions, Schoener (1971:375) states, "At the beginning of each, the animal assesses its strategy in the face of alternative future conditions whose probabilities are known (i.e. genetically programmed), but whose exact manifestation is unknown." The assessment includes the organism's immediate physiological state and its evaluation of present and impending environmental conditions. The environment changes as do the requirements of the organism during its life cycle. The strategy concept recognizes that behavior is patterned but that organisms need to evaluate and reach decisions appropriate to changing circumstances.

In the human case, it is usually not appropriate to rely on rates of genetic change under natural selection to establish the temporal parameters of the evolution of a behavioral strategy. Instead the focus must be on the long-term accumulation and integration of experience by cultural means. Information passed from generation to generation by culture provides much of the strategic framework within which specific choices and options are exercised by individuals or groups of human foragers. Thus the emphasis in ethnographic studies of optimal foraging is on the long term relative to sociocultural processes rather than to genetic processes.

Besides the evolutionary time scale of the strategy approach, there is another appropriate time interval for assessing aspects of behavioral optimization. This is the duration of the relevant behavioral pattern, its interval of recurrence (or, more precisely, the duration of the behavior's immediate and postponed effect on fitness or some other goal). An optimization interval may be based on an obvious environmental quality such as seasonality. But evolutionary processes are sometimes bound up with less easily recognized intervals which arise from the interactions between environmental variability and the life history processes affected by selection. It is usually assumed in optimal foraging studies that short-term maximization of net energy intake while foraging is an acceptable approximation of an organism's long-term goal, one producing optimal results over the longer periods as well. But this need not be the case. Assessment intervals are always important unless foraging "behavior at one point in time does not alter the optimal (foraging) behavior at a later point in time" (Pyke, Pulliam, and Charnov 1977:139; see also Katz 1974: 761).

Three situations in which short-term evaluation of foraging cannot be extrapolated in a simple manner to a longer time span are identifiable (Pyke, Pulliam, and Charnov 1977: 139-40): (1) First are cases where a behavior commits the organism to a particular activity or location for an extended period. Unless the fitness or adaptation results are uniform from beginning to end, evaluation should encompass the whole period. Foraging effects following from the choice of a camp or settlement location are an example. (2) In the second class the present behavior of the organism alters the environmental conditions which will affect later foraging efforts. For example, if there is exclusive use of a resource, the organism may adopt foraging behaviors which avoid complete local harvest in favor of returning at some future time. (3) The third class encompasses environmental changes which are independent of the organism's activity and more or less unpredictable. The organism may mix foraging with exploration, although the latter does not contribute in an immediate sense to energy maximization. Exploration behavior may reduce the efficiency of foraging but provide the organism with information instrumental in later foraging efforts.

Each of these three cases involves a more general observation: optimal strategy analysis is an attempt to specify the effects of complex fitness- or goal-related behaviors relative to theoretically derived predictions. This makes it important, with respect to both the predictions and the observations, to attend to the time interval over which the immediate *and* delayed costs and benefits accrue to the organism considered. Identifying these intervals can be difficult, and requires that the investigator know the "natural history" of the population being studied and the long-term properties of its environment (Winterhalder 1980b).

The strategy concept, and the necessity of evaluating behaviors over an interval that accurately represents their aggregate effect on the organism, introduce an effectiveness component into analysis by requiring that optimal (efficient) behaviors be evaluated over a relatively long time interval. Highly efficient short-term behaviors may not be effective over the longer period in which organismal or habitat variability occurs. Conversely, an effective adaptation over some time span may not always be the most efficient (Slobodkin 1973). In adaptation studies it is generally necessary to balance assessment of efficiency and effectiveness (Vayda and McCay 1975:295-97).

## Modeling

Behavioral phenomena combine multiple elements of ecology and population biology and genetics (Levins 1966:421). The problem is to simplify complex adaptive systems so that they retain essential and interesting (i.e., nontrivial) features, but at the same time become analytically tractable. Modeling has proven a useful solution. Levins (1966:422; cf. Schoener 1972:391) notes that ideally a model would simultaneously achieve generality, realism, and precision, but that this is rarely possible. Most types of modeling sacrifice one of the three qualities, with the choice depending on the nature and goals of the investigation. The models cited in this chapter emphasize realism and generality. They are expressed in differential calculus or graphical form, and functions are assumed to be linear, increasing or decreasing over some range--convex, concave, or the like--rather than having exact specifications. The resulting predictions are generally expressed as inequalities (Levins 1966:422-23) or in ordinal rather than cardinal rankings. The hypotheses are commonly comparative and qualitative.

The simplifying assumptions and constraints of all models make it possible that the results are an artifact of the procedure. Levins (1966:423) suggests a partial solution to this difficulty in characterizing models as "robust" or "nonrobust": "we attempt to treat the same problem with several alternative models each with different simplifications but with a common biological assumption. Then, if these models, despite their different assumptions, lead to similar results we have what we can call a robust theorem" (Levins

1966:423). Robustness is a quality of the modeling procedure, and hence somewhat independent of empirical confirmation or refutation of specific hypotheses. Most of the hypotheses outlined below come from models which are robust for biological applications. They may also be robust with respect to *some* aspects of human behavior, but testing will be necessary to establish that robusticity is correlated with empirical confirmation in both the nonhuman and the human cases.

A second important concept in modeling is that of "sufficient parameters" (Levins 1966: 427-30), abstractions of multiple, more detailed variables. For analysis it is necessary to generate sufficient parameters which (1) are reduced in number; (2) summarize most of the information at the level of concern; and (3) retain as much information from other, more detailed levels as possible. Examples of sufficient parameters in foraging analysis are resource qualities such as dispersion pattern or predictability, or adaptive criteria such as foraging efficiency or effectiveness. The utility of sufficient parameters lies in their condensation of information, but this also introduces imprecision and an inability to reconstitute lost information (Levins 1966:429).

In summary, there are three kinds of imprecision that enter into models emphasizing generality and realism: (1) They omit factors which have small effects or which have large effects but only in rare cases. (2) They are vague about the exact form of mathematical functions in order to stress qualitative properties. (3) The many-to-one property destroys information about lower levels (Levins 1966:429-30). The necessity to simplify, to stress qualitative properties, and to develop sufficient parameters gives foraging models a unique status. A model is not a theory or hypothesis, nor is it true or false. "The validation of a model is . . . that it generates good testable hypotheses relevant to important problems" (Levins 1966:430).

## Confirmation of Hypotheses

A strength of optimal foraging theory lies in its attention to hypothesis testing. Consequently, it is important how one confirms or refutes an optimal behavior hypothesis and how one interprets the meaning of either outcome. I will take up the latter point after discussing specific models; here I discuss tests and their interpretation (see also Dyson-Hudson and Smith 1978).

Cody (1974:1156-57) outlines two ways of testing for optimal solutions to the problems of time and energy allocation in natural situations. The first is comparative, and most valuable in situations where it is difficult to isolate the active selective forces or likely outcomes in order to build a model. In this instance one defines and measures several variables of interest in one locality. These could be community traits (e.g., number of species occupying a certain trophic level) or behavioral attributes of a population (e.g., diet breadth). The measured variables are then compared with those of a second, environmentally similar situation or species with an independent evolutionary history, and "if we find extensive similarities or convergences we can infer that selection has reached optimal solutions in both fields [cases], despite differences in history, time scales, and genetic origins" (Cody 1974:1157). This approach is widely used in anthropology, e.g., in the comparative studies of "band societies" (Damas 1969c; Lee and DeVore 1968).

An alternative test is to compare the natural situation with predictions based on models designed to replicate certain important features of the natural system (Cody 1974: 1157). This approach has been less used in anthropology.

Many foraging strategy models are based on geometric representations of the relationships of foragers to resources, with solutions found by graphs or by differential calculus

(Cody 1974:1157). Graphs have the advantage of simplicity. As an example, MacArthur and Pianka (1966:604) note that the details necessary to construct exact curves in their diet breadth models are usually unknown, and would vary from case to case in any event. Nonetheless, graphing allows the derivation of interesting results in the form of comparative and qualitative predictions. In complex mathematical models, predictions can easily become sensitive to poorly understood parameters (Schoener 1971:376). The proper analytic balance between simple and less simple models is for the investigator to judge, but "ultimately, our ability to test relationships like these [predicted by optimal foraging models] would seem to depend on retaining the simplicity in such models when confronting the real system" (Werner and Hall 1974:1044).

It is important when using this approach to recall that the model and hypothesis represent an analytic compromise mediated by the technical and logical constraints of analyzing the multiple interacting variables. The conflicts generated by the necessity to simplify and generalize are irreconcilable, but it is important that they are about methods, not reality, and that models are meant to assist understanding, not to duplicate nature (Levins 1966:431).

## Application of Optimal Foraging Models

### Choice of a Currency

According to Schoener (1971:369): "The primary task of a theory of feeding strategies is to specify for a given animal that complex of behavior and morphology best suited to gather food energy in a particular environment." Schoener identifies a three-step procedure: (1) a currency must be chosen; (2) an appropriate cost-benefit function must be adopted; and (3) the function must be solved for an optimum.

The first problem is to decide what is to be maximized or minimized, i.e., the currency must be identified (Schoener 1971:369). In biological terms, the most fundamental evolutionary property of an organism is reproductive fitness. It is rarely feasible to measure this. In foraging studies it is usually assumed that fitness varies directly with the rate of net energy intake which can be achieved while foraging (Pyke, Pulliam, and Charnov 1977:138-39; Krebs and Cowie 1976:99), although a variety of factors (summarized by Schoener 1971:372) can intervene to influence this relationship. An increased rate of energy intake while foraging can enhance viability of the organism or its ability to produce and provision offspring, but indirect effects are also significant. The time and energy that an organism invests in foraging are generally unavailable for other activities, and foraging may expose it to predation or other hazards. Thus "the profit an animal acquires in feeding must be weighed against the loss of time, while feeding, to participate in activities such as search for mates or predator avoidance" (Schoener 1971:371; see also Pianka 1978:148-49; Krebs and Cowie 1976:99; and Pyke, Pulliam, and Charnov 1977:139).

The sociocultural goals which pervade human behavior do not diminish the importance of efficient and effective foraging behavior in the maintenance of viable populations. Energy efficiency, assessed by a net rate of acquisition during foraging, need not be strictly covariant with human adaptive success, however defined. But it does provide a useful, proximate measure of adaptive behavior with both empirical and theoretical importance, and broad applicability (see Smith 1979b).

There are several rationales for emphasizing an energy currency. First, the environment may be one with absolute energy limitations, on either a periodic or a constant basis. This is especially likely for the larger omnivores or carnivores, including humans. General biome productivities (e.g., Leith 1973), however, are a very crude measure of the energy circumstances affecting a particular population.  Attention must focus on productivity available to the population, relative to its requirements.  Availability includes such factors as the absolute amount of the resource, fluctuations in its abundance, its distribution, difficulties of harvesting it, and the role of intra- and interspecific competitors. The case for energy limitations can be advanced if historical evidence shows shortages directly.  The converse, short-term studies indicating relative freedom of a group from energy shortages are not reliable evidence that selection pressures capable of influencing foraging behaviors do not or have not existed (Smith 1979b; cf. Vayda and McCay 1975).

Secondly, the relationship between energy and time on the one hand, and fitness or some other measure of goals, on the other, can be left hypothetical.  This procedure invokes the scarcity postulate of evolutionary (Pianka 1978:12) and microeconomic theory (Robbins 1932).  In this case the utility of that postulate in developing models is focal, and demonstration of absolute shortages is secondary.

Human behavioral flexibility expands the list of activities that compete with foraging for time and energy.  Included are behaviors not normally associated with fitness in nonhuman organisms--the desire for leisure, status, social interaction, and accumulation of wealth.  Humans must invest time and energy to maintain coherence and cross-generational continuity in their social and cultural systems, on which adaptive behavior depends.  Additionally, there is the manufacture of essential technologies.  These activities require time and energy, and thus contribute to the selective pressure for efficient foraging.

The operational reasons for using energy as a currency are also important.  Persistent or at least periodic energy shortages are likely to have been significant for human populations throughout their history and in many different habitats.  Adaptations producing efficient foraging should thus be a consistent aspect of hunter-gatherer behavior, and hence an important area for the comparative and historical investigation of human adaptation. This is not to assert the primacy of energy-related adaptations for all cases (Vayda and McCay 1975:295-97); rather it suggests that such adaptations will be, with fair regularity, important in many cases.  Energy flow is common to the functions and structural attributes of diverse human groups and ecosystems, and provides a quantifiable variable around which each can be analyzed within the context of the other (Adams 1978:298).

Finally, there is analytic convenience.  The energy currency is amenable to clear operational study and quantification; it is used frequently because it is a component of adaptation which can be isolated and reliably assessed.  The factors contributing to the observed behavioral variability within and among human foraging populations are multiple and interact in complicated ways.  A major operational merit of the energy currency is that it is possible to determine with some confidence to what extent optimization with respect to the energy efficiency of foraging is the operative influence on the formations of certain behaviors.

Energy is not the only significant aspect of food resources; nutritional qualities are important.  In most ecological studies it is assumed that energy is the most important component of food (Schoener 1971:369), and the significance of nutritional factors has rarely been established (Pyke, Pulliam, and Charnov 1977:139).  Pyke, Pulliam, and Charnov (1977: 138-39) conclude that the use of energy as the sole currency is justified for most of the studies they review, but there are cases where it is fairly clear that nutritional or other factors predominate, in avian species (Davies 1977:1026, 1032) and for humans (Harpending and Davis 1977:280; Keene 1980; Meehan 1977a; Montgomery 1978:64; Rappaport 1968).  It is possible that carnivores will be less influenced by nutrient constraints than are herbivores,

as the latter must cope with the complex allelopathic defenses of plants in addition to
their lower nutritional quality.

Optimal foraging models exist which take nutrients to be the currency (Belovsky 1978;
Keene 1979ab 1980; Pulliam 1975; Rapport 1971), and a goal of optimal foraging studies is
to develop models capable of handling currencies more complicated than energy (Pyke, Pulliam, and Charnov 1977). For the present, given the paucity of foraging studies on humans,
cautious use of an energy currency will be likely to produce extensive and fairly reliable,
if ultimately incomplete, insights.

## Cost-Benefit Functions:  General

Schoener (1971:177-79; see also Krebs and Cowie 1976:100; Pyke, Pulliam, and Charnov
1977:139-41) divides foraging into four decision sets:  optimal diet breadth; optimal foraging space; optimal feeding period; and optimal foraging group size. These categories
separate questions about (1) which items the forager will consume from those available;
(2) where in the spatial environment the forager will seek food resources; (3) the times
when foraging will occur; and (4) the circumstances in which foragers will form groups for
pursuit of food resources.

These decision sets and their arrangement in a hierarchy are for the convenience of
the investigator (Krebs and Cowie 1976:100). The categories may or may not approximate
those used by the organism as it assesses foraging decisions, although analysis using the
separate categories is based on an *assumption* that the forager makes decisions as if the
different sets are "approximately independent" (Pyke, Pulliam, and Charnov 1977:140). The
investigator should remain sensitive to the fact that the choice of a decision set, or, if
more than one is chosen, the arrangement of the sets in a hierarchy, and the design of a
model commit him or her to analytic constraints which may or may not be appropriate. Such
decisions must be justified with respect to the population and situation analyzed.

These analytic constraints are potential targets of criticism of optimal foraging
models (Krebs and Cowie 1976:98). In anthropology the problem has been cogently identified
by Sahlins (1976:82-83) in his criticism of "the fallacy of an a priori fitness course" in
evolutionary (or sociobiological) analysis. Lewontin (1977:28-29) criticizes the unwar-
ranted "*ceteris paribus*" assumption. Still, all behaviors are complex, and they are related
to multiple aspects of the environment and to other behaviors of the organism. Constraints
must be identified and their existence in analytic procedures accepted if evolutionary study
is to proceed beyond description and broad statements about functions. It is difficult in
any situation to decide what should be taken as constraint and what then analyzed as adaptation. The quality of the analysis depends on the thoroughness with which the researcher
knows the population and the skill with which that knowledge is incorporated into the analysis. Constraints can be chosen which reduce the problem in particular cases, but "in
general, there is no recipe for determining just what the currency and constraints should
be in a particular situation, and it will always be the job of the naturalist to understand
the biology of an animal sufficiently well to know which currency is being optimized" (Pyke,
Pulliam, and Charnov 1977:138; see also Crook, Ellis, and Goss-Custard 1976:265-66). Anthropological analyses of particular sociocultural groups do not escape this difficulty,
although research such as that reported in this volume should eventually provide some
general guidelines.

In the description of foraging models that follows I have adopted Schoener's (1971)
foraging decision categories, although models dealing with optimal feeding period will not
be discussed.

Optimal Diet

Models of optimal diet are concerned with the forager's choice of food items and with the range or variety of items that are harvested in different environmental circumstances. Most foragers are faced with a broad array of potential resources, and most are selective to some degree. Models of optimal diet analyze that selectivity. They are designed to predict for a given organism and habitat the answers to questions such as these: What items will a forager prefer? Which will be passed up even when located? Will the diet breadth be broad or narrow? In what environmental circumstances will the diet breadth expand or contract? Which items will be added to or dropped from a changing diet? Before discussing a model that helps to answer these questions, I must introduce some terminology.

First, a forager can be a generalist or a specialist. An organism is a generalist if it consumes a relatively large range or diversity of food types; if it has a variety of feeding behaviors; or if it is capable of extracting energy from diverse food sources, as is an omnivore (Schoener 1971:384). Specialists can be defined by any of the inverse qualities.

A second set of terms relates to spatial characteristics of the environment and an organism's behavior. The definitions used here follow Pianka (1978:263) and Wiens (1976: 82-84). Environments that are heterogeneous, having a discontinuous distribution or mosaic of resources, are termed patchy. Conversely, environments containing well-mixed, similar, or evenly distributed resources are homogeneous or uniform. Patchiness can exist on any spatial scale and can be defined with respect to multiple environmental features. Consequently, a definition of patches must be relevant to the organism and the behavior being analyzed (Wiens 1976:83); although patches are delimited by the physical differences in the environment, they must also reflect the array of resources and hazards influencing the organism and its evolution.

An important descriptive feature of patchiness is grain. Grain is a relative measure. It is determined either by comparing environments or by assessing the behavior of an organism or population in an environment. Organisms that structure daily activities so as to encounter and exploit different patches in the actual proportion in which they occur use the environment in a *fine-grained* manner. Conversely, organisms that make disproportionate use of certain components of heterogeneous environments employ space in a *coarse-grained* manner. These definitions refer to the extremes of a continuum of possible behaviors. Coarse- or fine-grained use may result because the scale of the relevant environmental features is very large or very small relative to the size and mobility of the organism. Thus patches such as a meadow and adjacent woodlot have a large grain size relative to a mouse but a small grain size relative to a human. Whereas fine- or coarse-grained behavior is based on functional aspects of an organism's behavior in an environment, small or large grain size expresses a structural relationship between the organism and its environment (see Wiens 1976:85).

The diet breadth model examined here was developed by MacArthur and Pianka (1966; MacArthur 1972:61; Pianka 1978:263-66) for an environment that is fine grained with respect to the organism's foraging movements. A random search by the organism would encounter the resources in the actual proportion in which they occur. Although the organism searches in a fine-grained manner, it selects only certain prey to pursue and exploit, and therefore harvests the environment in a coarse-grained manner (Pianka 1978:264). From an array of fine-grained encounters the diet breadth model is designed to determine the selectivity of resource use practiced by an optimal forager. The model also assumes that organisms consistently do or do not take a certain resource type.

The foraging effort is divided into two phases: time spent searching $(T_s)$; and time spent pursuing, capturing, and eating the prey $(T_p)$. The functional difference is that all items are searched for simultaneously but are pursued singly. When an item is encountered the forager must decide whether to pursue it or to continue searching for more desirable prey. If a forager has $n$ resource items in its diet, we can ask in what circumstances it should enlarge, or possibly reduce, the diet by one type. If prey are ranked by net rate of energy return from those with the highest to those with the lowest, the rule is that prey types should be added until the additional pursuit time necessary for including the next type is greater than the savings in search time.[1] At this point including an additional resource type produces a net increase in the cost per unit of resource intake.

The graphical form of this model is given in figure 2.1. Prey are ranked on the abscissa from highest to lowest yield per unit of time or energy cost. $\Delta S$ measures the *change* in search time per unit of harvest as the diet is enlarged, stepwise, to include a greater number of the resource types encountered. As more of the encountered items are pursued, the average time to find an acceptable item decreases. On the other hand, as less desirable or harder to catch items are added, the costs of pursuit increase. Thus the average pursuit time ($\Delta P$) grows as the diet breadth enlarges. The organism benefits-- in terms of net energy intake relative to time or energy investment in foraging--by expanding or contracting its diet breadth to that represented by the intersection of the $\Delta S$ and $\Delta P$ curves.

## DIET BREADTH MODEL

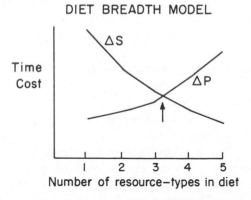

Figure 2.1. MacArthur and Pianka Optimal Diet Breadth Model. The $\Delta S$ curve plots decreasing average search costs, and the $\Delta P$ curve increasing average pursuit costs, as an increasing number of resource types are added to the diet. Cost here is expressed in terms of time, though it could be in terms of energy. Resources are ranked by their value to the organism in terms of the currency, or cost-benefit measure, adopted. The optimal diet breadth occurs at the intersection of the two curves. After MacArthur and Pianka 1966.

The predictions derived from this model are based on the positions and slopes of the $\Delta S$ and $\Delta P$ curves, or changes in these over time. A variety of influences on the forager's behavior can be conceived of as affecting or acting through these components of the model. For instance, if the encounter rate with items that are fairly easily pursued is low, the

---

[1]In their original model MacArthur and Pianka (1966) ranked prey types by numbers harvested per unit time. Schoener (1971:308) subsequently pointed out that this ranking implicitly assumes prey types are of equal value, and that the model does not guarantee an optimal solution if this condition is violated. The problem can be obviated if prey types are ranked by net energy gained per unit of pursuit time. Later formulations of the model (Pianka 1978:263-66; MacArthur 1972:61-62) point out that time and energy are interchangeable as measures of cost, and they measure returns in harvest or yield rather than numbers of prey.

search curve ($\Delta S$) will be high relative to the pursuit curve ($\Delta P$), and the organism should consume many of the prey types encountered. On the other hand, when encounter rates are high (the $\Delta S$ curve is low), the forager should be selective and pursue only the highly ranked prey. An optimal forager is selective in a rich environment; less discriminating in a poor one.

Changes in the environment, or in forager or prey behavior, can be reflected in the model's predictions. This is done by manipulating the curves to mimic the relevant factors. If, for instance, prey density increases, search time should decrease, shifting the $\Delta S$ curve downward and narrowing diet breadth. The $\Delta P$ curve remains stationary; pursuit time is not affected by prey density. The same change in the $\Delta S$ curve would occur if the forager became more efficient at searching. Converse circumstances would lead to an increase in diet breadth. This model also indicates that prey items should be added to or dropped from the diet sequentially and in the order of their ranking. Items taken by an optimal forager when the diet is narrow will continue to be taken as it enlarges; conversely, diet breadth will always decrease by a stepwise restriction to highly ranked items which were included in the more generalized diet.

In the results derived so far, we have assumed changes in prey species abundance to be proportionate for all resources. The environment became richer or poorer overall. But variation in the density of a single resource species will produce different effects depending on how the species is ranked. If the resource is highly ranked (within the existing diet breadth), an increase or decrease in its density should cause the diet breadth to contract or expand, respectively. If, however, it is ranked low, outside of the diet breadth, fluctuations in its abundance will have no effect on the optimal forager's diet. In terms of the model (figure 2.1), what happens to the $\Delta S$ curve to the right of its intersection with $\Delta P$ is irrelevant. In fact, "whether or not a food type should be eaten is independent of the absolute abundance of that type and depends only on the absolute abundances of food types of higher rank" (Pyke, Pulliam, and Charnov 1977:141).

The predictions about forager behavior which can be derived from the diet breadth model may be listed as hypotheses:

A. An optimal forager with a high search-cost/pursuit-cost ratio will tend toward a generalized diet breadth. Conversely, a forager with a high pursuit-cost/search-cost ratio will tend toward diet breadth specialization.
B. Any factor which causes an increase in the search costs of an optimal forager will produce a stepwise enlargement of its diet breadth. Conversely, a factor decreasing search costs will lead to a restriction of diet breadth.
C. Any factor reducing pursuit costs of the optimal forager will produce an enlargement of its diet breadth. Conversely, a factor increasing pursuit costs of a forager will produce diet breadth specialization.
D. An optimal forager highly specialized for searching, pursuit, or both will be relatively insensitive to factors affecting diet breadth. Conversely, organisms generalized for search, pursuit, or both will evidence fairly large changes of diet breadth in response to changes in search or pursuit costs.
E. The diet breadth of the optimal forager will be affected only by changes in the abundance of highly ranked resource items. In particular, if the absolute abundance of highly ranked resources is unchanged, the diet breadth of an optimal forager will not respond to an increase in the density of a resource which is ranked outside of its extant diet breadth.

Pyke, Pulliam, and Charnov (1977:141) note that similar results have been derived more or less independently at least nine times; they are therefore fairly robust. Reviews of field and laboratory analyses of foraging behavior using these hypotheses can be found in Krebs and Cowie (1976); Krebs (1977); Pyke, Pulliam, and Charnov (1977); and Davies (1977). Winterhalder (1977 n.d.b) applied this model in a detailed analysis of Cree foraging behavior and found a fairly strong confirmation of its hypotheses.

## Optimal Foraging Space

Optimal foraging space models examine the spatial characteristics of an organism's foraging relative to particular resource distributions (Schoener 1971:386). Some models also consider the spatial aspects of inter- and intraspecific interactions stemming from resource use. Specific questions include home range size (Clutton-Brock and Harvey 1978b: 192; Hamilton and Watt 1970; McNab 1963); whether a forager should or should not be territorial (Brown 1964; Hamilton and Watt 1970; Verner 1977); selection of foraging areas in a heterogeneous environment (MacArthur and Pianka 1966; Pianka 1978:265-66); and selection of a foraging pathway (Charnov 1976a; Charnov, Orians, and Hyatt 1976).

If prey are motile two extreme types of strategy can be identified: "sit and wait" and "widely foraging" (Pianka 1978:260-62). The former is expected when prey are dense and highly mobile, and the predator has a low resting energy requirement. In contrast, the widely foraging strategy is appropriate for an organism with a high resting metabolic requirement (including the energy requirements of nonforaging dependents), or one which depends on sedentary and low-density prey. Foraging space models indicate that territories (defended areas) should arise for individual foragers only when resources are of intermediate density and sufficient stability that the organism can acquire a net energy gain from exclusive use (Brown 1964; Hamilton and Watt 1970). Both ethnographic (Dyson-Hudson and Smith 1978) and primate (Clutton-Brock and Harvey 1977:16) studies provide evidence in support of this model. The models discussed below address two questions: choice of feeding areas in a patchy habitat, and choice of an optimal foraging pathway.

Many environments are characterized by a discontinuous, coarse-grained array of the resources or factors that affect the forager, and organisms should have behavioral patterns which reflect the heterogeneity of environmental conditions that facilitate or impede their essential activities. A model proposed by MacArthur and Pianka (1966) specifies the number of patch types that an optimal forager would include in its foraging itinerary (see figure 2.2). This model assumes that the environment is coarse grained, that patch types have different resource qualities, and that the mosaic is of a scale which affects the organism. The forager searches for the patch types in a fine-grained manner, but searches for and pursues prey only within certain patch types. Thus exploitation of patch types is coarse grained.

Patch types are ranked on the abscissa from the most to the least productive, measured by decreasing "expectation of yield" relative to time or calorie costs (Pianka 1978:265-66). Again, foraging is divided into two phases. Hunting time (or energy) within a patch type represents both search time and pursuit time (or energy) as defined in the model in figure 2.1 (Pianka 1978:265). Average hunting time ($\Delta H$) increases with the number of patch types included in the foraging itinerary because progressively less suitable patch types are harvested. $\Delta T$ represents the time spent traveling between or searching for acceptable patches. $\Delta T$ is a decreasing function of the number of patch types the organism includes in its foraging itinerary out of those that it must traverse.

This model predicts that the optimal forager will expand the number of patch types

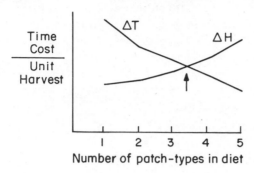

PATCH USE MODEL

Time Cost / Unit Harvest

Number of patch-types in diet

Figure 2.2. MacArthur and Pianka Optimal Patch Choice Model. The $\Delta T$ curve measures decreasing average between-patch travel time, and the $\Delta H$ curve increasing average within-patch foraging time (both per unit of resource taken), as an increasing number of patch types are added to the foraging itinerary. Cost here is expressed in terms of time, though a measure of energy could be used. Patch types are ranked by their value to the organism in terms of the currency, or cost-benefit measure, adopted. The optimal set of patch types for the forager to harvest is indicated by the arrow. After MacArthur and Pianka 1966.

included in its foraging itinerary until the increase in the average hunting time or energy (per unit yield) within the next patch type is greater than the average decrease in travel time or energy (per unit yield) between patches achieved by adding that next patch type. In graphical terms (figure 2.2) the optimal diet includes all patch types up to the intersection of the $\Delta T$ and $\Delta H$ curves.

This model is not fully analogous to that for diet breadth. We cannot substitute patch types, which may be relatively stationary, for motile resource items, because the forager can learn the location of favorable patch types in its range and adjust its "search" pathway accordingly (Pyke, Pulliam, and Charnov 1977:144). The nonrandom search path among patches implied by such learning is a violation of the fine-grained search assumption of the model. If favorable patch locations are known, the forager can reduce its average travel costs by avoiding encounters with unfavorable patches. Thus the outcome of knowing the location of high-ranked patch types is a greater specialization of patch type use.

The hypotheses that can be derived from the patch use model are more complicated than those in the diet breadth case. A uniform increase of resource density lowers both $\Delta T$ and $\Delta H$ curves, making predictions about changes in optimal patch use difficult. $\Delta H$ is lowered because the search within a patch becomes easier; $\Delta T$ is lowered because patches included in the foraging itinerary will be productive for a longer period of time, reducing the amount of travel between patches. Organisms which are pursuers (have a large pursuit-time/search-time ratio) should be relatively more affected by the decrease in travel time than by the decrease of hunting time within a patch. (Within the patch the greatest portion of their time is spent in pursuit.) Consequently, they are more likely than searchers to specialize with respect to patch types as food density increases (MacArthur and Pianka 1966:606; Pianka 1978:266). Increased mobility of the forager has the same effect as increasing the density of prey, and would thus generate the same prediction.

The relative size of patches (grain size) is also important in this model. If two environments are similar in the proportion (by area) and quality of their patch types, but differ in the size of patches, the model predicts that a forager will use the environment with the larger patches in a more specialized way. The reasoning behind this is explained by Pianka (1978:266).

Charnov (1976a; see also Charnov, Orians, and Hyatt 1976; Parker and Stuart 1976) has formulated a model predicting how an optimal forager will move in a patchy habitat. While the MacArthur and Pianka (1966) model cited above specifies which patch types an optimal forager will include in its diet, Charnov's "marginal value theorem" predicts when a forager should leave the patch that it is in. The theorem thus helps to determine the optimal forager's pattern and rate of movement among the patches being harvested.

This model is based on the observation that the activities of a forager often reduce the numbers or capturability of prey in its immediate vicinity. Charnov, Orians, and Hyatt (1976:247-48) call this "depression." It can occur in three ways. "Exploitation depression" results from the depletion, by harvesting, of the resources at a site. If easily discovered resources are taken first, then concurrent with diminishing abundance the forager must obtain its harvest from a residue of items that are increasingly difficult to locate or capture. "Behavioral depression" results from the increased wariness of prey which become aware of the forager's presence. "Microhabitat depression" results when alerted prey move to habitats where they are less conspicuous, or otherwise more protected. This kind of movement is expected to result from the coevolution of the forager and the prey. In each of these cases the marginal value theorem is applicable.

Charnov (1976a) begins with these assumptions: Food is encountered by the forager within patches. The forager must also travel between acceptable patches. Within a patch the forager "depresses" the rate of food intake as it forages; the quantity of food harvested rises over time to an asymptote, at which point the patch is exhausted and the rate of intake zero. Patch types are distributed randomly in the habitat, and the forager has a low probability of return in short time intervals to any one. Finally, the forager behaves so that its net rate of energy intake while foraging is maximized.

With these assumptions Charnov (1976a:131-33) derives the following theorem: "The predator should leave the patch it is presently in when the *marginal capture rate in the patch . . . drops to the average capture rate for the habitat*" (italics in original). This result is depicted graphically in figure 2.3. The average capture rate is represented by a straight line, with positive slope. The net energy intake for each of two patch types (A and B) is also shown. These curves represent assimilated energy less the costs of search, pursuit, and capture. The $x$-coordinates of the points of tangency of lines parallel to the average capture rate ($T_A$ and $T_B$) represent the optimal time to spend in each patch. If the organism remains beyond these times, its net rate of energy intake drops below the habitat average or what it could expect if it moved on. Thus an optimal forager abandons patches before they cease to be productive, and abandons them sooner the higher the overall quality of the environment. An optimal forager also leaves in its trail a series of patches of uniform quality (Krebs and Cowie 1976:102).

The marginal value theorem highlights the knowledge that a forager must have in order to forage optimally. To assess the point at which to leave a patch the organism must "know" how well it is doing in that location (i.e., the shape of the depression function) and on average how well it could expect to do in surrounding patches (Charnov, Orians, and Hyatt 1976). This implies that considerable information about the environment is stored by the organism. The advantage of familiarity with habitat patchiness is one reason to expect a violation of the fine-grained search assumption of the MacArthur and Pianka patch use model (figure 2.2).

Resource depression, and the microgeographic experience required to adjust to it, raise the question of the exclusive use of foraging space. The interval between depression of a patch and the time when it can again be profitably foraged is called "return time"

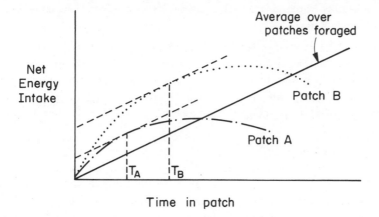

Time in patch

Figure 2.3.  Charnov Marginal Value Theorem.  Net energy intake within a patch for two
patch types is shown as a function of time (curves *A* and *B*).  Energy intake within a patch
grows at a decreasing rate as the forager depresses the resource availability for that location.  The straight line from the origin represents the average capture rate assessed
over the full set of patch types included in the foraging itinerary.  The optimum time to
spend within a patch type is found by constructing the highest tangent to the patch depression curve that is parallel to the line representing the average capture rate for the patch
types visited.  In this case the optimum times to spend in patch types *A* and *B* are represented on the *x*-axis by $T_A$ and $T_B$, respectively.  After Charnov 1976a.

(Charnov, Orians, and Hyatt 1976:256).  A forager must in some sense "know" an area in
order to adjust its return times to patch recovery and hence optimal use, giving an advantage to foragers maintaining home ranges or territories (Steward 1977:53).  Charnov, Orians,
and Hyatt (1976:256-57) suggest that this kind of reasoning may help account for "passive"
territoriality.  In addition, the forager remaining in a certain range can become familiar
with locations which provide shelter, escape, or other microgeographic advantages (Orians
1971:531).  It is important that humans can, if they wish, share information with immi-
grants.  Thus people can shift around over the landscape without suffering a shortage of
the information needed to forage optimally, so long as at least one person maintains continuity of knowledge about an area.

In summary, the MacArthur and Pianka model specifies how an optimal forager chooses
which patches to harvest from the larger habitat mosaic; the marginal value theorem model
specifies the way in which an optimal forager moves among those patches.  The hypotheses
which can be derived from these models are as follows:

A.  An optimal forager with a high pursuit-cost/search-cost ratio will react to an increase
    in resource density by a stepwise decrease in the number of patch types included in the
    foraging itinerary.
B.  An optimal forager in a habitat with small-grained patch types will tend toward gener-
    alized use of available patch types.  Conversely, a forager in a large-grained habitat
    should tend toward specialized use of patch types.
C.  An optimal forager will abandon a locality or patch before its resources are depleted,
    and specifically will abandon it at the point that the marginal return in that patch
    is equal to the average return from the set of patch types being foraged.
D.  The optimal forager leaves behind it a foraging pathway of patches of uniform resource
    quality.

E. An increase in resource densities will reduce the amount of time that an optimal forager spends in a given patch, i.e., will increase its rate of movement among the set
   of patch types being foraged.

Experimental or field studies on optimal foraging responses to patchy environments
are summarized in Pyke, Pulliam, and Charnov (1977); Krebs and Cowie (1976); and Cowie
(1977). Winterhalder (1977 n.d.b) found that the constraints incorporated in the patch
use model are not always appropriate in the context of Cree foraging; the same analysis
produced indirect and qualitative support for hypotheses derived from the marginal value
theorem.

## Group Formation and Optimal Foraging

Much recent work in evolutionary ecology attempts to isolate ecological factors which
affect individuals through the context of their group membership and which can be incorporated into models predicting group size and structure. Initially three hypotheses are
pertinent: (1) group formation may hinder individual foraging but has other, compensatory
effects; (2) groups form in response to concentration of food without an effect on the efficiency or effectiveness of individual foragers; and (3) aggregation increases the efficiency or effectiveness of individual foragers (Schoener 1971:392).

The third hypothesis is the most interesting in the present context. Smith (1980),
for instance, has gathered extensive field data showing that Inuit hunting group size is
adjusted so as to maximize the net energy return per individual for a variety of hunt types.
There are a number of ways that group foraging could be of advantage to individual foragers
(Orians 1971:538-41; Schoener 1971:393-96). Clumped foragers may increase the effective
density of prey by flushing, or groups of foragers may be able to take larger prey by cooperative search or pursuit. A third advantage of group foraging may lie in an increased
ability to defend an area for exclusive use (Hamilton and Watt 1970; Schoener 1971:394).

A fourth advantage of group foraging is the prevention of foraging overlap. If a
population of foragers in a certain area moves through it as a group they will more likely
encounter, or be able to adjust their routes to encounter, areas not already searched by
individuals and discovered to be empty, or areas already harvested and to some extent depleted. Individuals foraging alone (and not in territories) will always encounter a habitat with resources fairly uniformly depleted by other individuals foraging singly (uniform
depletion is predicted by the marginal value theorem). Thus individuals foraging in groups
should in some circumstances be more efficient because groups are more effective at locating undepleted resource areas (Cody 1974:1162-64).

A fifth potential advantage of group foraging is the ability to monitor a large area
for prey and to exchange information at a central place. This situation is most likely
when the resources are heterogeneously and erratically distributed, but abundant relative
to the requirements of the group being considered (Schoener 1971:395-96; Clutton-Brock and
Harvey 1977:15).

In the cases cited the benefits of group formation accrue to foragers that obtain and
consume their own food. By contrast, in hunter-gatherers and some social carnivores
(Thompson 1975), there is often a widespread sharing of foodstuffs and a division of foraging labor, mediated by cultural systems of reciprocity in the case of humans (Sahlins
1972). The effects of such differences in behavior on the use of these models are difficult to specify outside of particular cases. I simply point out that certain features of
human behavior could constitute a problem vis-à-vis the human application of some models.

The model of group formation that I will discuss (see figure 2.4) is adopted from

Horn (1968; see also Orians 1971:532-36). It varies the distribution and predictability
of food resources relative to the dispersion of the foraging population in four cases. The
geometric distance from the forager to a food source, weighted by the probability of finding food at a particular point, is established for each case. The optimal pattern of
forager dispersion is the one which requires the individual organisms to travel the smallest distance to locate food successfully. The actual or potential resource points, the
number of foraging organisms, and the quantity of food resources are the same in all cases.

## STABLE, EVENLY DISPERSED FOOD SOURCES

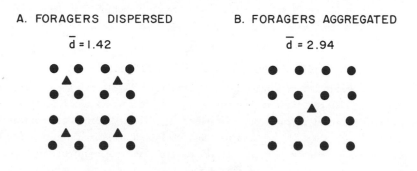

## MOBILE, CLUMPED FOOD SOURCE

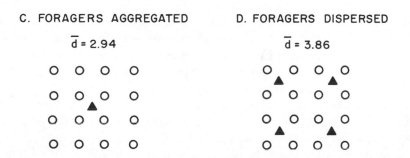

Figure 2.4. Horn Model for Optimal Forager Group Size and Dispersion. Triangles represent
foraging group locations; solid circles the locations of dispersed, stable resources; and
open circles the transient locations of clumped, mobile resources. The mean round-trip
distance from forager to resource points weighted by the probability of successfully locating food is given by $\bar{d}$. After Horn 1968.

If food resources are evenly distributed and stable, optimal foragers will then tend
toward regular dispersion of individuals or small social units (figure 2.4A; $\bar{d}$ = 1.42),
rather than toward aggregation at a central point (figure 2.4B; $\bar{d}$ = 2.94). Conversely, if
resources are mobile and unevenly distributed or clumped (i.e., concentrated transiently
at only one of the resource points and moving unpredictably among all of them), the optimal
strategy is aggregation of the foraging population at a central location (figure 2.4C;
$\bar{d}$ = 2.94), rather than toward dispersion (figure 2.4D; $\bar{d}$ = 3.86).

The mathematical interpretation of this model assumes that no information is exchanged
among the foragers. Horn (1968:690) notes, however, that if the distribution of resources
is aggregated and their location unpredictable, then the exchange of information at a

central location gives an added advantage to the aggregation of foragers. The human ability to communicate about situations displaced in space and time thus favors aggregation in this case. The situation producing dispersion of individual foraging organisms or units is also that which favors the evolution of territorial behavior (Orians 1971:533-35). Foraging from a central place, or refuging, is the subject of a number of interesting models (Hamilton and Watt 1970; Morrison 1978; Orians and Pearson 1979). Wilmsen (1973:6-10; Heffley, chapter 6, below) has considered the anthropological application of this model in detail; its hypotheses are the following:

A. Optimal foragers living in an environment with evenly distributed and stable resources will tend toward regular dispersion of the smallest viable social units.

B. Optimal foragers living in an environment with resources which are clumped and unpredictably located (mobile) will tend toward aggregation of social units at a central place.

## Interpreting Confirmation and Refutation

The foraging models outlined provide fairly realistic hypotheses about the characteristics of foraging, given optimization assumptions. The predictions about forager behavior in different environmental circumstances are based on a limited number of sufficient parameters, and to a large extent the success of the technique hinges on the nature of these parameters. They are amenable to quantitative research, and are also general enough to serve as vehicles for a variety of specific effects that could be important in the development of foraging behaviors. Thus search and pursuit times can be observed and measured, and they can carry into the model consideration of factors as diverse as changing prey densities or improvements in forager technology.

In this section I want to outline the possible interpretations that can accompany the confirmation or refutation of an optimal foraging hypothesis. The discussion assumes that the relevant parameters have been estimated or measured, including information on the microgeography or patchiness of the forager's habitat; on prey densities and population qualities such as distribution and fluctuations; and on the time and energy costs and energy returns of different aspects of foraging behavior. The actual foraging patterns of the organism should also be known, and the analysis should cover a suitable time interval. Not all studies will or can meet these conditions, but they should receive attention, since a strength of optimal foraging theory is its operational assessment of alternative hypotheses. The approach generates an agenda of information necessary for ecological analysis of complex behaviors; often the requisite data only partially overlap with those usually collected in human ecology studies.

It is initially necessary to decide what constitutes an acceptable "fit" between predictions and observation. This is largely a matter of judgment. Rarely will fit be exact, nor should it be. The models consider evolutionary tendencies or trends; they isolate single-goal behaviors from the larger arena of behavior; they analyze portions of those goals (represented by certain cost-benefit functions which are possibly interacting or hierarchical); and they abstract from the complex, fluctuating environmental situation wherein the organism is subject to competing goals and constraints. The logical limitations of the approach and the necessity to abstract from a complex situation are matched by the difficulties of gathering exhaustive and accurate field data. Nonetheless, to avoid vitiating the heuristic strengths of optimal foraging theory, it is necessary to demand a fairly close fit when testing a hypothesis. It is essential to maintain a balanced commitment to the situation and to ideas about how it can be described and analyzed, and to preserve regard for complex and sometimes recalcitrant data in the fact of a simple but comprehensive and compelling theory. This can be accomplished in evolutionary studies only by a continual reluctance to be comfortable with a fit that is close or suggestive (see also Schoener 1972:389-90).

On the other hand, confirmation of the fit between a prediction and observation is not in itself a fully reliable test of a hypothesis, unless the prediction is unique (not possibly generated by other models, currencies, or factors). This is rarely the case. Confirmation cannot prove that the factors identified in the model are the causative ones in the formation of the behavior because it does not exclude all alternative hypotheses (Charnov 1976b:149-50; Krebs and Cowie 1976:112). The methodology of optimal foraging research and its operational specificity, however, allow one to search for ways by which apparently complementary hypotheses can be distinguished (Krebs 1977; Verner 1977). This provides a way of evaluating the relative contributions of differing factors or processes to the evolution of observed behaviors.

A failure to confirm an optimal foraging hypothesis can initiate a series of procedures which themselves provoke insights. The model or its sufficient parameters may fail to capture essential elements of the situation. The constraints affecting the immediate behavioral capabilities of the organism and its evolutionary history, or the effective features of its environment, may be inadequately recognized. Adjustments designed to achieve a better fit must be done with a careful interplay of the theory and the data. There is a temptation to correct deficiencies of a model in ways (e.g., by incorporating additional variables) that make its predictions less specific and therefore less amenable to refutation, whatever their improved accuracy (Lewontin 1979a).

It is also possible that the environment in which the assessment is made is not similar to the one in which the behaviors evolved. In effect the test conditions may not be appropriate (Krebs and Cowie 1976:113). An organism's environment and the qualities of its food resources are continually changing, so that the extant situation is never precisely that in which selection acted to produce existing behaviors (Orians 1971:516). Deciding what constitutes or has constituted the natural or significant habitat of an organism is a difficult task (Krebs and Cowie 1976:113; Winterhalder 1980b). This problem can be avoided to some extent by choosing appropriate time intervals for assessing foraging behaviors and their evolution, a procedure greatly assisted in the human case by historical records.

Another possibility is that the wrong optimization goal or currency has been chosen. The nutrient or some other, perhaps social, value of food resources may be more important than calories in certain cases. When the assumed selective influence is stated through a simple, operational model that yields hypotheses amenable to refutation, it is possible to demonstrate that one selective influence (e.g., energy capture) is of less importance than another. Belovsky (1978) and Caraco and Wolf (1975) provide excellent examples of this point. The predictions of the models with certain assumptions will not always be correct, but if carefully evaluated even incorrect predictions can usually prove informative, and assist in disentangling the multiple interacting factors affecting human behavior.

Use of this approach in data collection and interpretation, then, results in a test of the assumptions and constraints contained in the model and the procedure used to evaluate specific hypotheses. Such tests can be informative about the evolution and function of behavior, but do not confirm the general proposition that nature optimizes or that behavior is adapted (Maynard Smith 1978).

## Conclusion

There is considerable disagreement in anthropology about the best sources of information for gaining insight into the hunting and gathering adaptation of prehistoric hominids. Hall (1977) and Thompson (1975), and earlier Schaller and Lowther (1969), have emphasized the usefulness of analogies with social carnivores, while Washburn and DeVore (1961), Reynolds (1966 1968), and Teleki (1975) have focused on various primate species, especially baboons and chimpanzees. A generalized ecological approach, based on vertebrate ecology, was suggested by Bartholomew and Birdsell (1953). Ethnographic information has always been used more or less explicitly in the formulation of conceptual models about early hominid lifeways (Martin 1974; Ember 1978). And, increasingly, systematic observations of extant hunter-gatherers are being used to develop concepts and data that will assist archeologists in the interpretation of prehistoric remains (R. A. Gould 1978; Jochim 1976; Yellen 1976). There is little way of deciding a priori which information source provides the greater or more accurate insights. It is certainly not clear that contemporary hunter-gatherers should be our preferred or exclusive models. Extant populations of foragers exist only in certain habitats, and their lifeways have been altered by contact with agricultural and industrial peoples. Aside from the difficulty of representativeness, there is simply little good information on contemporary hunter-gatherers.

The usefulness of diverse information sources is not always recognized, perhaps because an encompassing framework for ecological and evolutionary analysis has not been developed in anthropology. Washburn (1976:xv-xvi) insists on the uniqueness of human foraging with the claim that it is unlike that of any other social carnivore or primate. At one level this is undeniable. However, little is gained by emphasizing uniqueness at the expense of valuable sources of theory and information which arise in comparative studies of ecological adaptation. With respect to foraging behaviors, where similar conditions of resources pertain, all species, including humans, face the common problem of their efficient and effective harvest. The research approach developed here does not claim behavioral similarity of different foragers, but it does assert comparability with respect to the ecological factors affecting their behavioral variability. In place of assertions that hominids behaved *as if* they were baboons, or social carnivores, or !Kung San, we need an evolutionary framework which can (1) relate behavioral patterns to environmental properties through realistic models; and (2) encompass the diverse and individually only partially satisfactory information sources available to anthropologists interested in elaborating and refining understanding of hominid adaptive behavior.

Evolutionary ecology will not resolve the differences among these information sources; it does provide a framework of sufficient breadth and cohesiveness to pursue their systematic study. Useful results will probably emerge through the eclectic use of families or clusters of interrelated models, where each model is simple, analytically tractable, and addressed to a specific and fairly limited topic, and where as many as possible are robust or achieve robusticity through their overlapping relationships with one another (Levins 1966:430-31; Schoener 1972:391).

Optimal foraging theory is rich in the need for empirical confirmation. The analytic choices open to the investigator are many, indicating both the operational breadth of the approach and a present shortage of suitable information about human foraging. The investigator can choose among different currencies, different cost-benefit functions, different (perhaps hierarchical) combinations of those functions, or short- or long-term optimization approaches. Each choice will reflect initial impressions about important selective factors or adaptive goals, the significant environmental features or qualities of the forager, the differential importance of various kinds of foraging behaviors or kinds of behavioral optimization, and the temporal qualities of the behaviors and their development.   It may become possible to identify a particular currency that accounts for a major portion of the behavioral diversity in most cases, or to conclude that some models are more commonly applicable or reliable than others, or to isolate the conditions under which short-term models are sufficiently accurate for analytic purposes.   Advances such as these, with the insights they imply, will come primarily from ethnographic and archeological research using the perspective discussed here.

# 3

# The Application of Optimal Foraging Theory to the Analysis of Hunter-Gatherer Group Size

Eric Alden Smith

The size and composition of social groupings among human hunter-gatherers, and in particular the ecological determinants of group size and structure, have been topics of theoretical interest in anthropology for quite a number of years (Steward 1936; Birdsell 1968; Yellen and Harpending 1972; Damas 1969c; Wobst 1974). This chapter presents the general approach developed by evolutionary ecology (Emlen 1973; Pianka 1978) to explain group size, emphasizing the models and ideas falling under the rubric of optimal foraging theory (Pyke, Pulliam, and Charnov 1977; Schoener 1971). In addition, comparable as well as contrasting positions taken by anthropologists are surveyed. Finally, in order to demonstrate more clearly what the application of evolutionary-ecological theory to an anthropological problem might entail, one simple hypothesis on foraging group size is derived and subjected to empirical test with data drawn from recent fieldwork on Inuit (Canadian Eskimo) hunting strategies.

## The Evolutionary Ecology of Group Size

The evolutionary-ecological theory of social groups begins with the assumption that groups are expected to form only when group membership is on the average associated with greater reproductive success for each individual group member than is solitary living (Brown 1975:72ff., 134ff.; Alexander 1974:328). Evolutionary ecology so far recognizes four major forces leading to the formation of groups: (1) foraging strategies; (2) reproductive strategies; (3) predator avoidance; and (4) certain types of competition. Changes in any or all of these selective categories can affect the costs and benefits of various forms of social organization. Although I will be stressing foraging strategies, I want to emphasize that we can expect several factors to interact in any specific case. Thus, the different categories of selective forces may select for different types of group structure in the same population; for example, foraging considerations might favor solitary living, reproductive advantages might be associated with small groups of kin, and predator pressures might select

I am grateful to the following individuals for assistance with the research and/or for comments on this chapter: John Atkins, Lorraine Brooke (and other members of the Northern Quebec Inuit Association staff), Ruth Buskirk, Tom Caraco, William J. Chasko, Bill Durham, Rada Dyson-Hudson, Steve Emlen, Lazarusi Epoo, Davydd Greenwood, Henry Harpending, Marshall Hurlich, the Inukjuamiut Community Council, Robert Jarvenpa, Bill Kemp, Dick Nelson, Inukpuk Naktialuk, Gordon Orians, Ron Pulliam, Tom Schoener, Brooke Thomas, Lucasi Tukai (and members of his extended family), Danieli Weetaluktuk, Bruce Winterhalder, and the foragers of Inukjuak. Field research was supported by NIMH predoctoral fellowship No. 1 F31 MH05668, and by the Arctic Institute of North America (with the financial assistance of the Firestone Foundation). Carol Poliak made it all worthwhile.

for very large aggregations of randomly related individuals. The expected group size would
then represent a compromise of conflicting selective forces--and possibly of individual members' conflicting optima as well (Bertram 1978:96).

Recognizing that various selective forces interact, evolutionary ecologists keep in
mind that specific models consider only isolated portions of the selective context, and that
real populations should be expected to evolve toward a compromise or *optimum* group size and
structure, with all the costs and benefits derived from different selective factors being
summed (see figure 3.1). However, the usefulness of the optimality concept is entirely dependent on the availability of a valid common currency that can be used to measure these
various costs and benefits and sum them to obtain a net result. Without such a common currency, no way is left to weight the different selective forces and decide their relative
importance when they predict contradictory or nonidentical results. In theory, no problem
exists, since natural selection theory provides the deductive framework for evolutionary
ecology, and it is clear that all costs and benefits should be measured in terms of the net
effect on an individual's inclusive fitness. In practice, the fitness value of specific
choices, traits, or even alleles is extremely difficult to sort out, since many of each are
summed in any individual's life history. This problem is only compounded when dealing with
a long-lived, multiple-breeding, behaviorally complex species such as *Homo sapiens*.

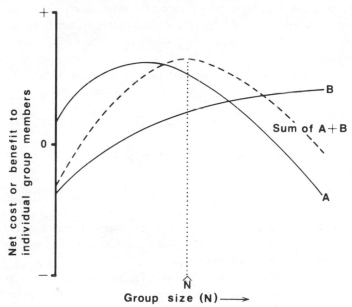

Figure 3.1. General Graph of the Interaction between Two Selective Forces in Determining
Optimal Group Size. Since factors $A$ and $B$ select for different group sizes, selection will
ultimately favor individuals who belong to groups approximating the compromise optimal size
$\hat{N}$. The value of $\hat{N}$ is obtained by summing the cost-benefit curves of each factor to obtain
a weighted mean cost-benefit curve that plots the net effect. Selective pressures in similar "domains" (e.g., two aspects of foraging strategy) can sometimes be summed via an operationally defined common currency (e.g., net capture rate), but selection in different domains (e.g., foraging strategy versus predator avoidance) must be measured via a more
general currency, such as increments of inclusive fitness. This latter task presents
great methodological difficulties. After Wilson 1975:136.

It therefore becomes necessary to choose a *proximate* currency that is more amenable to direct measurement and that is believed, on theoretical or empirical grounds, to be highly correlated with fitness. Energy and time, as incorporated in a measure of energetic efficiency, have been widely employed as such proximate measures by both evolutionary ecologists and anthropologists concerned with subsistence strategies, though any presumed correlation with fitness was not necessarily made. Recently, the reasons for expecting such a correlation under specific circumstances have been made much more explicit (Schoener 1971; Pyke, Pulliam, and Charnov 1977; Smith 1979b). This correlation is seen to apply generally where either time or energy is a constraint on reproductive success. In dealing with foraging activities, then, this chapter will take energetic input and output *rates* as valid measures for both costs and benefits. The basic postulate will be that various selective forces will favor foraging strategies that maximize *the net rate of energy capture per individual while foraging* (Schoener 1971; Smith 1979b). In no way am I assuming that selection of alternative strategies must proceed by natural selection of genetic variants. Even animals with relatively simple behavioral machinery can drastically modify their behavior in strategically adaptive ways under the influence of different environmental circumstances (Seger 1976). Humans, of course, are highly flexible in their behavioral repertoire, and are subject to several types of selective forces. The minimum assumption made here is that these various selective criteria (genetic, ontogenetic, cultural-evolutionary, conscious) will be generally congruent with the criterion of fitness (as discussed in Durham 1976a and 1978).

The guiding framework for the evolutionary-ecological theory of social groups can be summed up under five main points:
1. Groups form only when solitary behavior leads to lower reproductive success.
2. Success is to be measured in terms of net benefits to individual group members, and not to the group per se.
3. Net benefits are conceived of in terms of fitness units, but in practice it is necessary to use presumed correlates.
4. Several types of strategic goals affect the determination of optimal group size and structure, of which foraging strategy is only one.
5. The net rate of energy capture while foraging is a generally (but not universally) valid proximate measure of foraging success.

With this guiding framework, we can now briefly consider the types of models and hypotheses that evolutionary ecologists have constructed about optimal group size, before turning to the application of this approach to human foragers.

At least three possible relations may exist between foraging strategies and group formation (modified from Schoener 1971:392). First, group formation may have a neutral or negative effect on individual foraging efficiency, but be selectively advantageous for other reasons, such as predator avoidance. Second, groups may aggregate in proportion to resource concentrations, with no individual benefit arising from cooperative foraging per se. Finally, group formation may involve cooperative foraging in some form, such that individuals foraging in groups are favored with a net increase in foraging efficiency. Examples of each of these cases may be found in the biological and anthropological literature, and a summary is provided in table 3.1. The first case will be most important to human foragers when the advantages for reproductive strategy or long-term social reciprocity outweigh immediate losses in foraging efficiency. The second case results in the dispersion of foragers matching the resource dispersion (Winterhalder 1977:26), but is relatively uninteresting because of its simplicity. Most of my discussion will deal with the third case, where we can expect foraging efficiency considerations alone to select for optimal group size.

*Table 3.1*
*Some Possible Relationships between Group Formation and Various Selective Factors*

| Advantages of Group Formation | Evolutionary Ecology | | Anthropology | |
|---|---|---|---|---|
| | Theory | Empirical Cases | Theory | Empirical Cases |
| I. Decline in foraging efficiency, compensating benefits due to: | | | | |
| A. Reproductive strategies | Wittenberger 1980 | Groups of lions (Caraco and Wolf 1975; Bertram 1976) | Williams 1974 | Copper Inuit "Autumn sewing aggregations" (Damas 1972) |
| B. Predator avoidance | W. D. Hamilton 1971 | Various species of birds (Pulliam and Millikan, in press) | | |
| C. Resource defense | Crook 1972 | Social carnivores protecting kills (Kruuk 1975) | Dyson-Hudson and Smith 1978 | Northwest Coast Amerindians? |
| II. Increased foraging efficiency not due to grouping per se | Horn 1968 | Great blue herons (Krebs 1974) | Harpending and Davis 1977 | Shoshone pinon harvests and fish run groups (Steward 1938) |
| III. Grouping increases foraging efficiency, because of: | | | | |
| A. Increased encounter rate | Schoener 1971 | Cormorants pursuing fish (Bartholomew 1942) | | Inuit breathing hole seal hunting (Damas 1972:14) |
| B. Increased capture rate | Schoener 1971 | Social carnivores (Kruuk 1975) | | Shoshone game drives (Steward 1938 1955:109) |
| C. Increased prey size taken | Bertram 1978 | Social carnivores (Alcock 1975:350; Kruuk 1975) | Any text on human evolution | No. Alaskan Inuit whaling (Rainey 1947) |
| D. Reduction in foraging area overlap | Cody 1971 1974 | Desert finch flocks (Cody 1974) | | G/wi decision making (Silberbauer 1972:290) |
| E. Passive information sharing | Ward and Zahavi 1973 | Flock foraging in birds (Horn 1968; Krebs, et al. 1972) | Winterhalder 1977 | |
| F. Active information sharing | Schaffer 1978 | Chimpanzees foraging on fruiting trees (Reynolds 1965; but cf. Wrangham 1977) | Wilmsen 1973 | Shoshone winter village "chiefs" (Steward 1955:115) |
| G. Risk aversion | Pulliam and Millikan, in press | Simulations of bird flocks (Thompson, et al. 1974) | Durham, chapter 10, below | !Kung sharing networks (Wiessner 1977; Cashdan 1980) |

Note: Each possibility is matched with references from the literature that provide example of relevant evolutionary-ecological theory, anthropological theory, and proposed empirical cases from nonhuman species and human foragers.

Source: Schoener 1971.

If we consider only the third case, then, cooperatively foraging groups may gain more benefits than individual foragers (or other groups of nonoptimal size) for a number of possible reasons (based on Orians 1971:538-41; Schoener 1971:393-96; Winterhalder 1977:26ff.):

1. Groups encounter more prey per individual forager in a given habitat.
2. Groups capture a greater proportion of the prey encountered.
3. Groups are able to capture larger prey, and this increases the average foraging efficiency per individual.
4. Group foraging reduces the overlap of foraging areas, thus increasing the return per unit time foraged.
5. Groups foraging from a central place and specializing in large, spatiotemporally unpredictable food concentrations have increased individual capture rates as a result of *passive* (observational) information sharing.
6. Groups foraging under environmental conditions similar to (5) above have increased individual capture rates due to *active* food sharing and/or information sharing.
7. Group foraging decreases the *variance* in food intake rates, and this "risk aversion" is adaptive when food storage or central place sharing yields fewer benefits.

It must be remembered that other (nonforaging) selective advantages and disadvantages of different group sizes and structures can modify these results in complex ways.

## Application to Human Foragers

The application of the concepts developed in optimal foraging theory to human foraging populations demands a recognition of the complexity of human social structures, and an attention to possible ways in which humans uniquely violate the key assumptions of a neo-Darwinian approach (Winterhalder 1977:19f; Durham 1976a:102ff.). However, because of the key role given to environmental and behavioral variation by evolutionary-ecological theory, it offers definite advantages for dealing with human behavioral flexibility as compared with the more genetically oriented, static equilibrium focus of other neo-Darwinian approaches to behavioral analysis (Emlen 1980; Durham, chapter 10, below).

The analytical scheme that evolutionary ecologists have developed for the analysis of group formation, as summarized in table 3.1, suggests that several different levels of cooperation may be distinguished with reference to foraging strategy. With specific reference to human foragers, I want to define four levels of group organization that are heuristically and analytically useful for investigating the types of hypotheses developed in optimal foraging theory. I suggest that, for most or all populations of hunter-gatherers, we can distinguish the following:

1. Foraging groups: any group of individuals directly engaged in the cooperative procurement of a resource or set of resources.
2. Resource-sharing groups: any group within which a particular resource at a particular time is actually distributed, prior to consumption.
3. Information-sharing groups: any network of individuals through which information about spatiotemporal characteristics of a particular resource is transmitted, within a recent time period prior to the harvesting of this particular resource.
4. Coresident groups: any group of individuals residing together at a particular time and place.

These four types of groups are proposed as organizing concepts only, and are not highly original. The foraging group corresponds to Helm's (1968) "task group" in most attributes, and will generally refer to hunting parties, gathering groups, and so on. The coresident group is that group usually termed a camp or "local band," but no territorial identity or fixed membership is implied here. Resource-sharing and information-sharing groups are less common in the anthropological lexicon, and may prove harder to define operationally, though I have attempted to be explicit here.

I want to make some clarifying points about this organizing scheme, prior to exploring its relevance to hunter-gatherer group size and foraging strategy. First, while I believe that these four levels of organization will occur in most or all hunter-gatherer societies, many, and perhaps most, hunter-gatherer societies will include other functional units as well (such as resource-controlling groups, ritual groups, lineages, and councils), and all foragers belong to demes (breeding populations). Other organizational or classificatory schemes have certainly been proposed for hunter-gatherers (Steward 1936; Service 1962; Birdsell 1968; Damas 1969c; Williams 1974; King 1978), but for the purposes of this chapter these other schemes have less utility. On the one hand, the universal status of groups such as connubia, regional bands, and patrilocal bands is quite controversial. In addition, most of these other types of groups are more relevant to investigations of reproductive strategy and mating systems (Wobst 1974; Williams 1974) than of foraging strategy, which concerns us here. While I recognize that regional networks or group processes may be important for some aspects of foraging strategy, especially long-term strategy (Lee 1972a; Wiessner 1977; King 1978), the present classification system seems adequate to deal with such regional phenomena under the categories of information-sharing groups (cf. Moore, chapter 9, below), resource-sharing groups, or coresident groups (Lee 1972a; Harpending and Davis 1977) in which individual and family mobility facilitates rapidly changing membership.

A second general point concerns the distinction between different group levels, and their identity through time. The four group levels I have defined above definitely need *not* be mutually exclusive in any particular population of foragers. For instance, foraging groups may usually be made up of subsets of local (coresident) groups; but for certain resources, such as big game herds, a foraging group may include all members of a coresident group, or even members of several such groups. In light of the general postulate that group size and structure will be adjusted toward optimal levels under the selective influence of resource distributions, mating strategies, and so on, we have to take care not to reify these group categories into fixed units. Evolutionary ecology leads us to expect time-stable and space-stable groups only in spatiotemporally homogeneous environments--a rare if not nonexistent category. So, rather than fixed groups, each of these group levels should be considered situation specific.

For each of these four levels of group organization, it is possible to outline relevant evolutionary-ecological hypotheses that relate specific resource characteristics and foraging strategies to optimal group sizes. I will discuss each group level in turn, relating each to qualitative predictions about variance in optimal size generated from considerations of optimal resource utilization, as specified by both anthropological and evolutionary-ecological models. It is expected that optimal size at one level will often constrain optimal size at another level (for instance, optimal foraging group size for a critical resource may help determine optimum camp size, and vice versa); I will take note of evidence for this in specific cases. Other selective factors besides foraging strategy will be mentioned only briefly if at all, though they may be crucial in any particular case.

Foraging Groups

Foraging groups are by nature transitory, and we can thus reasonably expect a close fit between resource characteristics and the size of the foraging group. Accordingly, initial modeling and empirical research should focus on the simplest hypothesis: variance in foraging group size will be adjusted to the specific resources or patch types being exploited, in such a way as to produce a maximal net rate of energy capture per individual while foraging (see figure 3.2). We can expect this simple hypothesis to be modified or rejected in cases where materials other than energy are critical attributes of the resource being sought (such as specific nutrients or raw materials). This will require changing the currency to match more accurately the goals of the foragers (cf. Keene 1979a). We can also expect the hypothesis to be modified in cases where other selective forces are important determinants of optimal group size (such as risk factors, resource competition, cooperative defense, and so on).

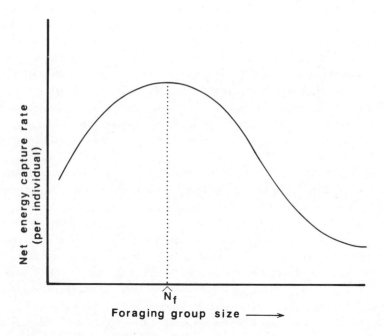

Figure 3.2. The Elementary Hypothesis That Optimal Foraging Group Size ($\hat{N}_f$) for Any Particular Type of Resource is Determined by Simple Covariance with Individual Energy Efficiency (as measured by net capture rate per individual forager).

Research on foraging group size that relies on the elementary hypothesis of foraging efficiency maximization is useful even in cases where this hypothesis fails to explain all or most of the variance in group size, *if* researchers are led to investigate other selective forces or strategic goals (cf. Caraco and Wolf 1975). In other words, the foraging efficiency assumption can be employed not only as a hypothesis subject to confirmation or refutation in specific cases, but also as part of a research strategy that generates different hypotheses and (because of its quantitative test implications) helps guide future research (Charnov 1976b). This applies to all types of research guided by any sort of optimization theory (Maynard Smith 1978).

In cases where the initial hypothesis of energy efficiency maximization *is* borne out, more specific hypotheses can be examined in an attempt to account for variation in foraging group size in greater detail. In light of the material summarized in table 3.1, some of these specific hypotheses can now be mentioned. First, the optimal size of foraging groups might vary so as to maximize the encounter rate for different prey, especially cryptic ones. One might expect that cryptic and aggregated prey types would be sought by larger groups, who could increase the encounter rate per forager by flushing and/or driving these prey to nets or ambush stations (e.g., Turnbull 1968:135 on Mbuti net hunting; Steward 1955:109 on Shoshone rabbit drives). On the other hand, cryptic but solitary prey might be more easily approached by small groups or individual foragers (e.g., Harner 1972:57ff. on Jivaro hunting methods). Certain prey can present unique encounter problems, such as arctic seals using a set of breathing holes in an unpredictable sequence; this has often been argued as a case where large foraging groups have much higher encounter rates per individual forager (Boas 1888; Balikci 1970:58; Damas 1972:14). I present an empirical test of this argument below.

The optimal size of foraging groups might also vary so as to maximize the *capture* rate for different prey species. In general one might expect that concentrated and mobile prey would be sought by larger groups than dispersed and/or sessile prey. Thus, the variance in foraging group size within any one society might often be tied to variance in the density and spatial predictability of specific resources, as these would directly affect the efficiency with which individuals and groups of various sizes could harvest the resources. Some evidence in support of this hypothesis has been summarized by Steward (1938 1955) for the Shoshone; he describes dispersal into family units for foraging on seeds and roots, but communal hunts of certain species, with larger groups being associated with prey species of greater density. Rogers (1972:111) has described variation in the size of Mistassini Cree hunting parties, with caribou herds being exploited by larger groups than more solitary moose (except when moose aggregate in deep snow conditions, at which time foraging group size increases). On the other hand, frequent descriptions of group foraging by parties of women gathering plant foods (e.g., Lee 1972b:345; Woodburn 1972:198) seem to conflict with the hypothesis that more dispersed and sessile resources will be exploited by smaller groups, especially when in the same societies men hunt large game in smaller groups.

At present, it is difficult to evaluate the explanatory adequacy of hypotheses on optimal foraging group size for a large sample of hunter-gatherer populations. Testing hypotheses (as opposed to making plausibility arguments) requires detailed and quantitative data of a type rarely available in the literature. Anthropologists themselves have devoted little effort to the construction or testing of hypotheses concerning the determinants of foraging group size. This is probably because variance in group size is generally seen as obviously tied to the efficient procurement of specific resources, with no need for detailed and critical examination (e.g., Helm 1968:121; Woodburn 1972:198; Lee 1972b:345-46). The problem of requisite data is also acute in the case of hypotheses about group size at other levels of organization, as will be apparent below.

## Information-Sharing Groups

Using ideas first discussed by Crook (1965) and Horn (1968; see also Ward and Zahavi 1973), we can predict that as the spatiotemporal unpredictability of any resource increases, larger information-sharing groups will have an improved chance of locating the ephemeral resource points. However, individuals are not expected to expand their information-sharing network indefinitely, as eventually any resource concentration could thereby attract too many individuals, and the benefit to individuals (in terms of resources obtained per unit time) would decline. Accordingly, optimal size of information-sharing groups should be set by an interaction of resource predictability and within-patch resource density (Dyson-Hudson and Smith 1978:25-26). In addition, one can predict that mobility costs will often contribute to variation in the size of information-sharing networks, as these affect not only the costs (e.g., in energy and time) of sharing information with distant foragers, but also the costs of exploiting larger foraging areas covered by larger information networks. Among human foragers, mobility costs can be lowered by certain modes of transport (watercraft, dog teams, horses). Higher population densities can also lower the costs of sharing information with greater numbers of people (because of the reduced size of per capita foraging area). In summary, high predictability of resources in space and time, as well as low population densities, reduces the advantages of large information-sharing networks, while lowered mobility costs and the concentration of resources into ephemeral "superabundances" favor increased information sharing about resource locations.

Another way that resource distribution can favor increased size of information-sharing groups is suggested by Cody's (1971 1974) idea of group foraging to reduce foraging area overlap. His model argues that, where critical resources are relatively evenly dispersed and are slowly renewing, foragers moving through an area individually and at random will "depress" the resource content fairly evenly and thus face increasingly poor returns on the time and energy they spend foraging (cf. Charnov, Orians, and Hyatt 1976). Group foraging, on the other hand, allows the same area to be more systematically cropped, since individuals need not search over an area already depressed by another independent forager; the result under these conditions should be a higher net rate of energy capture for individuals foraging in groups. Cody developed this model to account for certain types of bird flocking, but Winterhalder (1977:282f.) has pointed out that human language would allow the same kind of reduction in foraging overlap even for individuals who forage alone, if they engaged in systematic sharing of information about areas recently foraged or planned for foraging. Such advantages to information-sharing groups, then, would apply under the conditions of resource dispersion and slow renewal noted above, and would be more important to "searchers" (foragers with a large search-time/pursuit-time ratio) than to "pursuers."

Wilmsen (1973) has suggested some important applications of the information center concept to human foragers. He has generalized that "increased chances of hunting success for all hunters are obtained by co-operative search procedures for resources located at an unknown single point" (Wilmsen 1973:9) and suggests that gregarious, mobile herd animals have the characteristics that favor such cooperative search, while solitary animal species and plant foods do not. Yellen and Harpending (1972:247) have also argued that hunter-gatherer groups are adaptively important for information sharing about unpredictable resources.

Actual descriptions of information sharing about resource locations seem to be relatively rare in the hunter-gatherer literature, and it is clearly a difficult process to measure with any precision. However, the concepts and models discussed above suggest under what conditions we should look for intensive information sharing (see also Heffley, chapter 6, and Moore, chapter 9, below). It should be emphasized that the hypotheses noted above predict that the size of information-sharing groups should generally be resource specific, and thus that such groups should to some extent vary independently of the size of coresident groups. Steward (1938 1955) has presented qualitative evidence on Great Basin Shoshone information sharing, and these data are consistent with the idea that spatiotemporal predictability of resources is a major determinant of the degree of information sharing about resource locations (Steward 1955:107-11). Silberbauer (1972:290) has reported an example of information sharing in the prevention of foraging area overlap among the G/wi San:

> Most hunting is done by men working in pairs, making sorties of a day or less from the band's camp. Before going out, the hunters discuss their intentions and arrange their plans so as to avoid interference of one party by the others. There are seldom more than four pairs in the field on the same day, and there is usually more than one area in which game is to be found within the fifteen-mile operational radius of a daily hunting party.

While these empirical cases are suggestive, the lack of quantitative data on either the degree of information sharing or the resource characteristics and foraging efficiencies associated with each case argues for caution in interpreting the reports as support for the concepts of foraging efficiency maximization or optimal group size, or for specific models of information sharing.

## Resource-Sharing Groups

Cooperative food sharing extending beyond the bounds of a foraging group has often been cited as a hallmark of human foragers (Lee 1969; Washburn and Lancaster 1968; Isaac 1978). Evolutionary theory leads us to expect active resource sharing only under special conditions, and indeed it occurs among very few species (Schaller and Lowther 1969; Thompson 1975). While there is little formal ecological theory concerning the adaptive determinants of food sharing, it seems reasonable to extend some of the hypotheses concerning information sharing to this phenomenon (but see Schaffer 1978 and Harpending, in press). Any resources that are relatively rare and are highly unpredictable in space and time will have an erratic frequency of capture by any one individual or foraging group. A number of anthropologists have suggested that hunter-gatherer food sharing is adaptive in smoothing out the variation in food availability per capita, especially in the case of large game (Yellen and Harpending 1972:247; Woodburn 1972:199; Jochim 1976:68).

This hypothesis has generally been stated in a way that equates the coresident group (camp) with the food-sharing group. For example, Woodburn (1972:199) argues that "living in a large camp does not only increase the frequency of hunting kills: it also reduces the unpredictability," and that "where the number of hunters is greater, the intervals between kills are not only smaller but are more equal in length." Having established a rationale for increased group size with erratically obtained resources, Woodburn goes on to argue for a limit in the possible size of this group due to diminishing returns per individual, stating that if the camp size gets too large, the portion of meat each individual receives from a kill drops "below an acceptable quantity." However, it should theoretically be possible for a coresident group too large for optimum food sharing (as defined by minimum portions of meat per kill per individual) to restrict food sharing to groups less inclusive than the coresident group: these two group levels need not be isomorphic for any particular resource type.

Aside from the degree to which a resource is erratically captured by any one individual or foraging group, we can expect that the amount of the resource captured in relation to the consumption needs of the foraging unit, whether individual or group, will affect food-sharing practices. Accordingly, we can predict resource sharing beyond the foraging unit to be more common for resources that represent superabundances for that unit. The larger a resource packet (as measured by weight, or preferably calories), the more likely is it that it will be to a unit's advantage to share it with other reciprocating units. This general hypothesis should be reinforced when the unit's capture is erratic (as discussed above), but countered by its ability to store superabundances for long periods. If there is a shortage of individuals for some reason (e.g., camp size is very small), the advantage of low-risk, low-return resources (e.g., fish, plant foods) over relatively high-risk (erratic) resource types will be increased; thus, constraints on the possible size of resource-sharing groups can in turn affect prey choice.

Unlike information sharing, food sharing is relatively easy to observe and quantify. It has been repeatedly described in hunter-gatherer ethnography, and in some cases quantitative or semiquantitative generalizations indicate that variation in packet size is correlated with variation in the size of the sharing group (Lee 1972b:348; Graburn 1969:66-67; Gould 1967:58f.; Binford 1978:472), or that increased storage capabilities are associated with a reduced radius of food sharing (Binford 1978:140). Again, these cases were not tied to direct tests of optimal group size hypotheses, but are only suggestive.

## Coresident Groups

A large anthropological literature exists on the subject of coresident groups among hunter-gatherers (see Damas 1969c and references therein). Here I will deal only with the role of foraging strategy in determining the size of coresident groups. In general, we can expect that coresident group size will have a more complex set of ecological determinants than the group levels discussed above, so that predicting the size and structure of local bands or camps from resource characteristics alone will rarely be satisfactory. Since coresident groups are generally less temporary than the other groups I have discussed, and the costs of radically altering their size and structure over short periods of time are much higher, we might expect them to be less finely tuned to specific resources, and to represent more of a compromise of various strategic goals. In addition, conflicts of interest between coresident individuals are quite likely to occur (see Durham, chapter 10, below), and the resultant compromise group size may not be "optimal" for anyone. I will discuss coresident groups in terms of several limiting cases, where one or two factors at a time can be assessed as to their probable role in determining variance in coresident group size, but it should be kept in mind that any empirical case will probably be considerably more complex.

The first possibility we will consider is that variance in coresident group size is determined primarily by the optimal size (and age-sex structure) of the foraging groups exploiting the most critical resources (or the resource requiring the largest foraging group). Steward (1936 1955) was one of the first anthropologists to argue that foraging strategies adjusted to specific resource types would tend to determine the social organization of human foragers (in fact, many of his arguments anticipate the models of evolutionary ecology by about thirty years). Briefly, Steward argued that a principal reliance on wild plants and small game would favor a family-level organization; that a primary reliance on prey living in small, nonmigratory bands favored a patrilineal band organization and coresident groups of moderate size; and that a bilateral or composite band organization arises when the principal resource is game grouped into large, migratory herds.

The idea that optimal foraging group sizes will directly determine coresident group sizes cannot be ruled out. As an example, the desired composition of coresident hunting groups among the Mistassini Cree is said to have been four families, "so that the four males could hunt and trap as a group or in pairs" (Rogers 1972:121). Martin (1973) has coupled the optimum foraging group argument to a demographic model in order to predict the variance in size of Pai Indian local groups. In general, however, it seems likely that foraging group size will constrain only the *lower* limit of coresident group size, and that much of the variance in local group size will thus be due to other determinants.

Coresident groups are the source not only of most foraging parties, but of information-sharing and resource-sharing groups as well. Yellen and Harpending (1972:247) argue that camps or local bands are adaptive in permitting information sharing about unpredictable resources, thus "increasing hunting efficiency," as well as in smoothing variation in per capita meat availability. (However, they do not directly state that these factors alone will determine optimal camp size.) Wilmsen (1973), in applying Horn's (1968) geometric model for dispersion and aggregation of foragers according to resource predictability and concentration, has made a rather strong argument that optimal band size is primarily responsive to these parameters of resource distribution (see Heffley, chapter 6, below). The Horn model specifies that stable-dispersed resources are most efficiently harvested (in terms of the distance traveled) by a population dispersed into individual territories (or, in Wilmsen's application to the human case, "minimal work units"), while unpredictable-clumped resources are best captured by central place foraging, leading to population aggregation and the probable absence of territoriality (cf. Dyson-Hudson and Smith 1978).

The geometry of foraging may be hypothesized to affect optimum coresident group size by setting a limit on the area exploited from the home base, depending on mobility costs and resource densities. Steward (1955:125) argued that sparse and scattered resources lead to a low hunter-gatherer population density, and that "this prevents indefinite enlargement of the band because there would be no means of transporting the food to the people or the people to the food." The same point is made by Jochim (1976:66). These arguments are useful in defining an *upper* limit to coresident group size, but whether this limit will be operative would depend in each case on whether other determinants set a *lower* limit. Hassan (1975:40), using quantitative data on hunter-gatherer population density, has shown that the radius of a foraging area should rarely be a critical factor in determining local group size (see figure 3.3). A geometric model of foraging predicts that when resources tend toward homogeneous distribution, coresident groups as small as families or individuals are most efficient for minimizing mobility costs (Smith 1968; Horn 1968). It might be possible to test the hypothesis that mobility costs directly limit coresident group size by examining the correlation between resource density, foraging area, and group size among hunter-gatherer populations, holding mobility costs constant.

As a related case, optimal size in local groups can be modeled in terms of territorial units. Crook (1972:258) has argued that "optimum group size (in primates) will be that at which the defensible area provides an adequate provision of food under the normally existing range of conditions" (see figure 3.4). Thus, he treats group size as a function of resource defense capabilities, predator avoidance, and minimum range size for adequate per capita food supply. The conditions under which territorially exclusive groups of human foragers would be favored are controversial, and have been extensively discussed (e.g., Lee 1972a; King 1976; Dyson-Hudson and Smith 1978, and references therein). In general, the resource conditions favoring territoriality (relatively dense and predictable resources) also favor small group size, though humans can confound this generalization via cooperative perimeter defense (cf. Hamilton and Watt 1970).

A final way in which foraging strategy considerations might affect optimal coresident group size is via a direct matching of population concentrations and resource concentrations. Thus, Jochim (1976:66) notes that increased spatial concentration of resources will support a larger coresiding group. The examples he cites, and others occurring in the hunter-gatherer literature (e.g., Damas 1972:23-24; Yellen and Harpending 1972:246), seem

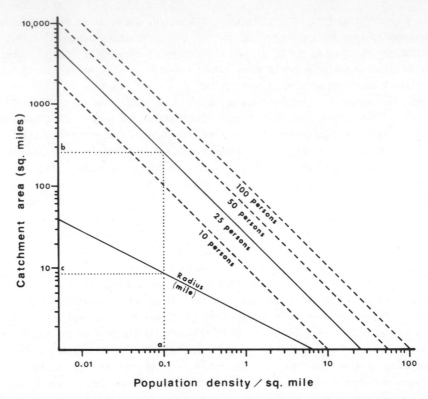

Figure 3.3.  Graph for Numerical Determination of the Relationship between Population Density, Catchment Area, and Coresident Group Size.  For example, for a hunter-gatherer population with a mean density of 0.1 persons per square mile (a), and a mean group size of 25, the catchment area averages 250 mi² (b) with a radius of 9 miles (c).  Double-log scale. After Hassan 1975:figure 2.

to indicate the aggregation of individual foragers at resource-rich locations, rather than cooperative foraging.  Although this sort of situation seems analytically simple, aggregation and dispersal of minimal units (e.g., extended or nuclear families), according to the concentration or scarcity of resources, may yet be found to account for a large part of the variance in coresident group size among many populations of human foragers.  Harpending and Davis (1977) have employed a very sophisticated approach to this issue, focusing on the "spatial phasing" of different resource types as the critical variable.  Their analysis suggests that "group size should be small when there is little spatial variation in resources," and that with high levels of spatial variation "large groups should aggregate when resources are in phase," but variation with resources out of phase "should lead to hyper-mobility and poorly-defined local groups" (Harpending and Davis 1977:283).

Now that we have considered a range of factors postulated to affect the size of hunter-gatherer groups, it should be evident that the data presented are weak and allow only a plausibility argument to be made in support of the optimal foraging theory of group size. In addition, ecological factors other than those based on foraging strategy must be kept in mind as strong candidates for determining variance in group size and structure.  Many anthropologists have stressed "social factors" as determinants of group aggregation and fission in foraging societies (e.g., Turnbull 1968; Woodburn 1968:106; Damas 1972:24). These need not be viewed a priori as alternatives to adaptive explanations; many social

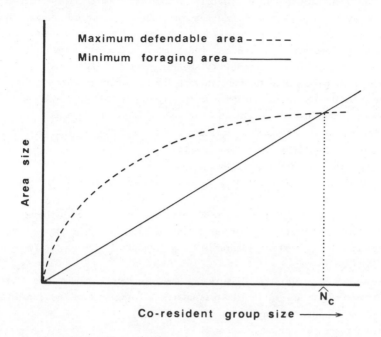

Figure 3.4.  Predicted Relationship between Foraging Area Requirements and Economic Defendability Measures in Determining Optimal Group Size, under Conditions of Group Territorial Defense.  Coresident groups of size $\hat{N}_c$ obtain maximum net benefit (utilizable resources minus costs of defense); groups smaller than this are possible, but suffer from inadequate territorial defense; larger groups are not viable because the required foraging area is not economically defendable.  All costs and benefits are assumed to be measurable in terms of energy rates per individual group member (time and energy expended on territorial defense, net energy captured per unit foraging time).  After Crook 1972:259.

factors affecting group size could be closely tied to reproductive advantages associated with particular social groupings in particular social environments.  While the tendency has been to rely on extremely simplistic descriptions of environmental variables in refuting the idea of ecological determinants of group size, we should also acknowledge that ecological models will probably account for only a portion of the variance in any sphere of human activity.  It seems likely that future progress in this area will attempt to consider various other factors *along with* foraging strategy models in the attempt more fully to explain variance in group size (as well as other aspects of hunter-gatherer socioecology).

## Summary of Optimum Group Size Hypotheses

A summary of the hypotheses on optimum group size derived from optimal foraging theory (and related anthropological research) might be outlined as follows:

A.  Optimal size of foraging groups $(N_f)$
1.  Variance in $N_f$ is adjusted to the specific resources or patch types being exploited in such a way as to produce a maximal net rate of energy capture per individual.
2.  $N_f$ varies so as to maximize the encounter rate for different resources.
    a.  Cryptic-aggregated prey are driven and flushed by larger groups.
    b.  Cryptic-solitary prey are sought by smaller groups or individuals.
3.  $N_f$ varies so as to maximize the capture rate for different resources.
    a.  More concentrated and mobile prey are pursued by larger groups.
    b.  More dispersed and/or sessile prey are sought by smaller groups.
    c.  Larger groups form to capture larger prey when and if this increases the net capture rate per individual group member.
B.  Optimal size of information-sharing groups $(N_i)$
1.  As the spatiotemporal unpredictability of any resource increases, the optimal $N_i$ for this resource also increases.
2.  As the average packet size for any resource increases relative to the needs of individual foraging units, the optimal $N_i$ increases.
3.  Decreases in mobility costs, by expanding the economical size of the foraging range, favor an increase in $N_i$.
4.  Where resources are relatively dispersed, slowly renewing, and involve a large search-time/pursuit-time ratio, the prevention of foraging area overlap favors the formation of information-sharing groups.
C.  Optimal size of resource-sharing groups $(N_r)$
1.  For resources with a more erratic frequency of capture per foraging unit, $N_r$ is larger (smoothing out variation in individual access).
2.  Resources with a very large packet size relative to the needs of foraging units (superabundances) are shared more widely.
3.  Increases in the ability to store food favor a decreased $N_r$.
4.  Constraints on the maximum $N_r$ may increase the advantage of reliable (low risk) resources relative to erratically captured ones.
D.  Optimal size of coresident groups $(N_c)$
1.  Variance in $N_c$ may be determined primarily by variance in the optimal $N_f$ (and age-sex structure) of a foraging unit for any one season or critical resource.
2.  Variance in $N_c$ may be determined primarily by considerations of optimal information-sharing or food-sharing networks.
    a.  Reliance on stable-dispersed resources favors a smaller $N_c$.
    b.  Reliance on unpredictable-clumped resources favors a larger $N_c$.
3.  The upper limit to $N_c$ may be set by the increased mobility costs of exploiting larger ranges (as determined by resource densities).
4.  Economically defendable (predictable-dense) resources combined with cooperative perimeter defense favor a larger $N_c$.
5.  Variance in $N_c$ may be determined primarily by the costs and benefits of aggregating at resource concentrations, when these concentrations are ephemeral superabundances (i.e., are not economically defendable).

Note that these hypotheses are not fully developed here with respect to operational definitions or test implications. This further development depends in part on the specific characteristics of the empirical cases one wishes to investigate. An example of how such investigations can be carried out, with respect to the first hypothesis on this list, will occupy the remaining sections of this chapter.

## Foraging Group Size:  A Case Study

I conducted fieldwork among contemporary Inuit (Canadian Eskimos) in order to generate data on a number of topics (foraging strategies, subsistence economics, group structure, and demography).  Among the hypotheses tested (Smith 1980), the one that will be discussed here concerns the relation of foraging group size to efficiency.  Specifically, I seek to test the hypothesis that foraging group size will be adjusted among different hunt types so as to maximize the net rate of energy capture per individual hunter while foraging.  The following sections discuss the model that formalizes this hypothesis, the methods of data collection and analysis employed, the results obtained for different types of hunting, and the values and limitations of the research.

## The Model:  Explicit and Implicit Contents

In this case study, the primary approach is that of modeling hunting strategies, and then comparing model predictions with the real world.  The strengths and weaknesses of ecological modeling in general, and foraging strategy models in particular, have been discussed by Winterhalder in chapter 2, above.  Briefly, it is assumed here that any model is a simplified and "artificial" version of reality, but useful nonetheless because of its logical clarity and direct (and in this case quantitative) test implications.  Model construction involves three important aspects:  major assumptions, key parameters, and the actual model structure.  Each of these must be assessed in evaluating any particular modeling exercise.

Three major assumptions underlie the research reported here.  First, I assume that a moderate level of statistical predictability applies to critical variables in the Inuit foragers' environment, such that the average forager can draw on a body of information (developed both through personal experience and via longer-term cultural storage) that will allow reasonably accurate estimates of the expected foraging success of alternative group sizes under varying conditions (cf. Nelson 1969).

A second major assumption is that the costs and benefits of different group sizes should be measured per individual; in other words, the model defines the optimum group size in terms of maximizing the net benefit per individual group member, and no assumption is made about the relation of individual benefit to total group benefit.

The third major assumption is that energetic efficiency, as defined below, is a suitable cost-benefit currency for analysis of Inuit foraging group size.  There are several justifications for this:  such a general measure allows comparability with other aspects of Inuit socioecology and with other studies of foraging; it is easier to define operationally than some alternative measures (e.g., fitness), and more analytically tractable than others (e.g., complex nutrient compositions); and it allows costs of foraging to be measured in the same currency as benefits--a problem with many alternative formulations.  Energetic efficiency measures are not without their problems, however.  The two most immediate problems concern cases where foragers are not food-limited, and cases where even though food may be a limiting factor, nutrients other than energy are binding (Keene, chapter 8, below).  The first objection can be partially met by using energy *rate* measures (rather than input/output ratios), since energetic efficiency can be favored if time is limited or foraging is riskier than nonforaging, even when energy is not in short supply (see discussion in Smith 1979b).  The second objection is an important one; my view is that the Inuit diet probably approximates the simplifying assumptions of energy maximization more closely than the diet of most human populations, because the fresh animal foods they rely on generally contain sufficient amounts of protein, fat, vitamins, and other nutrients

(Mann, et al. 1962; Heller and Scott 1967; Draper 1977; cf. Keene 1979a for an opposing view).

Because of the great complexity of human foraging strategies, it is necessary to model aspects of foraging using what Levins (1968:6ff.) has termed *sufficient parameters*, which reduce analytic complexity without (one hopes) ignoring it. Sufficient parameters act by subsuming many interacting determinants in a relatively simple but adequate fashion, for purposes of the topics addressed by any specific modeling exercise. (For example, when foraging time and associated energy expenditure and capture rates can be directly measured, the resultant parameter subsumes many of the troubling variables that Keene, because of the problems inherent in archeological data, is forced to estimate in chapter 8, below.)

The major sufficient parameters in the present study are group size, energy expenditure rates, energy capture rates, and hunt type. Group size, as employed here, ignores the variables of age and sex in foraging group composition (though these are accounted for in the energy expenditure parameter). Energy expenditure rates subsume a variety of lower-order variables (work effort, duration, age, sex, mobility costs, etc.), while energy capture rates subsume the variables determining caloric value of prey (tissue composition, edible portions, mean weight of harvested age-sex classes), as well as those determining forager-prey encounter rates (forager searching velocity and tactics; prey mobility, density, aggregation, spatiotemporal predictability, evasion abilities, etc.). The parameter of hunt type is the most complex and problematic; it aims to subsume the criteria used by foragers in making decisions about group size and prey choice. A discussion of how the hunt type classification of the present study was generated is given in the methods section, below.

Having discussed the major assumptions and parameters of the model, I shall now briefly define its actual structure, and derive hypotheses. Its variables and parameters are the following (see also Smith 1980):

$E_a$ = total metabolizable energy acquired on any foraging trip

$E_e$ = total metabolic energy expended on any foraging trip

$t$ = total duration of any foraging trip

$n$ = total number of foragers for any foraging trip or set of foraging trips

$R$ = per capita net capture rate for any foraging trip = $(E_a - E_e)/tn$

$\overline{R}_{ij}$ = mean per capita net capture rate for the $i^{th}$ group size of the $j^{th}$ hunt type

$(\overline{R}_j)_{max}$ = maximum mean net capture rate achieved by any group size of the $j^{th}$ hunt type

$\hat{N}_j$ = optimal group size of the $j^{th}$ hunt type, that achieving the maximum value of $\overline{R}_j$ varying $i$

If individuals seek to maximize net gain, and net gain is defined as energy captured minus energy expended per unit time, then the strategic goal is to maximize $R$ in the equation

$$R = \frac{E_a - E_e}{t} \qquad (1)$$

where $E_a$ is the total metabolizable energy acquired on a foraging trip, $E_e$ is the total metabolic energy expended on that trip, and $t$ is the total duration of the trip. $R$ is thus the net rate of energy capture while foraging, the efficiency measure that is usually maximized in optimal foraging theory models.

In terms of group size, individuals should attempt to forage in groups of a size that will maximize their net capture rate. If proceeds are equally shared (as they generally are in the Inuit case), or in any case where one wishes to calculate an average success rate per forager, equation (1) can be modified accordingly:

$$\overline{R} = \frac{\sum\limits^{n}(E_a - E_e)}{t \cdot n}$$
(2)

where $n$ = the total number of foragers, and $\overline{R}$ thus expresses the average net rate of energy acquisition *per forager* for the duration of the foraging period (e.g., kcal/hunter/hour).

A measure like $\overline{R}$ can be calculated not only for single instances of group foraging, but for any case where some set of foraging results needs to be analyzed in terms of an average net capture rate: the set of hunts of a specific type or period, particular group sizes of any hunt type, and so on. We can expect that optimal (maximally efficient) group size will often vary according to the spatiotemporal distribution of the species being sought, habitat conditions, methods of search and capture, and so on--what has been sub-sumed here under "hunt type." Equation (1) can be modified in order to specify optimal group size, as follows. Let hunt $ijk$ be the $k^{th}$ hunt of type $j$ and size $i$. For hunts of category $ij$, the mean per capita net capture rate is then

$$\overline{R}_{ij} = \frac{\sum\limits_{k=1}^{r}(E_a - E_e)_{ijk}}{n \cdot t_{ijk}}$$
(3)

The mean per capita net capture rate can also be defined for hunts of size $i$ or of type $j$, respectively, as follows:

$$\overline{R} = \frac{\sum\limits_{i=1}^{q}\overline{R}_{ij}}{q}$$
(4)

$$\overline{R}_j = \frac{\sum\limits_{i=1}^{p}\overline{R}_{ij}}{p}$$
(5)

For a particular hunt type $j$, the hypothetically optimal (maximally efficient) group size $\hat{N}$ is indexed by that value of $i$ (not necessarily unique) for which $\overline{R}_j = \max\limits_i \overline{R}_j$.

These simple mathematical formalisms are presented here for the purpose of clarifying and making explicit the procedures and assumptions that are involved in using an energy cost-benefit analysis to predict the choices individual foragers will make with respect to foraging group size. Using this formulation, we can derive various hypotheses to predict the variation of foraging group size under differing conditions and simplifying assumptions. (The full range of alternatives will not be discussed here, but see Smith 1980, chapter 8.) The following three hypotheses are subjected to test below:

$H_1$: Within any hunt type, the modal (most frequent) group size is that which is most energy efficient (maximizes $\overline{R}_j$ varying $i$).

$H_2$: Within any hunt type, the rank order of net capture rates (for each hunt) and the rank order of the observed frequency of each group size are positively correlated, such that the more efficient a given group size is, the more frequently it will occur.

$H_3$: The variables of modal group size and optimal group size will be positively correlated across the array of hunt types.

These three hypotheses are not truly independent, although they are sufficiently dif-ferent in details such that they need not be coconfirmed (or corefuted) in any specific case--as will be empirically demonstrated. The test of $H_1$ requires a simple comparison of measured $\hat{N}_j$ to the $f_{ij}$ values, while $H_2$ and $H_3$ require a statistical test for correlation,

and a determination of significance levels.[1]  $H_3$ predicts the structure of group size variation *between* hunt types, while $H_1$ and $H_2$ are concerned with within-hunt-type variation in
group size.  Finally, $H_2$ is the most stringent test of the three, in that all of the variance in the sample data for each hunt type, rather than just the central tendencies, must
be taken into consideration.

Research Methods

Data on Inuit foraging practices were collected over a period of approximately one
year (July 1977 to August 1978) in and around the village of Inukjuak, Arctic Quebec.
This village, inhabited by over six hundred Inuit (Inukjuamiut), is located on the east
coast of Hudson Bay in a low-Arctic, wet tundra habitat.  The foraging economy is heavily
marine oriented in summer and fall, but terrestrial hunting in winter and spring accounts
for a greater portion of the total annual harvest.  Fox trapping, commercial soapstone
carving, wage labor, and government transfer payments are the main sources of cash income.
Virtually all foraging activities involve the use of mechanized transport (canoes with outboard motors, snowmobiles) and imported tools (rifles, fishnets, and so on).  While no
Inukjuamiut in the past two decades have relied exclusively on foraging for their suste-
nance, comprehensive statistics indicate an annual harvest of approximately 186,390 kg of
game (edible weight), which amounts to an average daily harvest of 0.96 kg (1,700 kcal)
per capita (NHRC 1979; Smith 1980:table 5.6).  Many further details concerning the physical
and biological environment, foraging patterns, and socioeconomic history of Inukjuamiut are
discussed elsewhere (Smith 1980).

The data used in this analysis were collected in two distinct ways:  via participant
observation of hunting trips (41 trips covering 51 days, for a total of 405 hours of direct
observation); and via a series of interviews to elicit recall data on hunting activities
(71 interviews with 35 different individuals) coupled with hunter-recorded diaries of hunting patterns and harvest results.  The combination of observation and interview generated
a sample of 687 hunts covering 25,597 hunter-hours (h-hrs) of foraging time.  The sample
is distributed over all twelve months (though weak for late summer and early fall), and includes over twenty-five hunt types (see below).  Additional data on the total (community-
wide) harvest of game are being gathered over a five-year period by research funded through
the northern Quebec native land claims settlement (NHRC 1976, and subsequent reports).  It
was not possible formally to randomize the sample of informants or hunts, but the NHRC data
(and other sources) allow a check on sample bias, and these indicate that my data base is
reasonably representative in most respects (see Smith 1980 for details).

In order to calculate net energy capture rates for foraging, data are needed on two
basic variables:  average rates of energy expenditure (specific to the age, sex, and activity patterns of the forager), and average measures of the caloric value of prey species.
Energy expenditure estimates are based on time-motion analysis coupled with published
tables of expenditure rates for standardized tasks.  Detailed minute-by-minute time-motion
records of foraging activities were gathered by direct observation, and the activities
classified into twenty-eight descriptive categories distributed into fifteen different
energy expenditure levels (differentiated further by age and sex; see table 3.2).  Published expenditure rate data on both European and Inuit populations (Durnin and Passmore
1967; Godin 1972; Godin and Shephard 1973), in conjunction with the situation-specific

---

1.  For $H_2$ and $H_3$, correlation is measured by Spearman's rank correlating coefficient
($r_s$), and the significance level is set at .05 (one-tailed), using the t-distribution with
n-2 degrees of freedom.

*Table 3.2*

*Activity Categories and Energy Expenditure Levels Used in Calculating Inukjuamiut Hunting Effort*

| | Expenditure Levels (kcal/min) | | |
|---|---|---|---|
| Activity Categories[a] | Men[b] | Women[c] | Subadults[d] |
| Sedentary<br>(sit and work) | 1.6 ± 0.3 | 1.2 ± 0.2 | 1.1 ± 0.2 |
| Light work<br>(canoe travel, snowmobile<br>travel, stand and work,<br>tea break, clean fish and<br>small game, stalking, repairs) | 2.7 ± 0.7 | 2.0 ± 0.5 | 1.9 ± 0.5 |
| Semilight work<br>(difficult snowmobile travel,<br>hunt preparation, setting<br>camp, open water netting) | 4.2 ± 0.7 | 3.1 ± 0.5 | 2.9 ± 0.5 |
| Moderate work<br>(loading, hauling,<br>butchering large game) | 6.2 ± 1.2 | 4.7 ± 1.0 | 4.3 ± 0.8 |
| Heavy work<br>(heavy loading, carrying) | 8.7 ± 1.2 | 6.8 ± 1.0 | 6.1 ± 0.8 |
| Very heavy work<br>(running on tundra) | 11.2 ± 1.2 | 8.6 ± 0.7 | 7.8 ± 0.8 |
| Other | | | |
|   Lying down | 1.2 + 0.2 | 1.0 ± 0.2 | 0.8 ± 0.1 |
|   Sitting quietly | 1.4 ± 0.3 | 1.1 ± 0.3 | 1.0 ± 0.2 |
|   Standing quietly | 1.7 ± 0.3 | 1.3 ± 0.3 | 1.2 ± 0.2 |
|   Walking (moderate pace) | 5.3 ± 1.2 | 4.7 ± 1.0 | 3.7 ± 0.8 |
|   Walking (difficult) | 7.6 ± 1.2 | 6.7 ± 1.0 | 5.3 ± 0.8 |
|   Sled travel | 3.6 ± 1.7 | 2.0 ± 0.5 | 2.5 ± 1.2 |
|   Jigging | 2.0 ± 0.7 | 1.6 ± 0.5 | 1.4 ± 0.5 |
|   Netting through the ice | 5.5 ± 1.7 | | |
|   Chipping ice holes | 7.1 ± 1.7 | 5.4 ± 1.3 | |
|   Building snow houses | 5.4 ± 1.2 | | |

[a]See Smith 1980:appendix B, for detailed justification.

[b]Values are for a standard 65-kg adult male with average RMR.

[c]Values are for a standard 55-kg adult or adolescent female with average RMR.

[d]Values are for a 30-kg boy, aged 9-11 yrs, with an RMR of 26 cal/min/kg.

Source:  Durnin and Passmore 1967:31-45; Godin 1972:65-69, 308; Godin and Shephard 1973:197; and Kemp and Smith, n.d.

time-motion data, allowed estimates of average energy expenditure that were sufficiently accurate for purposes of foraging strategy analysis. Mean expenditure rates were calculated for each observed hunt type, and the estimates show a fairly small range (2.3 - 4.5 kcal/min for adult males).  For good theoretical reasons, the caloric value of the fossil fuel inputs was *not* summed with metabolic work inputs.[2]

The energetic returns on hunting time and effort depend on the total mean weight of each resource species *as harvested*, the portion utilized as food (edible weight), and the caloric value of the utilized portion (which varies according to its nutritional composition)(see table 3.3).  While available information on each of these variables is inadequate for most arctic resource species, especially because of considerable regional variation in the anatomical composition of the prey and the consumption practices of the human foragers, a concerted effort was made to collate available data and derive careful estimates (Smith 1980:appendix A).  When possible, I have used data on weights and utilization patterns specific to the study site.

Since the model of optimal group size presented earlier gives a crucial role to the definition of an array of hunt types, the methodology used in establishing a hunt type classification for Inukjuamiut should be noted.  As a key sufficient parameter, hunt type is intended to subsume factors such as resource species, season of harvest, mode of capture, habitat type, hunting technology, and certain other specific constraints.  Intuitively, the concept seems clear enough:  the list of hunt types for any foraging society is a list of the seasonal round (e.g., goose hunting in the spring, jigging through the lake ice in winter, fall caribou drives).  However, there is an admittedly subjective aspect to any hunt type classification.  This is important in the present study because seemingly minor alterations in the hunt type classification adopted can strongly affect test outcomes for hypotheses about foraging group size (and other foraging strategy models).

While the subjective aspect of hunt type classification could be eliminated by investigating group size in relation to different resource *species*, this would not be a valid approach to Inukjuamiut foraging, for at least two reasons.  First, average encounter rates and capture rates for the same species can differ markedly for different seasons or patch types (e.g., in the case of seals, breathing holes vs. ice leads).  Second, more than one species is frequently encountered, and harvested, on any one hunting foray, so that species-specific hunt types cannot be defined (even seasonally) except in an artificial, statistical manner.  For similar reasons, a hunt type classification based on patch utilization would oversimplify Inukjuamiut foraging decisions, unless it were made highly

2. While it is methodologically feasible to add caloric inputs from fossil fuels (e.g., snowmobile and outboard fuel consumption), this drastically reduces the likelihood of correlating adaptive costs and benefits with energy ones, for reasons discussed in Winterhalder (1977:610ff.) and Smith (1980:section 5.B.1).  Very briefly, it seems inconsistent to add fossil fuel inputs while excluding other caloric inputs such as fire or solar energy by-products (e.g., wind); the value of fossil fuels is not their caloric (heat) energy but rather their ability to reduce human labor and time inputs; and the costs to the forager of fossil fuel inputs are not measured in calories, but rather in money, and/or in the time and labor necessary to develop purchasing power.  Elsewhere (Smith 1980:chapter 9), I have incorporated the value of fossil fuels and other purchased supplies and equipment used by Inukjuamiut foragers by transforming monetary costs into time and labor energy, according to the prevailing wage rates, and then adding these to the foraging inputs.  For example, a hunter on a breathing hole hunt may incur $11 in costs (fuel, equipment depreciation, and ammunition), and this would represent an input of 1.5 hr and 260 kcal of wage labor (at $7.50/hr and 2.9 kcal/min) in addition to time and energy directly invested on the hunt.  However, this refinement would have little effect on the group size analysis presented here, since such monetary costs differ considerably *between* hunt types but do not vary much, if at all, between group sizes *within* a hunt type (per hunter).

*Table 3.3*

*Major Inukjuamiut Prey Species, with Average Weights and Caloric Values*

| Prey | Latin Binomial | Inuttitut Name | Kg Live Weight | Kg Edible Weight | Kcal/kg[e] |
|------|----------------|----------------|----------------|------------------|------------|
| Ringed seal | *Phoca hispida* | Nassiq | 33[b] | 12.0[a,c] | 1,680 |
| Bearded seal | *Erignathus barbatus* | Ujjuk | 207[a] | 55.2[a,c] | 1,230 |
| Beluga whale | *Delphinapterus leucas* | Qilalugaq | 499[b] | 101.7[a,c] | 1,900 |
| Caribou | *Rangifer tarandus* | Tuktu | 103[b] | 54.3[a,d] | 2,760 |
| Arctic fox | *Alopex lagopus* | Tirraganiaq | 2.5[b] | 0.9[c] | 2,490 |
| Canada goose | *Branta canadensis* | Nirllik | 3.5[a] | 2.1[a,c] | 1,650 |
| Snow goose | *Chen hyperborea* | Kanguk | 2.7[a] | 1.6[a,c] | 1,760 |
| Eider duck | *Somateria mollissima* | Mittiq | 2.6[a] | 1.1[a,c] | 1,300 |
| Ptarmigan | *Lagopus* sp. | Aqikgik | 0.7[a] | 0.4[a,c] | 1,280 |
| Arctic char | *Salvelinus alpinus* | Iqalupik | 1.7[a] | 1.4[a,c] | 1,550 |
| Lake trout | *Salvelinus namaycush* | Isuralitak | 3.4[b] | 2.9[c] | 1,090 |
| Brook trout | *Salvelinus fontinalus* | Anaaqik | 1.0[b] | 0.8[c] | 1,010 |
| Whitefish | *Coreogonus* sp. | Kapisalik | 0.8[a] | 0.7[a,c] | 1,350 |

[a]Author's field notes.

[b]NHRC 1976.

[c]Kemp, et al. 1977; Kemp, n.d.

[d]Foote 1967.

[e]Average derived from values in Farmer and Neilson 1967; Heller and Scott 1967; Kemp, n.d.; Mann, et al. 1962; and Watt and Merrill 1963.

Note:   Edible portions are based on weight and composition of food portions actually utilized at present, as measured in the course of fieldwork or reported in the literature on contemporary Inuit.

time and situation specific, in which case the patch-based classification would converge on the more synthetic classification employed here.  However, the specification of hunt types employed in the present research is analogous in many ways to the specification of patch types in some models of optimal foraging (e.g., MacArthur and Pianka 1966).

The actual array of hunt types identified in the present research is discussed in much greater detail elsewhere (Smith 1980).  For present purposes, the list of defining characteristics of the set of hunt types that are analyzed here with respect to group size (table 3.4), along with a brief description of each hunt type (results section, below), should be sufficient to indicate how the classification was operationalized.

Results

The results of tests of $H_1$ and $H_2$ are summarized in table 3.5 and will be discussed for each hunt type.  Following this, the test of $H_3$, which deals with between-hunt type variation in group size, will be presented and discussed.

*Lake ice jigging* occurs over a wide time span (February through June) and a wide range of group sizes.  Lakes known or believed to contain lake trout are sought out, holes chipped through the ice (which can be more than a meter thick), and many minutes or even hours spent at each hole jigging with a baited hook.  Solo fishing is both the most common and the most energy efficient (42% of 60 cases), a result consistent with $H_1$.  Nevertheless, a wide range of group sizes occurs with no clear energy benefit.  Groups of two to

*Table 3.4*

*Inukjuamiut Hunt Types and Their Defining Characteristics*

| Hunt Type | Primary Season | Major Prey Species | Primary Habitat | Technology |
|---|---|---|---|---|
| Lake ice jigging | Feb-May | Lake trout | Frozen fresh water lake margins | Ice chisel, jigging line |
| Ocean netting | Jul-Aug | Arctic char | Coves and estuaries | Gill nets, canoe |
| Jig / goose | late May-Jun | Lake trout, Canada and snow goose | Lakes and streams | Jigging line, shotgun |
| Spring goose | May | Canada goose | Marshes, river margins | Shotgun, snow blind |
| Ptarmigan | Feb-early May | Rock and willow ptarmigan | Clumps of dwarf willow | .22 rifle, snowmobile |
| Lead / floe edge | Nov-Jun | Ringed seal, eider duck | Leads in pack ice, edge of fast ice | High-powered rifle, retrieval hook |
| Breathing hole | Dec-Mar | Bearded seal, ringed seal | New fast ice or frozen leads | High-powered rifle, harpoon |
| Canoe seal | Apr-freeze-up | Ringed seal, bearded seal, eider duck | Coastal waters | Rifles, harpoon, freighter canoe |
| Beluga | Jul, Sep | Beluga whale | River mouths, channels | Rifles, harpoon, freighter canoe |
| Winter caribou | Dec-Mar | Caribou | Interior, distant coast | High-powered rifle, snow-mobile, sled |

Note: Only those hunt types analyzed in terms of group size are included here.

*Table 3.5*

*Summary of Data on Foraging Group Size for Ten Hunt Types*

| Hunt Type | Mean Group Size | Modal Group Size | Group Size Range | $(\bar{R}_j)_{max}$ [a] | $\hat{N}_j$ | $(\bar{R}_j)_{mode}$ [b] |
|---|---|---|---|---|---|---|
| Lake jigging | 2.8 | 1 | 1-10 | 1,770 | 1 | Same |
| Ocean netting | 1.6 | 1 | 1-5 | 21,350 | 1 | Same |
| Jig / goose | 2.6 | 1 | 1-6 | 3,290 | 1 | Same |
| Spring goose | 2.4 | 1 | 1-7 | 3,410 | 3 | 3,400 |
| Ptarmigan | 1.5 | 1 | 1-6 | 1,170 | 1 | Same |
| Lead / floe edge | 2.7 | 1 | 1-10 | 2,340 | 2 | 2,210 |
| Breathing hole | 3.9 | 4 | 1-8 | 4,120 | 3 | 1,350 |
| Canoe seal | 2.9 | 2 | 1-8 | 3,980 | 1 | 3,400 |
| Beluga[c] | 10.3 | | 5-16 | 4,760 | 5-6 | |
| Winter caribou[c] | 4.0 | 3,5 | 1-7 | 12,710 | 6-7 | 10,500 |

[a] $(\bar{R}_j)_{max}$ is the net capture rate (kcal/h-hr) averaged by the most efficient group size for the $j$th hunt type; $\hat{N}_j$ is the group size that achieves $(\bar{R}_j)_{max}$.

[b] $(\bar{R}_j)_{mode}$ is the net capture rate averaged by the modal (most frequent) group size for the $j$th hunt type; when the modal group size is also the most efficient, $(\bar{R}_j)_{mode} = (\bar{R}_j)_{max}$.

[c] No modal group size occurs in the sample of beluga hunts; group size frequencies peak bimodally for winter caribou hunts; $(\bar{R}_j)_{max}$ is averaged over two group sizes for both of these hunt types, in order to meet a sample criterion of at least two hunts.

four are roughly equivalent in efficiency, but larger groups suffer from greatly reduced capture rates. Little cooperative foraging activity occurs on jigging trips, though in mixed parties men may chip most or all the ice holes. The occurrence of large groups suggests that in many instances recreational rather than foraging goals are primary; groups of kin or friends often travel and fish together in the fine spring weather. Though larger groups were observed to disperse over a lake, the data indicate that they still suffer from interference. A test of $H_2$ indicates moderate support with this hunt type, with a Spearman rank correlation coefficient ($r_s$) of .401 (table 3.6).

*Ocean netting* is the primary form of fishing during the summer months. Gill nets are set in coves and at river mouths for anadromous fish (mostly arctic char, but some whitefish as well). Travel to and from nets is by canoe, with outboard. Very high efficiencies are obtained by individual fishermen (table 3.5), and moderate but consistently declining rates for larger groups. Solo fishing strongly predominates (67% of 69 sample trips), as predicted by $H_1$. Field data on the composition of groups indicate that they often include one or more adolescent boys, who are presumably gaining fishing experience. $H_2$ is rather strongly supported ($r_s$ = .676; p < .001).

*Jig/goose* is a mixed hunt type that occurs when poor weather, or the dispersion of geese at the end of the spring migration, reduces the return rates for pure goose hunting. Energetic efficiency drops off monotonically as group size increases. A modal group size of 1 is again consistent with $H_1$, but a secondary peak at N=3 is not matched by any rise in net capture rate. As with pure jigging trips, jig/goose trips are often considered recreational activity for families or other moderately large groups, and this probably accounts for most of the larger groups in the sample. The rank correlation test ($H_2$) indicates a

*Table 3.6*

*Summary of Hypothesis Testing for Relation of Foraging Group Size and Energetic Efficiency (within hunt type variation)*

| Hunt Type (sample size in parentheses) | Modal Group Size Test $(H_1)^a$ | Correlation Test $(H_2)^b$ ($r_s$ value in parentheses) |
|---|---|---|
| Lake ice jigging (60) | Supported | Supported (.401, p < .401) |
| Ocean netting (69) | Supported | Supported (.676, p << .001) |
| Jig / goose (25) | Supported | Supported (.448, p < .01) |
| Spring goose (53) | Indeterminate[c] | Supported (.232, p < .05) |
| Ptarmigan (27) | Supported | Supported (.435, p < .01) |
| Lead / floe edge (54) | Not supported | Not significant (.169) |
| Breathing hole (19) | Not supported | Not significant (-.006) |
| Canoe seal (36) | Not supported | Not significant (.109) |
| Beluga (6) | Indeterminate[d] | Not significant (0) |
| Winter caribou (10) | Not supported | Not significant (-.284) |

[a]$H_1$ is supported *iff* the most frequently occurring group size for a hunt type is the maximally efficient group size.

[b]$H_2$ is supported *iff* the linear correlation (measured by $r_s$, the Spearman rank correlation coefficient) between the observed frequencies and net capture rates for each group size is positive and statistically significant (p < .05, one-tailed $t$-test, n-2 d.f.).

[c]Net capture rate averages for the modal group size (N=1) and for N=3 are virtually identical; see text for discussion.

[d]Test could not be performed because of a lack of any modal group size.

moderate correlation between group size frequencies and net capture rates (table 3.6).

*Spring goose* hunts occur at the height of the spring migration of Canada and snow geese, and dominate Inukjuamiut foraging activity for a few short but intense weeks. The geese are most densely concentrated at this time by the scarcity of marsh or pond locations, and goose hunting is a very efficient hunt type relative to alternatives in late spring. Solo hunters generally travel a short distance from the village and return in the same day; group hunts often last longer and extend farther afield. The data on foraging efficiency indicate that group sizes of one and three are approximately equal in efficiency (table 3.6) --so close that the measured difference (10 kcal/h-hr) is certainly much less than sampling error. Thus, the decision to hunt alone or in small groups is in one sense a decision on whether to hunt nearby and face greater competition for resources, or to travel farther and have a somewhat richer resource base but somewhat greater foraging costs (monetary and energetic) (Smith 1980; cf. Hamilton and Watt 1970). In any case, the wide range of group sizes observed for this hunt type, and the moderate differences in net capture rates between them, result in a low correlation for the test of $H_2$, though the correlation is still positive and significant, and thus consistent with $H_2$ (table 3.6).

*Ptarmigan* are often harvested in conjunction with other hunt types (such as fox trapping and jigging), but at times they are the object of specific hunts, especially in the late winter and early spring when other game is scarce: here we are concerned with this specific hunt type. Search is by snowmobiles; hunters travel to patches of dwarf willow along river banks and in hollows, where ptarmigan are generally localized until the late spring breeding season; a .22 rifle is usually employed. Solitary hunting clearly predominates (64% of 27 cases), and groups larger than two are rare (7%). Both group size frequencies and efficiency curves peak at N=1, and decline monotonically, as predicted by $H_1$ and $H_2$. The correlation between the rank orders of the two variables is only moderate ($r_s$ = .435).

*Lead/floe edge* hunting is focused on seal, primarily ringed seal. In the literature on Inuit hunting, this hunt type has been portrayed as highly individualistic (Balikci 1964: 89) or even competitive (Nelson 1969:261-64), in strong contrast with breathing hole sealing. Inukjuamiut data are in part consistent with this portrait, but there are complexities. While solitary hunting predominates (41% of 54 cases), group hunts are the majority, and group sizes of up to ten occur in the sample. Furthermore, for the sample period at least, groups of two are slightly more efficient than solo hunters ($\bar{R}$ = 2,340 and 2,210, respectively) (table 3.5). Although for my interviews I defined groups as consisting of individuals who consciously cooperated and hunted together, some of the larger group sizes for this hunt type may be very loose groups resulting from proximity hunting when seal density is locally high. While pairs of hunters may increase per-hunter efficiency through the use of retrieval boats, I know of no major cooperative tactics or division of labor employed by larger groups. A large amount of variance in net capture rates resulted in a very low and statistically nonsignificant correlation, and thus a lack of confirmation for $H_2$ (table 3.6).

*Breathing hole* hunting occurs in the same general habitat as lead/floe hunting, and overlaps in time (though breathing hole hunting starts a little later in the winter, and ends sometime in March when breathing holes become difficult to locate in accumulating snowdrift). While lead/floe hunting involves scanning open water at the edge of ice in search of surfacing seals, breathing hole sealing requires the location of apertures actively maintained by seals in relatively thin ice. In the Eskimo literature, this is the classic case (along with caribou drives) of the alleged need for cooperation among a group of hunters in order to increase the harvest for all (Boas 1888; Nelson 1969:240; Balikci 1970:58; Damas 1972:14). Because a seal maintains several breathing holes in an area and visits any one somewhat rarely and unpredictably, both Inuit hunters and anthropologists state that a group of hunters must cooperate, distributing themselves at as many holes as possible.

Of course, the optimum (maximally efficient) number of cooperating hunters depends on the number of holes, but it should probably be less, and perhaps much less, than this maximum, if the measure of efficiency is net capture rate per individual rather than per group. To my knowledge, empirical data bearing on this question have never before been published. The Inukjuamiut data base is small (19 hunts) and covers only one season. The modal group size is four hunters, and hunts with three or more hunters account for eighty-four per cent of the sample (vs. only 41% for lead/floe hunts, a clear and significant difference).[3] Solo hunts are rare (one case, 5% of the sample) and considered somewhat offbeat by informants. However, energetic efficiency peaks at N=3, rather than N=4, as predicted by $H_1$ from

---

3. $x^2$ = 10.088, p < .005, 1 degree of freedom (chi-square test adjusted for contiguity).

the graph of group size frequency in figure 3.5, which is unaccountably shifted to the right of the graph of group size. As a result, the correlation between these two variables approaches randomness for this small sample, and $H_2$ is not confirmed.

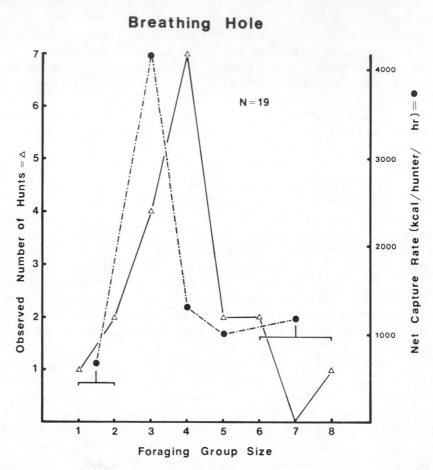

**Breathing Hole**

Figure 3.5. Frequency Distribution of Foraging Group Size in Relation to Mean Net Capture Rates for Inukjuamiut Breathing Hole Hunts. For group sizes represented in the sample by only one hunt (N = 1, 8), net capture rates have been averaged with adjacent group sizes.

Anthropological arguments on the causes of Inuit winter aggregation into relatively large villages (in the central and eastern Arctic) have often pointed to the need for a large pool of seal hunters to cooperate in breathing hole hunting as the primary cause for the size of these coresident groupings (e.g., Balikci 1970:58; Damas 1973:283). (Note that this would correspond to hypothesis D.1 in the previous section.) If the Inukjuamiut data are at all representative, they would indicate that groups much larger than four or five would be suboptimal for breathing hole hunting; relevant demographic data and models suggest a camp of 20-25 Inuit could supply 4-5 adult males (Weiss 1973:table 25-40; Keene 1980: table III). This is much smaller than the 50-200 range argued by Damas (1973:283) as characteristic of central Inuit winter sealing villages. Thus, we might want to reconsider the adaptive significance of these aboriginal winter aggregations.[4] Alternatively, the

4. The Inukjuak data indicate breathing hole hunting is highly uncertain, with 26% of the sample reporting zero success. This could possibly make large coresident groups

Inukjuamiut data might not be representative of central and eastern Arctic conditions, because of either sampling error or local differences in hunting tactics or seal densities (cf. Damas 1972:n.5).

*Canoe seal* hunting occurs in three seasons, but spring hunts require launching the canoe off the floe edge and must cope with the hazards of fog and drift ice; fall and especially summer hunts are more productive and more common. In the present sample, hunts involving the pursuit of caribou sighted along the coast, and beluga pods hunted after fortuitous encounter, have been removed, as these contingencies affect group size and efficiency variables. The remaining thirty-six hunts present a fairly consistent picture with respect to group size, with sixty-nine per cent of the sample consisting of groups of 2-3 hunters. In terms of energy, the picture is quite complicated, with average net capture rates for the different group sizes varying widely and in no consistent direction.

While the modal group size is two (15 cases), and solo hunting is relatively uncommon (4 cases), $\bar{R}$ peaks at N=1 and declines to about 500 kcal/h-hr for N=2 (table 3.5), a result inconsistent with $H_1$. The higher efficiency of solo canoe hunting is surprising, given the teamwork generally involved with pairs (the sternsman maneuvering the boat and helping to sight and shoot seals, while the bowman sights, shoots, harpoons, and secures). Informants indicate that solitary canoe travel is considered somewhat more dangerous than traveling in pairs, possibly accounting for the failure of the energy efficiency hypothesis; alternatively, the results could be due to sampling error (and a 500 kcal/h-hr difference is not large in light of the possible sources of such error or of measurement error). The test of $H_2$ results in a low and nonsignificant correlation (table 3.6).

*Beluga* whale hunting occurs in two varieties: special purpose long-distance trips to known concentrations at estuaries in early summer, and opportunistic hunting of fortuitously encountered pods of whales (primarily during their fall migration). Only the former is considered here, reducing the sample to a mere six hunts (but with a total of 4151 h-hrs). Group size is equimodal, with six different sizes spaced rather evenly between five hunters and sixteen, while efficiency declines linearly from small to large groups. It is of course impossible to assess to what degree these results are artifacts of small sample size, and to what extent they reflect real attributes of Inukjuamiut beluga hunting. There is a possibility that the relevant adaptive goal for beluga hunting is maximization of total harvest (which is shared rather evenly throughout the entire village) rather than maximization of individual efficiencies (Smith 1980).

*Winter caribou* hunting is also inadequately sampled in this study, with only ten hunts, resulting in a great deal of variance in group size frequencies and mean capture rates. The mean group size of 4.0 is larger than that for any hunt type except beluga (10.3); groups of 3 and 5 are modal (3 cases each), while efficiency peaks at 6-7 hunters (table 3.5). Thus, while neither $H_1$ nor $H_2$ is supported by the meager data, it seems probable that moderately large groups are more efficient than the smaller group sizes that predominate with most other hunt types.

To sum up the results discussed so far, it is evident that the present data do not provide overwhelming support for the general idea that group size will be tightly optimized to maximize individual energetic efficiency. For the hypothesis that the most frequent group size will be the most efficient ($H_1$), support was forthcoming in four cases, two cases were

---

adaptive for minimizing variance in food supply through resource sharing, along the lines suggested by hypotheses C1 and D2 outlined above. However, food storage, easily accomplished by freezing during the breathing hole hunting season, would seem to obviate this advantage of large coresident groups.

indeterminate, and a contrary result was obtained for four hunt types (table 3.6). The relatively more complex hypothesis that the rank orders of foraging efficiency and frequency of occurrence for each group size would be positively correlated ($H_2$) fared only slightly better, with five cases indicating positive and statistically significant correlations ranging between .2 and .7, while the remaining five hunt types did not register any significant correlation, positive or negative (table 3.6). Three of the five negative cases for both tests were rendered somewhat ambiguous by very small sample sizes.

However, these results are arguably more encouraging for optimal foraging theory than would first appear. The first hypothesis, in predicting an exact match of modal group sizes with maximal efficiencies, gives no role to year-to-year fluctuations in resources, or assumes perfect tracking of shifting optima. We can expect that human foraging decisions, based as they are on individual foragers' memories of past years plus culturally stored information, will often be keyed to fairly long-term expectations of payoffs for alternatives (for example, it *might* be the case that with breathing hole seal hunting, the long-term optimum *is* groups of four, but that unusual conditions in the study period shifted the return rate curve to the left). The test results for the second hypothesis of rank order correlation indicate support in 5/10 of the cases, with no statistically significant *negative* correlations. The probability of getting five significant positive correlations and no negative ones, by chance alone, is very small indeed (H. R. Pulliam, personal communication).

The final hypothesis tested here concerns variation in group size and energetic efficiency *between* hunt types (rather than within each hunt type). $H_3$ predicts that variation in modal group size will be linearly correlated with variation in optimal (maximally efficient) group size over the set of hunt types. Dropping the beluga hunt type (where there is no variation in the first variable), we have nine hunt types for which a Spearman rank correlation coefficient can be calculated. The result is a moderate correlation ($r_s$ = .611, p < .05, 7 d.f.) for the two variables. If we keep in mind the small sample size (9 in this case), and the large number of rank ties for modal group size (6 cases of N=1), this level of correlation seems rather strong, and increases our confidence that there is some meaningful relationship between Inukjuamiut foraging group size and energy efficiency, even if this relationship appears to be more complex than can be comprehended with simple optimal foraging models alone.[5]

## Conclusions

If optimal efficiency models of foraging group size are only partially successful in the present case, this need not be seen as a weakness of the optimization approach. First, failure to confirm is just as valuable a result as confirmation, if it leads to further investigations into the determinants of group size--a matter not pursued here because of space limitations. Second, empirically testable optimization models, by explicitly specifying the results expected from theory, can lead to a more rapid development of a field of inquiry than less rigorous research programs (see chapter 10, below). As we have seen in this chapter, many previous anthropological analyses of hunter-gatherer group size have asserted support for generalized "adaptive function" arguments on the basis of loose plausibility arguments and anecdotal (rather than quantitative) evidence. If such previous

---

[5]For both $H_2$ and $H_3$, the occurrence of rank ties in either or both variables was accounted for, and $r_s$ was calculated using the special formula available for such situations (Thomas 1976:402).

analyses of adaptive variation in group size have seemed tidier, they were perhaps less deserving of our confidence.

When efficiency measures fail to predict closely the empirically observed situation, there are several possible explanations: (1) the currency (e.g., net capture rate/individual) may be inappropriate, or the model structure faulty in some other way; (2) errors, either systematic (due to sample design) or stochastic (due to sample size) may significantly bias the data base; (3) the time period may be unusual and thus unrepresentative (this implies the priority of long-term optimization, and a failure to adjust to short-term variance of a certain magnitude); (4) the analytical design (e.g., the present hunt type classification) may be faulty; or (5) less efficient group sizes may have a number of non-energetic functions (e.g., reduced risk, learning situations, "social rewards" of larger groups). When subsequent research or analysis based on such alternative possibilities is carried out, nonconfirmation of the original hypothesis will have played an important scientific role.

As evolutionary ecology begins to be rigorously applied to human cases, the complexities and inconsistencies between theory and data that are certain to arise may be taken by many as evidence that "deterministic models of human behavior" (that perennial anthropological whipping boy) are inadequate *because of* the unique properties of culture or some other human attribute. As argued elsewhere (chapter 1, above; Winterhalder 1977:21), such a conclusion would be premature. The question of the degree to which humans are less likely to achieve optimal solutions to "biological" problems cannot be decided a priori--culturally determined behavioral flexibility may on the contrary make the development of optimal patterns *more* likely than in other species. It is sobering that, in the few available empirical tests of optimal group size models for social predators, confirmation has generally been no stronger than in the Inukjuamiut case (cf. Kruuk 1975 on hyenas; Caraco and Wolf 1975 on lions; Busse 1978 on chimpanzees). If predicted optima are not always met in future anthropological tests, we need not automatically ascribe this to culture autonomy or human capriciousness.

# 4

# Foraging Strategies in the Boreal Forest:
# An Analysis of Cree Hunting and Gathering

Bruce Winterhalder

## Introduction

Hunter-gatherers, or foragers, live in environments characterized by diverse and heterogeneously distributed resources. From the array of potential food species, foraging locations, and pathways, the forager can choose combinations which more or less effectively and efficiently procure subsistence. The forager's choices make up a strategy of adjustment to ecological conditions, an adaptive pattern resulting from evolutionary processes and the constraints of situation, time, and chance. Analysis of form and dynamics of these strategies in specified environmental situations is of interest not only to ecological anthropologists, but also to prehistoric archeologists and paleontologists studying the ecological circumstances affecting the evolution and expression of hunter-gatherer behavior. These strategies are the subject of the socioecological analysis presented in this chapter.

This chapter is intended as an analytic and empirical companion to the more theoretical and programmatic content of chapter 2, above. It is heuristic in intent. It attempts to evaluate the applicability of optimal foraging theory to human foraging behavior, and to assess the predictive reliability of hypotheses derived from particular models. These models provide alternative hypotheses for testing and clear guidelines about the kinds of information required to evaluate them. The structured nature of the approach means that confirmation or refutation can be used to reflect on the premises and constraints incorporated into the modeling effort.

The data are based on Cree hunting and gathering in a particular environment, the boreal forest of northern Ontario, but the analysis is directed to learning what the approach can help us to understand about foragers, and what an understanding of foragers can help us to appreciate about anthropological applications of the theory and methodology. The goal then is a general assessment of the usefulness of this theory to ecologically oriented anthropologists and prehistorians.

Throughout the analysis two questions are central to the proposed evaluation: Does use of this approach help in identifying the ecological variables affecting foraging behavior decisions? And, does the optimal foraging approach reliably specify the manner of their action?

The research reported in this paper was supported by the National Science Foundation (Grant No. SO 38065 to Ted Steegmann, Jr., SUNY at Buffalo). It was conducted with the permission and assistance of the Cree People of Muskrat Dam Lake, Ontario. The information and ideas presented here owe a great deal to these people: Sara DeGraff, William H. Durham, Davydd Greenwood, Marshall Hurlich, H. R. Pulliam, Eric A. Smith, Ted Steegmann, Jr., and R. Brooke Thomas.

66

## Study Orientation and Hypotheses Examined

The most general assumption invoked here is that adaptive processes produce behaviors which allow organisms to achieve specified goals efficiently and effectively. For human biocultural behavior the processes producing adaptations are not fully understood (cf. Durham 1976a; Thomas, Winterhalder, and McRae 1979). However, the assumption that behaviors develop toward optimization relative to adaptive goals is a reasonable one for building testable theory. The optimization assumption in the present instance is this: hunter-gatherers will develop behaviors which maximize the net rate of energy capture while foraging. This isolates energy capture as a measure of adaptation, and net acquisition rate as the criterion of success. Other measures—or "currencies" (Schoener 1971:369)—could be used, such as nutritional quality, and other assessment criteria adopted, such as an output-input (acquisition efficiency) ratio. But energy is measurable and of general significance, and the net rate criterion appears to be the best way of relating energy capture to adaptedness (Smith 1979b).

A case for the importance of maximizing the net rate of energy capture while foraging can take several forms: (a) the population may be constantly or periodically energy limited; (b) the population may be energy or time limited, in which case a high net rate of energy capture releases time for performance of essential activities besides foraging; or (c) the population may suffer a greater than average exposure to hazards while foraging, in which case improvement in the net rate of capture will reduce exposure to those hazards. Further, it is reasonable to suppose that hunters who survive to a large extent on a carnivorous diet readily obtain essential nutrients and minerals, so that in a first approximation the nutritional aspects of food resources can be overlooked.

There is ethnohistorical and dietary evidence to support the use of these assumptions in this study. Cree populations in the boreal forest faced periodic food shortages and occasional starvation throughout the historical fur trade period, and presumably before (Bishop 1974; Leacock 1973; Ray 1974; Rogers and Black 1976). When food supplies were adequate in quantity, evidence shows that the traditional Cree diet of meat, fish, and small amounts of vegetable matter provided sufficient amounts of minerals and vitamins (Berkes and Farkas 1978:156). This information confirms the proposition that periodic resource shortages had serious consequences in terms of energy for human foragers in this environment up to the early twentieth century, and consequently supports the expectation of finding foraging behaviors stressing energy efficiency.

The present analysis relies on the belief that these patterns have persisted into the present, when food shortages are not imminent, in part because the energy goal is substantially the same for the contemporary Cree hunter exercising personal skill in the capture of game. The desire to have leisure time within the village and to be with a family, to appear a competent and effective hunter and trapper, and to consume "healthy" bush food all contribute to the pressure to forage optimally, even though food may be available at a local store.

Given the assumption of maximization, a currency (energy), and a parameter (net capture rate), graphical or mathematical models can be constructed which produce hypotheses about foraging behavior. These models use qualities of resources and the environmental mosaic as independent variables (Pyke, Pulliam, and Charnov 1977; Schoener 1971). Tests of those hypotheses should identify ecological factors affecting behavior, or help to isolate historical constraints or competing goals which limit maximization with respect to particular behaviors or goals (Cody 1974).

The hypotheses examined here arise from models discussed in Winterhalder (chapter 2, above), and can be grouped under diet breadth, patch selectivity, and forager movement among patches.

## Diet Breadth

Humans have evolved the capability to extract food energy and nutrients from a variety of plant and animal sources. This omnivory is expressed differently, and with differing degrees of selectivity, depending on habitat and situation. Optimal diet hypotheses attempt to determine the items, and, in general, the number of items, that will be included in an optimal forager's diet in given ecological circumstances.

In the diet breadth model (MacArthur 1972; MacArthur and Pianka 1966; Pianka 1978) resources are ranked by their value to the forager. Foraging is divided into two phases: search costs (time or energy) to encounter each unit of potential resource species, and the pursuit costs for each unit. Search and pursuit costs are the variables which carry into the model a variety of considerations, and their manipulation is the basis of hypothesis construction. The operational distinction between these foraging phases is this: all organisms are searched for concurrently (the environmental mosaic of resources is fine grained, Wiens 1976); but pursuit involves selection. An optimal diet is one that adds resources to those pursued in decreasing rank order until the last resource added creates a loss in the average pursuit costs that is not compensated by savings in average search costs, both measured per unit of resource captured. Factors which cause large or increasing search times will result in relatively broad, or increasingly broad, diet breadths. Conversely, a situation in which the forager has high or increasing pursuit costs will result respectively in a relatively narrow or decreasing diet breadth for the optimal forager.

Diet breadth, then, is the set of prey types that a forager will pursue if they are encountered during a search. If a sufficient time period or number of foraging trips is analyzed in given environmental conditions, diet breadth will be the same as the resources actually captured and consumed. By definition, in this study search costs end and pursuit costs begin when a species is located by sight or by definitive sign of its presence nearby. The operational distinction between search and pursuit in the model is that between the attempt to locate any of the species in the diet, and a commitment to capture a particular individual or group of individuals of that species. That transition most often occurs for the Cree when fresh tracks or some other sign (a beaver lodge, for instance) are located.

Application of this model requires information on the relative net energy value of prey species, and search and pursuit costs associated with each.

## Patch Selectivity

Nearly all environments have an uneven distribution of resources. This almost ubiquitous spatial heterogeneity (Wiens 1976) can arise from habitat patchiness, from intraspecific social factors or habitat qualities affecting the dispersion of mobile prey, or directly from activities of the forager, such as localized depletion of prey. Environmental patchiness should affect the number and types of habitats within which a forager seeks resources, patterns of movement over the environmental mosaic, and the forager's influence on the resources themselves.

The patch selectivity model (MacArthur and Pianka 1966) assumes that the forager's effective resource habitat is discontinuous. There are a number of different patches, or patch types, each having a somewhat different quality. The organism moves over the landscape, randomly encountering patches, but is selective about the ones it forages within.

Patches are ranked by their quality to the forager.  The foraging phases in this model are travel between patches (lost time and energy), and foraging time within patches which are harvested.  The optimal forager includes patches in its foraging itinerary until the use of a low-quality patch lowers the average foraging return by an amount not compensated by the reduction in travel costs.

This model predicts that organisms living in a relatively small-scaled environmental mosaic will develop a broad use of habitats; they will be patch type generalists.  Conversely, those exposed to a large-scaled resource environment will specialize and forage within relatively few habitats.  As scale increases the optimum patch choice shifts toward specialization (Pianka 1978:266; Winterhalder, chapter 2, above).

The model in this case requires information on the relative value of patch types, and on the costs (per unit of resource captured) of traveling between and foraging within different types.

## Movement among Habitats

The third set of hypotheses derive from the marginal value theorem (Charnov 1976a). This model complements the previous one in that it assumes the forager has already settled on an optimal set of patch types to harvest.  The model posits that the net rate of harvest of a particular patch decreases, or is "depressed" (Charnov, Orians, and Hyatt 1976:247), with time.  This happens because (a) the forager progressively depletes the resources in that locale; (b) the forager picks the more accessible resource initially and thus must harvest items increasingly difficult to locate or capture; or (c) the forager may inadvertently alert prey, which then emigrate or conceal themselves.  The model predicts when, in terms of the depression curve for a particular patch type, the forager should leave that patch and search for one that is undepleted.

In this case two versions of the basic hypothesis, the second more strict in its test implications, can be considered:  (1) Foragers abandon the harvest of patches or local resource aggregations prior to their depletion.  (2) Foragers abandon each patch at the point at which its marginal return falls to the average habitat return.  The second form of this hypothesis implies that in richer habitats, where the average foraging return is relatively high, patches will be abandoned sooner and depleted relatively less.  In addition, the optimal forager leaves a trail of patches of uniform quality with respect to the resources it harvests from them.

In analyses using the marginal value theorem the following information is required: the average foraging return for the set of patches harvested, and the resource depression curve for each of the patches visited.

It should be apparent that the hypotheses developed in these models are generally qualitative rather than quantitative.  Ideally they should be confirmed on a comparative rather than single-case basis.  Given the exigencies of data collection and the complexity of the variables involved, the diet breadth model does not, for instance, allow one to hypothesize and test that the optimal strategy for organism $X$ in circumstance $Y$ is four resource items.  Rather, diet breadth hypotheses are comparative in the following ways: (a) one can predict the change in foraging behavior as the organism moves from one environmental situation to another, spatially or temporally, or (b) one can predict foraging changes as the functional abilities of either the predator or the prey change with respect to search and pursuit costs and success.  Despite this, in the present and most other analyses, some comparisons are only implicit.

The remainder of this chapter uses information gathered on Cree foraging to evaluate these models and hypotheses.

## Methods

### The Study Site

The data presented here are drawn from a year-long study (calendar year 1975) of hunting and gathering in the northern Ontario Cree community of Muskrat Dam Lake (Winterhalder 1977). The population of the community averaged about a hundred people, in two extended families and seventeen households. The community was initiated as an offshoot of Bearskin Lake ten years before fieldwork, in an area of the hunting ranges of some, but not all, contemporary residents. Currently the community is served by two small native-owned stores, selling foodstuffs, petroleum products, and a limited variety of hardware; an Anglican church with a native pastor; and a day school with a nonnative teacher. The nearest settlement is Round Lake (65 km air distance); intercommunity travel is usually by unscheduled, single-engine bush planes. The monetary income of the community is based on occasional wage labor (construction and fire fighting), some trapping, various grants (e.g., community development projects), and social services extended by the federal government of Canada (family allowance, unemployment, old age pensions).

In general social, cultural, and economic respects, Muskrat Dam Lake is similar to other Cree settlements in eastern boreal Canada (Black 1970; Dunning 1959; Rogers 1962). It differs from surrounding communities in being smaller, more recent in development, and somewhat more cohesive in social structure.

Snowmobiles are used in Muskrat Dam for winter travel and occasionally for searching for resources, but not for the pursuit of game. They allow a hunter to get away from the village, and perhaps to locate tracks along a river or lake shore, but hunting in the bush is done by snowshoe. Snowmobiles cannot be used off the hard-packed snow or ice surfaces of lakes and rivers unless a trail is packed in advance; they are too noisy to be useful in the direct location and pursuit of boreal forest animals. In summer, canoes with outboards replace snowmobiles to the same effect: they facilitate travel and increase search velocity, but they are not used for pursuit. The effects of these technologies on foraging will be examined below.

### Data Collection and Presentation

Data were gathered in three ways: (1) I participated in and directly recorded hunting, fishing, and trapping trips; (2) I discussed specific instances of foraging with recently returned hunters; and (3) I kept notes of hunting activities in the community and discussed procedures formally and informally with a group of diverse people. The first two sources of information are based on intensive work with six hunters. This sample covers ages eighteen to sixty, and was chosen to represent people of above average bush skills and hunting and trapping abilities, and who spent an above average time foraging. The data are not representative of the population in general, but come from experienced and committed hunters of different ages.

When directly observed, hunting activities were timed by wrist- and stopwatch in categories which differentiated tasks and energy expenditure levels. Foraging routes and the locations of significant events were recorded on topographic maps (1:250,000 scale) or on acetate sheets over a black-and-white air photo mosaic (1:59,000 scale). Discussion of the hunt--weather, tactics, animal behavior, clues as to location and movement of prey, and reasons for success and failure--was recorded, as were the type, number, and, in some cases, weight of game located and captured. In the case of nonobserved trips, the foragers provided similar but less detailed information, sometimes based on simple time diaries which they recorded for me. This information expanded the sample, but was invariably less complete and detailed than that obtained by participation. The Cree educate young hunters by providing extensive experience with little verbal instruction; they were most comfortable, and my education was most productive, when I learned in the same way. Several older hunters were willing to discuss and be questioned about hunting at length (and through a translator), and thus provided historical information not otherwise obtainable.

The data presented here are selective with respect to the economic and in some cases ecological activity of the community. The focus is primarily on the foraging decisions made after a person has decided to hunt. This excludes analysis of decisions between hunting and other forms of productive activity, and it restricts attention to behavior of individuals or small groups of hunters, excluding community-level phenomena such as exchange of hunting and trapping products. More importantly, I will not consider the capital and immediate monetary costs and rewards of foraging associated with the use of outboard motors and canoes, snowmobiles, steel traps, repeating rifles and shotguns, and nylon fishing nets, and the sale of pelts. This can be done without compromising the present analytic focus because: (a) each of the hunters studied has, or has access to, the necessary equipment, purchased with wage earnings or social service payments; and (b) while the cost of fuel and ammunition may influence the overall amount of hunting, it does not strongly affect decisions to hunt particular species, in particular locations, with particular patterns of movement. Equipment, fuel, and ammunition costs are, therefore, fairly neutral factors with respect to the specific foraging decisions examined here, although they would certainly enter into a more complete human ecology analysis. The sale of pelts may have influenced the food quest in several specific ways, noted below. This selection of data is necessary to test the foraging hypotheses under evaluation.

It is also the case that the Cree are subject to, and observe, legal (provincial) restrictions on the trapping of fur bearers. They are, however, exempt by treaty from most regulations placed on sport hunters. As a result, game hunting regulations are not of large consequence to the data base used in this analysis.

## Energy Calculations

The energy costs of foraging were calculated by timing foraging activities, assigning the activities to standardized energy expenditure levels for adult males or females (Durnin and Passmore 1967:47 and passim; Godin 1972), and aggregating the energy expenditure over the time, activities, and persons involved.

The energy value of various game species was determined using field measurements or published values of weights for the species in boreal Canada (e.g., Banfield 1974; Bellrose 1976; MacCay 1963), corrected in the case of larger, slow-growing species for the age structure of the harvest (NHRC 1976a). The composition and caloric value of various tissues for boreal species (Farmer, Ho, and Neilson 1971; Farmer and Neilson 1967; Ho, Farmer, and Neilson 1971; Mann, et al. 1962), the proportion by weight of the animal represented in these tissues (Kemp, unpub.; Spector 1956; Stewart and Stahl 1977; White 1953), and the tissues consumed under culturally prescribed "full use" were considered in calculating the caloric value of harvested organisms. Details of this procedure will be presented elsewhere (Winterhalder, in prep.); the caveat is stated here that the information available for these computations is partial and not always representative of the expected variation by season, sex, maturity, and health status of the animal. The net acquisition rate parameters used below are all calculated on a per forager basis, whether one or more persons participated in the activity. Energy values are expressed as kcal, or kcal/hr, as appropriate. Full details of the study location, sampling and recording procedures, and methods of calculation and data analysis can be found in Winterhalder (1977).

## Data and Results

### The Boreal Forest Environment

*Physical and climatic features.* The study area, Muskrat Dam Lake, is located on the Severn River. Geologically the area is in the Superior Province of the Precambrian Shield (Hewitt and Freeman 1972:72-85); floristically it is in the Northern Conifer Section of the Boreal Forest Region (Rowe 1972). The altitude is 300 m. The landscape is topographically muted and landforms are disoriented, a result of glacial disturbance (Bryson, et al. 1969), which left an irregular mosaic of subdued outcrops and glacial features (Prest 1965: 6-21). Moraines, kames, drumlins, and eskers separate kettle lakes in poorly drained depressions. Uplands rise 10-30 m above surrounding areas and represent either drift deposits or exposed Precambrian rock. These landforms constitute a small-scale irregular landscape.

The disorganized landforms, shallow slope toward Hudson Bay, and continuing isostatic uplift of Hudson Bay drainage basin have resulted in an impeded drainage (Andrews 1973:189; Terasmae 1970). Consequently much of the landscape is covered by numerous small lakes, or by hydrographic vegetation associations such as bogs or muskeg. Soils are mainly of the continental podsol type (Papadakis 1969). Specific soils are closely associated with landform features (Moir 1958:17; Rowe 1972; Tedrow 1970:203; Terasmae 1970).

The climate in winter is dominated by the dry, cold, and stable Arctic air masses (Bryson and Hare 1974:13). Days are short, typically clear and still, and acutely cold. Average nighttime lows and daytime highs are -29°C and -19°C, respectively. In summer the Arctic Frontal Zone is displaced north of Muskrat Dam Lake, to a position along the northern margin of the boreal forest. Air masses from the Pacific and Gulf regions mix frontally with Arctic air (Bryson 1966). Temperatures are warm, with an average daytime high of 21°C in July, and conditions typically are characterized by rain and thunderstorms, with occasional drizzle and fog. The pronounced seasonal cycle of the region is exemplary of a strong continental climate. Spring and fall mark the transition of the modal Arctic position from the southern to the northern margin of the boreal forest (Bryson 1966; Krebs and Barry 1970), and are characterized by cold, blustery weather. Hare and Hay (1974) and Hare and Thomas (1974) provide excellent summaries of the climate of this region.

Three secondary climatic features of this environment are of direct importance to foraging behavior, through their effects on game behavior, location, and accessibility to the Cree forager. These are freeze-up and break-up dates, snow cover profiles, and stream flow. These climatic features also show considerable year-to-year variability, variability which becomes important when evaluating the constancy of parameters incorporated into optimal foraging models.

The average and range of dates for initiation and conclusion of freeze-up and break-up are shown in figure 4.1. These environmental events are particularly important because they are phenological set points of the annual cycle, both for humans and for their prey, and because they mark the limits of a period of limited mobility, especially for humans.

Snow cover is the winter substrate of animals and humans (Formozov 1973; Pruitt 1970), and its depth and structure are critical to the movement of both over the boreal landscape. For instance, an increasingly deep snow cover, up to about 100 cm (chest height), progressively reduces the mobility of moose, an effect augmented by a crust on the snow (Coady 1974:423; LeResche 1974:406). But fairly deep snow and a light crust, or at least snow muffled by a light cover of powder, enhances the velocity and efficiency of human movement on snowshoes. As snow depth increases, moose are easier to pursue, but more difficult to

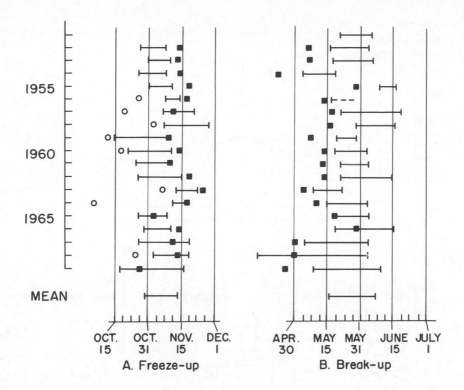

1955

1960

1965

MEAN

| OCT. | OCT. | NOV. | DEC. | | APR. | MAY | MAY | JUNE | JULY |
| 15 | 31 | 15 | 1 | | 30 | 15 | 31 | 15 | 1 |

**A. Freeze-up**          **B. Break-up**

Figure 4.1.  Freeze-up and Break-up Dates.  (A) Freeze-up:  The circles indicate the formation of ice that later melted completely; the horizontal lines show the interval between
the formation of the first permanent ice and complete freeze-over, excepting permanently
open areas such as falls; and the squares indicate that the ice became safe for light
ground or air traffic.  (B) Break-up:  The squares indicate the time at which the ice became unsafe for light traffic; the horizontal lines represent the interval between the
earliest date of the final thaw of the season (definite ice melt, cracks, movement or
water puddles) and the disappearance of fixed or floating ice.  Data from Allen and
Cudbird (1971).

locate because they become confined to small feeding patches and do not leave long trails
of easy-to-locate tracks (Bishop and Rausch 1974:571).  The quality of the snow cover thus
affects the ease and efficacy, and hence cost and likelihood of success, of searching for
and pursuing moose.  Variability from year to year in the snow cover (figure 4.2) causes
variability in the parameters incorporated in the foraging models.  Other examples could
be given for different species, and the relationship discussed is one of greater detail,
but the general significance to the human forager of variability in this secondary environmental factor should be evident.

Stream flow, and the level of lakes and rivers, are the third important factor (figure
4.3).  Among other things stream flow affects the distribution of fish, the migration of
waterfowl (especially whether dabbling ducks will stop over in the Muskrat Dam area during
migrations), and summer accessibility to game species and the habitat in general.  The boreal landscape is an irregular pattern of uplands scattered in a matrix of lakes and streams,
bogs and muskeg.  Movement on water by canoe is fast and efficacious, but movement by foot
through the bogs or muskeg is tortuously difficult.  As a consequence of this and the shallow nature of the topography, changes in the level of lakes and small streams can open or

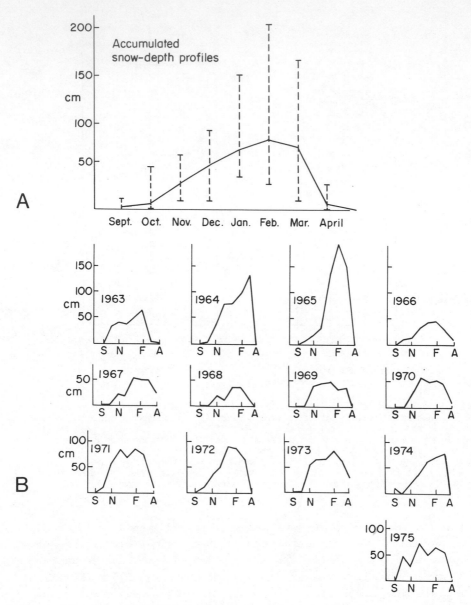

Figure 4.2.  Annual Variability in the Accumulated Snow Depth Profile for Big Trout Lake, Ontario.  (A)  Monthly mean snow depth for the period 1963-75.  The vertical dashed lines show the range of the monthly mean values.  (B)  Seasonal profiles for selected years. Data from Environment Canada, 1963-75.

close large areas to the only effective form of movement--canoe travel.  Again, moose can provide an example of the effect of this factor on animal distributions and mobility.  When summer water levels are high, moose can escape heat and insects and reach aquatic foods while well hidden in the extensive brushy bogs and muskegs lining streams and rivers.  Low water, however, forces them to seek the deeper streams for the same reasons, where they are easily searched for and readily seen.  Again, the importance of this secondary environmental factor is its high annual variability, especially in late summer and fall, and its effects on the parameters incorporated in foraging models.

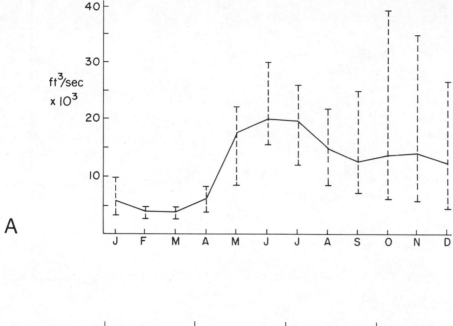

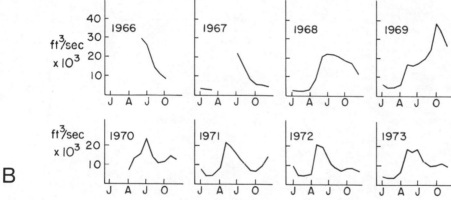

Figure 4.3. Annual Variability in Stream Flow. (A) Monthly mean discharge for the period 1966-73, measured at the outlet of Muskrat Dam Lake, on the Severn River. The vertical dashed lines show the range of monthly values. (B) Seasonal profiles for selected years. Source: Water Survey of Canada, Department of Environment, Guelph, Ontario.

*Flora: vegetation patchiness.* Two of the models analyzed here are concerned with a specific environmental property--spatial heterogeneity. The most obvious aspect of the boreal forest mosaic is the terrestrial-aquatic distinction. Topographic maps of the region show the forest to be studded with a myriad of small lakes, with a modal size in northern Ontario of 1.6 km$^2$ (Ontario Department of Lands and Forests 1971:6). Secondarily a complex and irregular, but distinct, set of vegetation patches is evident. The boundaries of these patches are defined by edaphic factors such as landform, soils, and drainage, and by ecological ones, primarily disturbance and succession. These patches differ in their species composition, physiognomy, and productivity, and consequently in the resources and shelter

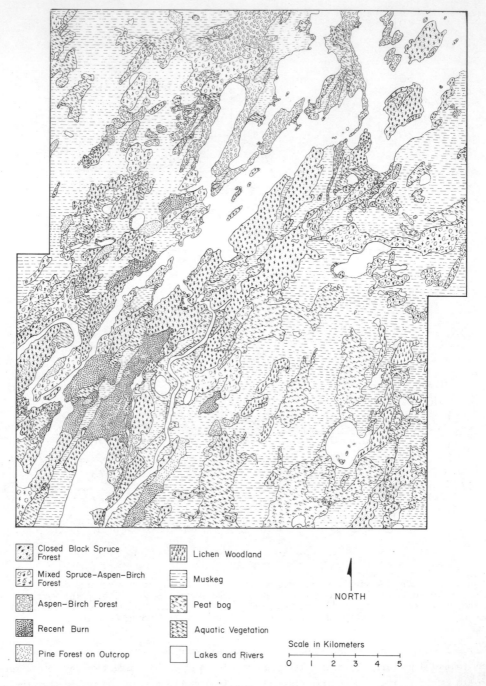

Figure 4.4. The Vegetation Mosaic. The definition and recognition of these associations are based on Ritchie's (1956 1958 1960) research in the Manitoba boreal forest, somewhat modified by field observations and by the work of the botanists Moir (1958) and Hustich (1957) within the Severn River drainage (see Winterhalder 1977:128-48). A stereoscopic interpretation of black and white air photos (provided by the National Airphoto Library, Survey and Mapping Branch, Energy Mines and Resources, Ottawa) was used in preparation of the map. The interpretation relied on (a) the author's familiarity with the area; (b) a series of low-level color air photos taken by the author at the autumn peak of vegetation color distinctions, which overlapped and could be correlated with the textural and tonal features of the high-altitude photos; and (c) reference to publications describing the preparation of similar maps of boreal forest vegetation (Larsen 1962 1972; Ritchie 1958).

they offer various animal species. Each has different qualities with respect to the game
it attracts, and the impediments it places between forager and prey.

   Figure 4.4 is a vegetation association map, based on air photo analysis, which demonstrates the pattern of ten patch types which can be distinguished by their composition and
physiognomy, and by their functional distinctions with respect to resources important to
Cree foraging.

   Table 4.1 is a quantitative analysis of the area depicted in figure 4.4. Several
things stand out. First, fifty per cent of the area is muskeg or peat bogs, relatively unproductive habitats for terrestrial mammals and difficult ones for the Cree forager in summer. Another eighteen per cent is covered by water. The remainder of the habitat is upland
patch types, for the most part in various stages of succession from recent burns to the
climax association for this area--closed black spruce forest. The exceptions are the rarely
occurring rock outcrops which support pine forests or lichen woodlands. Unlike the boreal
forest areas of either Manitoba or Quebec, northwestern Ontario, for climatic and edaphic
reasons (Ahti and Hepburn 1967:26-29, 52) does not have extensive areas of lichen woodland.

*Table 4.1*
*Vegetation Patch Types:  Number, Size, and Proportional Area*

| Patch Type | Number of Patches | Mean Size ($km^2$) | Total Area ($km^2$) | % of All Area | % of Upland (Successional) Area |
|---|---|---|---|---|---|
| Closed black spruce forest | 74 | .73 | 53.9 | 12 | 39 |
| Mixed spruce-aspen-birch forest | 55 | .64 | 35.1 | 08 | 26 |
| Aspen-birch forest | 29 | .76 | 22.1 | 05 | 16 |
| Recent burn | 10 | 1.38 | 13.8 | 03 | 10 |
| Pine forest on rock outcrop | 17 | .14 | 2.4 | 01 | 03 |
| Lichen woodland | 13 | .53 | 6.8 | 02 | 06 |
| Muskeg | 38 | 4.24 | 161.0 | 37 | |
| Peat bog | 57 | .99 | 56.4 | 13 | |
| Aquatic vegetation | 38 | .20 | 7.6 | 02 | |
| Lakes and rivers Muskrat Dam Lake | 1 | 63.10 | 63.1 | 14 | |
| Others | 54 | .30 | 16.4 | 04 | |
| Total | 386 | | 438.6 | 101 | 100 |

Note:  The sizes of individual patches were calculated by placing a transparent point grid,
calibrated on geometric shapes of known area, over the air photos used to prepare figure
4.4.  A regression equation established the relationship between point counts for patches
and their areas.  Source:  Winterhalder 1977:145.

   The scale of heterogeneity of this habitat is important. The mean size of the productive upland patches is small (generally < 1 $km^2$) relative to the range normally covered by
a human forager.  For instance, Rogers (1963:57) records family "hunting group" (3-5 families) areas of approximately 700 $km^2$ for the Pekangekum area of Ontario.

   The vegetation mosaic presented in figure 4.4 is a dynamic one. The large areas of muskeg, bogs, and fens have developed to their present state over a period of several thousand years (Terasmae 1970). But upland patch types have a high rate of repeated disturbance followed by succession. A given locality burns from natural causes every 100-150 years (Rowe and Scotter 1973:447; Viereck 1973:474). Away from population centers, lightning-caused fires predominate (Johnson and Rowe 1975:3; Viereck 1973:471). This ignition source guarantees the irregular distribution of early successional patches in space and time. Most fires are small: eighty-eight per cent of those in northern Saskatchewan burn less than forty-one hectares (Rowe and Scotter 1973:452). On this basis Rowe and Scotter (1973:453) state: "These figures suggest good reason for the patchiness of vegetation." The greatest area, however, is burned by the rare. large fire:

> But rarely do such conflagrations completely demolish the forest. Because of the vagaries of wind, and to some extent because of topography and the disposition of wetlands and water bodies, islands of undamaged vegetation escape. In fact some students of fire believe that the forest patchwork pattern is as much due to isolated remnants in a burned matrix as to spot fires in an unburned matrix. [Rowe and Scotter 1973:453]

Wind throw and snow throw (Pruitt 1958:169; Ritchie 1956:528) can also create successional gaps in the shallowly rooted trees of the spruce-dominated climax forest.

The result of these disturbances is a small-scaled mosaic of vegetation patch types, even-aged and homogeneous in composition, abruptly and irregularly bounded (Ritchie 1956: 532). The disturbances, and particularly fire, stimulate a flush of herbaceous and woody growth (Shafi and Yarranton 1973a 1973b), which represents quickly appearing and localized pockets of high and accessible productivity (Wright and Heinselman 1973:324-25), attracting a variety of animal species.

> Faunal succession follows plant succession, and there are optimum habitat or stages of plant succession for every animal species. Therefore, inasmuch as fire initiates and terminates succession it exerts both short-term and long-term effects . . . the conclusion must be that any influence tending toward diversifying the landscape at large and small scales will increase the diversity of the fauna as well as the population density of some species. By maintaining a mosaic pattern in the boreal forest, fire assists in the maintenance of diverse wildlife populations. [Rowe and Scotter 1973:457-58]

Within about fifty years a canopy forms and browse diversity decreases (Shafi and Yarranton 1973a:88). As noted earlier, the climax association, a spruce canopy over a feather moss mat, attracts few game species.

This vegetation dynamic has a scale roughly equivalent to the life span of the hunter, and draws the forager's attention closely to the microgeography of the vegetation landscape.

*Fauna: resource species population characteristics.* Currently the Cree of Muskrat Dam Lake depend entirely on fauna for their locally derived resources. Consequently the population and distributional characteristics of fish, waterfowl, and semiaquatic and terrestrial mammals are of central importance.

Table 4.2 summarizes, in highly condensed form, the population characteristics of major boreal forest resource species. This table is based on an extensive review of ecological and game management literature for this region, recorded in Winterhalder (1977). For the major species, biomass and density estimates, the stability of the population, the pattern of recurrence (recovery from depressions in population numbers), and the early winter group size are given.

*Table 4.2*
*Population Characteristics of Major Resource Species*

| | Biomass (kg/km$^2$) | Density (No/100 km$^2$) | Stability | Recurrence | Early Winter Group Size |
|---|---|---|---|---|---|
| Moose | 17.2 (+ -) | 5.6 | Moderate | Irregular Short-term | 680 kg (+ -) 1.8 individuals |
| Caribou | 0.7 (+ -) | 0.5 | Moderate | Irregular Long-term | 900 kg (+ -) 6 individuals |
| Beaver | 20.9 (+ --) | 185 | Moderate | Irregular Short-term | 100 kg (+ -) 5 individuals |
| Muskrat | 34.2 (++ --) | 3,800 | Low | Cyclic--10 yr Irregular | 0.9 kg individual |
| Hare | 1,610 - 18.2 | 115,000 - 1,300 | Low | Cyclic--10 yr | 1.5 kg individual |
| Ruffed grouse | 54.0 - 6.0 | 8,600 - 1,000 | Low | Cyclic--10 yr | 1.8 kg (+ -) 3 individuals |
| Spruce grouse | 18.5 - Low | 3,090 - Low | Low | Cyclic--10 yr | 1.8 kg (+ -) 3 individuals |
| Fish | 675 | | High | | |

Note:  The +'s and -'s in parentheses are meant to indicate especially broad upper and lower boundaries of persistence relative to the estimate.  The summary parameters used in this table (e.g., persistence, stability, and recurrence) are explained in Winterhalder 1980b.  Source:  Winterhalder 1977:275, with modification.

Several points stand out.  The biomass of the large mammals, moose and caribou, is low compared with that of the smaller organisms.  Cyclic, or periodic but irregular, population fluctuations are known to occur in all species, except fish.  Fish populations are fairly stable according to records from commercial fisheries in the north (MacKay 1963).  Northern Canadian mammals and game birds are known for their dramatic population fluctuations (Bulmer 1974; Elton 1942; Keith 1963; Winterhalder 1980a), documented in thorough historical records kept by the Hudson's Bay Company and its interior post traders, and more recently by the extensive zoological study which the cyclic fluctuations have stimulated (Keith 1974).  As a result, a long-term record is available on this natural resource base, unlike that available for most other habitats.

The amplitude, frequency, and regularity of population fluctuations for these species are important to the boreal forager, and are indicated by each species' population stability and by the regularity and rate of its recurrence from points of low population density (table 4.2).

The final column of table 4.2 roughly indicates the dispersion pattern of each species as it is affected by sociality.  Moose are predominantly solitary; woodland caribou are found in small herds.  Beaver occur in family groups, regularly dispersed over the landscape because of territoriality and the fairly even availability of lodge sites.  The remaining terrestrial mammals and game birds are either solitary or found in small groups during at least some seasons.  With the exception of caribou, which are of negligible biomass in this region, none of these animals is aggregated into large groups.  They are not, therefore, patchily distributed by virtue of social aggregation.

The habitat preferences of these species provide the key to their dispersion patterns (table 4.3).  Each species is associated with only certain vegetation patch types.  The Cree forager knows that each game species occupies certain landscape areas preferentially and can be found in specific types of habitats most of the time.  Table 4.3 also indicates

*Table 4.3*
*Habitat Associations of Major Resource Species*

| Resource | Patch or Vegetation Type Association | Notes |
|---|---|---|
| Moose Winter | Aspen-birch forest Recent burn Lake margins | Deep snowfall strengthens winter patch association |
| Summer | Aquatic vegetation Lake margins | Low water, heat, and insects strengthen summer patch association |
| Caribou Winter | Closed black spruce forest Pine forest on outcrop Lichen woodland | Deep snowfall strengthens winter patch association, especially for pine forest on outcrop |
| Summer | Peat bog | |
| Beaver | Aquatic vegetation Lake margins | |
| Muskrat | Aquatic vegetation | |
| Hare Winter | Aspen-birch forest Recent burn | Association with specific patch types increases during fall, winter, and spring, and when populations are low |
| Summer | Various | |
| Ruffed grouse | Aspen-birch forest Recent burn Lake margins | |
| Spruce grouse | Closed black spruce forest Spruce-aspen-birch forest | |
| Fish | Aquatic vegetation Open water | Association with the shallow water habitat is temperature influenced and increases in spring and fall and with spawning |

Source:  Winterhalder 1977:277.

that the associations change with the seasons, and that population density and secondary climatic factors can determine the probability that particular animals will be confined to distinct vegetation patches.  For instance, as noted earlier, as winter snow depth increases, moose are increasingly confined within small areas offering abundant browse, because of the difficulty and high energy costs of movement between preferred patch types. And in summer, high temperatures, thick insects, and low water levels increase the chance that moose can be found in or near aquatic habitats.  Resource patchiness for the Cree forager arises in the association of each animal species with particular vegetation patch types scattered over the boreal landscape.

The boreal forest presents a dramatic example of what is probably common to all habitats:  regular and irregular fluctuations of the biomass of game species, with week synchronization among species.  Each year the forager faces a somewhat different set of game densities.  Over a period of decades it is unlikely that the same proportional distribution of population densities repeats.  If the vagaries of resource densities are combined with those of the secondary climatic elements affecting foragers and game, and these are combined with changes in the environmental mosaic, an important conclusion emerges:  on the scale of a hunter's life span, and at the detail at which foraging decisions are affected, the constellation of environmental factors significant to foraging decisions is a nonrecurrent phenomenon.

## Applicable Foraging Hypotheses

In terms of the models, then, these points emerge concerning the effective environment of the Cree forager:

a. The boreal environment contains a large number of potential resources. Resource species are generally of fairly low density, scattered, and either solitary or in small groups. This leads to the expectation that the Cree will expend considerable energy searching for organisms, and, as a consequence, to the hypothesis that they have a generalized diet breadth.

b. In addition, the resources available are patchily distributed. Thus, the environmental conditions assumed in the models for patch selection and movement in a heterogeneous environment are present. The scale (or grain) of the environmental mosaic is small relative to the usual range of a Cree forager, and a generalized use of patch types is hypothesized.

The analysis of Cree foraging in terms of time and energy investment and energy return provides information on the ranking of different resources or patch types, and on the relative costs of searching for and pursuing various species. An evaluation of foraging in terms of the energy currency is the basic content of the parameters of the models examined here. Table 4.4 presents the net acquisition rate and net acquisition rate per unit of pursuit time for the foraging activities measured in 1975. The measurements are differentiated by species and in some cases by season or capture technique. Figure 4.5 presents a composite seasonal profile of the foraging energetics of major resource species, also for the year 1975. The curves are complete for all species except beaver. For this organism data were insufficient to make the seasonal extrapolations.

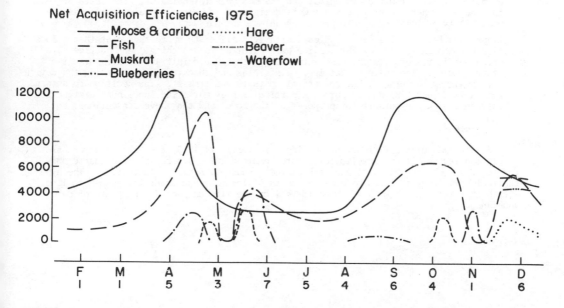

Figure 4.5.  Seasonal Net Acquisition Efficiencies of Foraging for Various Resources. All of the curves are complete for the year, with the exception of beaver.

*Table 4.4*

*Measured Net Acquisition Rate of Foraging for Various Resources*

| Resource and Dates | Net Acquisition Rate (kcal/hr) | Net Acquisition Rate/Pursuit Time (kcal/hr)[1] |
|---|---|---|
| Moose and caribou[2] | | |
| Winter | 6,050 | 8,220 |
| Early spring | 11,950 | 25,140 |
| Summer and fall | 5,920 | 95,600 |
| Fall (rut) | 11,280 | |
| Net fishing | | |
| Winter, net 1 | 1,060 | 1,790 |
| Spring, net 2 | 3,180 | 3,710 |
| Spring, net 3 | 9,680 | 11,660 |
| Summer, net 4 | 2,260 | 21,340 |
| Summer, net 5 | 5,320 | 34,000 |
| Fall, net 6 | 6,390 | 7,980 |
| Hare snaring[3] | | |
| Fall (measured) | 1,900 | 8,260 |
| Fall (hypothetical) | 8,180 | 15,220 |

1. Calculation of this parameter required separation of search and pursuit costs. The working distinction between these two variables was not always evident, necessitating the following conventions (Winterhalder 1977:600-601):

All foraging costs up to the point of deciding to pursue a particular animal, or unit of organisms if it was a herd, flock, or other group, were designated as searching. Pursuit costs began when an animal was located visually, by tracks, or by some other indication of immediate presence, such as a fresh sign at a beaver lodge. The travel costs of returning to a village following a successful or unsuccessful pursuit were allotted to searching. It was always possible that another prey organism would be located and pursued. For large game the costs of processing and retrieval were designated as pursuit. If pursuit of an animal was resumed on a following day, the costs of reaching the site where pursuit left off were designated as search. Again, there was the possibility of locating a more promising animal for pursuit.

Traps, snares, and nets were handled similarly. All costs up to the point that a location was chosen for the capture device were allotted to searching. Such devices are often set in response to the same animal signs that would initiate active pursuit of other species. The costs of setting, maintaining and checking, and resetting the device were assigned to pursuit, but not travel costs to and from it. The decision to suspend generalized searching and to pursue a particular prey marks the functional distinction between search and pursuit for purposes of the model and the above conventions.

2. See figure 4.6.

3. The measured efficiency of snaring hare refers to 1975, the first year of hare population recovery from a cyclic low. Hare remained quite scarce and were snared only for several weeks in the fall, the peak of their seasonal density fluctuation. The hypothetical efficiency is based on measured costs of locating and maintaining a snare line, with both effort and returns adjusted to reflect reported catches during years of hare abundance.

| Resource and Dates | Net Acquisition Rate (kcal/hr) | Net Acquisition Rate/Pursuit Time (kcal/hr)[1] |
|---|---|---|
| Muskrats[4] | | |
| Spring trapping, case 1 | 250 | 1,280 |
| Spring trapping, case 2 | 2,500 | 6,230 |
| Fall hunting, case 1 | 2,370 | 4,740 |
| Fall hunting, case 2 | 1,330 | |
| | | |
| Beaver[5] | | |
| Early winter trapping | 1,640 | 5,690 |
| Early winter trapping (est.) | 4,360 | 23,620 |
| Early winter trapping (est.) | 5,280 | |
| | | |
| Waterfowl | | |
| Pre-break-up | 720 | 3,000 |
| Post-break-up | 1,980 | |
| Pre-freeze-up | 1,190 | |
| | | |
| Game birds | | |
| Grouse, case 1 | | 1,740 |
| Grouse, case 2 | | 1,220 |
| | | |
| Vegetable foods | | |
| Blueberries | 250 | 650 |

4. The first case of spring muskrat trapping was described as unsuccessful; the second case is more representative of the expected efficiency of this type of foraging. Both instances of fall hunting fall within expected ranges of catch and effort.

5. The three values given for early winter beaver trapping represent three different cases. Time and energy costs, and returns, for the lowest efficiency case were measured in detail, but the effort was considered unsuccessful by the trapper. Consequently, two additional cases with more representative catches were recorded. The two estimated efficiencies then are calculated on the basis of known catches and reconstructed time and energy costs based on descriptions by the trappers involved.

Source:  Winterhalder 1977:486.

The full data base for the energy measurements recorded in table 4.4 will be presented elsewhere. Figure 4.6 demonstrates how the energy efficiency curve was derived for moose and caribou. The bottom graph shows the distribution of the sample of analyzed hunting trips. The solid horizontal lines in the middle figure show the measured net acquisition rate and the duration for the sample. In this case the year was divided into a winter period of hunting on snowshoes (November through the beginning of March); a spring period in April (when a unique set of weather conditions produced a hard, powder-covered snow crust and unusually favorable hunting conditions); a lengthy summer and fall period (May through October) when moose were sought along waterways from canoes; and a brief period (during September) when the rut again created a highly favorable hunting situation. Differentiation of these intervals is thus based on seasonality and aspects of the environment or animal behavior which made hunting unique with respect to tactics and success. The dashed line interpolates a seasonal profile from those data, based on the measured levels and diverse sources of less quantitative information about the factors influencing the costs and success of moose hunting (Winterhalder 1977). The top graph shows the annual distribution of the community moose harvest (only some of these animals were captured on hunts represented in the energy analysis sample).

This particular curve for moose and caribou, and the similar curves drawn for other organisms (figure 4.5), are to some extent unique to the sample year, 1975. The April peak of energy efficiency derives in part from the peculiar weather and snow crust conditions of this period. Such a peak may not occur in other years. Similarly, the low efficiency of the summer sample stems in part from the unusually high water levels of 1975. Cree foragers watched the river carefully for signs that the flow would recede and improve their chances of finding moose. In a summer with lower water levels the energy efficiency of moose hunting could be considerably greater for reasons cited earlier. Similar idiosyncracies affect the costs of locating and pursuing each species, and although they are cited as peculiarities, the numerous sources of variability affecting the forager in this environment ensure that each year is one of peculiarities.

In a fine-grained search situation, as postulated for the diet breadth model, pursuit efficiency takes on special importance. An alternative statement of the main hypothesis of this model is as follows: When an organism is encountered it should be pursued if, and only if, in the same interval the forager is unlikely to encounter and capture an organism with a greater net return (MacArthur 1972:62). This allows organisms to be ranked for purposes of the model by the efficiency with which they can be pursued. This is important, because pursuit efficiency for *individual organisms* is much more easily derived from field data than is acquisition efficiency. Table 4.4, then, also gives the net acquisition rate per unit of pursuit time. With a few exceptions this parallels the general net acquisition rate.

### Foraging Patterns in Relation to Those Hypothesized

In order to evaluate the optimal foraging predictions it is necessary to provide some general information on Cree hunting and gathering. The data used to construct figure 4.5 are based on isolated foraging trips. The net acquisition rate was determined from trips during which only one species was captured (although others would have been pursued had they been located), and, in effect, this sample draws on limited search success to isolate values for a particular species.

The important question in verifying the hypothesis of optimal diet breadth is not, What animals were successfully captured on a hunting trip? A given trip may result in the

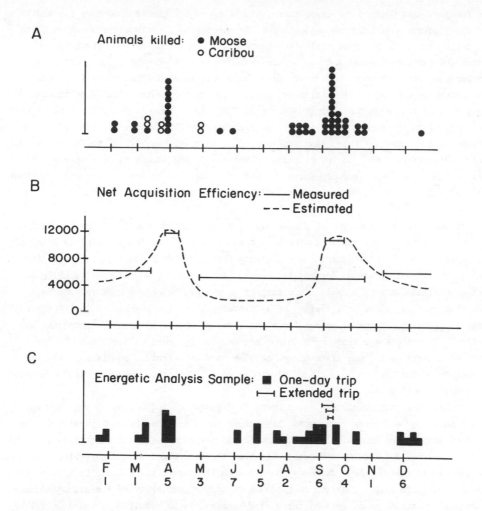

Figure 4.6. Calculations of Seasonal Energetics of Moose and Caribou Hunting. (A) Seasonal distribution, by week, of large game kills during 1975; (B) Measured and estimated net acquisition efficiency; (C) The energy analysis sample. The letters below the abscissa indicate months; the numbers the first date in each month that initiated a weekly sample period.

forager's encountering only a portion of the organisms in its actual diet breadth at that time. The appropriate question is, What organisms will the forager pursue if they are encountered? Determining this for nonhuman foragers is difficult. Anthropologists have the advantage of being able to ask. Or, even better, if differing technologies are used for various species then the equipment carried by the forager will be a fair clue to the organisms which will be pursued if located. The latter evidence is important in the Cree case. Each species (or species group in the case of waterfowl and fish) has its weapon, and although a hunter may say that the trip is for moose hunting, if a shotgun is included then ducks or geese will probably also be pursued if encountered. On a certain trip the forager may come back with the full complement of organisms being sought, but this is fairly rare.

Seasonally, the pattern of Cree hunting parallels fairly closely the acquisition efficiency ranking of prey species in figure 4.5 and table 4.4. Several examples will demonstrate this. In early winter trips (November-December), designated as beaver trapping,

Cree foragers also pursued (by trap, snare, or rifle) moose, grouse, and hare (in addition to the furbearers muskrat, mink, and otter). In the period shortly after break-up (late May, early June), the array of rifles and capture devices taken and the actual species pursued and captured indicated that, besides waterfowl, muskrats and beaver were pursued when located, and that moose would have been pursued if located in an accessible aquatic area. These species were potential prey, part of the diet breadth, along with the water-fowl and loons that were the express objects of the trips. Moose and caribou hunting trips usually focus on these animals in winter and early spring, but beaver snare wire is often included in the materials taken, and grouse will be shot (with a .22) if the noise is not likely to interfere with locating or pursuing moose. During summer trips, expressly for moose hunting, a shotgun is included, and adult waterfowl are hunted if encountered. What-ever the stated purpose of a foraging trip, the Cree hunter is rarely without a .30-.30 for moose.

Although the set of curves in figure 4.5 is assembled from hunting trips in which only one or a few species were captured, the diet breadth of the Cree forager closely parallels that suggested by the net acquisition efficiency rankings. On a hunting trip at a given point in the annual cycle the forager is prepared to pursue the set of species which have a net acquisition rate of roughly 1,500 kcal/hr or better. When the capture rate falls below this general value, dissatisfaction is expressed, and the pursuit of that species often stopped. The spring trapping of muskrats, and pre-break-up waterfowl hunting, are examples. The hare snare line, which had a net acquisition rate of 1,900 kcal/hr for a period of several weeks, was discontinued because hare were scarce, and it was felt that the success of the line would decline. For most of the year this foraging cutoff results in a moderate diet breadth.

Further confirmation of this point comes from table 4.5. The table gives four ways of ranking resources by their value to the forager in 1975: the actual harvest, biomass of the organisms, net acquisition rate, and the short-term reliability of capture once the organism is located. The table demonstrates that the rank order of the harvest corresponds more closely to that of the efficiency measure than it does to the biomass of the organisms present. Although this comparison overlooks much of the complexity of the situation, such as seasonal restrictions of some of the energy samples, these results are fairly striking. The net acquisition efficiency corresponds closely to the actual ranking of the harvest, and the harvest bears little relationship to biomass.

A familiarity with Cree hunting tactics provides substance and detail to this discus-sion. I will describe a foraging trip that occurred in late November, shortly after freeze-up. I accompanied another man. We traveled 12 km downriver by snowmobile and then left the snowmobiles to continue on snowshoe. The whole trip lasted 5 1/2 hours.

The trip was described as one for beaver trapping. But in the course of several hours we encountered tracks or sign of grouse, moose, wolf, hare, beaver, mink, otter, fisher, and muskrat. As each sign was located, the forager appraised the situation and decided whether or not to pursue the organism. The decisions were as follows: the grouse were shot with a .22; the moose was passed up, as the trail was old and the snow conditions poor for tracking it quietly; the wolf was passed up, because wolves move rapidly and al-though the trail was fresh, the wolf was probably distant; snares were set for the hare and beaver; and traps were set for the muskrat and otter. This example demonstrates the correspondence between the model parameters, especially the differentiation of search and pursuit, and the actual tactics of Cree hunting.

*Table 4.5*
*Four Ways of Ranking Resource Species in the Boreal Forest by Their Value to the Forager*

| Biomass (kg/km²) | Harvest (kcal×10⁶) | Activity and Net Acquisition Rate (kcal/hr) | Short-Term Reliability |
|---|---|---|---|
| Fish (675) | Moose (23.5) | Moose, spring (11,950) | Fish (high) |
| | | Moose, fall (11,280) | |
| Small mammals (110) | Beaver (6.9) | Fish, net 3 (9,680) | Hare (mod-high) |
| | | Fish, net 6 (6,390) | |
| Muskrat (34) | Fish (3.5) | Moose, winter (6,050) | Muskrat (mod) |
| | | Moose, sum-fall (5,920) | |
| Beaver (21) | Caribou (1.3) | Fish, net 5 (5,320) | Beaver (mod) |
| | | Beaver, est. (4,820) | |
| Hare (20) | Muskrat (0.4) | Fish, net 2 (3,180) | Spruce grouse (mod) |
| | | Muskrat, trap 2 (2,500) | |
| Moose (17) | Waterfowl (0.3) | Muskrat, hunt 1 (2,370) | Ruffed grouse (mod) |
| | | Fish, net 4 (2,260) | |
| Ruffed grouse (10) | Hare (0.2) | Waterfowl Post-break-up (1,980) | Waterfowl (mod-low) |
| Spruce grouse (10) | Ruffed grouse (?) | Hare, meas. (1,900) | Moose (low) |
| | | Beaver, meas. (1,640) | |
| Waterfowl (?) | Spruce grouse (?) | Muskrat (1,330) | Caribou (low) |
| | | Waterfowl Pre-freeze-up (1,190) | |
| Caribou (1) | Carnivores | Fish, net 1 (1,060) | |
| Carnivores | Small mammals | Waterfowl Pre-break-up (720) | |
| Passerine birds | Passerine birds | Muskrat, trap 1 (250) | |
| | | Grouse | |
| | | Grouse | |
| | | Blueberries (250) | |

Note: The relatively high harvests of beaver and muskrat reflect their value as furbearers in addition to the food resources they provide. Source: Winterhalder 1977:501, with modification.

These results provide a basis for examining historical evidence of changes in diet breadth. The sequential adoption by the Cree of two sets of foraging technologies--the earlier acquisition of improved pursuit devices such as muskets and repeating rifles, traps, and nets, and the more recent introduction of motorized transport, snowmobiles, and outboards--provides important comparative information. The earlier technologies improved the efficiency of pursuing prey species; the later the efficiency of searching for prey (figure 4.7). Here I focus primarily on the more recent change, that affecting the mobility and velocity of the search phase of foraging.

The optimal diet breadth model produces the hypothesis that an increase in the efficiency of searching should result in a constriction of diet breadth. Snowmobiles and outboard motors provide that increase. On a packed snow surface over ice, snowmobiles can reach a velocity of 20 - 35 km/hr, whereas a man walking on snowshoes averages about 5 - 8 km/hr. A light outboard (10 hp) can push a canoe at 20 km/hr; the same canoe paddled over long distances moves at a much slower velocity. In the comparison being made we can look

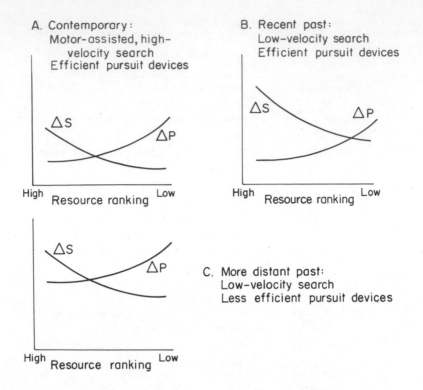

A. Contemporary:
   Motor-assisted, high-
       velocity search
   Efficient pursuit devices

B. Recent past:
   Low-velocity search
   Efficient pursuit devices

C. More distant past:
   Low-velocity search
   Less efficient pursuit devices

Figure 4.7.  Optimal Diet Breadths Hypothesized for Three Historical Periods.  (A) In the contemporary situation the use of outboard motors and snowmobiles and efficient steel traps, wire snares, and repeating rifles has kept search and pursuit costs low.  Short-term diet breadth is fairly narrow in these circumstances.  (B) Prior to the use of snowmobiles and outboard motors search velocity was lower and search costs in time and metabolic energy higher.  Pursuit costs generally would have remained the same, leading to the prediction of a more generalized short-term diet during this period.  (C) In the more distant past, prior to the widespread use of snare wire, steel traps, and repeating rifles, pursuit costs would be higher than in either the contemporary situation or the recent past.  Again, the prediction is for a fairly narrow short-term diet breadth, one which does not necessarily include the same species as in case A.

to the period prior to the use of these devices as one of much slower search movements, leading to the hypothesis of a broader diet breadth.  Outboards have come into use in northern Ontario within the past thirty years, and snowmobiles within the past 10-12 years, so that the changes they produced are well within the experience of older hunters and parts of the ethnographic record.

Several types of evidence confirm that the hypothesis accurately depicts this transition:  Foragers state that access to snowmobiles and outboards, and increased ability to purchase fuel, have changed their hunting habits.  There is a tendency to travel more and to do less looking for low-priority species.  This comment, in the context of a discussion of moose hunting, is typical: "Before, I had to get by with just a little gas.  I had to come back with something, like a beaver, or I didn't get any more gas.  It was true for other animals too."  The reduction in search time, and the reduced need of an immediate return, have limited the variety of animals sought on a given trip.  Foragers with high mobility give little thought to traveling 30 km to a good location to look for moose, or to traveling that far to find moose tracks, while passing by evidence of other, less valued, species. Foragers on snowshoes, or paddling a canoe, pursued such species long before these distances were traveled.

The hunting trip described above can be taken as indicative of an older style of foraging. A snowmobile was used to travel to a trail distant from the village, but the search and pursuit were done on snowshoe in areas not accessible to snowmobile travel. Velocity was slow, and a variety of animals were sought; the diet breadth was fairly wide. Older trappers comment that they always took a variety of traps and snares and used them for the different animals as they were located.

But ethnographic evidence is generally not of the right kind or of sufficient detail to determine the short-term diet breadth of boreal foragers. An exception is Rogers's weekly account (1973:table 4) of the game taken by a hunting group of Mistassini Cree with whom he traveled during the winter of 1953-54. At this time the Mistassini used outboards to travel between camps, but when hunting they paddled. Winter travel was by snowshoe, with the occasional assistance of a dogsled (Rogers 1973:7). In his report Rogers lumped fish species, and separated avian species into loons, geese, ducks, grouse, terns, and owls. Thirteen additional species were listed separately. Over a thirty-nine week period an average of five different species were captured each week. Presumably the diet breadth was larger than this; the game searched for and perhaps even located and pursued was more various than that captured in a given week. For instance, although moose were taken in only six of the sample weeks, it is probable that this animal was included in the diet breadth throughout the period. All of the species or species groups were harvested at some point, with the exception of weasel, fox, and tern.

The diet breadth of the foraging effort in this case is greater than that at Muskrat Dam Lake today, and species were taken that would not be taken today (e.g., squirrel, bear), even though encountered in the course of foraging. Again, this is consistent with the hypothesis. Other anthropologists working in northern Canada have observed that the introduction of snowmobiles has led to more specialized hunting (Hurlich, pers. comm.; McCormack, pers. comm.).

A fourth kind of evidence can be cited on this point--the qualities by which older Cree judge a hunter. One stands out: "A good hunter is someone who knows how to hunt all of the animals." People said that today the younger men know how to hunt or trap one or two animals, and that they are sometimes proficient at capturing those. But by an older standard this is not equated with being competent in the most desirable sense: "The good hunter . . . knows how to catch all of the animals, even if he isn't too good at any one of them." This is an evaluation made most emphatically by the older adults, and it lingers from a period when game was sought by snowshoe or paddle.

There is, then, good evidence to substantiate the hypothesis that diet breadth was wider prior to the use of snowmobiles and outboards.

A third and earlier situation can be envisioned, without motorized transport, but also without the pursuit efficiency afforded by repeating rifles, steel traps, and nylon fishnets (figure 4.7). In the nineteenth century and earlier, the bow and arrow, muzzle-loading rifle, pole snares, handwoven nets, weir fish traps, and deadfall traps were used. These are all technologies which are either less effective or less convenient to use, or which require greater effort in construction or maintenance than present devices and techniques. Relative to the contemporary situation, it would have been a period when high search costs (due to the absence of motorized transport) were matched by fairly high pursuit costs. In this circumstance the diet breadth model predicts a constriction in diet breadth, coupled generally with less efficient foraging.

I have not yet tested this hypothesis, although the extensive ethnohistorical (and ethnoecological) evidence available for the Canadian North makes is probable that information is available for at least a partial confirmation or refutation.

The patch use model produced the hypothesis of a generalized use of the habitat mosaic. In fact, the foraging behavior of the Cree does not fully bear this out. Foraging itineraries touch on relatively few patch types. In part this is owing to the high mobility of contemporary hunters. Snowmobiles and outboards greatly reduce the cost of travel between productive patches. This reduction, which does not affect hunting costs, should favor specialization, and it appears to do so. Cree foragers know the location of favorable patches and can travel to them quickly. As with diet breadth, there is some evidence that Cree hunters sought resources in a broader variety of patch types prior to motorized transport and when the food quest was more important. Older hunters, for instance, recall that caribou were pursued into bogs and fens, a practice now abandoned because of its difficulty. But some other factors operate as well, making the predictions of the patch use model less reliable ones.

The impression of somewhat restricted habitat use is based partly on this observation: Cree seek particular prey species in fewer patch types than the species are known to inhabit at a given time. For example, it is known that moose frequent certain habitat areas near water in the summer, but they are sought only in or from the aquatic habitat. The limitation in this and other cases is a physical one: hunters avoid some patch types (e.g., bogs or muskeg) either because of the difficulty and high cost of moving about there, or because the noise of doing so, and the limited visibility (as in brushy areas), preclude finding an unalerted animal. The patch use model assumes that different patch types are homogeneous with respect to travel costs and the physical impediments they create for search and pursuit tactics, but this is not the case in the boreal forest. Different habitat types are unequal with respect to travel or foraging conditions.

In practice, however, the main reason that this model is less satisfactory arises from the implications of tracking. For some smaller species, such as muskrat, the Cree forager moves in the patch-to-patch fashion envisioned in the model. These animals are localized in discrete habitats, mainly the aquatic vegetation found in shallow, sheltered areas along river and lake shorelines. However, in the case of moose and caribou and some of the widely foraging carnivores (the furbearers), the prey species themselves move from patch to patch. Moose, for instance, will enter a small feeding patch and spend several days there, but move with regularity between such patches. In these instances the Cree forager, rather than seeking to locate the animal within a patch, searches instead for tracks located between patches. The Cree adopt an "interstice" foraging pattern. They follow the creeks and lakes of the drainage pattern, moving along the matrix which surrounds the more productive upland patch types.

The difference between a patch-to-patch and an interstice pattern is illustrated in figure 4.8. Moose move between patches fairly frequently relative to the duration of the trail they leave behind, and the number of animals is low compared with the number of patches they might inhabit. The Cree forager's tactic in this circumstance is to attempt to cross and thus discover old trails rather than to locate the moose directly within a patch.

This pattern has advantages besides shortening the travel route of the forager. With or without motorized transport, it is much easier to travel on the ice and hardpacked snow (or on the water) of streams and lakes than to enter the brushy upland habitats where the

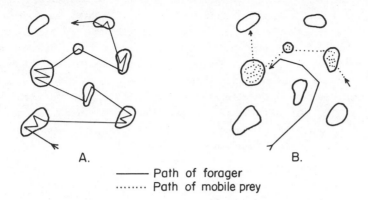

——— Path of forager
········ Path of mobile prey

Figure 4.8. Alternative Foraging Tactics in a Patchy Environment. (A) In the MacArthur and Pianka (1966) model it is assumed that the forager moves from patch to patch in search of prey. (B) This research suggests a somewhat different model, in which the forager seeks mobile prey by moving in the interstices of the patches being visited by the resource organism. This kind of adaptation arises when prey spend time within, but regularly move among, small patches; the prey organisms (or groups if they are aggregated) are not abundant relative to the number of patches they are associated with; the forager relies on locating tracks or a trail as part of its search procedure.

snows are deep and soft and movement is slower and more costly. Second, for many prey species it is essential to anticipate the location of an unseen animal before the final stages of the pursuit. For example, a successful moose hunter must know the animal's location before coming too close to it. This is done by searching for tracks in habitats that the animal is traversing (rather than feeding in) and then adjusting the pursuit tactics to the location of feeding patches which the animal is likely to visit. Cree foragers have developed this technique to a high level of skill.

The interstice pattern presumably applies for any carnivore that preys on organisms that (a) themselves respond to patchy habitats of small grain size; and (b) move between patches in a regular manner. Because the pattern of interstice movement partially obviates the assumptions of the patch use model, it illustrates the importance of examining the constraints built into the models with field observations, and the value of field evidence to modeling in general. It should be possible to define the conditions under which the patch-to-patch pattern would, optimally, switch to the interstice pattern. The number and size of patches, the density of prey, the time prey animals spend within a patch, the frequency of movement between patches, and the life span of the trail left behind would be key variables.

The data gathered on Cree foraging are not sufficient to make a quantitative test of the marginal value theorem. They do provide anecdotal support for the hypothesis that foragers leave patches before they are depleted of the resource(s) being sought there. Thus, in 1975 visits to patches to snare hare were stopped in the late fall in favor of other foraging activities, even though the patches continued to produce animals. Referring to previous years, foragers described abandoning a snareline set around a felled tree for a fresh location, even though the original site continued to be productive. During spring trapping, only the most favorable muskrat push-ups were chosen for trap sets, and then the trapper moved to another patch to pursue only the most promising set locations. In the fall, muskrat are shot with .22s as they sit on the newly formed ice mats found over aquatic habitats along river banks. Several animals would be taken from each area, but a patch was abandoned when the muskrats became scarce (but not entirely depleted) in favor of other patches where they were more abundant because not recently hunted. Finally, although a beaver house may have 3-5 underwater shoots (openings), snares are set at only two or three of these, suggesting that the return is greater on two snares at the next beaver house than on the additional snares at a house which already has some. In each of these examples the forager moved to the next patch before exhausting the resources or capture opportunities of the one being foraged. This is the pattern suggested by the marginal value theorem, but how closely the marginal return at the point of a decision to move on approximates the average return from the habitat is not known.

## Discussion

### Theory Assumptions, Models, and Tests of the Hypotheses

The models and variables applied in this specific analysis of Cree foraging are general ones. Search and pursuit time, patchiness, prey stabilities and distributions are variables --"sufficient parameters" in Levins's (1966) phrase--with wide applicability. Thus the broader lessons of these results apply beyond the temporal and geographic limits of ethnographic analysis in the boreal forest. It may also be true that some of the more specific points--for example, about nonrecurrence of the forager's environment--are similarly general.

The choice of an energy currency to measure subsistence goals produced good results. Energy effectively subsumed the complex set of variables that go into a forager's appraisal of resource opportunities: the size and quality of game species; their nutritional value; and the social rewards of their capture. And, for analysis of foraging, energy gave a fairly complete accounting of both sides of the cost-benefit ratios central to optimal foraging theory. Cultural constraints on energy optimization did not prove critical, although it should be stressed that these hypotheses were chosen for examination precisely to minimize this type of constraint.

The results obtained in the energy analysis of contemporary Cree foraging and the data available from historical sources confirm the hypotheses of the optimal diet breadth model. The dynamic expressed in the model itself conforms well to the practice of Cree foraging. This appears to be a model, with some qualifications noted below, that can be reliably applied in anthropological research.

The hypotheses about patch selectivity performed less well. The original model structure assumes a homogeneous space with respect to travel, and does not allow for alternate foraging patterns based on tracking of mobile prey. The first problem could be unique to the boreal forest; other biomes may have patch types less differentiated in these respects. The problem of tracking, however, may prove to be a more general deficiency of the model. Assessment of these qualifications will require more analyses in different environments.

Qualitative evidence supports the marginal value theorem, but the data are not complete enough to confirm the hypothesis in its stronger form. Unlike the models that make dichotomous, or simple, qualitative predictions (generalized versus specialized diet breadth; dispersed versus aggregated settlement pattern), this model focuses on a decision point in the middle of a range of complicated values. Given the complexities of foraging, and the vagaries of data collection, this type of hypothesis is less amenable to verification.

For the marginal value theorem it is useful to emphasize that most of its assumptions (see below) and constraints, and the goals the model assumes, are indirectly confirmed by this research. The data *suggest* that the hypothesis is a reliable one.

The time interval used to assess foraging in this study--one year--is short given the temporal scale of human foraging activities and the dynamic qualities of the boreal forest over time intervals longer than the seasonal one. Three situations were identified which may compromise the validity of short assessment intervals (Winterhalder, chapter 2, above) --the effects of extended foraging in a limited area; delay of harvest for resources which are used exclusively; and investment in exploration. Although the general importance of these situations cannot be judged from the present study, two comments can be made. First, there is an obvious example of delay of harvest in the boreal forest: the beaver. Beaver lodges and their resident populations are visible, and sufficiently permanent in location and stable in number, that Cree foragers "manage" the harvest of those over which they have exclusive control. This is an alternative explanation for the use of fewer snares than there are snare locations at a beaver lodge, a practice cited above as possibly confirming the marginal value theorem. Second, although the dynamic quality of the boreal habitat, and particularly of its patch structure, makes exploration important, two considerations diminish the impact of this requirement on short-term foraging optimization: (a) By the time that a Cree forager is recognized as proficient, long experience within a given range has provided him or her with detailed knowledge of it. This is particularly evident in the density of ecologically and historically informative names which are applied to the micro-geography (Winterhalder, unpubl.). (b) Because of the extensive nature of searching, and the fine grain of the habitat structure, considerable information can be maintained incidentally to the regular foraging effort. Occasionally a forager deviates to check on a beaver lodge or notice how the browse is growing on a recent burn, but for the most part this information can remain current without much special effort. The maintenance of extensive habitat information by experienced foragers entails little cost exclusive of foraging itself.

The intimate knowledge the Cree forager has of an area raises a question about the random search assumption of these models. With the exception of beaver, the mobility and dispersal of prey and their association with a fine-grained habitat make the random prey encounter assumption a reasonable one. This is not the case, however, for patches. Cree foragers know the distribution of patches in their hunting areas closely. They can often choose foraging pathways which avoid encountering patch types which are not productive in a given situation. This does not compromise the applicability of either the patch use model or the marginal value theorem, provided that the effect of nonrandom searching on the model parameters is noted. In both cases habitat knowledge decreases the travel time which would otherwise be lost in encounters with unproductive patches. This implies greater specialization. In terms of the marginal value theorem, because the average return over the set of patches visited is somewhat greater, each patch should be abandoned somewhat sooner along the depression curve.

Fairly specialized use of habitat patches is the case for Cree foraging: the efficiency gained by knowing patch locations complements that of motorized transport for covering the intervening spaces. As noted earlier, the results obtained here are not sufficiently detailed to make a quantitative test of the effect of habitat knowledge on the marginal value theorem. In the case of muskrat hunting, cited earlier, when the hunter decided to leave one patch, the next productive location was already in mind.

Another factor not considered explicitly in foraging strategy theory, but of immediate concern in Cree foraging decisions, is short-term risk with respect to a return on foraging effort. Moose and hare are examples. In some instances moose will have a higher net energy efficiency than hare, but, even so, a hunter could go for days or weeks without successfully capturing a moose. In contrast, a few hare will, with fair regularity, turn up in a snare line each night. Although possibly of lower efficiency, a foraging effort invested in hare snaring will produce food consistently and with less risk of shortages on a day-to-day basis. Grouse provide a second example. Although the net acquisition rate for their pursuit is fairly low by Cree standards (table 4.4), if grouse are encountered in the course of moose hunting they are usually shot. Grouse are reliably captured, and at the end of the day it is sometimes better to have a few grouse than an abstract vision of an efficiently sought but elusive moose.

Other things being equal, species with a low short-term risk of capture failure will be ranked preferentially to those with a higher risk. In the boreal forest, and perhaps elsewhere, these tend to be the smaller herbivores (table 4.5).

It should be evident by now that although the independent variables in these models are environmental, their action cannot be understood in complete ignorance of the specifics of foraging. It is not heterogeneity, the size or density of prey, or prey distribution *per se* that generate hypotheses, but rather these environmental parameters as they relate to foraging. The "independent" environmental variables become relevant with sufficient empirical understanding of foraging behavior to evaluate their relationship to the models. For example, prey must be ranked according to energy costs and benefits, and this involves evaluation of the forager's behavioral and technological capabilities for capturing each animal. Although the models and parameters are based on highly generalized ecological parameters, these parameters can be utilized only with some knowledge about the skills and behavior of the foragers.

Finally, there is a question of the independence of models, or alternatively, of the interrelationships among separate "decision sets" (see Winterhalder, chapter 2, above). Diet breadth and use of a patchy environment are the decision sets covered in this report. Actually, the information provided here does not suggest clear general conclusions concerning their adequacy or importance relative to one another. Are these decision sets conceptually appropriate? And if the decision sets are in conflict, which will take precedence? In this analysis the small grain size of the habitat structure does not diverge strongly from the fine-grained assumption of the diet breadth model, making it difficult to appraise these questions. Cree foragers *are* excluded from certain habitats that contain resources within their diet breadth, but the causes of this may be specific to the boreal forest. Indeed, it may not be feasible to seek a general resolution to these questions.

In the environmental analysis I stressed two sets of properties in the boreal forest that are highly variable and that directly affect foraging: secondary features of the environment (freeze-up and break-up, snow conditions, stream and lake levels), and the strong fluctuations in animal populations. The analysis of moose foraging gave several examples of how these environmental factors affect foraging, examples that could be multiplied for moose and extended to other species. It is apparent that the parameters of foraging models may be dynamic in ways not appreciated in the model itself, and any long-term view of foraging must take this into account. The search costs and pursuit costs of individual species may vary seasonally and on the longer term, with effects on diet selectivity and breadth. As the environment of the boreal forest is nonrecurrent, so too on a year-to-year basis are the details of foraging. This situation does not reduce the value of the foraging model, but it does indicate that such models should not be applied in static interpretations based on a normative description of the environment (Winterhalder 1980b). Indeed, a virtue of these models is that they allow predictions to track such environmental variability.

Some experience with the details of Cree foraging, combined with analysis and interpretation using optimal foraging models, makes it possible to predict with some confidence the effect on foraging behavior of diverse environmental situations which may occur in the boreal forest. Optimal foraging strategy models provide that capacity by virtue of their realism and dynamic incorporation of a limited set of apposite environmental variables.

This analysis has demonstrated that the optimal foraging approach, the form of specific models, and the constraints contained in their structure and parameters are heuristically valuable for the analysis of human foraging behavior. Several hypotheses gained support, and others did not, for reasons which became evident during analysis, and which are informative in their own right. It is important to be candid about the strength of the case. Much of the field data were consumed in identifying the correct hypotheses, and in estimating model parameters. In an ideal scientific world independent data would be used to test hypotheses, but that has not always been possible in this chapter. There is another shortcoming of the energy efficiency results presented--I was able to measure the efficiency only of activities that were actually performed. Although considerable evidence indicates that they ceased to be performed because efficiency decreased below a certain point, short of experimental intervention, direct demonstration of this is impossible. For instance, while the biomass of very small mammals in the boreal forest is quite high (109 kg/km$^2$ for 4 species--squirrel, shrew, and two voles--in Alaskan boreal forest [Grodzinski 1971]), presumably they cannot be captured with sufficient efficiency for the Cree forager to pursue them. Ecological information can be developed to make this a reasonable argument, but for obvious reasons direct energy measurements are impossible.

What has emerged, then, is a strong case for analytic efficacy, for the use of the optimal foraging approach as a research procedure which can produce reliable predictions with conscientious application.

## Implications for Archeology and Paleontology

Foraging strategy models have a variety of implications for interpretations of prehistoric human ecology, and for data gathering and analysis in prehistoric archeology. The support that the optimal foraging strategy approach has received here and in the rest of this volume charter a guarded license for application of this reasoning in prehistoric contexts. Caution is necessary because this theory, like other forms of adaptive optimization arguments (e.g., sociobiology), can readily stimulate the production of "just-so" stories (S. J. Gould 1978; Lewontin 1979b) of questionable analytic merit. Nevertheless, some points can be developed with fair reliability, and are an improvement over the more intuitive assertions which permeate the literature, and with which foraging strategy hypotheses sometimes differ.

Optimal foraging models can apparently predict the effects of technological changes such as the introduction of firearms or motorized transport, because these have specifiable impacts on model parameters. They should also be applicable to the analysis of other technological and morphological changes where similar foraging effects can be specified, such as alterations in stone tools or the development of bipedalism.

Perhaps the most important point is this: optimal foraging models do help identify the environmental variables affecting foraging behavior (see Sih 1979) and the manner of their action, and should do so in diverse situations.

There are a number of such possible variables: the relative abundances of game species; their absolute abundances; the size of the available organisms; or the distribution or behavior of the organisms. Analyses of hunter-gatherer behavior are not consistent in the importance assigned to the variables mentioned. Archeologists and others (e.g., Simenstad, et al. 1978:405) sometimes assume, for instance, that harvest is proportional to biomass. These foraging models make it clear that prey abundance is only indirectly involved in foraging decisions. The effectiveness of searching for prey, and especially the costs of pursuing and capturing different species, are also determining parameters. In particular, changes in the abundance of species ranked outside of a diet breadth in a given situation should have no effect on whether or not they are included in the diet. And an increase in the abundance of highly ranked species may decrease diet breadth, but the forager will drop species from the diet in rank order, even though their particular abundances may not have changed.

Another common assumption, that larger species are always more efficiently hunted than smaller ones, is not supported by this research. In years in which hare are abundant, for instance, their net acquisition rate per unit of pursuit time (15,220 kcal/hr) is almost twice that recorded for moose (8,220 kcal/hr).

The approach developed here isolates a limited set of variables, and directly establishes their relevance to foraging behavior. It is evident in considering wider use of these models that we need to develop measurements of the energetics of different foraging activities in diverse environments; of the costs of travel and manufacture and use of pursuit technologies for different prey species; of the energy and nutritional value of various game species; and of the effectiveness and short-term risk of various foraging tactics. The literature records too little quantitative information of sufficient detail on any of these points.

The models used here examine very specific aspects of the behavior of individual foragers. I suggest that this microecological approach and data gathering are necessary to develop correct interpretations of the macroecological topics frequently discussed in ethnographic and prehistoric analyses. Several examples can be cited.

The optimal hunter in a fine-grained environment takes a variety of game species determined by the conjunction of prey ranking and search and pursuit costs. If the optimal diet breadth is fairly broad, efficiency is achieved only if each hunter or contiguous hunting group is general in its hunting. In this circumstance individual specialization and camp exchange will not achieve the same end. Thus in fine-grained environments there is an ecological or energy disadvantage to the "division of labor" often postulated to be the basis of hominid sociality. In contrast, the ability to specialize and then exchange goods at a central location may be of advantage in a coarse-grained environment, with separate foragers behaving optimally by seeking resources in a few geographically separated and ecologically distinct types of patches.

The patch use model demonstrates that if a situation arises which compels highly efficient foraging, such as diminished resource availability due to environmental changes or to competition from other species, the optimal forager may restrict the portion of habitat it uses. Habitat selectivity is thus critical to archeological applications of the carrying capacity concept, or to paleontological applications of the competitive exclusion principle. For instance, Wolpoff (1971 1976) argues that competition between two hominid species will necessarily select for more generalized use of resources and habitat. This increased competition, in his view, will result in the inevitable extinction of one species. Foraging behavior models--in particular the "compression hypothesis" (MacArthur and Pianka

1966)--produce the opposite prediction (see Winterhalder 1980c n.d.c).  Further, foraging
models outline the specific types of dietary "character divergence" which are likely to
result.

The marginal value theorem has similar implications.  For instance, it indicates that
the foraging behaviors implied in the Pleistocene extinction ("overkill") hypothesis (P. S.
Martin 1973), as applied to the North American megafauna, are not likely.  The overkill
hypothesis posits highly efficient hunters moving through a heterogeneous environment of
abundant and easily pursued game.  The marginal value theorem indicates that this is just
the situation in which localized depletion of game populations does not occur.  Efficient
Pleistocene hunters entering the North American continent would have skimmed the most
easily obtained animals from a location before moving on.  With high average habitat returns, an optimal forager moves out of a given patch early along the depression curve (see
figure 2.2) and leaves behind a breeding stock.  This theorem, incidentally, may help explain the apparently very rapid migration over, and hence population of, the continent.

The apparent population stability of hunter-gatherers may be due to a related consideration.  It is sometimes stated that hunters developed behaviors which promoted the management of game species and hence their conservation.  The marginal value theorem makes it
apparent that it would be difficult for hunters to act otherwise.  Most environments are
heterogeneous to some degree (Wiens 1976).  The forager attempting to deplete localized
populations fully must act in a manner that is not energy efficient in order to do so.
The marginal costs of fully "depressing" the resources of a patch and thereby depleting
the breeding stock are high compared with those of moving to the next patch to continue
foraging.  In effect, conservation may (among other things) be the *incidental* effect of
efficient foraging in a heterogeneous habitat.  A consequence of this is a reduced possibility of crashes in human population due to serious decreases in game supplies.

While these are brief and somewhat speculative examples, they demonstrate the potential of applying carefully verified foraging models to interpretations of prehistoric
hunter-gatherer behavior.

## Conclusions

Optimal foraging theory can link theory and field data of diverse sources in a program
to improve both; it is an operational approach to analysis of hunter-gatherer behavior.
The models examined here provided, for the most part, a reliable analysis of the ecological
factors affecting Cree behavior.  The approach has some important kinds of generality; it
can be applied in ethnographic or prehistoric situations; and it can be applied to topics
other than those discussed here (e.g., territoriality and group formation).  It is versa-
tile and should help to organize the rather disparate sources of information available to
anthropologists for inferring the adaptations of early hominid species (e.g., primate and
social carnivore behavior; ethnography of hunter-gatherers; archeological information).
In general the results presented here begin to substantiate the optimistic assessment of
these models presented in chapter 2, above.

Careful testing of this theory is important to its use.  Some model hypotheses have
emerged in this analysis as more reliable than others.  The diet breadth model and hypotheses were confirmed here without major qualifications; the patch use model, in contrast,
made assumptions about the structure of the forager's environment, and about the tactics
of foraging itself, that were not appropriate.  This work, in combination with other analyses using these models, can eventually be used to illuminate the peculiarities of individual

models and to evaluate them by their reliability in circumstances where information is incomplete, as in most archeological or paleontological analysis. Wider application of this approach will require the production of types of data which are not routinely generated in research on human ecology, ethnographic or prehistoric.

# 5

# Alyawara Plant Use and Optimal Foraging Theory

James F. O'Connell and Kristen Hawkes

## Introduction

Various authors (e.g., Golson 1971; Lawrence 1968; Meggitt 1964; Tindale 1977) have remarked on the importance of seeds in the pre-European diet of central Australian Aborigines. The Alyawara, an Arandic-speaking group, were typical in this respect. They collected edible seeds from nearly half the eighty-five plant species in their traditional subsistence inventory. In the past thirty years, Alyawara subsistence practices have changed dramatically because of the availability of European foods. Nevertheless, native foods continue to play a small but important role in the economies of some communities. Curiously, seeds are now seldom taken by the modern Alyawara, although they are often very abundant and readily accessible. We argue here that this phenomenon is best accounted for by models drawn from the theory of optimal foraging, which seeks to explain subsistence patterns in terms of the costs and benefits of exploiting various resources. Specifically, we maintain that since seeds are expensive to take relative to their nutritional value, they should be used only when the returns from other resources are very low, regardless of their own absolute abundance. This explanation appears to account for the modern Alyawara situation. It also contradicts the commonly accepted notion that hunter-gatherers take plant and animal foods in direct proportion to their abundance or nutritional value, except where considerations of palatability, or "cultural" preference or prohibition, intervene (e.g., Harpending and Davis 1977; Jones 1978; Yellen 1977:64-65).

Having presented this argument, we then consider some more general implications of optimal foraging theory: first, for the explanation of intergroup variation in diet among central Australian Aborigines; then, for current thought about seed exploitation in Australia, its history and its significance for ideas about the pattern and rate of continental colonization. We conclude with some comments about the general value of optimal foraging theory in anthropology.

The fieldwork reported here was supported by the Department of Prehistory, Research School of Pacific Studies, Australian National University, and by members of the MacDonald Downs community. The assistance of Mr. and Mrs. M. Chalmers, K. and M. Morton, and J. Jones was especially important. Critical data, useful comments on early drafts, and general encouragement were provided by J. Allen, J. Beaton, R. Bettinger, K. Cummins, W. Denham, D. Grayson, R. Gould, D. Heskel, K. Hill, K. Jones, D. Kimber, R. Maguire, N. Peterson, M. Schiffer, S. Simms, E. Smith, J. P. White, and L. Zaleski-Daley. We especially thank E. Charnov and P. Latz for their generous assistance and for access to unpublished data. The manuscript was typed by S. Arnold and U. Hanly; W. Mumford and M. Horne prepared the illustrations.

The Alyawara Case

Environmental and Ethnographic Background

The Alyawara are a regional population who define themselves by a common language, a dialect of Aranda called Alyawara or Iliaura. Their traditional homeland is centered on the Sandover River, about 250 km northeast of Alice Springs, central Australia (figure 5.1). Most of this country is a rolling sand plain or dune field dotted with low, isolated sandstone ridges, and covered with vast stands of tussock grass and scattered, sometimes sizable patches of scrub forest. The climate is warm and dry (Slatyer 1962). Summer (December-

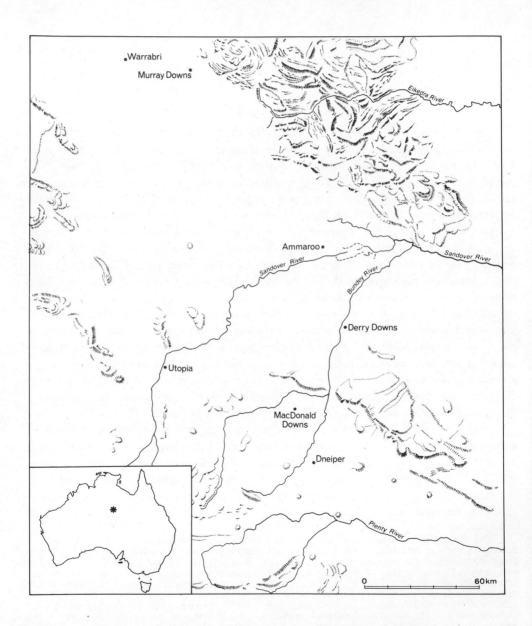

Figure 5.1.  Traditional Alyawara Territory and Locations of Modern Settlements.

February) high temperatures average 37°C, and often exceed 40°C for days at a time.  Nighttime lows average 22°C.  In winter, daily highs average 21°C, nightly lows about 3°C.
Average annual precipitation is about 300 mm (12 in), most of it falling in violent summer
thunderstorms.  Seasonal and annual totals are both highly variable.

In pre-European times, the Alyawara lived in small, widely scattered groups, each consisting of a few closely related families.  Regional population density was low, probably
about one person per 50-90 km$^2$.  Subsistence economy was based entirely on hunting and
gathering.  Local groups moved frequently from site to site over a wide area during the
course of a year, depending on the distribution of food and water (see Gould 1969; Spencer
and Gillen 1927; Strehlow 1965 for comprehensive descriptions of traditional life among
neighboring groups).

Some aspects of Alyawara life have changed dramatically in the past half-century,
largely because of the establishment of local European cattle stations (Stanley 1976;
Stevens 1974).  Most Alyawara now live in semipermanent settlements of 20-200 people located near station homesteads on or just outside the limits of their traditional territory.
Some are employed in the cattle industry, but most are heavily dependent on government welfare for basic subsistence.  Apart from these changes, the Alyawara remain strongly traditional in many respects.  Alyawara itself is still the basic language although English is
spoken by many.  There has been little exposure to European religion or formal education.
Traditional marriage and kinship systems are essentially intact.

Until the mid-1970s, the Alyawara were scarcely reported in the anthropological literature.  Early research among southern bands is described by Tindale (1931) and Cleland (1932).
More recently, Yallop (1969 1977) and Denham (1972 1974ab 1975 1977 1978; Denham, et al.
1979) have published major works on language, territory, population structure, kinship, and
nonverbal behavior.  The data presented here were gathered in the course of sixteen months
of ethnographic and archeological fieldwork during 1973-78 in the area around MacDonald
Downs homestead (O'Connell 1977abc).

## Traditional Subsistence

In pre-European times, Alyawara diet included more than 120 species of native animals,
insects, and plants.  There are no quantitative data on the relative importance of various
taxa, but informants raised under traditional conditions consistently identify eight marsupials, two birds, two or three lizards, cossid larvae (also known as witchitty grubs),
about fifteen seeds, two roots, and four to six fruits as having been eaten regularly (see
table 5.A.1 in the appendix to this chapter).  Nearly all these species were once encountered throughout Alyawara territory, but most of the marsupials (with the exception of red
kangaroo and euro) are now locally extinct or much reduced in number.  Large animals and
birds were taken by men armed with spears and throwing sticks; burrowing animals and roots
were dug by men and women alike with wooden scoops and digging sticks.  Seeds were collected
by women and processed with a variety of tools and facilities, including seed beaters, win-
nowing trays, threshing pits, grinding slabs, and handstones.[1]  None of these foods was
stored, with the exception of some fruits which were occasionally kept dried in small quantities for brief periods (see Cleland 1932; O'Connell, Latz, and Barnett, n.d.; Spencer
and Gillen 1899 1927; Tindale 1974 for detailed descriptions of traditional hunting, collecting, and processing techniques and technology).

---

1. The terms *forage* and *collect* and their respective derivatives are used here syn-
onymously, not in the sense of Binford (1980).

## Modern Subsistence

Since the mid-1950s, when the native welfare system came into effect locally, Alyawara diet has consisted largely of European foods distributed in the form of weekly rations. The kinds and quantities of items given to each household vary somewhat depending on its size and composition, but the average family of five or six, including two adults and three to four children, receives about 20 kg flour, 2 kg treacle or jam, 5 kg refined white sugar, 1.5 kg powdered milk, 0.5 kg tea, and a small quantity of plug tobacco. Households with cash incomes from wages or welfare benefits also purchase extra ration items, as well as tinned fruit and meat, sweet biscuits, candy, and soft drinks at the small stores run by most cattle station operators. Fresh beef is frequently available for sale in many settlements. In 1974, average weekly sales were as high as 1.0-1.5 kg per capita.

Hunting continues to play an important role in some communities, especially those along the southern tier of Alyawara territory. Men armed with small-caliber rifles and shotguns regularly take red kangaroo, euro, and bustard, an activity which contributes up to seventy per cent of total per capita meat intake. Women still forage for native foods, though far less often than they did under traditional conditions, largely because of the availability of rations. Even the most active collectors seldom go out more than once a week, and many women rarely go. The return from this activity is relatively low, probably about five per cent of total food intake in those households where it is most important.

## Plant Collecting at Bendaijerum

The best available data on Alyawara plant collecting are from the settlement known as Bendaijerum or MacDonald Downs (Denham 1975 1978; O'Connell 1977c). In 1974-75, this community included a European homesteader and his family and about 100-125 Alyawara and eastern Aranda. The European employed about 10-15 Aborigines as stockmen and also distributed rations and welfare checks and ran a small cash store. Many of the Aboriginal men hunted regularly on foot in the area immediately around the settlement and by car in the grasslands 20 km to the southwest. Both men and women collected plant foods, the women far more often than the men.

Plant collecting took place in three major plant communities or habitats (figure 5.2). *Mulga woodland.* The mulga woodland community covers about seventy-five per cent of the area within 10 km (two hours walking distance) of Bendaijerum. The dominant species is mulga (*Acacia aneura*), a low scrubby tree 3-6 m high, typically distributed in dense linear groves 200-400 m long and 10-100 m wide. Groves are separated by open lanes, or "intergroves," which are several times larger and covered by low shrubs (especially *A. kempeana* and *Cassia* spp.) and grasses (especially *Eragrostis eriopoda*, *Panicum* spp., and *Astrebla* spp.).

*Riverine floodplain.* Bendaijerum sits between two major watercourses, Bundey and Frazer creeks, which run together about 15 km northeast of the settlement. These streams carry runoff for brief periods after rain, but are otherwise dry, at least on the surface. Their channels are lined with gallery forests of river red gum (*Eucalyptus camaldulensis*), coolibah *(E. microtheca),* and ghost gum *(E. papuana)*; their broad floodplains covered by open park lands in which ironwood (*Acacia estrophiolata*) and coolibah trees and various grasses (especially *Panicum* spp.) are prominent elements. This community covers twenty-five per cent of the area within two hours walking distance of Bendaijerum.

*Sandhills.* A prominent sandstone ridge 12 km north of Bendaijerum marks the southern limit of a broad, rolling sand plain which stretches more than 100 km north across the heart of Alyawara territory. The primary plant cover is spinifex, a collective term for several

species of tough, spiky tussock grasses (*Triodia* spp., *Plectrachne* spp.).  The most common
trees are scrubby acacias and eucalypts, notably *A. aneura, coriacea, cowleana, dictyophleba,*
and *kempeana,* and *E. gamophylla* and *pachyphylla.*  Where the climax community has been disturbed, especially by fire, bush potato (*Ipomoea costata*), native tomato (*Solanum* spp.),
and various grasses are usually abundant.  Low-lying areas, where runoff from ridge lines
and other high ground collects after rain, are covered by dense stands of mulga woodland.
The sandhill community is about two hours walking distance from Bendaijerum, but may be
reached by car within thirty minutes.[2]

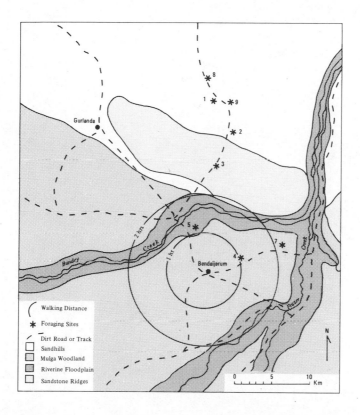

Figure 5.2.  Plant Communities (habitats) near Bendaijerum (MacDonald Downs).  Site 6 is
in the sandhill community west of the area covered by this figure.

    The condition of plant resources in these communities during 1974-75 is summarized in
figure 5.3.  The data are incomplete in that not all resources were monitored consistently
throughout this period, but the information available should be sufficient for this discussion.  Quantitative analyses of plant collecting are based on a sample of nineteen foraging
events, eighteen of which took place between May 1974 and March 1975 (table 5.A.2).  The
sample is small, representing only 12%-15% of the estimated 100-125 collecting trips originating from Bendaijerum during the May-March interval; and some of the trip records are
incomplete.  Still, casual observations of collecting activities over a five-year period

    2.  Though distinctive in some respects, vegetation on the sandstone ridges at the
southern edge of the sandhill community (figure 5.2) can be considered the equivalent of
that in the latter area for purposes of this analysis (Perry 1962).

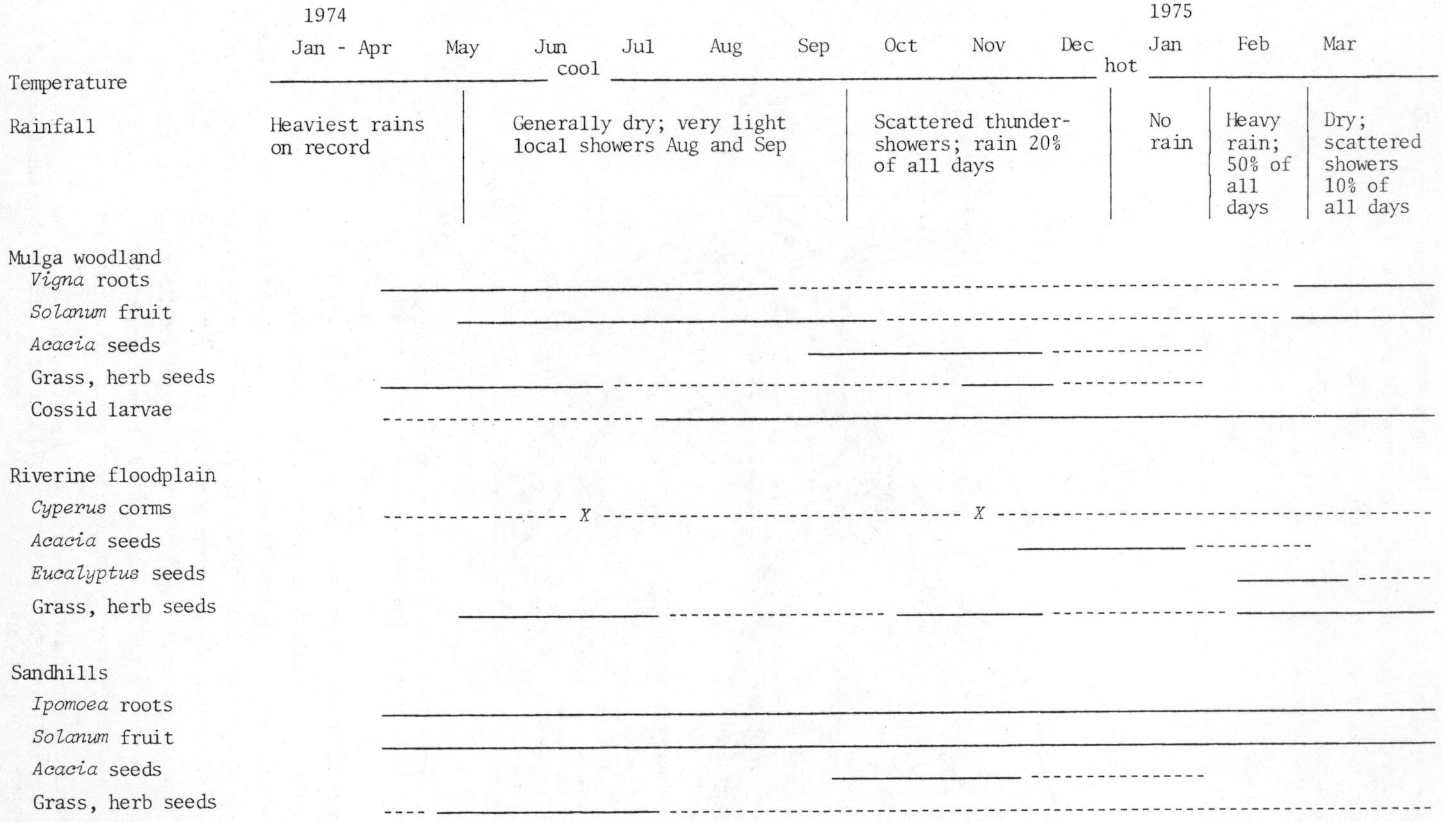

| | 1974 | | | | | | | | | 1975 | | |
|---|---|---|---|---|---|---|---|---|---|---|---|---|
| | Jan - Apr | May | Jun | Jul | Aug | Sep | Oct | Nov | Dec | Jan | Feb | Mar |
| Temperature | | | cool | | | | | | hot | | | |
| Rainfall | Heaviest rains on record | | Generally dry; very light local showers Aug and Sep | | | | Scattered thunder-showers; rain 20% of all days | | | No rain | Heavy rain; 50% of all days | Dry; scattered showers 10% of all days |

Mulga woodland
Vigna roots
Solanum fruit
Acacia seeds
Grass, herb seeds
Cossid larvae

Riverine floodplain
Cyperus corms
Acacia seeds
Eucalyptus seeds
Grass, herb seeds

Sandhills
Ipomoea roots
Solanum fruit
Acacia seeds
Grass, herb seeds

Figure 5.3. Availability of Traditional Plant Foods in Plant Communities near Bendaijerum, 1974-75. Solid horizontal lines indicate periods when resources were observed to be available; dashed lines mark periods when resources were likely to be available given rainfall and temperature conditions. X = isolated observations.

in the same area have convinced us that the sample is broadly representative. It is notably exceptional only in that it includes a disproportionate number of trips in which a motor vehicle was used for transportation. In all these instances, the vehicle was the long-wheel-base Toyota Land Cruiser belonging to one of the authors. Except as otherwise indicated in the notes on table 5.A.2, Alyawara collectors initiated the planning for these trips and made all decisions about destination, route, and length of stay at the collecting site. As we shall see, the use of the vehicle, though unusual, actually enhances our understanding of the principles which underlie foraging decisions (see also Winterhalder, chapter 4, above).

Some additional comments on table 5.A.2 are in order. When the vehicle was used for transportation, the party traveled to one or more specific foraging sites. These are numbered on table 5.A.2 and keyed to figure 5.2. When the party traveled on foot, resources might be collected at any time; thus a general area (e.g., mulga woodland east of Bendaijerum) is indicated rather than a specific site. Number of collectors is the number of individuals actually engaged in food collecting. If others were present, as they often were, they are listed in the notes on the table. Main items collected are those gathered and brought back to the settlement. Other resources were occasionally taken in small quantities and eaten in the field; these too are listed in the notes. Total trip time is that between the time the party left the settlement and the time it returned. Time on site is total time spent at each collecting site; this was not recorded for trips made entirely on foot. Processing time is that spent preparing resources for consumption after they had been collected. It includes cleaning, separation of seeds from pods or chaff, grinding, and cooking. Calories per forager hour is the average return in energy per unit of time spent traveling, collecting, and processing.

During late fall and winter (May-July) 1974, plant foods were abundant in all habitats near Bendaijerum owing to very heavy rains during the preceding summer. Alyawara women foraged on foot in the mulga woodland north and east of the settlement, some as often as once or twice a week. Their primary target was *Vigna lanceolata*, or "native yam," a carrot-sized root found in small numbers in moist, well-shaded spots throughout the area. They also collected two species of lizard (*Amphibolarus* sp., *Varanus* sp.), small quantities of *Solanum* fruit, *Lysiana* berries, and tender *Leichhardtia* leaves, all whenever encountered. *Leichhardtia* leaves, *Lysiana* berries, and most *Solanum* fruit were eaten at the collecting site; *Vigna* roots and lizards were brought back to the settlement, as were *Solanum* fruit if available in any quantity (say, more than 0.5 kg). *Vigna* and lizards were roasted in the ashes of hearths; solanums were rubbed by hand to remove any grit and eaten without further preparation. Total returns for these trips were about 2.5-3.0 kg per active collector, or about 0.4 kg per collector-hr, including travel, collecting, and processing time.

Collectors visited the floodplain community far less often. Only one trip (event 7) was recorded in the four-month period May-August, and we doubt that more than one or two others, if any, were taken. The principal target of the recorded trip was *Cyperus* sp., a small corm roughly the size of a shallot, found in some abundance in small patches where the soil is fine, moist, and well shaded. In the one instance observed, five collectors brought 8.0 kg back to camp after eight hours total time in the field, for an average of 1.6 kg per collector, or 0.2 kg per collector-hr.

Whenever the ethnographer's vehicle was available, women organized trips to locations in the sandhill community north and west of the settlement to collect *Ipomoea*, or "bush potato," a large tuber up to 1.0 kg in weight which is common in disturbed areas in this habitat.  Their favorite collecting spot was a large abandoned campsite (site 1), about 25 km north-northwest of Bendaijerum; but on one occasion they insisted on traveling to a site on the Sandover River (event 9, site 6), 95 km west of Bendaijerum where they thought *Ipomoea* would be particularly abundant.  On nearly all these trips, collectors took *Solanum* (esp. *centrale), Vigna, Leichhardtia* (both fruit and leaves), and *Varanus* whenever encountered.  Some *Solanum* and all *Leichhardtia* were eaten in the field without preparation, while *Ipomoea, Vigna,* lizards, and *Solanum* were brought back to camp.  *Ipomoea* were scraped with sticks or knives or rubbed by hand to remove grit, and cooked for 15-20 minutes in small, specially prepared roasting pits.  The other resources were treated as described above. The return on these trips was relatively high.  Average weight of all foods brought to the settlement was 5.5 kg per collector, or about 0.7 per collector-hr.

Trips to the sandhills were also made under other circumstances.  Alyawara men occasionally visited these areas while working as stockmen, or when acting as guides or ethnographic informants, or in the course of infrequent long-range hunting trips.  In these situations, they collected *Ipomoea* and *Solanum* whenever possible, often in substantial quantities.  Also, individual families sometimes arranged trips to the sandhills in their own vehicles.  In May 1974, for example, several families traveled by car to a site near Derry Downs, 50 km north of Bendaijerum, where they stayed more than a week collecting *Ipomoea* and *Solanum,* both of which were very abundant there.  When these resources were exhausted, the people returned to Bendaijerum.  Although many Alyawara own cars or light trucks, trips like this are not common because the vehicles are generally in poor condition and are rightly considered unreliable on the badly maintained tracks one must travel to reach the more productive sandhill patches.

From late winter through midsummer (January 1975), women continued to forage primarily in mulga woodland, generally traveling on foot, but sometimes in the ethnographer's vehicle. Their primary target was cossid larvae, which they dug from the shallow roots of cassia and acacia shrubs.  *Solanum* and lizards were also taken, as was the occasional *Leichhardtia* fruit.  The average return from these trips was 1.5 kg per collector, or about 0.2 kg per collector-hr.

There were no visits to the floodplains during this period, and only three recorded trips to the sandhills.  One (event 13) was made to collect the large but still unripened seeds of *A. coriacea*; and on another (event 16), the target was *Solanum centrale*.  Both trips were organized by the ethnographer.  Collectors were given choice of habitat and site on the first trip, but site only on the second.  The third incident (event 12) took place on a plant-collecting trip organized for botanist Peter Latz, when a sizable patch of *Ipomoea* was discovered unexpectedly.  Two of the men acting as guides quickly collected 4.0 kg of *Ipomoea* and a small quantity of *A. coriacea* seeds.  This was the only time *Ipomoea* was collected that season.

During  February 1975, heavy rains prevented supplies from reaching Bendaijerum for nearly two weeks, and ration stocks became depleted.  In response, women foraged more frequently, this time exclusively in mulga woodland.  Though the ethnographer's vehicle was available at this time, roads were so wet that it could not be used.  Cossid larvae were the principal prey, although *Vigna* roots were collected again for the first time since the preceding winter.

## Summary

Though admittedly limited, these observations present us with a very striking fact.

Of the eighty-five plant species identified by the Alyawara as edible, less than a dozen were collected during the study period, and of these, only three (*Ipomoea*, *Vigna*, and *Solanum centrale*) were regularly taken in any quantity.  The nearly complete absence of seeds from this group is most surprising.  Of the thirty-nine seed-producing species on the traditional list, only one--*Acacia coriacea*--was ever collected by choice, and then only during a brief period just before the seeds became fully ripe.  Two other species were also taken (*A. aneura*, event 11; *A. cowleana*, event 13a), but only because of the ethnographer's request for a demonstration of processing and collecting techniques.  Although the importance of seeds in the pre-European diet cannot be assessed in strictly quantitative terms, every knowledgeable informant insists that they were eaten regularly and in substantial quantities.  Tindale (1974 1977 n.d.) and other observers who visited the Alyawara under traditional conditions make the same observation.  This makes the recent lack of attention to seed resources all the more remarkable.

The failure to take seeds cannot be explained by lack of availability or access.  At least five edible species (including *Acacia aneura* and *kempeana*, *Eucalyptus microtheca*, *Eragrostis eriopoda*, and *Panicum* spp.) could have been collected within a 10-km radius of Bendaijerum, and an additional four or more (including *Acacia cowleana* and *dictyophleba*, *Eragrostis* spp., *Panicum* spp.) were within easy reach by car.  Moreover, the unusually heavy rains of late 1973 and early 1974 had produced abundant seed crops in all species, especially the acacias.  Differences in the palatability of seeds relative to other foods are also unlikely to provide an explanation.  Though we recognize that cross-cultural assessments of taste appeal can be misleading, one of us (JOC) would argue that seed paste is at least as tasty as *Vigna* or *Ipomoea* roots.  More important, the Alyawara themselves never expressed any negative attitudes toward seeds as food.  Finally, we note that the availability of flour as a ration item also fails to explain this behavior toward seeds.  As we shall show, seeds have been used in the recent past when flour was as available as it was during 1974-75.

We are left with two intriguing questions:  Why ignore seeds that were traditionally important, currently abundant, and immediately available, in favor of grubs, roots, and fruit that were less common and could be taken only by walking or driving long distances?  Why take one seed species (*A. coriacea*) found no less than 25 km away rather than several others which were abundant less than one kilometer from the settlement?  We think both questions can be answered through an application of optimal foraging theory.

## Optimal Foraging

### The Optimal Diet Model

We use two models derived from optimal foraging theory in the analysis of Alyawara plant use.  One describes optimal diet in a uniform or fine-grained environment; the other pertains to choice of foraging sites or areas in a "patchy" or coarse-grained environment.[3] The optimal diet model predicts that in an area or "patch" where resources are encountered

---

3.  Both are reviewed in detail elsewhere (see Winterhalder, chapter 2, above, and references).  In applying them here, we assume that human hunters maximize energy return relative to time invested, and that behavioral or technological practices which increase the likelihood of procuring a particular resource or reduce the time required to take that resource will spread.  The first of these assumptions may seem inconsistent with the common ethnographic observation that hunters spend relatively little time on the food quest (Lee 1965; Sahlins 1968 1972).  However, energy may be maximized *either* by taking the greatest amount of energy possible in the time available, *or* by investing the least time necessary to obtain given amounts of energy (Schoener 1971).  The latter strategy matches the behavior observed among most modern hunters.

at random in proportion to their abundance, a predator will take a resource item only if
the returns gained from collecting and processing, or "handling," it are greater than those
likely to be gained from searching for and handling an item of higher rank, that is, one
which produces a better return from the investment made in collecting and processing. If
the return from the item at hand is less, the model predicts that it will be ignored and
that the predator will continue to search for higher-ranked resources. If time and energy
are used as convenient measures of costs and benefits, this means that resources are included in or excluded from the diet as a function of (1) their rank in terms of energy
gain per unit of handling time relative to other resources; and (2) the abundance of higher-
ranked resources, or, more precisely, their encounter rate. As the encounter rate for high-
ranked resources goes up, low-ranked resources will be eliminated from the diet, and conversely, regardless of the absolute abundance of the low-ranked resources (MacArthur and
Pianka 1966; Emlen 1966; Schoener 1971; Charnov and Orians 1973; Pyke, et al. 1977). At
the same time, even very rare resources will be included in the diet, provided they produce
a relatively high return on handling time (Royama 1970). The model also leads to the expectation that foragers may react quite differently to the same resource, depending on the
characteristics of other resources available in a given situation.

   If Alyawara collectors are foraging optimally, the resources they take in each patch
will depend on the relative energy return per unit of handling time for each resource, and
the average return from collecting in that patch. Any resource which yields a return on
handling time higher than the average return for the patch will be included in the diet;
any resource with a lower return will be excluded. This can be stated formally:

   For all items in the optimal set,

$E^*_i/h_i \geq E_p$ where

$E^*_i$    = energy (kcal) per unit weight (kg) of resource $i$

$h_i$    = gathering and processing time ($g_i + p_i$, in hr) for each resource $i$

$E_p$    = $E/(T_s + T_g + T_p)$

$E$    = total energy in resources gathered per collector

$T_s$    = total search time within patch

$T_g$    = total gathering time per collector for all resources gathered

$T_p$    = total processing time per collector for all resources gathered

If the encounter rate for high-ranked resources goes down, then search time goes up, the
average return for the patch falls, and new items are added as their rank $E^*_i/h_i$ equals or
exceeds $E_p$, and conversely (Charnov and Orians 1973; Charnov 1976b; Pulliam 1974; Schoener
1971; MacArthur and Pianka 1966; MacArthur 1972).[4]

   For purposes of this discussion, we assume that despite minor nonrandom variation in
the distribution of resources, the mulga woodland around Bendaijerum can be considered a
single patch. Sandhill habitats are more complex in that they contain relatively small,
bounded areas in which the climax plant community has been disturbed by various processes
(notably fire or human occupation) in such a way as to permit the growth of potential subsistence resources, including *Ipomoea*, *Solanum* spp., and various seed-producing grasses.
These disturbed areas are the focus of Alyawara foraging activities in the sandhill habitat,

---

   4. Note that travel time to and from the patch is not included in this model. If it
were, one would predict that, all else being equal, increasingly lower-ranked resources
would be added to the diet as travel time to patch increased. On the contrary, foragers
should choose *only* that set of resources which produces the best return per unit of time
expended once they enter the patch, regardless of the distance traveled to reach the
patch.

and are called sandhill *patches* to distinguish them from the climax grassland, which is comparatively poor in resources. The small stands of mulga woodland found in sandhill country are also distinguished as separate patches. Floodplain habitats are not considered in this discussion for lack of data.

Energy returns per forager-hour ($E_p$) in mulga woodland and sandhill patches are listed in table 5.A.3 along with energy returns per unit of handling time ($E^*_i/h_i$) for each resource collected. Estimates of handling time were difficult to derive since the field notes did not consistently separate this value, except in the case of seeds. Nevertheless, we have arrived at rough but reasonable approximations of these figures by considering the general features of each resource (e.g., average size of individual units) and the time limits suggested by the events sampled. These figures are presented in table 5.A.4. Comments on their derivation are found in the notes for that table.

Now consider the foraging behavior in each patch type. On eleven visits to sandhill patches (excluding event 13a, a seed-processing demonstration), energy returns ranged from about 750-5,200 kcal per forager-hr searching, collecting, and processing. Eight visits produced returns in 2,000-4,000 kcal-per-hr range. Resources taken in quantity were *Ipomoea* roots, *Solanum* fruits, and unripened *A. coriacea* seeds. In each instance, returns per unit of handling time for the resource were well above the average returns for the patch. Although several species of ripe seeds were available in these patches (see figure 5.3) and often encountered, they were never taken because returns from other, higher-ranked resources never fell low enough. *A. coriacea* seeds (event 13b) were collected only in the brief period after they reached maximum size and before they hardened, when handling time is relatively low and energy returns correspondingly high. Foraging behavior in this habitat is clearly consistent with the predictions of the optimal diet model.

Returns from foraging in mulga woodland are low compared with those from the sandhills. Totals for ten incidents ranged about 200-800 kcal per forager-hr in patch, and in all but one case they were less than 600 kcal per hr. *Vigna* roots, cossid larvae, and lizards (*Amphibolarus*, *Varanus*), all of which have $E^*_i/h_i$ values greater than 1,400, were the principal resources taken.[5] With one exception (event 11, a collecting demonstration), ripe seeds were ignored entirely even though $E_p$ values in eight of the nine other cases were equal to or less than those to be gained from handling seeds (500-600 kcal/hr). This suggests that foragers would have been acting more efficiently by including these resources in their diet, especially in the spring (October-November) when acacia seeds were extremely abundant in the area immediately around Bendaijerum. In other words, Alyawara foraging behavior in these eight events fails to fit the optimal diet prediction about the threshold at which lower-ranked resources will be added.[6]

---

5. The shift from *Vigna* to cossid larvae in late winter and back again in late summer deserves special comment here, in that it probably reflects small but important variations in encounter rate and forager search patterns. *Vigna* roots are marked above ground by a distinctive vine which flourishes during wet periods, but dies back as conditions become drier, making the roots more difficult to locate. Grubs, on the other hand, are found in the shallow lateral roots of acacias and cassias, which are hard to spot when the soil is moist. As it dries, however, fine cracks appear on the surface just above the root line, and are easily seen by experienced collectors. During the first few months after the heavy rains of summer and early fall, 1974, foragers took *Vigna*, but no grubs. As the ground dried during midwinter, *Vigna* became progressively more difficult to find, even though the roots themselves were still present. Foragers apparently reacted by shifting their attention to grubs. This pattern continued till the following summer when the heavy rains of mid-February prompted renewed growth in *Vigna*. As soon as the vines became visible, collectors began taking this resource again.

6. It is interesting to note that more kinds of resources are consistently collected in the mulga woodland than in the sandhills. This expansion in diet diversity where average returns per forager are lower is the pattern predicted by the optimal diet model.

One explanation for this apparent inconsistency is that the cost of collecting seeds has been underestimated, at least in this particular situation. During 1974-75, the standard plant-collecting kit maintained by women at Bendaijerum included a metal digging stick and one or more carrying devices, such as a wooden tray, plastic bucket, billy can, or some combination of these. With this kit, a woman could collect and process roots, burrowing lizards, and cossid larvae, but not seeds. The manufacture and maintenance of seed-grinding tools would have increased the cost of handling seeds, at least initially.

If this were true, we would expect that where the encounter rate for higher-ranked resources was lower, or foraging activity more intensive (a factor which would both deplete the high-ranked resources *and* spread the cost of maintaining seed-processing gear over a larger number of collecting incidents), seeds would enter the diet. In this connection, it is interesting to note that seed-processing tools are common in household camp debris at Gurlanda B, an abandoned settlement thirty kilometers northwest of Bendaijerum (figure 5.2), occupied in 1971-73. Because of the distance to the store and the limited availability of reliable transport (Denham, n.d.), residents of this settlement had no regular daily access to European foods, though they still received weekly rations, including flour. They may have relied more heavily on native plant resources than did the people at Bendaijerum, but, more important, the abundance of these resources had been reduced by drought conditions which had prevailed in this part of central Australia for several years (Denham, n.d.). Under these circumstances, energy returns from the sandhill and mulga woodland patches around Gurlanda probably fell low enough that it became efficient to take seeds. As the preceding discussion has indicated, the drop need not have been far below 1974-75 levels to make these resources part of the optimal diet. Though the data are limited, they suggest that Alyawara foraging behavior may be explained by a cost-benefit analysis which adds the cost of manufacturing and maintaining processing gear to the variables of the optimal diet model.

These same data also indicate why seeds were so important in the traditional diet. In the absence of European foods, the pressure on native plant resources would have been much greater. Moreover, collectors can apparently deplete certain high-ranked resources with surprising speed, even in a good year. In the next section, for example, we suggest that *Ipomoea* may have been cropped completely from a one-kilometer-square patch after only three visits by collectors. Given this, it should not be surprising that seeds were a central element in past diets.

## The Patch Choice Model

Now consider a second closely related question. In situations where resources are differentially distributed in kind and quantity among a series of habitats or patches, as is the case at Bendaijerum, how do foragers decide which patches to exploit? Optimal foraging theory predicts that under such circumstances, collectors will operate in that patch or set of patches which produces the best return in energy for time spent traveling to the patch, searching it, and gathering and processing the resources found there (Charnov and Orians 1973; MacArthur and Pianka 1966; Pyke, et al. 1977; Orians and Pearson 1977). Stated formally, foragers will maximize $E_n$, where

$$E_n = E/(T_t + T_s + T_g + T_p)$$

$E$ = total energy gained from all resources gathered per collector

$T_t$ = total travel time to and from the patch

and $T_s$, $T_g$, and $T_p$ are defined as above. Within each patch, resource exploitation should follow the predictions of the fine-grain, random encounter model. As relative returns from different patches change over time (e.g., with the seasons, or as the forager depletes resources), the optimal choice will change accordingly.

If Alyawara foraging behavior is consistent with the optimal diet model, we might expect it to fit the patch choice model as well. $E_n$ values for six trips to sandhill patches alone range about 800-1,950 kcal per forager-hr (events 2, 4, 9, 12-13, 16; see table 5.A.2). All these trips involved the use of the ethnographer's vehicle for transport. Eight trips to mulga woodland alone yielded only 250-850 kcal per forager-hr (events 5-6, 10-11, 14-15, 17-18). Three of these trips were by car; the other five were on foot. These figures suggest that foragers operating from Bendaijerum should visit the sandhills whenever they have access to motor vehicles.[7] On nine occasions when the ethnographic vehicle was available, *and* the choice of destination left entirely to the foragers, they elected to travel to sandhill patches five times.

Among these five, events 8 and 9 merit special comment. Event 8 was the third occasion after the beginning of the 1974-75 study period that foragers had visited site 1, an abandoned settlement twenty-five kilometers north of Bendaijerum. On the first trip (event 2, table 5.A.3), they gathered 5.0 kg of *Ipomoea* per collector in a 500-m$^2$ area, for a return of more than 5,200 kcal per hour spent searching, gathering, and processing. On subsequent trips, returns fell below 2,600 kcal per hour searching and handling, and the area searched steadily increased to more than 60,000 m$^2$. On the afternoon of event 8, foragers abandoned the search for *Ipomoea* and walked to a nearby patch of mulga where they collected *Vigna*. The next time they had access to the vehicle, they traveled not to site 1, but to site 6, ninety-five kilometers west on the Sandover.

Although the data are admittedly slender, we suspect foragers had exhausted *Ipomoea* at site 1 by midday on the third trip, or at least reduced its abundance to the point that *Vigna* in the adjacent patch became the optimal choice. If so, the subsequent trip to site 6 makes sense. Having depleted one sandhill patch, foragers then shifted their attention to another more distant one, where returns were better.[8]

Now let us examine the four cases which seem to be inconsistent with the patch choice model.

*Event 3a.* Foragers traveled to an isolated patch of mulga woodland (site 2), located about twenty kilometers north of Bendaijerum, well inside the sandhill habitat. There they spent more than an hour searching for *Vigna* and lizards, but with little success. The take was barely 200 kcal per forager-hr searching and handling (table 5.A.3). En route back to the settlement, they stopped to collect *Ipomoea* in a sandhill patch (event 3b, site 3) that they all knew well and through which they had passed on route to the mulga. There the

---

7. In spite of the fact that the sandhill habitat is 9 km, or about two hours walk from Bendaijerum, foragers might still be expected to travel there on foot rather than operate in mulga woodland, at least under certain circumstances. Assuming the average return ($E_n$) from foraging in mulga woodland is 500 kcal per hr, a trip to the sandhills would have to yield better than 4,000 kcal in an eight-hour period to surpass the yield from the same time spent in the mulga. The average $E_p$ value for sandhill patches listed in table 5.3 is about 2,900 kcal per hr, which means that foragers could travel up to 3.25 hours (ca. 16 km) to reach such a patch, spend no more than 1.5 hours searching and collecting, and still gain an $E_n$ greater than 540 kcal per hr. Still, Alyawara foragers never traveled to the sandhills on foot from Bendaijerum during the study period. Whether this reflects a failure to conform to the predictions of the patch choice model or the absence of productive sandhill patches within a 3.0-3.5-hour radius of Bendaijerum is not clear, though for reasons outlined later in the text, we suspect that suitable patches were in fact not present.

8. If we are right, these two interpatch moves are consistent with the predictions of Charnov's (1976a) marginal value theorem (see Winterhalder, chapter 2, above).

take was more than 2,300 kcal per collector-hr on site, or about 2,000 kcal per hr, counting processing. Moreover, it had been less than a month since members of the same party
had visited another sandhill patch (site 1, event 2), less than five kilometers beyond the
mulga, where they gained the 5,200-kcal-per-hr return mentioned above. As records of subsequent visits to this site (events 4, 8a) clearly show, there was still much more to be
collected there. Even if *Vigna* had been so abundant in the mulga patch as to require no
search, the best return possible would have been no better than 1,700 kcal per hr, somewhat
less than that available in adjacent sandhill patches.

Forager behavior in this instance might be seen as an attempt to obtain information
on resource conditions as an aid to planning future trips. Foragers certainly knew that
*Ipomoea* would ultimately be exhausted in patches near Bendaijerum, and, when it was, information on the availability of alternate resources would have been essential to future
planning. Reconnaissance visits like these are to be expected, even though the immediate
returns may often be comparatively low. As J. Maynard Smith (1978:34) says: "Optimal behavior depends on a knowledge of the environment, which can only be acquired by experience;
this means that in order to acquire information of value in the long run, an animal may
have to behave in a way which is inefficient in the short run" (see also Hitchcock and
Ebert 1980).

*Events 15 and 17.* The exceptions in the case of events 15 and 17 may be more apparent
than real. We note that from August through December, energy returns from grub-collecting
trips in mulga woodland nearby doubled relative to time spent searching and gathering
(table 5.A.5). This probably reflects a reduction both in search time as local soils dried
and cracked over grub-infested roots, and in handling time as grubs grew in size toward
the end of the larval stage (Tindale 1953). By mid-November, foragers could probably have
expected average returns greater than 800 kcal per on-site hour in the mulga near Bendaijerum. If we assume they could reach productive areas in an hour's travel time, and that
they could anticipate at least four hours time on site collecting, the minimum return would
have been 3,200 kcal per collector-trip, or about 533 kcal per collector-hr ($E_n$).

Trips to sandhill patches earlier in the year certainly produced better results. On
four occasions from June through August (table 5.A.3), returns from *Ipomoea* alone averaged
about 2,700 kcal per collector-hr on site, or about 2,300 kcal per collector-hr, counting
processing. At this rate, collectors could have driven 2.5 hours each way, spent only 1.5
hours on the patch, and still gained a net return better than 530 kcal per hour, including
processing time. Even if the trip were extended to nine hours (at or near the maximum for
both the ethnographer and the Alyawara), 2.2 hours collecting would have yielded an $E_n$ return greater than 560 kcal per hr, and a total trip return greater than 5,000 kcal. This
allows about 3.4 hours travel time each way. If foragers had targeted *Solanum centrale,*
and located a patch which produced at the same rate as did those visited on 28 December
1974 (table 5.A.3), they could have traveled more than 3.75 hours to reach the patch, collected for less than 1.5 hours, and still gained better than 650 kcal per hr, or about
6,000 kcal total for the trip.

The problem lies in finding the appropriate patch. As we have already said, *Ipomoea*
and *Solanum* are not uniformly or randomly distributed in the sandhill habitat, but are
found in abundance only in disturbed areas, such as recently abandoned habitation sites or
localities swept by bush fires. There were only two of the former in sandhill country
near Bendaijerum. As we have already mentioned, one (site 1) may have been cleared of
*Ipomoea* by mid-July. The other (Gurlanda) was seldom visited for fear of dangerous spirits,

and in any case had been so thoroughly searched during the years it was occupied that it may not have had sufficient time to recover.[9] Fire-scarred sites at various successional stages are found throughout sandhill country, but are difficult to monitor. Only one road, barely passable by four-wheel-drive vehicle, transects the sandhills directly north of site 1, and it is seldom traveled. Though *Ipomoea* and *Solanum* were probably common at some sites within 3.5-4.0 hours by truck from Bendaijerum, actually *locating* one in that time would have been a chancy business. The fact that collectors were willing to travel three hours to a site 95 kilometers west of Bendaijerum (event 9) seems to us an indication of the risks involved in foraging in the sandhills north of site 1.

Given this line of reasoning, it should not be surprising that foragers collected in the sandhills only three times after August, twice in the course of trips in which the destination was determined by the ethnographer (events 12, 16), once when they evidently chose a site on the basis of information gained on a previous trip (event 13). Without such information, foragers were more assured of a good return in mulga woodland, even if they had access to a vehicle; or at least so the data suggest.

*Event 10.* On the occasion of event 10, women used the ethnographer's truck to reach a grub-collecting site in mulga country, but recovered only 418 kcal per collector-hr for the entire trip. Since the event took place after the apparent depletion of nearby, well-known sandhill patches, it is consistent with the argument just outlined for events 15 and 17. The implication is that the anticipated encounter rate for high-ranked sandhill resources was very low indeed.

*Summary.* Although the data are few, Alyawara foraging behavior seems to fit the patch choice model fairly well. On nine occasions in which foragers had free access to the ethnographer's vehicle, they made what appear to have been optimal choices concerning patch type at least five times, and possibly as many as eight times. Even the ninth case (event 3) can be seen as consistent with the model, when the need to gather information on resource condition is considered. We conclude that optimal foraging theory is likely to provide a useful framework in which to consider Alyawara subsistence strategy and tactics. Certainly it merits a more comprehensive test. The analysis also shows that the presence of motor vehicles (and other items of European technology) need not inhibit the investigation of hunter-gatherer ecology. In this case, the vehicle simply added to the range of foraging options open to the Alyawara, thereby enriching the "experimental" dimensions of the situation.

## Some General Implications

To this point, we have confined our discussion of hunter-gatherer subsistence practices and optimal foraging to the Alyawara case. We now turn briefly to two more general issues: regional variation in diet, and long-term change in diet and patch use among Australian Aborigines.

### Regional Variation in Diet

A comparison of the lists of plant foods used by various central Australian tribes

---

9. The Gurlanda locality, which includes four separate sites (Z, A-C), was occupied from 1969 to 1973. All sites show evidence that seeds were exploited during occupation, which implies heavy pressure on higher-ranked resources. Each site was abandoned because of the death of one of its occupants, a common practice among Australian Aborigines. The death which led to the abandonment of site C, the last site occupied, was of a particularly influential senior man, and informants were openly afraid of visiting this site or the surrounding area, lest they provoke the man's spirit.

shows that certain species common throughout this region were heavily exploited by some groups but ignored by others. Examples include nardoo (*Marsilea* spp.), which produces a seedlike sporocarp often identified as a staple south of the Macdonnell Ranges, 200-400 kilometers south of Alyawara territory (Horne and Aiston 1924:52-57; Spencer 1928:34-35; Worsnop 1897:81-82); and ironwood and deadfinish (*Acacia estriophiolata* and *tetragonophylla*), the seeds of which were used by the Walbiri and others in and around the Tanami Desert, 200-300 kilometers west of Alyawara country (Meggitt 1957:143 1962:5). All three species are found in the upper Sandover and Bundey river drainages, but none are identified there as edible. Nardoo even lacks a specific Alyawara name. It seems unlikely that the Alyawara fail to recognize the potential utility of these plants, especially since many are well aware of their use among other groups. In spite of this, they maintain that the plants are "not food" and refer to those who eat them as *urrupana* or "poor buggers." Similar differences in the use of plants are reported on an even larger, subcontinental scale by Golson (1971), Lawrence (1968), and Meggitt (1964). Golson, for example, says that as many as forty-five species of tree and grass seeds taken by central Australian groups are ignored by the natives of Arnhem Land, even though common there.

These differences could be attributed to cultural preference but this begs the question. We suggest that in these and other similar cases, plants are included in or omitted from the list of species culturally designated as edible on the basis of the same criteria which determine optimal diet, i.e., net returns on handling time and the abundance and accessibility of higher-ranked resources. If high-ranked resources are so abundant that returns never fall to the point where it becomes efficient to include lower-ranked items in the diet, there is no reason to define the latter as food, all else being equal. If this hypothesis were valid, we would expect that a species common in two areas but eaten in only one would have relatively high gathering and processing costs. We would also expect that lower-cost resources were more common in the area where the species in question was not used. It is interesting in this light to recall Spencer's (1928:35) remarks on nardoo. He notes that it is heavily used by the Urabunna and Dieri around Lake Eyre, but ignored by the Arunta (Aranda) farther north in favor of manyeroo (*Portulaca oleracea*, an important Alyawara seed food), "probably because [the latter] is more common and more easily collected." Spencer's observation is anecdotal, but consistent with expectations. It would be most interesting to pursue this line of argument further, not only in Australia, but with data from other hunter-gatherers, such as the !Kung, among whom dietary differences of this type are well documented (e.g., Lee 1979).

## Long-Term Change in Diet and Land Use

In recent years, an interesting controversy has developed over the pattern and rate of human colonization of Australia. Birdsell (1957) originally argued that within five thousand years after man's initial landing, an event now thought to have taken place at least fifty thousand years ago (Jones 1979; White and O'Connell 1979), all parts of the continent, including the continental islands of New Guinea and Tasmania, were already populated at levels approaching those recorded at the time of European contact. This idea seems to have been accepted tacitly by prehistorians, who until recently treated the archeological record as if it provided incomplete but plausible support for Birdsell's position (e.g., Jones 1973:281; Mulvaney 1975:161).

Bowdler (1977) has challenged this line by arguing that the available archeological data are better seen as showing that the earliest Australians occupied coastal and riverine habitats first, and only later moved to other areas, including the arid central desert,

probably after 15,000 BP.  Jones (1979) rightly remarks that although occupation of the
continental core is indeed late (no earlier than 10,000 BP on present evidence; see Gould
1977), the archeological record shows that several areas which were neither coastal nor
riverine were inhabited before 20,000 BP, including the mountains of New Guinea and east
central Queensland (White, et al. 1970; Mulvaney and Joyce 1965), the Nullarbor Plain of
south Australia (Wright 1971), and parts of southwestern Australia (Dortch 1976).  Jones
and Bowdler agree that there is probably a causal connection between the beginning of a
period of widespread aridity dated 16,000-17,500 BP (Bowler, et al. 1976), the first use
of seeds, as evidenced by the discovery of grinding tools in 15,000-18,000-year-old deposits
in western New South Wales and Arnhem Land (Allen 1972 1974; Kamminga and Allen 1973, cited
in Bowdler 1977:235-36), and the initial occupation of the central desert, but they are not
specific about the details of this relationship.

Optimal foraging theory gives us some insight into the processes which might have
been operating in this situation.  We suggest that on landing, Australian Aborigines first
occupied only those habitats which produced the best return for foraging effort.  More
precisely, the order in which habitats or habitat types were occupied should have varied
directly with the net energy gained from exploiting them, and inversely with their distance
from the original landing point(s).  Habitats in which energy returns were comparatively
low should have remained unoccupied until returns in "better" habitats fell to the same
level (Fretwell and Lucas 1969).  Movement into new habitats should have been a function
of (a) population increase which depleted resources in occupied habitats to the point where
such movement became more efficient, or (b) climatic or other environmental change which
either differentially reduced returns in the occupied habitats, or increased those available in the unoccupied ones.  Within each habitat, resources should have been exploited in
order of net return on handling time, highest-ranked resources first.  The same pattern
should be evident on a continental scale as well, i.e., low-cost/high-return resources
taken relatively early in the past, high-cost/low-return resources relatively later.  Again,
depletion of high-ranked resources through population growth or environmental change should
have been the critical factor forcing increased diet breadth.

All this means that although coastal and riverine habitats may have been *among* the
first occupied, it need not have been to the exclusion of other habitats, nor need it have
been the result of a "preadaptation" to aquatic resources, as Bowdler (1977:221) implies.
Energy budgets are more likely to have been important here than any presumed traditional
economic orientation.  On the other hand, these same propositions are consistent with
Bowdler's suggestion that central Australia was unoccupied until quite late.  In light of
the Alyawara data, it seems unlikely that Aborigines could have lived there (certainly not
at the densities recorded historically) unless they had access to seeds, which should also
be late.  We propose that the onset of arid conditions 17,000-18,000 BP led to critical
reductions in the abundance of high-ranked foods and favored the adoption of more expensive
items, including seeds.  Once the technology for processing seeds was available, it was
possible for Aborigines to move to previously uninhabited or sparsely inhabited parts of
the continent.  It is consistent with expectations based on the optimal diet model that
seeds were subsequently the first resources dropped from the diet when European rations
(which are high ranked in cost-benefit terms relative to native resources) became available
in quantity.

It is interesting to note that cycads (*Macrozamia* spp., *Cycas* spp.), a seasonal staple
in many areas of tropical Australia, but one which may be even more expensive than seeds

because of the elaborate processing it requires, first appears in the Australian diet even later than seeds, possibly as late as 5,000 BP (Beaton 1977). This also seems consistent with expectations based on the optimal diet model. We wonder how widely this model can be applied in the explanation of long-term changes in diet, including those involving the adoption of domesticates.

## Summary

We began this chapter by asking why the Alyawara had effectively stopped eating native grass and tree seeds, resources which had been staples in the traditional diet and which continue to be locally abundant today. Analysis of the available data on modern plant collecting practices strongly suggests that this behavior can be understood in terms of a model of optimal diet derived from the theory of optimal foraging. It further suggests that the choice of location in which to search for plant foods can be explained in terms of a second model (i.e., patch choice) also derived from this theory. Having presented this argument, we then considered its implications for the explanation of synchronic and diachronic variability in seed use by Australian Aborigines. Although our treatment was cursory, it was sufficient to suggest that optimal foraging theory may provide a useful means of investigating such variability.

Overall, this discussion provides empirical support for the argument that hunter-gatherer subsistence practices can be viewed profitably in terms of the same general theory now being applied by evolutionary ecologists to the study of feeding strategies among nonhuman organisms. This does not mean that such theory will necessarily provide complete and comprehensive explanations for the full range of foraging practices observed or inferred for past and present hunters. Other social and cultural variables will certainly have structured these practices to a significant degree. The value of such theory lies in its role as a reference dimension, as a source of testable hypotheses about the organization of subsistence-related behavior in a wide range of environmental, technological, and social circumstances. By testing such hypotheses, we should be able to distinguish those aspects of behavior motivated by the principles of optimal foraging from those which are shaped by other variables, and, having isolated the latter, seek explanations for them in other terms.

*Table 5.A.1*

*Some Animal and Plant Foods of the Alyawara*

---

ANIMALS

  Mammals (> 15 species)

| | |
|---|---|
| Red kangaroo | *Megaleia rufa* |
| Euro or wallaroo | *Macropus robustus* |
| Hare wallaby | *Lagorchestes* spp. |
| Nail-tailed wallaby | *Onychogalea* sp. |
| Rat kangaroo | *Bettongia* spp. |
| Bandicoots | *Perameles* sp. |
| | *Macrotis lagotis* |
| Brush-tailed possum | *Trichosurus vulpecula* |

  Birds (> 10 species)

| | |
|---|---|
| Emu | *Dromaius novae-hollandiae* |
| Plains bustard | *Eupodotis australis* |

  Reptiles (> 5 species)

| | |
|---|---|
| Pirenti | *Varanus giganteus* |
| Sand goanna | *V. gouldii* |
| --- | *Amphibolarus* sp. |
| Carpet python | *Aspidites* sp. |

  Insects (> 5 species)

| | |
|---|---|
| Witchitty grubs | *Cossidae* (larvae, probably *Xyleutes* sp.) |

PLANTS

  Seed producers (39 species)

| | |
|---|---|
| Acacias | *Acacia* spp., esp. *aneura, kempeana, coriacea, cowleana, dictyophleba* |
| Kurrajong | *Brachychiton gregorii* |
| Gums or eucalypts | *Eucalyptus* spp., esp. *microtheca* |
| Chenopods | *Chenopodium* spp. |
| Grasses | *Eragrostis eriopoda, leptocarpa Panicum australiense, decompositum* |
| Manyeroo | *Portulaca oleracea* |

  Root producers (5 species)

| | |
|---|---|
| Bush potato | *Ipomoea costata* |
| Native yam | *Vigna lanceolata* |

  Fruit producers (27 species)

| | |
|---|---|
| Native plum | *Canthium latifolium* |
| Native oranges | *Capparis* spp. |
| Konkaberry | *Carissa lanceolata* |
| Solanums | *Solanum* spp., esp. *centrale* |

---

Note: Figures in parentheses indicate the total number of species identified as edible.
Named taxa are those most often mentioned by informants in response to questions about pre-
European diet. Most plant species listed were probably staples. Sources: O'Connell, Latz,
and Barnett, n.d.; Allen Newsome, personal communication.

Table 5.A.2

Quantitative Data on Some Plant Collecting Trips Originating at Bendaijerum, 1973-75

| Event | Date | Habitat | Site | Distance Traveled (km) | Total Trip Time (hr) $[T_t + T_s + T_g]$ | Mode of Travel | Time on Site (hr) $[T_s + T_g]$ | No. of Collectors | Main Items Collected | Kg/Collector | Additional Processing Time (hr) $[T_p]$ | Kcal/kg $[E^*_i]$ | Kcal/Forager-hr, incl. Travel, Search, Gathering, and Processing $[E_n = E/(T_t + T_s + T_g + T_p)]$ |
|---|---|---|---|---|---|---|---|---|---|---|---|---|---|
| 1 | 2 Sept 73 | SH | 1 | 50 | | V | 1.5 | 5 | Solanum centrale | 2.0 | 0.0 | 2992 | |
| 2 | 11 May 74 | SH | 1 | 50 | 3.5 | V | 1.0 | 3 | Ipomoea | 5.0 | 0.5 | 1563 | 1,954 |
| 3a | 2 Jun 74 | MW | 2 | 45 | 6.0 | V | 1.17 | 4 | Vigna | 0.13 | 0.0 | 862 | 617 |
| | | | | | | | | | Varanus | 0.13 | 0.0 | 1050 | |
| 3b | 2 Jun 74 | SH | 3 | | | | 1.5 | 3 | Ipomoea | 2.3 | 0.23 | 1563 | |
| 4 | 28 Jun 74 | SH | 1 | 50 | 7.5 | V | 4.5 | 7 | Ipomoea | 8.9 | 0.89 | 1563 | 1,658 |
| 5 | 6 Jul 74 | MW | 4 | | 5.0 | F | | 7 | Vigna | 2.14 | 0.0 | 862 | 413 |
| | | | | | | | | | Amphibolarus | 0.14 | 0.0 | 1050 | |
| | | | | | | | | | Varanus | 0.07 | 0.0 | 1050 | |
| 6 | 10 Jul 74 | MW | 4 | | 8.0 | F | | 4 | Vigna | 2.25 | 0.0 | 862 | 325 |
| | | | | | | | | | S.cf.ellipticum | 0.25 | 0.0 | 508 | |
| | | | | | | | | | Amphibolarus | 0.13 | 0.0 | 1050 | |
| | | | | | | | | | Varanus | 0.38 | 0.0 | 1050 | |
| 7 | 10 Jul 74 | FP | 5 | | 8.0 | F | | 5 | Cyperus | 1.6 | 0.4 | 3326 | 634 |

| | | | | | | | | | | | | | |
|---|---|---|---|---|---|---|---|---|---|---|---|---|---|
| 8a | 15 Jul 74 | SH | 1 | 50 | 8.0 | V | 3.0 | 8 | *Ipomoea* | 5.5 | 0.55 | 1563 | 1,039 |
| 8b | 15 Jul 74 | MW | 1 | | | | 0.6 | 6 | *Vigna* | 0.33 | 0.0 | 862 | |
| 9 | 10 Aug 74 | SH | 6 | 190 | 9.0 | V | 3.0 | 7 | *Ipomoea* | 5.0 | 0.5 | 1563 | 823 |
| 10 | 22 Aug 74 | MW | 7 | 25 | 6.75 | V | 4.5 | 7 | *Cossidae* | 1.0 | 0.0 | 2600 | 418 |
| | | | | | | | | | *Amphibolarus* | 0.14 | 0.0 | 1050 | |
| | | | | | | | | | *Varanus* | 0.07 | 0.0 | 1050 | |
| *11 | 7 Oct 74 | MW | 7 | 25 | 4.5 | V | 3.5 | 2 | *Acacia aneura* | 0.5 | 2.0 | 3778 | 579 |
| | | | | | | | | 5 | *Cossidae* | 0.72 | 0.0 | 2600 | |
| *12 | 23 Oct 74 | SH | 8 | 60 | 4.5 | V | 1.5 | 2 | *Ipomoea* | 4.0 | 0.4 | 1563 | 1,276 |
| *13a | 7 Nov 74 | SH | 2 | 60 | 5.0 | V | 0.25 | 2 | *Acacia cowleana* | 0.1 | 0.4 | 3589 | |
| 13b | 7 Nov 74 | SH | 8 | | | | 1.0 | 8 | *A. coriacea* (unripe) | 1.4 | 0.0 | 2600 | 787 |
| 13c | 7 Nov 74 | SH | 9 | | | | 0.33 | 3 | *Ipomoea* | 0.17 | 0.02 | 1563 | |
| 14 | 14 Nov 74 | MW | 4 | | 6.0 | F | | 6 | *Cossidae* | 1.1 | 0.0 | 2600 | 520 |
| | | | | | | | | | *Amphibolarus* | 0.25 | 0.0 | 1050 | |
| 15 | 15 Nov 74 | MW | 7 | 30 | 7.0 | V | 5.0 | 5 | *Cossidae* | 1.54 | 0.0 | 2600 | 587 |
| | | | | | | | | | *Varanus* | 0.1 | 0.0 | 1050 | |
| *16a | 28 Dec 74 | SH | 2 | 45 | 3.5 | V | 1.0 | 3 | *S. centrale* | 1.5 | 0.0 | 2992 | 2,052 |
| 16b | 28 Dec 74 | SH | 3 | | 5.5 | | 0.75 | 5 | *S. centrale* | 0.9 | 0.0 | 2992 | |
| 17 | 30 Dec 74 | MW | 7 | 30 | 8.5 | V | 4.5 | 4 | *Cossidae* | 1.75 | 0.0 | 2600 | 827 |
| 18 | 19 Feb 75 | MW | 4 | | | F | | 7 | *Cossidae* | 0.66 | 0.0 | 2600 | 251 |
| | | | | | | | | | *Vigna* | 0.14 | 0.0 | 862 | |
| | | | | | | | | | *Amphibolarus* | 0.14 | 0.0 | 1050 | |
| | | | | | | | | | *Varanus* | 0.14 | 0.0 | 1050 | |
| 19 | 27 Feb 75 | MW | 4 | | | F | | 2 | *Vigna* | 0.5 | 0.0 | 862 | |
| | | | | | | | | | *Amphibolarus* | 0.75 | 0.0 | 1050 | |

Notes on Table 5.A.2

## Abbreviations

SH = sandhills
MW = mulga woodland
FP = riverine floodplains
V = motor vehicle
F = foot
$T_t$ = time traveling to and from foraging site(s)
$T_s$ = time searching foraging site(s)
$T_g$ = time gathering resources
$T_p$ = time processing resources for consumption after collecting
$E^*_i$ = mean calories (kcal) per kilogram of resource type $i$ (see table 5.4)
$E^i$ = total calories recovered per collector per trip
$E_n$ = ratio of energy gained per unit of time invested in foraging, including travel time to foraging site(s)

Starred trips (*) are those in which the ethnographer played a significant role in determining destination and/or resources taken.

## Collecting events

1.  Site 1 is an abandoned campsite. *Ipomoea* and *Solanum* flourish there after rain.
2.  Collectors arranged trip late in the day; traveled direct to the collecting site. The encounter rate for *Ipomoea* was at its highest. Collectors dug all roots within 500-m$^2$ area. Collecting stopped because of darkness. Total party: 7 women, 5 children.
3.  Collectors traveled to a patch of mulga woodland in sandhill country; foraged on foot for *Vigna* over 75,000 m$^2$ area; ate small quantities of *Carissa* and *Lysiana* berries while walking. At end of walk, they expressed surprise at low returns. On route back to Bendaijerum, they collected *Ipomoea* in a 500 m$^2$ patch along the roadside. Time on site at this location includes about one hour search time. Total party: 8 women, 5 children, 1 infant.
4.  Collectors traveled directly to site. Foraged on foot over 20,000 m$^2$; gathered 6.3 kg *Ipomoea* per collector in 2.17 hr. Foragers ate small quantities of *Solanum* fruit and *Leichhardtia* leaves encountered while walking. After a 30-min lunch break, they foraged over 25,000 m$^2$; took 1.5 kg *Ipomoea* per collector in 1.75 hr. Total party: 7 women, 7 children, 1 infant.
5.  Site 4 is in mulga woodland east of Bendaijerum. No data on location or size of specific site(s) visited by foragers. Total party: 7 women, 1 infant.
6.  *Solanum* cf. *ellipticum* was originally identified as *S. cleistogamum*, but the latter does not appear in Chippendale (1971). The species collected resembles *ellipticum*. Note also that the caloric value reported for *ellipticum* (508 kcal per kg, ref. Dadswell 1934, cited in N. Peterson 1978:28-29) is low by comparison with other solanums, especially *S. centrale*. A value equivalent to the latter would raise the $E_n$ figure to 402 kcal per collector-hr. Total party: 4 women.
7.  Site 5 is on the Bundey River, west of Bendaijerum. Total party: 6 women, 5 children, 1 infant.
8.  After arrival at the collecting site, operators foraged over 60,000 m$^2$, recovered 5.5 kg *Ipomoea* per collector in 3 hr. Ate small quantities of *Solanum* fruit (both *centrale* and *ellipticum*) and *Leichhardtia* fruit and leaves as they walked. After a brief meal stop, collectors moved into a stand of mulga woodland, took 0.33 kg *Vigna* per collector in 0.6 hr. All *Vigna* were eaten at collecting site. Total party: 8 women, 6 children, 3 infants.
9.  Collectors traveled 95 km by road to a site west of the Sandover River, well known to several members of party. Spent only three hours on site before returning to Bendaijerum. Total party: 9 women, 4 children, 3 infants.
10.  Collectors visited two sites in mulga woodland. On arrival at first, collectors dispersed. One group of three collectors dug 1.5 kg grubs from 17 shrubs (all *Acacia kempeana*) scattered over 10,000 m$^2$ in 1.5 hr. One-third of the total was taken from roots of first shrub, remainder from the other sixteen. About 2-5 min were spent digging at each shrub. Children collected 3.0 kg *Leichhardtia* fruit at this site. Entire party then moved to a site 1 km distant where more grub collecting took place. Total party: 8 women, 7 children.
11.  Women offered to demonstrate collecting techniques for *Acacia aneura*. Party traveled by truck to a point about 12 km east of Bendaijerum, where two women spent 1.82 hr gathering 1 kg of seed (see notes, table 5.3; also O'Connell, Latz, and Barnett, n.d.). Other women in party observed demonstration for a time, then went off to collect cossid larvae. Four women took 2.4 kg grubs in 1.7 hr; one woman took 1.2 kg in 1.75 hr. Total party: 7 women, 2 children, 2 infants.
12.  *Ipomoea* tubers were unexpectedly encountered just north of site 1 on a trip organized by O'Connell and botanist Peter Latz for purposes of collecting plant specimens. Two Alyawara men acting as guides and informants collected tubers plus small quantities of unripened *A. coriacea* seed.

13.  Women were asked for a second demonstration of seed collecting.  At their request, they were driven to the sandhill habitat north of Bendaijerum, stopping twice en route to collect *A. cowleana* seeds.  Two women performed each demonstration; all others in party observed.  On arrival at site 8, the same one visited on event 12, all debarked and spent ca. 1 hr collecting unripe *A. coriacea* seed pods.  Total 34 kg pods, containing an estimated 7-10 kg seeds, were loaded for return trip, but large numbers were also split and the seeds eaten on the spot.  On return trip, women stopped briefly at site 9 to look for *Ipomoea*. More than 8,000 m[2] were searched, but though plants were common, tubers themselves were few.  Total party:  8 women, 6 children, 2 infants.

14.  Total party:  6 women, 1 infant.

15.  Total party:  6 women, 4 children.

16.  Total party:  6 women, 3 children, 1 infant.

17.  Total party:  4 women, 9 children.

18.  Total party:  8 women, 1 infant.

19.  Total party:  2 women.

*Table 5.A.3*

*Energy Returns from Sandhill and Mulga Woodland Patches*

| Patch Type | Event | Date | Site | Main Item Collected | Kcal/Forager-hr in Patch, including Processing $[E_p = E/(T_s + T_g + T_p)]$ | $E^*_i/h_i$ |
|---|---|---|---|---|---|---|
| Sandhill | 1 | 2 Sept 73 | 1 | *Solanum centrale* | 3,989 | 5,984 |
| | 2 | 11 May 74 | 1 | *Ipomoea* | 5,210 | 6,252 |
| | 3b | 2 Jun 74 | 3 | *Ipomoea* | 2,077 | 6,252 |
| | 4 | 28 Jun 74 | 1 | *Ipomoea* | 2,576 | 6,252 |
| | 8a | 15 Jul 74 | 1 | *Ipomoea* | 2,422 | 6,252 |
| | 9 | 10 Aug 74 | 6 | *Ipomoea* | 2,232 | 6,252 |
| | 12 | 23 Oct 74 | 8 | *Ipomoea* | 3,290 | 6,252 |
| | 13a | 7 Nov 74 | 2 | *Acacia cowleana* | 552 | 552 |
| | 13b | 7 Nov 74 | 8 | *Acacia coriacea* | 3,640 | 4,333 |
| | 13c | 7 Nov 74 | 9 | *Ipomoea* | 759 | 6,252 |
| | 16a | 28 Dec 74 | 2 | *Solanum centrale* | 4,488 | 5,984 |
| | 16b | 28 Dec 74 | 3 | *Solanum centrale* | 3,590 | 5,984 |
| Mulga woodland | 3a | 2 Jun 74 | 2 | *Vigna* | 212 | 1,724 |
| | | | | *Varanus* | | 4,200 |
| | 5 | 6 Jul 74 | 4 | *Vigna* | 413 | 1,724 |
| | | | | *Varanus* | | 4,200 |
| | | | | *Amphibolarus* | | 4,200 |
| | 6 | 10 Jul 74 | 4 | *Vigna* | 325 | 1,724 |
| | | | | *S. cf. ellipticum* | | 504 |
| | | | | *Varanus* | | 4,200 |
| | | | | *Amphibolarus* | | 4,200 |
| | 8b | 15 Jul 74 | 1 | *Vigna* | 474 | 1,724 |
| | 10 | 22 Aug 74 | 7 | *Cossidae* | 418 | 1,486 |
| | | | | *Varanus* | | 4,200 |
| | | | | *Amphibolarus* | | 4,200 |
| | 11 | 7 Oct 74 | 7 | *A. aneura* | 529 | 580 |
| | | | | *Cossidae* | | 1,486 |

*Table 5.A.3 (continued)*

| Patch Type | Event | Date | Site | Main Item Collected | Kcal/Forager-hr in Patch, including Processing $[E_p = E/(T_s + T_g + T_p)]$ | $E^*_i/h_i$ |
|---|---|---|---|---|---|---|
| Mulga woodland (continued) | 14 | 14 Nov 74 | 4 | *Cossidae* *Amphibolarus* | 520 | 1,486 4,200 |
| | 15 | 15 Nov 74 | 7 | *Cossidae* *Varanus* | 587 | 1,486 4,200 |
| | 17 | 30 Dec 74 | 7 | *Cossidae* | 827 | 1,486 |
| | 18 | 19 Feb 75 | 4 | *Cossidae* *Vigna* *Varanus* *Amphibolarus* | 251 | 1,486 1,724 4,200 4,200 |

Note:  Time spent traveling to and from patch not included in calculation.

*Table 5.A.4*

*Quantitative Data on Collecting and Processing Time:  Net Energy Returns for Some Alyawara Plant and Animal Foods (W = winter, S = spring and/or early summer)*

| | Collecting and Processing Time (hr/kg) $[h_i = g_i + p_i]$ | Kcal $[E^*_i]$ | Net Return Rate on Resource Once Encountered $[E^*_i/h_i]$ | Rank | Period Available W | Period Available S |
|---|---|---|---|---|---|---|
| **Sandhill** | | | | | | |
| *Ipomoea costata* | 0.25 | 1,563 | 6,252 | 1 | X | X |
| *Solanum centrale* | 0.50 | 2,992 | 5,984 | 2 | X | X |
| *Acacia coriacea* (unripe) | 0.60 | 2,600 | 4,333 | 3 | | X |
| *Varanus* sp. *(cf. gouldii)* | 0.25 | 1,050 | 4,200 | 4 | X | X |
| *Vigna lanceolata* | 0.50 | 862 | 1,724 | 5 | X | X |
| *A. coriacea* (ripe) | >5.25 | 3,551 | < 676 | | | X |
| *A. aneura* | 6.50 | 3,778 | 580 | | | X |
| Grass seeds | 6.00 | 3,450 | 575 | 6 | X | X |
| *A. cowleana* | 6.50 | 3,589 | 552 | | | X |
| Other acacias | 6.50 | 3,500 | 538 | | | X |
| **Mulga woodland** | | | | | | |
| *Amphibolarus* sp. *Varanus* sp. | 0.25 | 1,050 | 4,200 | 1 | X | X |
| *Vigna lanceolata* | 0.50 | 862 | 1,724 | 2 | X | X |
| Cossid larvae | 1.75 | 2,600 | 1,486 | 3 | X | X |
| *A. aneura* | 6.50 | 3,778 | 580 | 4 | | X |
| Grass seeds | 6.00 | 3,450 | 575 | | X | X |
| **River floodplain** | | | | | | |
| *Cyperus* sp. | 0.75 | 3,326 | 4,435 | 1 | X | X |
| Grass seeds | 6.00 | 3,450 | 575 | 2 | X | X |

## Notes on Table 5.A.4

### Caloric Values

Caloric values for reptiles *Amphibolarus* sp. and *Varanus* sp. are taken from Meehan (1977b); those for *Vigna*, *Acacia coriacea* (ripe), *A. cowleana*, "other acacias," grass seeds, and solanums from N. Peterson (1978); those for *Ipomoea*, *A. aneura*, *A. coriacea* (unripe), *Cyperus* from P. Latz and P. Maggiore (Latz, personal communication). Values for cossidae calculated as follows:

1. Cossid larvae are said to contain about 50% fat, 50% protein (A. Hamilton 1971, cited in N. Peterson 1978:28-29). We assume these are dry weight proportions.
2. The moisture content of morphologically similar "meal worms" (species unknown) from a Salt Lake City pet store was found to be about 60% (A. Mahoney, Department of Nutrition and Food Sciences, Utah State University, Logan; personal communication).

3.  Standard caloric equivalents for fats and proteins are about 9 kcal/g and 4 kcal/g, respectively (Merrill and Watt 1955).

Thus, we estimate 1,000 g live weight of cossid larvae equal 400 g dry weight, including 200 g fat and 200 g protein, or about 2,600 kcal. Cummins and Wychuck (1971:128-29) calculate a similar figure for larvae of "grain beetles" (*Tenebrio* spp.).

## Collecting and Processing Time

Estimates for seeds are based on controlled demonstrations. They include collecting and processing time $(g_i, p_i)$, but no search time $(T_s)$. Estimates for all other resources are based on observations in which search time and collecting time were not always clearly separated. Note: $h_i$ (handling time) = $g_i + p_i$.

*Amphibolarus* sp., *Varanus* sp.: These are small lizards, average weight 0.5 kg, often encountered in mulga woodland and sandhill country. Once spotted, they are treed, or trapped in burrows, and killed, usually within 5 min of contact. They are roasted whole in ashes on open hearths. Est. $h_i$ = 0.25 hr/kg.

Cossid larvae: These are small grubs, 4-10 cm long. They are dug from shallow roots of *A. kempeana* or *Cassia* spp., lightly roasted in hot ashes. $p_i$ is minimal; $g_i$ estimated from two incidents:
1. Event 10:  3 collectors took 0.5 kg larvae from roots of one *A. kempeana* shrub in 0.33 hr. $T_s$ = 0.0; thus, $g_i$ = 2.0 hr/kg.
2. Event 15:  5 collectors foraged for grubs in mulga woodland. $T_s + g_i$ were recorded for each collector during two separate foraging bouts:

| Collector | | hr | kg | $(T_s + g_i)$/kg |
|---|---|---|---|---|
| Minnie | am | 2.2 | 0.76 | 2.89 |
| | pm | 1.8 | 0.53 | 3.40 |
| Angelina | am | 2.33 | 1.10 | 2.12 |
| | pm | 2.25 | 0.71 | 3.87 |
| Maggie | am | 2.33 | 0.32 | 7.28 |
| | pm | 2.25 | 1.00 | 2.25 |
| Elsie | am | 2.33 | 0.32 | 7.28 |
| | pm | 2.25 | 1.20 | 1.88 |
| Dollie | am | 2.2 | 1.20 | 1.83 |
| | pm | 1.8 | 0.53 | 3.40 |

The range is wide, but minimum $T_s + g_i$ figures are less than 2.0 hr/kg; thus we take $g_i$ = 1.75 hr/kg as a best approximation for this resource.

*Ipomoea costata*: These tubers grow on rooted stems of rhizomes which extend from a central bush or shrub, and are found ca. 0.6-1.0 m below ground surface. Tubers vary greatly in size but average 0.4 kg each. During event 2, three women collected 15 kg in one hour. $T_s$ = 0.0; thus $g_i$ = 0.2 hr/kg. Tubers are scraped free of grit and roasted in small, specially prepared pits. We estimate $p_i$ = 0.08 hr/kg. $g_i + p_i = h_i$ = 0.28 hr/kg; rounded to nearest quarter hour, 0.25 hr/kg. Data from event 3 yield the same estimate.

*Solanum centrale, ellipticum*: These small fruit (ca. 2 cm dia) are found on low bushes and are picked individually by hand. Bushes were common at sites 2 and 3 on 28 Dec 74 (event 16), and search time was correspondingly quite low. At site 2, three women took 4.5 kg *S. centrale* in one hour; thus $T_s + g_i$ = 0.67 hr/kg. At site 3, five women took 4.5 kg in 0.75 hr; thus $T_s + g_i$ = 0.83 hr/kg. Therefore, we estimate $g_i$ alone = 0.50 hr/kg, rounding to nearest quarter hour. Once collected, fruit were always eaten without further processing, thus $g_i + p_i$ = 0.5 hr/kg.

*Vigna lanceolata, Cyperus* sp: *Vigna* are 15-20 cm long, 2-4 cm in diameter; *Cyperus* are 1-2 cm in diameter. Both are found close to the ground surface; *Vigna* usually as an isolate, *Cyperus* often at high densities. We estimate $g_i$ greater than that for *Ipomoea*, or about 0.5 hr/kg. *Vigna* requires no processing other than hand rubbing to remove grit; thus $g_i + p_i$ = 0.5 hr/kg. The thin skin on *Cyperus* must be rubbed off by hand. Estimated $p_i$ = 0.25 hr/kg; thus $g_i + p_i$ = 0.75 hr/kg.

*Acacia* spp: Seeds occur in pods 2-20 cm long, depending on the species. When pods are dry, collectors pull boughs from tree, beat with sticks to separate pods, beat and crush pods to release seeds, winnow seeds from pod fragments in carrying trays. Seeds are parched in ashes; then ground on flat or grooved slabs with handstones. Quantitative data on these observations come primarily from three incidents:
1. *A. aneura*/event 11:  two women gathered and winnowed 1 kg seed in 1.82 hr ($g_i$ = 3.64 hr/kg). Many pods were too green to be cracked, and were set aside to dry. If collectors had returned to gather seeds from these, the same amount would have been recovered in half the time. Thus $g_i$ (combined) = 2.64 hr/kg. Parching time = 0.06 hr/kg. Brief demonstration of grinding indicates est. rate of 165 g/hr or 6.06 hr/kg. P. Latz

(personal communication) says this figure may be too high. His experiments suggest a grinding rate of 3 hr/kg. Combining these data with our own, we estimate $p_i$ (including parching) = 4 hr/kg; thus $g_i + p_i$ = 6.64 (rounded = 6.5 hr/kg).

2. *A. cowleana*/event 13a: two women collected and winnowed 200 g of seed in 0.25 hr ($g_i$ = 2.5 hr/kg). Assuming $p_i$ the same as that for *A. aneura*, $p_i + g_i$ = 6.5 hr/kg.

3. *A. coriacea* (ripe)/event 13b: two women collected and winnowed 600 g of seed in 0.375 hr ($g_i$ = 1.25 hr/kg). Assuming $p_i$ the same as that for *A. aneura*, $p_i + g_i$ = 5.25 hr/kg. Since *A. coriacea* seeds are very hard, grinding may be preceded by a pounding step. Processing time will be correspondingly higher.

Most other acacias should have seed-handling times comparable to *A. cowleana*. Note that *A. coriacea* seeds can also be eaten without grinding, just before they ripen fully. Seeds are collected in pods, warmed or lightly parched in ashes, then stripped out by hand and eaten. During event 13b, eight women collected more than 34 kg of pods in 1 hour, stripped and ate many more while doing so. Very little search time was involved. We estimate $g_i + p_i$ = approx. 0.60 hr/kg.

Grass seeds: No quantitative data available for the Alyawara. Figures reported by Brokensha (1975:25) from elsewhere in central Australia, coupled with Tindale's (1974:94-106 1977 n.d.) descriptive comments indicate $h_i$ = approx. 6.0 hr/kg.

*Table 5.A.5*

*Energy Returns per Forager-Hour on Site for Trips in Mulga Woodland Involving Motor Vehicle Transport*

| Event | Date | Kg/Collector | Time on Site Away from Vehicle (hr) | Kcal/Forager-hr on Site |
|-------|------|--------------|-------------------------------------|--------------------------|
| 10 | 22 Aug 74 | 1.0 | 4.5 | 572 |
| 11 | 7 Oct 74 | 0.72 | 3.0* | 624 |
| 15 | 15 Nov 74 | 1.54 | 5.0 | 806 |
| 17 | 30 Dec 74 | 1.75 | 4.5 | 1,014 |

Note: Returns listed are for cossid larvae. Travel to and from collecting site not included in calculation. *Estimate omits time collectors spent watching seed collecting demonstration.

# 6

## The Relationship between
## Northern Athapaskan Settlement Patterns
## and Resource Distribution:
## An Application of Horn's Model

Sheri Heffley

### Introduction

For many years anthropologists and archeologists have attempted to understand the variability in settlement pattern exhibited among and within hunter-gatherer societies. Notable of those who have followed this line of investigation are Steward (1955), Chang (1962),
Beardsley (1956), Helm (1968), Damas (1969c), and McKennan (1969). All have stressed the
resource-specific aspect of variance in settlement pattern. Other investigators have
stressed other determinants of observed group size and location (Woodburn 1968; Williams
1968).

Despite the diversity of approaches, many of the explanations have suffered from a too-
particular or a too-general approach. Although some of the schemes have enjoyed widespread
use, mechanisms of universal application have not been provided. The present chapter represents an attempt to evaluate the use of a general model with a clearly defined mechanism
for the interpretation of hunter-gatherer settlement pattern.

This chapter examines the ecological basis of settlement patterns among northern
Athapaskan hunter-gatherers. A general ecological model is applied to ethnographic data
for Athapaskan populations. The model, first formulated by Horn (1968), proposes that an
optimal relationship exists between group size and location (i.e., settlement pattern) and
resource distribution. The model considers the adaptive advantage of different forms of
social spacing in relation to food resource availability.

Horn's model can be used to interpret ethnographic Athapaskan settlement patterns as
behavorial responses to both predictable-stable and uncertain-mobile food resources. The
settlement patterns are analyzed as flexible strategies which put Athapaskan groups in optimal spatial and temporal positions for the exploitation of uncertain-mobile resources
such as caribou and stable, evenly spaced resources such as small game and moose. The
analysis also shows the importance of foraging patterns as communication networks.

Northern Athapaskan groups lend themselves in two ways to such analysis: first, there
is a great diversity in Athapaskan adaptations; second, reconstruction of general settlement patterns from the aboriginal situation is possible. Diversity of Athapaskan adaptations is discussed by VanStone (1974), who states that even the casual observer will notice

I would like to thank Bill Durham for encouraging me toward publication and for his
helpful suggestions and editorial assistance. Thanks to John Rick for producing the fine
graphs. I especially wish to acknowledge the support and encouragement of my husband,
Bob, and my daughters, Pamela, Jennifer, and Deborah, and I thank them.

a striking relationship between the Athapaskans' behaviors, particularly subsistence activities, and their environment.  The reconstruction of precontact settlement patterns
draws on accounts of explorers and traders, and the ethnologies of early investigators
(Osgood 1940 1958 1959; McKennan 1959).  Although these sometime lack specific quantitative
data, they adequately reflect the diversity of behavorial patterns and provide information
about the subsistence emphasis of each group here analyzed.

Graburn and Strong (1974) have also discussed the cultural ecology of Athapaskan
groups in relation to their natural resources.  These authors state that the main independent variable is the "richness" of an area in resources (Graburn and Strong 1974:76).  Dependent variables are the sizes of the regional and local bands and the degree of mobility
of each group.  A drawback to such analysis is the operational imprecision of a concept
like "richness"; an advantage to a model such as Horn's is that it formulates the independent variables in terms of specific and measurable resource quantities:  location (distribution), size, and predictability.  The dependent variables in Horn's model are the location
and size of foraging units able to exploit the resource efficiently.

In this chapter I first present the theoretical background for this interpretation of
settlement pattern.  A general description of the Athapaskan environment follows.  Three
groups of northern Athapaskan Indians are chosen to analyze settlement pattern and resource
base.  Horn's model is compared with the variability of settlement pattern among Athapaskan
groups.

## Theoretical Background

The model used here was proposed by Horn in 1968 in an analysis of colonial nesting in
Brewer's blackbirds.  The general form of the model is:

$$\overline{d} = 2kT\sum_i\sum_j t(x_i y_j) \ \sqrt{(x_i - x_o)^2 + (y_j - y_o)^2}$$

$\overline{d}$        = average round-trip distance between a user and resource points

$k$        = number of foraging trips per unit time

$T$        = total time under consideration

$t(x_i, y_j)$ = proportion of time during which foraging is better at $(x_i y_j)$ than at
any other point in the area

$(x_o, y_o)$  = coordinates of user location.

For evenly dispersed, stable resources, a strategy of small units of users evenly
spaced is almost twice as efficient (in terms of average round-trip distance) as a strategy
of central location for all users.  On the other hand, when resources are mobile, clumped,
and unpredictable, the central user location is more efficient.  Two assumptions about the
resources are made:  (1) resources at stable, evenly distributed points are simultaneously
available, and (2) resources at mobile, clumped resource points are available at only one,
or at the most a few, of the points (Wilmsen 1973:3).  Horn's model weights the distances
traveled in exploiting mobile, clumped food with the predictability of finding food at a
particular point.

The value of this model is its generation of hypotheses about behavior based on a
generally applicable analysis of resource distribution and availability.  The hypotheses
predict an optimal foraging strategy for each resource situation (Wilmsen 1973:8):  "Foragers depending largely upon resources that are evenly-spaced and stable will tend toward

a dispersal of small social units.  Foragers depending largely upon resources that are clumped and mobile will tend toward aggregations at a central location."

As mentioned above, the analysis of the relationship between resources and the organization of human social groups is not new.  However, the application of a general model to explain the variability of social groupings is new.  Selection for optimal foraging efficiency should be considered in relation to other human behaviors.  There are many activities that compete with the time and energy investment involved in the food quest.  The maintenance of the social continuity requires time and energy which can, along with other nonforaging selective forces, alter observed behaviors, thus compromising foraging efficiency.  However, without a minimum net energy return from a foraging strategy, a society is not viable.  Optimal foraging theory is a heuristic tool from which this further behavioral variation may be studied.

## Athapaskan Ecology

The great expanse of the Athapaskan region provides many environmental contrasts (figure 6.1).  The land rises from a coastal plain in the west into rugged coastal mountains.  After these mountains and their intermontane plains come the Rocky Mountains, followed by an expanse of lowlands dominated by the Mackenzie River Basin.  North to south the land of the Athapaskans runs from the Arctic Circle to the beginnings of the great plains of the mid-continent.

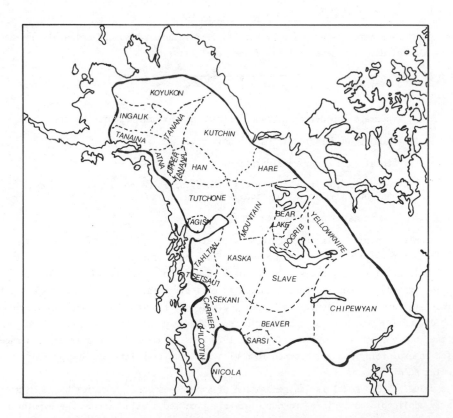

Figure 6.1.  Northern Athapaskan Indian Groups.  The figure shows the geographical distribution of northern Athapaskan Indians as they were identified by Osgood (1936).

The Athapaskans are characterized as a mountain people who have spread from the cordillera into the diverse environments surrounding it.  Five contiguous physiographic units have been distinguished within the current Athapaskan area.  They are (1) Arctic drainage lowlands; (2) cordilleran; (3) Yukon and Kuskokwim river basins; (4) Copper River; and (5) Cook Inlet-Susitna River Basin (McClellan 1970:x).

Three areas among these five have been selected for analysis.  These regions and the three Athapaskan groups chosen from them show the contrasts that existed within aboriginal subsistence patterns.  These groups are representative of their areas, well documented, and evince the three most basic adaptations within the region as a whole.  Two groups in Alaska are discussed.  The Upper Tanana subsistence was keyed to the broad resource base of the inland riverine environment; the hunting of a variety of animals is the basic subsistence pattern (see figure 6.2).  The Ingalik are representative of those groups which depended upon the great runs of salmon in the rivers of the Pacific drainage area (see figure 6.3).  The Chipewyan of northeastern Canada depend upon the large herds of caribou for the greatest part of their diet and material culture.  The settlement patterns of each are shown to approach the predicted optimum for efficiently exploiting these resources.

*Varieties of Atha. subs./selle*

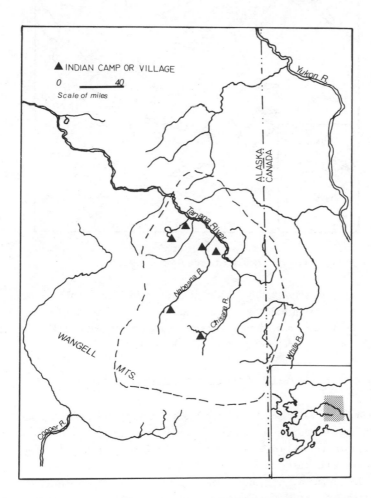

Figure 6.2.  Upper Tanana Territory.  Modified from McKennan 1959.

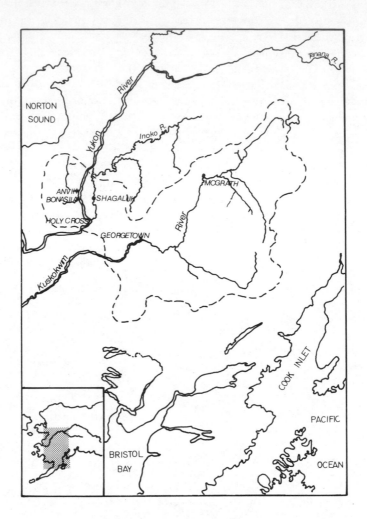

Figure 6.3.  Ingalik Territory.  Modified from Osgood 1940.

The environment of the area is thought to have stabilized for the ancestors of the ethnographic groups between 8,000 and 6,000 years ago.  The various groups of Athapaskans were formed in and became adapted to a subarctic taiga/tundra environment not greatly different from the one they occupy today (VanStone 1974:5).

## Arctic Drainage Lowlands: Chipewyan

### Environment

The region is the major portion of the Precambrian Shield west of Hudson Bay.  The soils are thin with the bedrock near the surface or outcropping.  The topography is characterized by a plateau covered with lakes and connecting rivers.  The standing water is caused by the discontinuous permafrost rather than by precipitation, which is limited to about fifteen inches annually.  Winters are long and severe with temperatures dropping to -21°C.  Throughout most of the region snow is on the ground from October until April or

early May.  Rivers and lakes freeze in early November, and not until late May does break-up
occur.

Three major ecological zones make up this vast lowland area.  In the north is the
tundra, the barren ground.  In favorable but limited areas there are stunted stands of
forest well north of the treeline, usually along the shores of lakes and rivers.  Species
include black spruce, tamarack, and some alder and willow.  The tundra proper is covered
mainly with mosses, lichens, grasses, a few woody shrubs, and a few flowering plants.
Lichens are the main food for the summering herds of migratory barren-ground caribou
(*Rangifer tarandus*).

Along the treeline is the taiga or transitional forest, an area where boreal forest
outliers and tundra patches meet and trees are stunted because of the reduced growing season and the effects of the permafrost (McCormack 1975:193).  This is the Indians' "land of
the little sticks" (J. G. E. Smith 1975:399).  In addition to the black spruce and other
tundra trees, the taiga has stands of birch, jack pine, aspen, and poplar.

The boreal forest is the third ecological zone.  Until recently it has not been inhabited by the traditional Athapaskan Indian group and has not played a large role in the
subsistence patterns of the Chipewyan groups discussed here.

## Resources

Tundra resources are generally limited to those available during the summer.  Although
small game in restricted numbers, musk ox, and fish of a number of species were present in
the winter, their low availability apparently made subsistence unreliable.  The caribou is
the single most important inhabitant of the tundra.  The tundra is the animal's summer
range with a few animals remaining in favorable areas during the winter (Banfield 1954b).

The only small animal of subsistence importance found on the tundra is the Arctic hare.
Rock ptarmigan are present in the summer only.  Fish that are available in large numbers
during the summer runs are whitefish, grayling, and lake trout.

The main resource in the taiga is also the barren-ground caribou, which uses the area
as its wintering range.  Rodents such as beaver, muskrats, and porcupines are found in the
area, but they become increasingly sparse as the tundra is approached (J. G. E. Smith 1975:
399).  Fish are found in the taiga in larger numbers than on the tundra mainly because the
larger lakes are located in the southern part of the Arctic lowlands region.

## Resource Distribution

Small animals and fish are distributed evenly on the tundra and in the taiga.  Fish
are available in abundance during summer runs and through the ice or at rapids during the
winter.  The most important resource from the viewpoint of human subsistence needs is the
barren-ground caribou.  It winters within the taiga and summers on the tundra.  Within
their ranges the caribou disperse into bands and subherds.  The behavior of the caribou, as
it pertains to human exploitation, will be discussed below in greater detail.

## Yukon and Kuskokwim River Basin: Ingalik

### Environment

The area consists of two extensive lowland valleys formed by two rivers.  It includes
the valley of the Yukon, from the mouth of the Tanana River to the westernmost extension of
the Athapaskan-speaking peoples, and the valley of the Kuskokwim, from its headwaters at
Lake Minchumina to about half of its distance to the Pacific coast.  The Ingalik group in-
habits the middle Yukon and the upper Kuskokwim valleys.  The climate of the area is coldest

in the eastern mountains and warmest (probably the most moderate of the interior of Alaska) in the west.  With considerable rainfall in the summer, the country is well timbered with heavy spruce and birch forests, especially around the rivers.  Poplar, tamarack, and alder are also present.  Alder occur near the treeline at 2,500 feet, and tamarack and willows occupy swampy areas in the lowlands.  There are patches of tundra and taiga at higher altitudes.

## Resources

Animals of economic importance to the Indians of central Alaska include small mammals such as snowshoe hare, squirrels, lynx, muskrats, and beaver.  Large animals taken with regularity are caribou, moose, and bear.  Salmon runs provide the greatest part of the food resources, for the fish are taken in great numbers during the runs and stored.  Throughout the year fish are harvested from the rivers and streams for fresh supplies.  Game animals are used as a supplement to the fish and to add variety to the diet.

## Resource Distribution

All of the animals listed above are distributed evenly throughout the area except the caribou, which travel through the region on seasonal migrations in the spring and fall. Moose are evenly distributed and harvested whenever the opportunity arises.  The availability of fish at many well-known spots along the rivers and streams provides a widely distributed and generally predictable resource.

## The Cordilleran:  Upper Tanana

### Environment

The cordilleran region is characterized by the mountain chain that runs in a north-to-south direction through it.  The climate is dry except for a moderate snowfall.  The temperature differences are extreme:  from -18°C in the winter to 38°C in the summer in some areas.  The region is well timbered for the most part, as it lies within the circumpolar boreal forest.  The great differences in elevation created by the rugged mountains produce an environment with habitats much like those of the Arctic drainage lowlands but on a much smaller scale.

The area of study is encompassed by the Tanana River watershed, a zone of discontinuous permafrost where glaciers occur along the southern boundary.  In the north is an area of low, rolling hills between the Tanana and Yukon rivers.  The greatest density of vegetation occurs in the bottomland near the Tanana and its tributaries.  This spruce-poplar forest is confined to broad floodplains, low river terraces, and more deeply thawed south-facing banks of the major rivers.  The upland tree species are fewer, as are other types of vegetation.  Moist tundra is found in the foothills and alpine tundra in the high mountains where bedrock is near the surface.  The region is geographically separated from the coast and has an interior climate owing to the Wrangell Mountain Range.

### Resources

Caribou are an important game animal but are found in the area in large numbers only during their seasonal migrations.  White mountain sheep occur in the mountains, and moose are found in riparian willow stands in the winter and in the upland forests in the summer (LeResche, et al. 1975).  Of small mammals, the rabbit, which is periodically abundant, is the most important.  Muskrat, ground squirrel, and porcupines are also used as food resources.  Whitefish, which run in the summer, are the most important fish species.

## Resource Distribution

Caribou generally provided a large migratory source of food.  Moose were hunted by the Indians almost year-round because of their predictable habits and high yield.  Mountain sheep were taken when they were accessible, that is, before winter made travel into the mountains impossible.  The fish runs of early July provided an abundant resource, but because of the glacial nature of the streams in the Upper Tanana territory, they were available at only a few places (McKennan 1959:21).

## Resource Classification

Horn's model classifies resources as either evenly spaced and stable, or clumped, mobile, and unpredictable.  Wilmsen (1973:8) describes evenly spaced, stable resources as those animal species with restricted individual movements and localized spacing patterns.  Their habits can be used to predict availability throughout the year.  Conversely, migratory herding species are the principal example of mobile, clumped resources.  These animals favor certain environmental conditions, and this offers a certain degree of predictability about their availability.  However, spatial and temporal fluctuations in the size and location of animal aggregations make their exact whereabouts at any one time uncertain.

Because of the large number of rivers, streams, and lakes found in the Athapaskan territory, fish may be classified as an evenly spaced, stable resource.  However, availability depends upon season and the physical nature of the rivers, streams, and lakes.

Small animals have small-scale dispersal patterns in particular habitats.  This dispersal provided, overall, an evenly spaced and stable resource.  The fluctuations in the populations of small animals will not be dealt with here, although this aspect is an important part of availability.

Moose, mountain sheep, and bears also prefer particular habitats and are not migratory.  Although their numbers are small compared with the smaller animals, their size makes them desirable resources.  Because they remain in restricted habitats, they are classified as evenly spaced, stable resources.

From the above, a preliminary classification of available resources would be:  (a) mobile, clumped, and unpredictable--Barren-ground caribou; (b) evenly spaced and stable-- fish, small animals, mountain sheep, moose, bear.

## Behavior of Barren-Ground Caribou

Because caribou are such a widespread resource in the circumpolar region, they have played an important role in the cultures of all northern Indian groups.  The details of their behavior are important for understanding the settlement patterns of the human groups which depend upon them for any degree of subsistence.  For this reason caribou behavior is treated separately in this section.

Caribou behavior has been studied extensively over the past twenty years, and much has been learned about it.  The caribou is a gregarious animal which congregates in organized groups of varying sizes:  the band, the herd, and the migratory herd.  Bands consist of about five to one hundred individuals.  A herd is composed of several bands loosely associated into groups of between a hundred and two or three thousand animals.  The migratory herds may number more than a hundred thousand (Banfield 1954a:17).  Dispersal of the animals in the summer and winter ranges occurs with the break-up of the large migratory herd into smaller herds and bands.  The size of these subgroups is dependent upon the availability of forage and the severity of the winter (J. G. E. Smith 1978:72). Forage areas tend to be used for several years in a row, and these areas are known to the Indians.

Burch (1972) has made an extensive study of the caribou as a human resource. He has identified two techniques for locating caribou. The first is the "head-em-off-at-the-pass" technique (Burch 1972:346), which is used everywhere caribou are hunted. The spring and fall migrations make this technique efficient for the interception of the caribou. Herd behavior also provided some degree of predictability within and between the winter and summer ranges. Finding the animals depended on a thorough knowledge of their behavior given the current environmental conditions. It has been observed that the large herds favor level ground and areas without thick brush or timbered areas. Also, when moving along the shores of large lakes, the herds bunch up and stick to the shore until a projection into the lake is found. Narrows of large or swift-flowing rivers are also preferred paths.

The second hunting technique depends upon the degree of sedentism of the animals and their preference for certain environmental conditions. During their dispersal in the summer range, caribou are plagued by warble flies. They prefer areas of stiff wind and patches of unmelted snow where flies are less concentrated. In the winter, caribou are restricted by snow conditions, especially as those conditions affect the availability of forage (Pruitt 1960). The caribou often make beds on lakes in areas where snow is neither deep nor hard. These environmental preferences increase the chances of finding caribou.

The following description from Banfield (1954b:30) summarizes the seasonal movements of the caribou:

> The movements of the barren-ground caribou are best described as nomadic. As a gregarious species, the herds are continually in random movement seeking an adequate supply of food. Superimposed upon these local movements are the annual travel requirements. Annual shifts in food preferences and available forage encourage travel. In summer the herds seek the relatively cool, dry tundra with taiga where the snowfall is less, the temperature is milder, and lichens and twigs are plentiful. The rut and the fawning seem to require a tundra location. Local weather and physiography affect routes and periods of movements.

The herds of the Arctic drainage lowlands generally separate into four distinct groups (Gordon 1975:76). Two of these regional herds and their areas of exploitation are shown in figure 6.4. The map shows the summer and winter ranges, migration routes, and the calving grounds for each. The herds within these regions have the same pattern of movements whether they are compact or spread out (Banfield 1954a:18).

The "centers of habitation" of the Alaskan herds are shown in figure 6.5. The centers serve as focal points for population buildup and dispersal and are areas of optimal habitat (Skoog 1968:662). The Alaska caribou normally spends at least three-fourths of its time in treeless areas. The availability of suitable alpine or tundra areas largely determines centers of habitation for the six major herds of caribou in Alaska. The range boundaries shown in figure 6.5 pass through areas that are mostly devoid of resident caribou. The animals are in the area only in transit between the summer and winter habitats.

## The Chipewyan

The area inhabited by the Chipewyan in prehistoric and historic times extends west from Hudson Bay to the drainage of the Athabasca and Hayes rivers and north from the Churchill River drainage to the Arctic Circle (J. G. E. Smith 1975:395). The area encompasses the winter and summer ranges of the barren-ground caribou. The Chipewyan have been characterized as the "edge-of-the-forest people" (J. G. E. Smith 1975). There is an intimate relationship between the Chipewyan and the caribou which traverse this area twice a year. Chipewyan

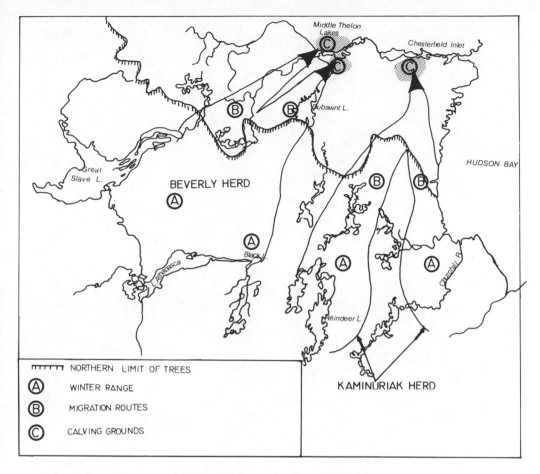

Figure 6.4. Major Caribou Herds in the Chipewyan Territory, Keewatin Region. Two major herds of caribou were exploited by the caribou-eater Chipewyan. The figure shows the distribution of those herds within the Chipewyan territory. Source: Modified from Banfield 1954a and Kelsall 1960.

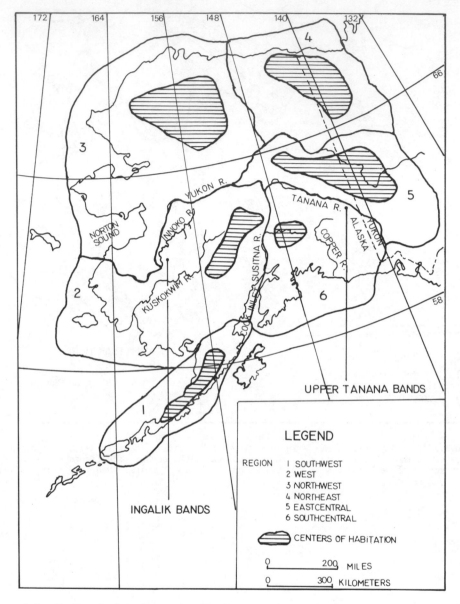

Figure 6.5. Caribou Regions in Alaska. Skoog (1968) has identified several regions of caribou habitation in Alaska. These regions are shown with an indication of their proximity to the two Alaskan Athapaskan groups discussed here.

spoke of themselves as living "like the caribou" or "like the wolf" which is the other main
predator of the caribou (J. G. E. Smith 1975:392). The people went where the caribou were
abundant. Although fish and small game were eaten, the caribou provided at least ninety
per cent of the diet of the people. The number of animals taken for food is impossible to
estimate. When abundant, only choice morsels were eaten, while the remainder of the carcass
rotted (J. G. E. Smith 1975:406).

The continuing importance of caribou to the Chipewyan is illustrated by VanStone's
(1963:12) study of the Snowdrift Chipewyan. The Snowdrift group has been engaged in fur
trapping as the primary subsistence activity for many years. Still, for many of the Indians,
looking for caribou is the most important thing to do on a trap line, and always takes precedence over trapping. Some men in the village in the early 1960s were unwilling to leave
the village for trapping if no caribou had been reported in the area of their trap lines.

Aboriginally, caribou were hunted in a variety of ways depending upon their degree of
aggregation or dispersal. Surrounds were used to snare and then kill large numbers of animals at the times of migrations. The surrounds were placed along migration paths and were
used year after year, as long as the caribou favored the route. Large numbers of men,
women, and children were necessary to use this method effectively. The method was also
used when large subherds moved about within the summer and winter ranges. The efficiency
of the method was noted by the early explorer Hearne, who wrote that many families were
able to subsist by it without having to move their camp more than once or twice during the
course of a winter (in J. G. E. Smith 1975:408).

The Chipewyan also hunted caribou singly or in pairs with bow and arrow, or from
canoes with spears. While the bulk of caribou was taken by communal methods, the more individual methods were used when the animals were dispersed in the summer and winter ranges.
Hunting dispersed caribou often led to the discovery of a large subherd.

Settlement Pattern

The close historic relationship of the Chipewyan to the caribou was expressed in the
varied concentrations or dispersals of people coinciding with the seasonal concentrations
of caribou (J. G. E. Smith 1975:425). The largest concentrations of Chipewyan occurred for
the exploitation of large migrating herds of caribou. When caribou concentrations fell off
between migrations, the larger groups of Chipewyan broke up into smaller units. These
changes formed the basis for the settlement pattern. While other nonfood resources were
important, the primacy of the caribou is revealed by Sharp (1977:n.5): "The Chipewyan
choose dwelling locations on the basis of terrain, wind, firewood availability, and water,
but choose the area on the basis of caribou."

Chipewyan social organization consisted of regional bands, local bands, and hunting
groups.[1] J. G. E. Smith (1978:76) describes the hunting group as the primary subsistence
unit. In the period just after contact, it varied from eleven to forty-one persons (from
3-8 nuclear family households). Each local band consisted of several hunting groups and numbered anywhere from fifty to two hundred people (J. G. E. Smith 1975:426). The large size of the

1. The terms "local" and "regional" bands will be used here to describe the sizes of
settlements as they relate to the larger human population of a region. Helm (1968) has defined these two terms elsewhere. Their use here is for convenience. Other settlements
will be described using the terms from the ethnographies of the groups. These are descriptive terms usually related to location and season. The purpose of this chapter is not to
establish another classification for settlements, but rather to show that settlements described in the literature can be related to a specific resource base using a general model.

local band was based upon the numbers necessary to exploit the aggregated caribou.  The regional band varied in size from two hundred to four hundred or more individuals (J. G. E.
Smith 1975:453), with even larger concentrations found occasionally in the early contact
period.  The band range was not clearly defined and not associated with a formal territory.
A range identified by tradition and use was based upon caribou migration and foraging areas
exploited by the band.

Chipewyan camps were used as long as they provided a strategic striking location relative to caribou movements.  Those occupied for at least a season over many generations were
(1) near the spring migration path; (2) near the late fall migration path; and/or (3) in
the areas where large numbers of animals habitually foraged for long periods in the winter
J. G. E. Smith 1975:437).

Although caribou provided by far the greater part of the Chipewyan subsistence, alternative resources were also important.  Fish were a major alternative.  They were numerous
in spawning seasons, and were taken in gill nets in great numbers (J. G. E. Smith 1978:72).
Often good fishing spots coincided with major migration routes.  The centers of local and
regional band activity were often near good fish lakes (J. G. E. Smith 1978:76).  However,
fish populations fluctuated and, in winter, ice made them inaccessible at all but a few
places.  Thus, they did not offer a particularly reliable resource (McCormack 1975:208;
J. G. E. Smith 1978:72).

Discussion

The observed diversity of size of Chipewyan settlements represents a flexible adaptation to resource availability.  Changes in group size throughout the annual cycle coincided
with the population size, concentration, dispersal, and predictability of the barren-ground
caribou.  Figures 6.6 and 6.7 compare the relative aggregation of caribou with the changes
in settlement size of the Chipewyan over the year.  Horn's model can be used to interpret
this relationship.

The Chipewyan exploited few resources that were evenly spaced and stable.  Ninety per
cent of their food resources were mobile, clumped, and unpredictable.  Regional and local
bands were located central to possible resource points of migrating caribou or aggregations
of subherds.  The difference between the two settlement sizes was dependent upon the size
of the clumped resource.  Information about size and location of caribou was furnished to
the larger groups by the smallest exploitative unit, the hunting group.  Hunting groups
were dispersed from local and regional bands in search of caribou.  The sizes of the three
groups varied greatly.  This variation was in a great part linked to the availability of
caribou.  Hunting groups and nuclear families moved between settlements with whom they
shared broad social ties (J. G. E. Smith 1978:68).

The dispersal of hunting groups from the local and regional bands was crucial to the
exploitation of the nomadic, often unpredictable caribou.  These groups kept track of the
caribou movements before seasonal migrations.  Hunting groups provided a communications
network that kept all members of the bands apprised of caribou movements when the animals
were at maximum dispersal.  As the animals aggregated for their seasonal migration, the
general direction of movement was noted by hunting groups, the information was shared, and
the larger regional bands were able to come together in an area that anticipated the migration route.

The importance of the information network cannot be overemphasized.  Without knowledge
of herd movements, the larger groups probably could not have come together with the cer-
tainty of resource availability.  This interaction between foragers when a resource is not

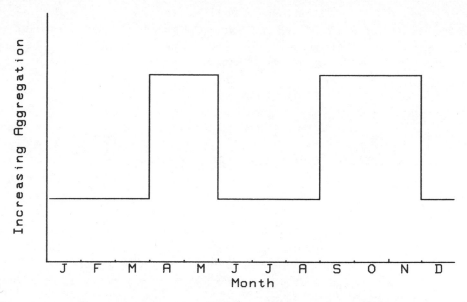

Figure 6.6. Caribou Aggregation over the Year. Jan-Mar: bands and subherds. Apr and May: migrating herds. Jun-Aug: bands and subherds. Sept-Nov: migrating herds. Dec: bands and subherds. Source: Banfield 1954ab; J. G. E. Smith 1975.

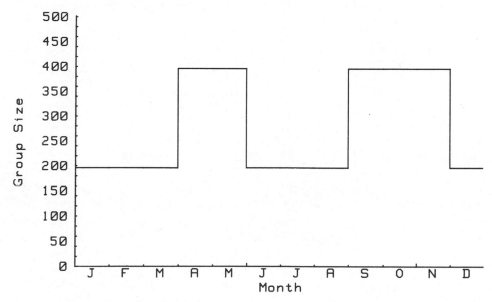

Figure 6.7. Chipewyan Group Size. Jan-Mar: local bands (50-200). Apr and May: regional bands (200-400). Jun-Aug: local bands. Sept-Nov: regional bands. Dec: local bands. Source: J. G. E. Smith 1975.

temporally or spatially predictable is the basis for an added advantage to central place foraging (Horn 1968:690). The Chipewyan have been characterized as a gregarious people (J. G. E. Smith 1978:81). Visiting was common between dispersed hunting groups and local and regional bands. Overlapping areas of resource exploitation facilitated this communication.

The Chipewyan exploited the caribou on a year-round basis. The centers of band activity were located at the transition between the taiga and the tundra. From this location the hunting groups were able to disperse into both the winter and the summer ranges of the caribou. Some groups followed the caribou well into the forest in winter and far out on the tundra in summer (J. G. E. Smith 1978:84). This dependence on a mobile, clumped, and unpredictable resource is reflected in the large size of settlements, and also in their central location.

## The Upper Tanana

The territory of the Upper Tanana Indians includes the headwaters of the Tanana River in Alaska and a portion of the headwaters of the White River extending into Canada. The total area was never entirely occupied but was the hunting range of the group, small bands of which wandered over it at will (McKennan 1959:17).

McKennan (1959:32) describes the Upper Tanana Indians as a culture "centered around a nomadic hunting existence." The major large food animals were caribou, moose, and sheep. Fish, small game, and birds were important at certain times of the year. The procurement of food governed the movements of the people within their territory. The food quest was well summarized by an informant in the following way (McKennan 1959:46):

> In the old days the people seldom stayed in the village. Always they were on the trail hunting and camping. In July whitefish were dried and cached at the Fish Camp. Then the people went moose hunting, caching the meat. In winter they visited the caches and then when the caribou came they killed caribou. After the moose season the people went to the head of the Nebesna to secure sheepskins for the winter. Then they would return to the village, make their clothes and then take the winter trails to Ladue Creek, the Chisana basin, and the White River. In the spring when the leaves were coming out they returned to the village. They would take birchbark and sew it together to make new tents and then wait for the caribou to come back again.

The diversity of the food quest is apparent here, as is the degree of mobility of the people.

McKennan (1959:47) saw the economic life of the Upper Tanana as centering on the caribou. When he did his field work in 1929-30, he noted that large numbers of migrating caribou were found in the area in May and again in November. In December hundreds of caribou were in sight daily. The Upper Tanana ate and utilized almost the entire animal: meat was frozen in winter and dried in summer, and fat was either dried or rendered for future use. Clothing, shelter, and boats were made from caribou hides. These migrating caribou were taken in communal effort by the use of the surround. This method provided most of the caribou harvest for the year.

Skoog's (1968) extensive studies of caribou indicate that the animal's populations fluctuate markedly. From the historical accounts, he has determined that the past hundred years have seen major population changes in the Upper Tanana area (Skoog 1968:304). During the period of McKennan's study the caribou were at a population peak, following a low at the turn of the century. Migrating herds in the year 1929-30 were the largest known in the history of interior Alaska.

Skoog's study and the timing of McKennan's seem to indicate that the caribou were the

basis of Upper Tanana economic life, especially when caribou were at population peaks.  At
other times the Indians must have relied more heavily on other, more evenly spaced, resources.  In fact, Skoog (1968:267) mentions that early explorers noted that the Upper
Tanana were clothed in moose skins, and that they used moose skins in many of the same
ways that McKennan recorded of caribou hides.

Moose have long been residents in much of Alaska, and particularly in this south central area (LeReshe, et al. 1975).  In winter, moose tend to congregate in riparian willow
stands, such as those found along the Tanana River and its tributaries.  The Indians periodically burned the hillsides to provide feeding places for moose, as willows grew to suc-
ceed the burned forest (McKennan 1959:49).

Moose hunting was most important to the Upper Tanana in the late summer and early fall
(after the disappearance of the whitefish) and in the winter and early spring (when winter
stores were running low) (McKennan 1959:34).  Moose were captured in snares in combination
with small fences, and hunted by individuals who ran them down on snowshoes and killed them
with a bow and arrow.  Small animals and mountain sheep were also captured in snares.

## Settlement Pattern

The seasonal resource exploitation pattern described above can be related to the
settlement pattern of the Upper Tanana.  McKennan (1959:18) found five bands of Indians in
the region in 1929.  All but one had semipermanent settlements.  The Indians "repaired" to
these settlements at intervals.  The band members were scattered in the woods in smaller
units during most of the year (Guedon 1974:40).  Temporary hunting dwellings were set up
along the trails, and these usually accommodated two families (McKennan 1959:73).

The semipermanent villages were located at the fishing weirs used for the early July
run of whitefish.  Since the number of places where fish could easily be taken was limited,
the fishing villages acted as nucleating centers for the local band.  The smaller winter
camps were located where hunting was good, and these were occupied for much shorter periods.

McKennan (1969:102) has estimated the size of aboriginal Upper Tanana bands to have
ranged from twenty to seventy people.  The bands came together for the caribou migrations
to maintain and use the fences, and for the July fish run to maintain and use the weirs.

The basic exploitative unit at other times of the year was the two-family hunting
group (8-20 people) (Holmes 1975:40).  When the available resources were moose, sheep, and
small animals, these smaller groups scattered into the forest, coming together only when an
exceptionally good kill had been made.

The area of the Upper Tanana supported these local bands and constituted the distinctive range of the regional band (McKennan 1959:21; Holmes 1975:100).  The regional band did
not form as an exploitative unit, however; the largest such unit was the local band.  Membership in local bands was flexible, and families could shift from one locality to another
(McKennan 1959:19).  However, the summer fishing group was generally made up of the same
individuals as exploited the caribou at the winter hunting village.

## Discussion

The Upper Tanana adapted their foraging strategy to a mixed resource base.  They exploited mobile, clumped, and unpredictable resources as well as evenly spaced, stable ones
and adjusted their settlement pattern to accommodate this strategy.  Clumped, unpredictable
caribou were hunted by aggregated hunters in spring and fall.  The local band provided the
level of aggregation for this strategy, and the larger villages reflected this.  Fish runs
in July nucleated the Upper Tanana at the few available fishing spots.  The local band was
the exploitative unit at this time also.

Evenly spaced, stable resources were exploited by smaller units, for the most part two nuclear families. These units dispersed into the forest and returned periodically to the village where food was cached from the caribou hunts and fish runs. The smaller units moved over the area throughout the late winter. The groups might change their location five times during the winter, and even daily if prey animals were not available in the area (Guedon 1974:40).

Figure 6.8 shows the seasonal availability of resources and classifies them along the lines of Wilmsen (1973), mentioned above. The change in settlement size over the year is shown in figure 6.9. Comparing the figures shows the relationship of population aggregates to the classification of resources.

## The Ingalik

The Ingalik inhabit the basins of the middle Yukon and the upper Kuskokwim rivers. The Ingalik have been subdivided, primarily on the basis of language, into four regional units. Three of the units, Anvik-Shageluk, Bonasila, and Holy Cross-Georgetown have centers in the western half of the territory; the McGrath group occupies the Upper Kuskokwim and its tributaries. Osgood's (1940 1958 1959) monographs take their data from the first of these groups. Each of the regional bands had populations of more than five hundred people (Graburn and Strong 1974:75). During his travels in 1842-44, the Russian explorer Zagoskin reported the total population in the area of Osgood's study as 770 (Graburn and Strong 1974:71).

As a group, the Ingalik provide a sharp contrast with the Chipewyan and Upper Tanana. Large, permanent villages were inhabited by more than a hundred people at a time. The majority of the population of the local band remained there for nine months of the year, and it was the source of smaller settlements found in the local band territory throughout the year. The aggregation of people was not an exploitative unit for much of the nine months it was together but depended upon the stores of fish cached there as its main resource. The harvest of this resource was done when the people were at their maximum dispersal.

The Ingalik depended upon the runs of salmon in the Yukon and Kuskokwim rivers for their main food resource. The fish were harvested throughout the summer and dried for winter use. The presence of this predictable resource "made possible a relatively settled way of life not possible in the areas where people followed the seasonal movements of large game animals" (VanStone 1974:31). The winter village was occupied from August until May. But, in addition to the large settlement, there were other settlements more characteristic of the flexible Athapaskan subsistence pattern.

Osgood (1958:38-45, 236-48) has separated the resource procurement activities of the Ingalik into "village behavior" and "individual behavior." Individual activities included the numerous fishing methods and the hunting of dispersed small and large game.

Fish were caught beginning with the break-up of the ice in late April or early May. Individual fishermen set traps and used dip nets or seine nets to catch fish available in the main channels of the major rivers. Each man had rights to a good spring fishing site as well as one or two other sites (Osgood 1958:237). In summer a man set his traps at the principal of these sites. While traps filled, the fisherman and his wife captured additional fish with nets. Fish were also taken with traps set through the ice in winter, when they provided a welcome fresh supplement to dried stores.

Moose were pursued whenever the opportunity presented itself. Black bear, beaver, muskrat, lynx, rabbit, porcupine, and ground squirrels were also significant as food, and all were taken by individual effort (Osgood 1958:281).

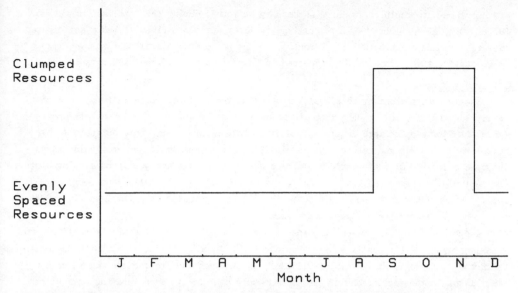

Figure 6.8. Upper Tanana Resource Availability. Jan-March: moose and small game. Apr and May: migrating caribou. Jul: whitefish runs. Aug-Sept: moose, sheep, and small game. Oct-Dec: migrating caribou. Source: McKennan 1959 and Holmes 1975.

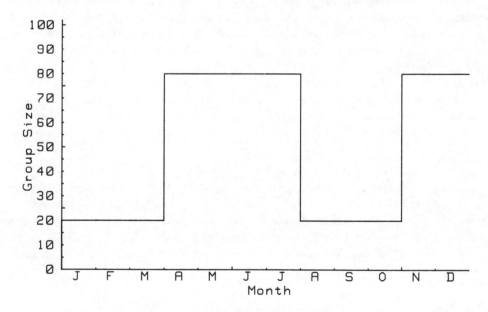

Figure 6.9. Upper Tanana Yearly Settlement Pattern. Jan-Mar: small two-family units. Apr-Jul: local bands. Aug-Oct: small two-family units. Nov-Dec: local bands. Source: McKennan 1969; Guedon 1974; Holmes 1975.

Caribou were captured in large numbers by surrounds during the late fall migration. Large groups of men left the winter village to intercept the caribou at their anticipated migration routes through the area. Because of the peripheral position of the Ingalik (figure 6.5), the region could be expected to have caribou as migrant inhabitants only.

## Settlement Pattern

The main settlement of the Ingalik was the winter village. Life centered on each family's cache of fish, brought from the summer fishing camps. These large settlements (more than 100 people) were located at intervals along the rivers where suitable sites were found. Distributed between the large villages were the small summer fishing camps. These were located so that people could take advantage of the numerous good fishing spots. For most of the summer one or two families lived in each of the small camps (Osgood 1958: 158). As described by Osgood (1958:27), "in all the intervals along the main rivers, small villages . . . and large villages" were located.

Two other types of settlements, the spring canoe village and the winter hunting camp, were important to the Ingalik subsistence strategy (Osgood 1958:42, 169). Both decreased the numbers of people at the winter village. In the weeks before the ice melted on the small lakes in the region, one or two groups would haul their canoes and the necessities for a camp on sleds to one of the small lakes six or seven miles away. Fish traps were set at the narrow outlets to the lakes as soon as the ice began to break up.

These spring camps were difficult to get to and establish, and they were rather uncomfortable owing to the early spring sleet and rains and melting snow and ice. The impetus for them must have been strong, and indeed this was a time of low rations and, sometimes, starvation (Graburn and Strong 1974:70). After the rivers became clear of ice, the excess dried fish were taken to the summer fish camps where preparations were made for the summer fish runs.

Winter hunting camps were farther from the winter village and were generally established early in the season. Hunting groups were always small, only one or two families. The small groups would move into an area where the hunting had been reported to be good.

## Discussion

If this settlement pattern is compared with the main Ingalik resource distribution (figures 6.10 and 6.11), the importance of the stored fish is apparent. Population aggregations were maintained during much of the winter. It is important to note that when stored resources were inadequate to maintain the group, parts of it set off in small groups to exploit evenly spaced, stable resources. The timing of the movement from summer camps to the winter village also coincides with the anticipated arrival of the mobile, clumped migrating herds of caribou.

## Summary and Conclusions

The key to northern Athapaskan settlement patterns for all the groups examined was flexibility. Each group was able to change settlement size and location depending in part upon the resources it exploited. Settlement patterns chosen over the year appear to be, in many cases, those which minimized travel costs (energy and time), given the foods available and their distribution.

Horn's (1968) model separates resources into two classifications: (1) clumped, mobile, and unpredictable; and (2) evenly spaced and stable. For each resource class, Horn has shown that there is an optimal strategy for the distribution of users (hunters and

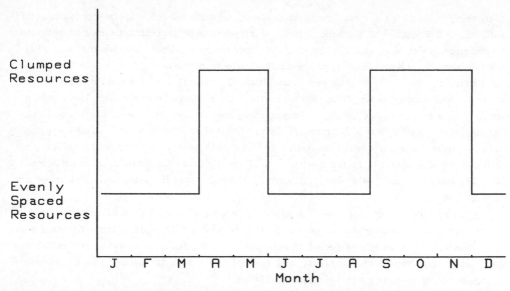

Figure 6.10. Ingalik Resource Availability. Jan-May: moose, fish, and small game. Jun-Aug: fish runs. Sept-Nov: migrating caribou. Dec: moose, fish, and small game. Source: Osgood 1958.

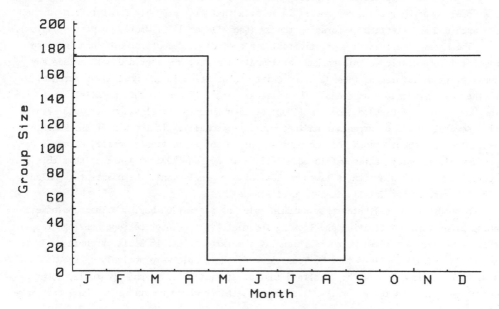

Figure 6.11. Ingalik Yearly Settlement Pattern. Sept-May: winter village 33-170. Jun-Aug: fishing village 6-12. Source: Osgood 1958; Graburn and Strong 1974.

gatherers). Resources for each group of northern Athapaskans fell within the two classifications. As predicted by the model, large settlements were centrally located in relation to resources which were clumped, mobile, and unpredictable. Small settlements were dispersed in the exploitation of evenly spaced, stable resources.

There are two cases of food resources which did not fit into the Horn model classification. Both cases concern fish, in one instance as a stored resource (Ingalik), and in another as a resource that, though evenly spaced, had limited spatial availability (Upper Tanana). In both instances the resource is clumped and predictable, and allowed aggregations of users in a pattern not accounted for in Horn's model. A revised classification that may be more suitable in the application of the model to the human case would therefore be: (1) evenly spaced and stable; (2) mobile, clumped, unpredictable; and (3) clumped and predictable.

Caching food of any type seems to allow for a central aggregation of people not participating in the food quest. As we saw in the Chipewyan case, information sharing can be greatly enhanced by increased social interaction. Cached food, by allowing for relatively large and semipermanent aggregations, must have played a role in the development of information networks in many hunter-gatherer societies.

In the Chipewyan case, we saw that information networks allowed systematic flux in forager aggregation. Other than to mention the added advantage information exchange can give to centrally aggregated foragers, Horn (1968) did not incorporate this process into his model in any direct manner. This is an area that will probably benefit from further research and modification of foraging theory (see Wilmsen 1973; Moore, chapter 9, below).

The model's value as a heuristic tool can be further demonstrated by examining an earlier interpretation of Athapaskan settlement behavior, one that did not include any consideration of foraging theory. The society in question is the Peel River Kutchin, another Alaskan Athapaskan group. The basic structure of the Kutchin parallels that of the Upper Tanana. Richard Slobodin (1962) studied Kutchin social structure, and identified several levels of organization that varied seasonally. In the winter the Kutchin assembled into "meat camps" for the express purpose of exploiting a mobile, clumped, unpredictable resource--caribou (Slobodin 1962:58). Nelson (1973:304) argues that this large aggregation was maladaptive in times of low caribou populations. He blames this maladaptive behavior on the fatalistic nature of Athapaskans.

Slobodin (1962:69) notes that Kutchin tales of starvation begin: "The people were going along together starving and looking for meat." The winter caribou-hunting groups that formed at such times were traditionally the largest Kutchin social grouping. In fact, Nelson (1973:304) mentions that at least some of the people were actively engaged in a search for caribou--those who "declined to face starvation . . . and eventually found enough game to save the others." This suggests that such aggregations may have been more than a fatalistic exercise.

The size of the winter grouping, the degree of dispersal, mobility, and predictability of the caribou at this season, and the fact that it could be a time of low rations can all be incorporated into an adaptive interpretation of Kutchin behavior based on Horn's model. The model predicts that mobile, clumped, unpredictable resources such as the nomadic caribou are optimally located by large groups of foragers based in a central location; central aggregation is further favored when active information sharing is practiced. It seems likely that the Kutchin, far from engaging in a maladaptive activity, were employing a strategy which would markedly increase their chances of finding "meat." Horn's model thus provides explanatory insight not available to intuition alone.

Generally, Horn's model of spatial organization has been able to explain several aspects of the diversity evident in northern Athapaskan settlement patterns. Analysis of the three ethnographic cases shows that variation in settlement *not* accounted for by the model arose in two contexts: (1) when detailed information about resource locations was being actively shared; and (2) when clumped but predictable resources (including stored food) were being used. These are unique human capabilities, and while Horn's model does not explicitly allow for these factors, they can be incorporated into the analysis with little difficulty. The role of these additional factors has not been quantified here, but simply used to illustrate the necessity to take unique human capabilities into account when applying general ecological models.

# 7

# Archeological Applications of Optimal Foraging Theory: Harvest Strategies of Aleut Hunter-Gatherers

David R. Yesner

## Optimal Foraging Theory: An Introduction

Survival of all animal populations depends upon three factors: reproduction above a net replacement rate; adjustment to environmental stresses; and acquisition of adequate supplies of "limiting factors" (Odum 1971), such as water, energy (calories), and nutrients (protein, vitamins, and minerals). In particular, those populations that develop exploitative strategies which optimize ratios of energy consumption to energy expenditure will be more likely to survive over extended periods of time (Slobodkin 1962). The notion that animal populations tend toward optimization of foraging efficiency is, therefore, a direct corollary of Darwin's theory of natural selection.

Optimal foraging theory has been applied widely during the past decade to animal populations, including vertebrates and invertebrates, and primary and secondary consumers (Comins and Hassell 1979; Stenseth and Hansson 1979; Pyke, et al. 1977; Krebs 1977; Rapport and Turner 1977; Charnov 1976a; Pulliam 1974; Cody 1974; Rapport 1971; Schoener 1971; Emlen 1968). In order to approximate actual conditions as closely as possible, models assuming homogeneous resources or environments have usually been avoided; beginning with MacArthur and Pianka (1966), attention has been given to optimal exploitation of dispersed prey and "patchy," or spatially heterogeneous, environments. Applications of optimal foraging theory to animal populations have therefore focused on three aspects of exploitation strategies that satisfy the above requirements: (1) food preferences; (2) foraging patch selection; and (3) allocation of time to different patches during foraging. In all three cases, energy can be used as a "currency" to measure foraging efficiency and assess hypotheses (cf. Paine 1971).

## Optimal Foraging among Hunter-Gatherers

The above comments should apply equally to human hunters and gatherers, viewed as foraging animals. Approaches similar to optimal foraging--such as "least effort,"

---

Much of the Aleutian data discussed here were derived from research conducted under grants from the National Science Foundation and Connecticut Research Foundation to W. S. Laughlin and J. S. Aigner at the University of Connecticut. The computer centers of the Universities of Connecticut and Alaska kindly donated computer time for the analyses. The manuscript was proofread by K. Crossen and typed by N. Weed. Many of the ideas on optimal foraging reflected in this article received their initial stimulus through discussions over the last several years with R. B. Thomas, S. Cook, E. Wilmsen, S. Langdon, V. Reidhead, S. Perlman, and others. None of them would agree with all of the ideas included here, and those stubbornly retained are solely my own.

"strategizing," "minimax," or "satisficing"--have existed for some time in economic anthropology (e.g., Burling 1962; Prattis 1973).  The use of energy as a measure of cultural evolution can also be traced to the work of White (1959) and Harris (1971).  But early field applications of such concepts to hunter-gatherers were designed simply to determine the level of energy efficiency of day-to-day subsistence activities.  This resulted in the development of "input-output" methods, used by Lee (1969) in his energy studies of !Kung San populations in South Africa (later modified by Foley [1977]).  More complex models of energy flow were then proposed by Kemp (1971), Godin (1972), and others working with hunting and gathering groups (cf. Little and Morren 1976).

Few of these studies involved detailed tests of optimizing behavior with respect to specific aspects of hunting and gathering lifeways, be they food preferences, patch selection, or time allocation.  For example, food preferences have been described in detail for African hunter-gatherers such as the !Kung San (Lee 1965 1969) and Valley Bisa (Marks 1973 1976 1977ab), but systematic causes have not been sought for consumption in the amounts observed.  Similarly, settlement location has been described in detail for groups like the !Kung (Yellen 1977), but rarely have the reasons for moving camps to particular sites been equally well analyzed.  An encouraging recent trend, however, is the increasing willingness of anthropologists to use biological theory along with ethnographic evidence to derive subsistence behavior hypotheses.  The present chapter contributes to this trend through an archeological analysis of diet choice among the prehistoric Aleuts.

## Archeological Applications of Optimal Foraging Theory

Perhaps because living hunter-gatherers are becoming increasingly difficult to study, archeology has become a prime source for data to test optimal exploitation strategies (Nunley 1970).  Archeological data are, of course, subject to problems of taphonomy (degree of preservation, nature of postdepositional disturbance, and so on)--what Schiffer (1976) has termed "N-transforms" of the archeological record.  Archeologists also generally remain dependent upon ethnographic data on subsistence pursuits, such as time-motion studies, for much of their cultural interpretations (cf. Hill 1971; Perlman 1976).  Similar data, however, can be reproduced through experimentation, e.g., measuring energy and time inputs required in the use of "primitive" technologies (Carneiro 1979; Saraydar and Shimada 1971 1973).

Basically, archeological data provide a picture of past exploitational strategies, coupled with a limited amount of information on past environments.  Independent data on environment must be sought from materials not greatly affected by human activities (e.g., geomorphology and palynology).  This is critical, since developing tests of optimization behavior from prehistoric materials requires either:  (a) that the past environment be reconstructed in detail, including distinct microenvironments within the exploitational area; or (b) that ecological congruence between past and present environments be demonstrated, so that the modern environment may serve as a source of relevant biological data.  In addition, the "catchment" or exploitational area must itself be defined, along with the technological complexity (and therefore harvesting efficiency) of the population.  While the degree of technological complexity is usually recoverable from archeological data, the prehistoric "catchment" area is difficult to define with any degree of precision in most archeological situations.  However, in unusual circumstances, where natural regions are set apart by physiographic barriers, and where hunter-gatherer populations that exploited those regions prehistorically survive in situ to the ethnographic present, it may well be possible to reconstruct catchment areas with a fair degree of confidence.  In any case, taphonomic factors are likely to set limits on the inferences that may be derived.

Assuming that defining the prehistoric catchment area, its biotic composition, and the technology of the group exploiting it can be accomplished, archeologists may then proceed to examine hypotheses about foraging behavior in basically the same way that ethnographers have in living populations. The specific goal of archeologists, using their own methodologies, would be to determine the accuracy of optimization hypotheses concerning food preferences, patch selection, and time allocation. Settlement pattern studies are the most developed of these subjects. They are analogous to studies of patch selection and time allocation among other foraging animals, in the sense that they help to identify how settlements are centrally located to take advantage of resources available at different times of year (Orians and Pearson 1978; Morrison 1978; Hamilton and Watt 1970). Site *location* analysis has received the bulk of recent attention by ecologically oriented archeologists (e.g., Jochim 1976), but site *seasonality* studies have a much longer history, using both faunal and floral remains as well as inferences drawn from site location and artifact functions.

Archeologists have not, however, developed rigorous, quantitative approaches to dealing with food preferences or prey selection. The remainder of this chapter will attempt to do so, using optimal foraging approaches. Two interrelated goals are involved: to determine prehistoric food preferences in a quantitative fashion; and to suggest the important factors underlying those preferences. For both of these goals, organic residues, particularly faunal remains, are the major data base (Yesner 1978).

## "Proportional" Hunting: Tests of Hypotheses

The range of foods eaten by different populations of animals or human hunter-gatherers depends on both the abundance and the "value" of available, edible resources (Sih 1979; Estabrook and Dunham 1976). "Value" may be defined as the net energy yield of a resource per unit of "handling time"; for human hunter-gatherers, the latter includes time devoted to the capture, retrieval, and processing of different foods. The result is that most foragers take an optimal range of resources, or optimal dietary breadth (Colwell and Futuyama 1971). When is a particular resource included in (added to) the optimal diet breadth? This appears to depend primarily on the "value" of that item, and both the abundance and the value of more valuable resources (Sih 1979). Thus, the value (handling time) of an item is the major factor, and abundance a secondary factor, in determining the resources "selected" to constitute an optimal diet.

Once dietary breadth has been determined, however, optimal foraging theory predicts that the species that fall within that breadth will be taken whenever encountered. Large, carnivorous foragers, such as humans, tend to exploit their environments in a "fine-grained" fashion, encountering and exploiting resources in the proportions in which they actually occur (Oaten 1977; Krebs, et al. 1974). Thus, for those species that are harvested, an optimal forager will take them in amounts representative of the biomass of that species in the (local) environment. In other words, while the spectrum of species eaten may not be a representative sample of all species available, among those that are eaten, harvested biomass should be proportional to that in the natural environment.[1] This concept can be framed

1. This concept of "proportional" hunting is somewhat similar to the concept of "random" hunting developed by Wilkinson (1976), which he defines as harvesting animals "more or less at random from the populations accessible to the hunters." My major disagreement lies in the use of the term "random," which implies no ranking of species "values." By using biomass units instead of animal numbers or frequencies, one can take into account both the abundance and the yield of different species (assuming caloric values are proportional to biomass).

as a "proportional hunting" hypothesis to test on archeological data. The appropriate hypothesis would be that species would rank similarly in terms of biomass in both the prehistoric diet and the natural environment. If such a hypothesis fails to account for specific cases, then specific secondary hypotheses based on nutrition, taste, or factors other than energy efficiency may be tested individually.

To test such a hypothesis it is necessary to obtain accurate biomass data for each species present in both the archeological faunal assemblages and the natural ecosystem. How does an archeologist go about obtaining biomass data, either from current animal censuses or from archeological faunal assemblages?

The archeological data are a little easier to come by than the animal census data. By examining the numbers of various skeletal elements representing each species, it is possible to estimate the "minimum number of individuals" (MNI) of each in a particular archeological unit. Zooarcheologists generally accept stratigraphic units as the most culturally meaningful units for the tabulation of MNIs (Grayson 1973). MNI values may be summed from all of the stratigraphic units in a given site to yield a somewhat artificial site MNI total. Whether or not such a total is archeologically meaningful depends on two factors: (1) whether the site was used consistently in the same manner over time, particularly in terms of season of occupation; and (2) whether differential preservation has affected various stratigraphic units. (This problem will be discussed in more detail later.) After MNI figures have been calculated for each stratum or site, biomass values can then be determined by multiplying the MNI for each species by the mass of that species.

Obtaining biomass figures for the natural ecosystem can be much more difficult. Quantitative animal censuses are available for some geographic regions where lands have been surveyed by government agencies. Otherwise, "analogous" census data may be used from geographically adjacent zones or similar ecosystems (Mohr 1940). However, direct animal census data should be sought for the region in question wherever possible, since it is difficult to establish exactly what degree of geographical proximity or "ecosystem similarity" (B. D. Smith 1979) allows for valid tests of hypotheses on selective resource utilization.

Direct census data come in different forms. Total numbers of animals is fine if either: (1) the census region coincides with the prehistoric catchment area; or (2) the area (in $km^2$) of the census is known so that density estimates (animals/$km^2$) can be derived (Grayson 1974). Densities or total numbers for each species can then be multiplied by the weight of each animal to yield a unit-area or total biomass figure (B. D. Smith 1979:157).[2]

These approaches work well for terrestrial hunter-gatherers whose catchment area is distinctly bounded in space, and for which animal densities can be readily determined. Except for populations exploiting caribou, bison, and a few other migratory species, most terrestrial hunter-gatherers have a diet composed largely of resident fauna. Although some principal food resources may fluctuate seasonally in availability (or biomass), rarely are these groups highly dependent on species present during limited portions of the year. But what of coastal hunter-gatherers? Some of the densest populations of hunter-gatherers have developed in coastal regions (Yesner 1980). For these groups, regional animal densities

---

2. Biomass figures may be converted into energy (calories) if the appropriate factor is known for each species. Caloric values for most wild mammals range ca. 1.5-2.5 kcal/g for flesh and subcutaneous fat, while those for wild birds range ca. 1.0-1.5 kcal/g; fish and shellfish are somewhat lower in caloric content; most species of fish range ca. 0.75-2.0 kcal/g, and shellfish ca. 0.5-1.25 kcal/g (Watt and Merrill 1963; Wooster and Blanck 1950). Actual values within any taxonomic group tend to be distributed normally, and determined primarily by the diet of the individual species (Prus 1970; Slobodkin and Richman 1961).

are not as meaningful, since their catchment area consists of the coastline and a strip of hinterland and ocean which varies in size, depending on the species being exploited. Fish, birds, and sea mammals are, furthermore, rarely confined to such a zone. Island species, in particular, are often migratory, inhabiting an island region for only a limited period during the year. Thus, in order to test foraging behavior hypotheses over the full range of hunter-gatherer adaptations, mechanisms must be developed for dealing with: (1) animal censuses which simply list relative species abundance (instead of density); and (2) seasonal variations in species numbers or biomass due to migration or local changes (cf. McCullough 1970; Yesner 1977b).

These procedures will be developed in the context of an example that will be used to test the hypothesis presented above.

## An Aleutian Example

The chief problems in testing optimal foraging behavior with archeological data include (1) accurate reconstruction of the paleoenvironment; and (2) accurate assessment of exploitation patterns, given that taphonomic or preservational factors may affect archeological faunal samples. The best results can be achieved when (1) little environmental change has occurred since the period of site occupation; and (2) faunal preservation is excellent, or at least there is little reason to suspect differential preservation within any class of fauna.

These conditions are met in the Aleutian Islands, an archipelago stretching more than a thousand miles from the coast of southwest Alaska (figure 7.1). The Aleutian Islands are a good area for testing hypotheses about prehistoric human ecology for several reasons. Like other island chains, they form a well-defined ecosystem, composed of distinct, naturally bounded units. The Aleutians have a relatively uniform (though severe) oceanic climate, and, although there is some east-west biogeographical variation within the archipelago (Yesner 1977a), the environment is basically homogeneous. The archipelago is isomorphic with the Aleuts, close relatives of the neighboring southwestern Alaskan Eskimos, but with a distinct population history for the past several thousand years. The Aleuts are indeed "survivors of the Bering Land Bridge" (Laughlin 1980); they have continued the same maritime hunting-and-gathering way of life relatively unchanged in this location for thousands of years (Aigner 1976; Laughlin 1972), surviving to be recorded by early missionaries and ethnographers (e.g., Veniaminov 1840; Dall 1877). The island chain itself is distinct from the neighboring ecosystem of southwestern Alaska, primarily because of a lack of trees and winter ice, so that substantial year-round populations of invertebrates, fish, and sea mammals have been able to develop in the area. In contrast, the terrestrial fauna is depauperate (foxes are the largest terrestrial animals on most islands), so that the Aleuts have an almost exclusively maritime orientation. Geological data (Black 1974 1975 1976) and palynological data (Heusser 1973; Nybakken 1966) suggest little environmental change in the region during the past few thousand years. This lends confidence to attempts to use the modern Aleutian environment as a source of data on prehistoric species abundance. Finally, the Aleutians fall almost entirely within a national wildlife refuge, where excellent studies have been undertaken of bird and mammal abundance, and the majority of Aleutian archeological sites are excellently preserved, partly because the remains of marine invertebrates (shellfish and sea urchins) eaten by the prehistoric Aleuts have neutralized the soil to the point where nearly all mammal and bird bone (and most, though not all, fish bone) has been preserved.

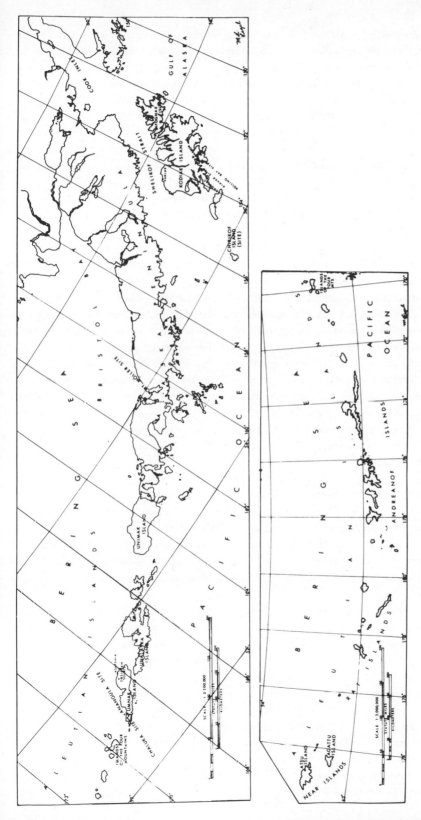

Figure 7.1. The Aleutian Islands. Copyright University of Wisconsin Press.

Extensive archeological work has been undertaken in the eastern Aleutian Islands since the 1930s, particularly in the region of southwestern Umnak Island, hypothesized as the southeastern terminus of the Bering Land Bridge (Aigner 1974; Laughlin 1974/75), and as a region of particularly high prehistoric population density, due to the richness of the up-welling system in Samalga Pass immediately to the west (Laughlin 1972; Yesner 1977c). The region is bounded naturally by a mountain chain to the east and ocean to the north, south, and west. While older sites were the original focus of archeological work in this area, four sites dating within the past four thousand years were excavated. All of these sites were thoroughly sampled by a combination of trenching, areal, and test excavation techniques (Yesner 1977a). Details of stratigraphy, dating, and excavation strategies may be found in Yesner (1977ac). Among other materials, a total of 12,260 faunal remains were retrieved from excavations at these four sites. These form the basis of the archeological portion of the following discussion.

It should be noted that this does not represent an exhaustive sample of sites in the southwest Umnak region; at least two other large coastal sites (at Sandy Beach and Driftwood Bay) and a number of smaller coastal and interior sites exist within the region. However, for reasons that will become apparent, the site sample was judged adequate for testing hypotheses about prehistoric Aleut foraging strategies. In addition, all of the sites excavated date to the period of relative geological and environmental stability within the past few thousand years. This means that: (1) eustatic sea level changes have not resulted in a great deal of site erosion; and (2) environmental change does not have to be considered as a major factor affecting the interpretation of faunal samples. Also, since invertebrates (shellfish and sea urchins) were available on coastal strand flats during the entire period of site occupation, differential preservation of site strata is likely to be minimal.

Four types of foods form the mainstay of the Aleut diet: fish, marine invertebrates, sea mammals, and birds. Each category has peculiar problems in censusing present-day numbers of individuals and in determining relative representation in the archeological sites. For this reason, one cannot compare directly the total biota of the region to the range of foods eaten by the prehistoric Aleuts. Each type of resource must be examined individually.

Fish abundance has not been accurately assessed in the Aleutian region. Escapements of salmon (five species are present in the Aleutians on a seasonal basis) have been measured for some streams, but the bottomfish (cod and halibut), also favored by the Aleuts, have not been similarly censused. In addition, skeletal remains of salmon are rarely preserved in archeological sites, so that comparisons of present relative abundance and past fishing patterns would be impossible.

Marine invertebrates, in contrast, are relatively easy to census. Shellfish, for instance, can be counted on strand flats at low tide with sampling procedures such as transect analysis. In fact, many previous attempts to estimate the resource base of coastal hunter-gatherers concentrate almost exclusively on marine invertebrates to generate biomass figures (cf. Shawcross's [1967 1972] studies in New Zealand). Using such methods, Love (1977) has calculated the invertebrate biomass for a strand flat on Umnak Island in the eastern Aleutians (table 7.1), associated with the prehistoric Aleut village of "Chaluka." Of the taxa listed in table 7.1, only sea urchins and mollusks were utilized by the Aleuts.

Sea urchins comprise ca. 93.8 per cent of the total biomass on the strand flat, while edible shellfish represent only ca. 5.4 per cent. Unquestionably, sea urchin tests comprise the bulk of marine invertebrate remains in the Chaluka midden. It appears, however, that shellfish represent far more than 5.4 per cent of the midden mass. Unfortunately, because

*Table 7.1*
*Invertebrate biomass: Nikolski Strand flat*

| Invertebrate Group | Biomass (g) | Density (g/m$^2$) |
|---|---|---|
| Crustacea | $6.21 \times 10^6$ (= $.01 \times 10^9$) | $2.23 \times 10^3$ |
|   Barnacles | $2.69 \times 10^5$ | $2.18 \times 10^3$ |
|   Amphipods and isopods | $2.41 \times 10^5$ | 12.2 |
|   Others | $1.11 \times 10^5$ | 18.4 |
| Echinodermata | $1.52 \times 10^9$ | $2.33 \times 10^4$ |
|   Starfishes | $3.11 \times 10^5$ | 33.8 |
|   Sea urchins | $1.52 \times 10^9$ | $2.32 \times 10^4$ |
| Mollusca | $8.79 \times 10^7$ | |
|   Mussels | $6.21 \times 10^7$ | $2.78 \times 10^4$ |
|   Limpets | $5.29 \times 10^6$ | 78.3 |
|   Periwinkles | $1.70 \times 10^7$ | 166.2 |
|   Whelks | $2.60 \times 10^5$ | 187.1 |
|   Chitons | $9.28 \times 10^5$ | 200.8 |

Source:   Love 1977.

adequate molluscan samples have not been retrieved from Aleutian middens, and because of difficulties in counting archeological individuals and converting these counts into biomass estimates (Kranz 1977), the relative biomass of each species present cannot be estimated with precision.  If--as appears to be the case--shellfish are represented in the midden to a greater extent than their natural biomass would suggest, there was some selectivity directed toward their collection from the strand flats.  How much selectivity we cannot determine at present.

In addition, there appears to have been selection among shellfish species.  For example, while conch-type gastropods (periwinkles and whelks) are relatively abundant on the strand flat, comprising about twenty per cent of the shellfish biomass, they are practically non-existent in the middens, and there is no ethnographic evidence to suggest that they were ever significant dietary items.  These species probably fall outside of the optimal diet, owing to the large time and energy expenditure required for their processing (handling costs).  They are smaller than the other shellfish species, and picks would have been required to retrieve the individually small amount of (low calorie) meat from them.  Other shellfish (mussels, limpets, and chitons) were harvested and appear to rank in popularity in the middens in the same order that they rank in biomass on the strand flats, as predicted.  However, this is a qualitative rather than a quantitative judgment.

Better estimates of prehistoric use can be made for the Aleutian sea mammals, but there are problems with obtaining accurate population data for all species.  For sea lions, hair seals, and sea otters, numbers have been established for various parts of the Aleutian chain (table 7.2).  For example, in the eastern Aleutians, there are about 55,500 sea lions, 16,000 hair seals, and 42,000 sea otters (Sekora 1973).  Conversion to biomass is not easy, since weights differ greatly according to sex and age.  I have therefore used the weight of an "average" adult of each species in my calculations.  On this basis, sea lions comprise 89 per cent of the biomass, hair seals 6.3%, and sea otters ca. 3.9% (see table 7.3).  I have used the eastern Aleutian figures here in order to make comparisons with four archeological sites on southwest Umnak Island in the eastern Aleutians (figure 7.2).

*Table 7.2*
*Mammal Population Densities by Region*

| Species | East | Central | West |
|---------|------|---------|------|
| Sea lion | | | |
| Numbers | 55,482 | 28,911 | 16,730 |
| Frequency | 54.9% | 28.6% | 16.5% |
| Density | 16.5/mi$^2$ | 23.4/mi$^2$ | 51.3/mi$^2$ |
| Hair seal | | | |
| Numbers | 16,000 | 10,800 | 2,000 |
| Frequency | 55.6% | 37.5% | 6.9% |
| Density | 4.8/mi$^2$ | 8.7/mi$^2$ | 6.1/mi$^2$ |
| Sea otter | | | |
| Numbers | 42,100 | 15,500 | 4,150 |
| Frequency | 68.2% | 25.1% | 6.7% |
| Density | 12.5/mi$^2$ | 12.5/mi$^2$ | 12.7/mi$^2$ |

Source:   Sekora 1973; Laughlin 1974/75.

We may now generate the required comparative biomass figures from mammalian bone remains in these four sites. The 5,079 bones from these sites represented 905 individuals (table 7.4). By multiplying the numbers of individuals by "average" (adult) species weights, we find that about 70.4 per cent of the archeological biomass (meat weight) is provided by sea lions, 12.2 per cent by hair seals, and 3.0 per cent by sea otters. The result demonstrates that these species do rank similarly in both natural (habitat) and archeological (harvest) biomass, suggesting that they were harvested as encountered, i.e., in proportion to their natural abundance.

One problem with the data used in this case is that the modern census covered a much larger area than that exploited by the prehistoric inhabitants of these sites. There is no clear way around this difficulty. Coastal hunter-gatherers use boats for hunting sea mammals, either at sea or at the rookeries that sea mammals occupy for varying periods. For example, we know that approximately 4,275 sea lions currently inhabit rookeries near the archeological sites on Umnak Island. (We have no such data for hair seals or sea otters.) If the sea lion figure is comparable to the past local abundance of sea lions, and if the Aleuts maintained an annual culling rate of 8%-10%, characteristic of seal exploitation elsewhere in the arctic (McLaren 1962), then the maximum sustained yield for the prehistoric villages in the region would have been about 350-425 sea lions per year. On several lines of evidence, a regional population of about one hundred persons can be suggested (Yesner 1977a), yielding 3-5 sea lions per Aleut per year (1,000-16,000 kg meat/person/yr from this source alone). This evidence is consistent with the idea that sea lions contributed the majority of the mammalian calories.

The archeological MNI percentages for sea lions, hair seals, and sea otters do not add up to 100%; fur seals, another species of significance in the prehistoric Aleut diet, contributed the remaining 14.3 per cent. Unlike the other sea mammals, fur seals are migratory, moving through the eastern Aleutians for short periods during the spring and fall. Surveys of mammalian abundance are usually taken in the Aleutians during the summer and do

*Table 7.3*

*Meat Yield of Aleutian Mammals*

| Mammal | Sex/ Age Div. | Average Live Weight (kg) | % of Usable Meat | Kg of Usable Meat |
|---|---|---|---|---|
| *Enhydra lutris*[1] | M | 34.47 | 70 | 24.13 |
| (sea otter) | F | 19.62 | 70 | 13.73 |
|  | M or F | 27.04 | 70 | 18.93 |
|  | Juvenile | 13.52 | 70 | 9.46 |
|  | Infant | 1.75 | 70 | 1.22 |
| *Eumetopias jubata*[2] | M | 725.76 | 70 | 508.03 |
| (sea lion) | F | 204.12 | 70 | 142.88 |
|  | M or F | 464.94 | 70 | 325.46 |
|  | Juvenile | 232.47 | 70 | 162.73 |
|  | Infant | 29.96 | 70 | 20.97 |
| *Callorhinus ursinus*[3] | M | 229.72 | 70 | 160.80 |
| (fur seal) | F | 63.00 | 70 | 44.10 |
|  | M or F | 146.36 | 70 | 102.45 |
|  | Juvenile | 73.18 | 70 | 51.23 |
|  | Infant | 9.43 | 70 | 6.60 |
| *Phoca vitulina*[4] | M | 116.00 | 70 | 81.20 |
| (hair seal) | F | 110.00 | 70 | 77.00 |
|  | M or F | 113.00 | 70 | 79.10 |
|  | Juvenile | 56.50 | 70 | 39.55 |
|  | Infant | 7.28 | 70 | 5.10 |
| *Vulpes vulpes*[5] (red fox) |  | 3.63 | 50 | 1.81 |

1. Murie 1940.
2. Fiscus 1961; Spaulding 1964; White 1953.
3. Kenyon and Scheffer 1955; White 1953.
4. Kenyon and Scheffer 1955; Usher and Church 1969.
5. White 1953.
Note: M or F category was used for determining "average" weights.

*Table 7.4*

*Southwest Umnak Faunal Sample*

| Archeological Site | Avian Remains | | Mammalian Remains | |
|---|---|---|---|---|
|  | Bones | MNIs | Bones | MNIs |
| Chaluka | 3,985 | 1,207 | 2,466 | 455 |
| Oglodax' | 2,086 | 586 | 1,942 | 242 |
| Anangula Village | 791 | 120 | 210 | 111 |
| Sheep Creek | 319 | 22 | 461 | 97 |
| Total | 7,181 | 1,935 | 5,079 | 905 |

Source:  Yesner 1977a.

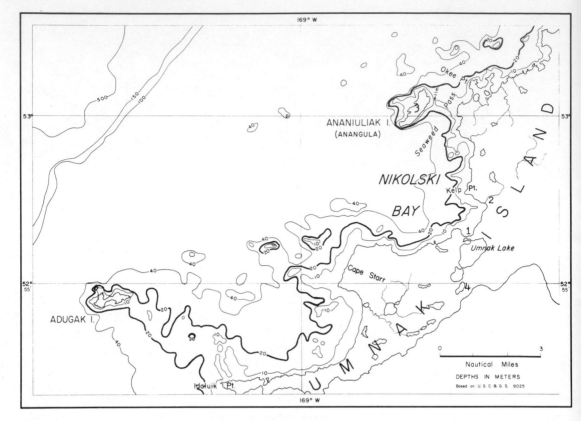

Figure 7.2.  Archeological Sites on Southwest Umnak Island,
Aleutian Islands.  (1) Chaluka; (2) Sheep Creek; (3) Anangula
Village; (4) Oglodax'.  Copyright University of Wisconsin Press.

not reflect the number of fur seals periodically in the region.  Whales also occasionally
move through the eastern Aleutians; they, again, have not been censused.  Nor have the
whalebones found in the archeological sites been quantified as MNIs because of the extreme
difficulty of applying this procedure to scraps of archeological whalebone (Turner, Turner,
and Richards 1975).  Furthermore, it is unclear if whales were actively hunted and eaten,
or if beached whales were scavenged for ivory and whalebone (used in tool making).  The
same is true of foxes, which are a minor fraction of the prehistoric biomass (0.1%) and

which may have been trapped for furs or may represent scavengers that died on the site, not eaten by the Aleuts at all.

Birds, however, do not suffer from the estimation problems that affect fish, inverte-brates, or sea mammals. Bird bones are excellently preserved in the middens, and there are apparently no problems in generating MNI figures from these bones resulting from differen-tial preservation of bird species. We also have some type of abundance estimate for all species of Aleutian birds, based on extensive research by the U. S. Fish and Wildlife Ser-vice in the area. Bird species diversity is very high in the Aleutians; 105 species of birds inhabit the Aleutians during some season of the year (Sekora 1973). (Common and scientific names of these species are listed in appendix 1.) Regional bird densities have been estimated from aerial transects with wide coverage, but these are not nearly as ac-curate as local shipboard censuses from which biomass figures can be generated (table 7.5).

*Table 7.5*

*Seasonal Seabird Abundance for the Bering Sea Coastal Domain*

| Ecological Group | Winter Data | | | Summer Data | | |
|---|---|---|---|---|---|---|
| | $\bar{X}$ birds/ Km$^2$ | Standing Stock | Biomass (tons) | $\bar{X}$ birds/ Km$^2$ | Standing Stock | Biomass (tons) |
| Diomedeidae (albatrosses) | 0.80 | 10,100 | 27.8 | 6.76 | 92,000 | 253,0 |
| Procellariidae (shearwaters) | 12.61 | 171,500 | 115.1 | 654.00 | 8,890,000 | 5,778.5 |
| Laridae/ Stercorariidae (gulls/jaegers) | 21.51 | 292,500 | 219.4 | 13.11 | 178,000 | 133.9 |
| Alcidae (large) | 13.38 | 182,000 | 172.9 | 26.35 | 358,000 | 300.0 |
| Alcidae (small) | 100.90 | 1,370,500 | 274.1 | 6.04 | 82,100 | 16.4 |
| Hydrobatidae/ Phalaropodidae (shorebirds) | 5.94 | 80,900 | 0.4 | 69.25 | 942,000 | 4.5 |
| Other | 5.85 | 79,500 | 47.1 | 3.00 | 40,800 | 24.5 |
| Total | 160.99 | 2,187,000 | 856.8 | 778.51 | 10,582,900 | 6,510.8 |

Source:   Sanger 1972:599.

Both procedures, furthermore, suffer from two deficiencies: (1) they are usually conducted during only one or two seasons of the year; and (2) they are usually conducted well off shore, thus seriously underestimating the densities of near-shore species such as certain waterfowl or cormorants. The Fish and Wildlife Service has also produced qualitative esti-mates of avian species abundance, based on island censuses as well as offshore transects. These reports (Sekora 1973) list birds as "abundant," "common," "occasional," "unusual," or "rare" during each of the four seasons. For this study, a method was therefore developed based on Fay and Cade (1959) to convert these qualitative assessments into numbers from which biomass estimates could be derived. A detailed description of this method is found in appendix 2. Biomass figures generated by this method for all avian species in the Aleu-tians can be found in Yesner and Aigner (1976).

Comparative avian biomass estimates were derived from faunal data from the four arche-ological sites on Umnak Island. As described above, MNIs were derived for each species from each archeological site stratum; these MNIs were summed over all strata to obtain a total value for each species from each site; and the MNIs were then multiplied by the average weight of each species to obtain a biomass estimate. The 7,181 avian remains recorded from all four sites constituted a total of 1,935 MNIs (table 7.4). MNI and biomass estimates for all avian species from these four sites may be found in Yesner and Aigner (1976).

Before comparing the natural biomass estimates with those from the archeological sites, a few words of caution are in order. First, as noted previously, site biomass estimates based on MNIs summed over various stratigraphic units are archeologically meaningful only if sites have been consistently used in similar fashion over time, particularly in terms of season of occupation. Our data suggest that, with few exceptions, sites were in fact used in such a consistent way. Using a variety of seasonal indicators, primarily birds but also migratory fur seals, we were able to establish that the Chaluka site was always occupied as a year-round, central base village (Yesner 1977a). Similarly, the Sheep Creek site was always used as a short-term encampment, predominantly for late summer to fall fishing, but for collecting other species as well. The Oglodax' and Anangula Village sites also show continuous seasonal use, although Oglodax' is the one site that apparently was used as a central base camp for only a temporary period ca. 1,000-2,000 BP (Yesner 1977ac). The fact that sites continued to be used in the same fashion over time can be shown quite nicely in a dendrogram of site strata, based on clustering the strata by species frequencies. With the exception of a few strata from the Oglodax' site, the strata of each site continue to cluster together even when all are thrown together in the analysis (Yesner and Aigner 1976).

Even under these almost "laboratory" conditions, however, there are likely to be a number of taphonomic factors affecting the faunal assemblages in different sites. For this reason, it would be unjustified to use raw MNI or biomass values as representative of true prehistoric hunting yields. B. D. Smith (1979) implies that direct comparisons can be made between raw biomass figures from both archeological and biological data to test hypotheses on resource selectivity, as long as a full range of possible modern biomass figures is indicated. However, the archeological values are not absolute, and measure only the relative yield from a species at a given location. Similarly, if qualitative data are used to generate biomass estimates from a natural ecosystem (as in the avian case), the resulting estimates are only relative measures of food availability. Therefore, all biomass estimates should be converted into ranks. The resulting ranked (ordinal) data are also more amenable to statistical testing.

Following this caveat, the biomass estimates for avian species derived from the Aleutian data were converted into ranks. Table 7.6 shows the twenty-five avian species that ranked highest in modern biomass on the left and averaged for all four sites on the right. A test of proportional hunting, then, is equivalent to testing a null hypothesis of equivalence between these two sets of biomass ranks. A Spearman rank correlation coefficient is the appropriate statistic to compare the two sets of ranks.[3] When applied, the result is a correlation coefficient of +0.554. A student's "t"-test for ranked data with twenty-four degrees of freedom is significant at the p = 0.05 level, but not below it. Overall, there

---

3. This statistic is of the form

$$r_s = 1 - \frac{6\Sigma d_i^2}{n(n^2 - 1)}$$

where $d$ is the difference between each set of ranks, and $n$ is the number of pairs of ranks. In this case, $n = 25$.

*Table 7.6*

*Comparative Archeological and Biological Avian Biomass Ranks*

| Species | Biological Biomass Rank | Chaluka | Oglodax' | Anangula Village | Sheep Creek | Mean Rank |
|---|---|---|---|---|---|---|
| *Phalacrocorax pelagious* | 1 | 7 | 4 | 5 | 1 | 3 |
| *Larus glaucescens* | 2 | 10 | 9 | 8 | 7 | 5 |
| *Uria* spp. | 3/4 | 3 | 13 | 9 | 10 | 6 |
| *Lunda cirrhata* | 5 | 8 | 14 | 15 | 9 | 8 |
| *Fulmarus glacialis* | 6 | 9 | 2 | 1 | 19 | 4 |
| *Anas Crecca* | 7 | - | - | - | 22 | 23 |
| *Diomedea albatrus* | 8 | 2 | 3 | 3 | 5 | 1 |
| *Haliaeetus leucocephalus* | 9 | 5 | 6 | - | 6 | 9 |
| *Histrionicus histrionicus* | 10 | 20 | 17 | - | 21 | 16 |
| *Rissa tridactyla* | 11 | - | 25 | 22 | - | 20 |
| *Gavia immer* | 12 | 16 | 10 | 10 | 16 | 10 |
| *Somateria mollissima* | 13 | 13 | 8 | 7 | 8 | 7 |
| *Phalacrocorax urile* | 14 | 4 | 7 | 2 | 2 | 2 |
| Misc. *Alcidae* | 15 | 14 | 21 | 12 | 15 | 13 |
| *Gavia stellata* | 16 | 23 | 18 | 20 | - | 17 |
| *Anas platyrhynochos* | 17 | - | - | 23 | - | 24 |
| *Corvus corax* | 18 | 19 | 16 | 24 | 20 | 15 |
| *Falco peregrinus* | 19 | - | 24 | - | 25 | 21 |
| *Haemateous bachmani* | 20 | - | 29 | 21 | - | 22 |
| *Olor* spp. | 21 | 12 | 5 | - | 11 | 12 |
| *Philacte canagica* | 22 | 21 | 11 | 11 | 4 | 9 |
| *Phalacrocorax auritus* | 23 | 11 | 23 | 6 | - | 14 |
| *Somateria spectabilis* | 24 | 15 | 12 | 13 | 13 | 11 |
| *Mergus merganser* | 25 | 27 | 28 | 14 | - | 18 |
| *Branta nigricans* | 26 | 29 | 24 | 19 | - | 19 |

Note:  Common names for species are listed in appendix 1.

appears to be a fair degree of association between the two sets of ranks.[4]

In spite of the somewhat ambiguous result of this statistical test, several important features of Aleut hunting strategies emerge from the analysis of avian exploitation.  They are as follows:

(1)  *Not all species* are included in the Aleut diet.  Of the 105 species of birds recorded for the Aleutian ecosystem (Sekora 1973), only 62 species, or 59 per cent were utilized by the Aleuts (Yesner 1977a).  It is unlikely that this is the result of environmental change, since no "alien" species (i.e., those not found in the region today) are present in the middens.  Furthermore, these 62 species represent the *maximum* number exploited at a given archeological site (Chaluka).  The dietary breadth reflected at other sites is substantially lower, as low as 31 species, or half the maximum number (at Sheep Creek).  The actual dietary breadth reflected at any given site is a result of both microenvironmental variation and length of time commitment of humans to a particular area--i.e., temporary hunting camps versus more permanent headquarters for "central base foraging" (Yesner 1977b).

(2)  Clearly, only those species of "value" to the Aleuts were included in the diet.  In particular, those species falling below an absolute minimum biomass of 100 g were not exploited at all by the Aleuts.  As was the case with the shellfish, the handling time (including retrieval and processing) is probably too large for these very small species

4.  Alternatively, an "electivity index," "forage ratio," or "preference coefficient" might be used to assess the deviance of each archeobiomass frequency from the modern biomass frequency of the same species (cf. Chesson 1978).

to make exploitation of them worthwhile, even if abundant, because of their low individual biomass yield. Because the bird species diversity is so high in the Aleutians, larger species apparently never became scarce enough to encourage the exploitation of extremely small ones (cf. Klopfer and MacArthur 1960).

(3) Larger species were almost always exploited, whether they were abundant or not. Because these are highly "valued" resources in the sense that they yield a high return for the required handling costs, they were evidently utilized even if present in relatively low frequencies in the Aleutian ecosystem. However, there are some exceptions to these overall trends. For example, certain species such as eagles were not heavily exploited, even though quite large in size. Other factors--such as taste, nonfood yields, or other values--have to be brought into account to explain such cases. These "exceptions" are explored below.

(4) Generally speaking, middle-sized species were probably pursued only when larger species were not sufficiently abundant at any given time. However, there are a number of exceptions to this general rule. Species such as waterfowl--probably important for reasons both of taste and of nonfood yields--were disproportionately favored (see discussion below).

(5) Occasionally, species only slightly smaller than the minimum exploited biomass were quite "popular" in the middens. These species are not reflected in table 7.6, which considers only the twenty-five most abundant species in the Aleutians. A case in point involves the shearwaters (*Puffinus* spp.). They have a very low biomass *only* because of their small body size. Their popularity may be accounted for by the fact that their numbers are extremely large on a seasonal basis (table 7.5), particularly in the late summer and early fall when their biomass in the Aleutians increases dramatically, and by the fact that they aggregate in these huge numbers in relatively localized areas (interisland passes) where they are relatively easy to exploit. Clearly, the "value" of these small species is enhanced by the ease with which they can be harvested (handled).

(6) Another feature of the Aleut exploitational pattern is what I term a "coharvesting" strategy. Optimal foraging theory predicts that any prey encountered that has a low handling cost, or a handling cost/benefit ratio below a given level, will be harvested. "Coharvesting" is a type of optimal foraging when additional species are obtained as part of the same general hunting procedure. For example, desert hunters returning unsuccessfully from a large mammal hunt may capture and kill a tortoise or porcupine that they discover along their path, so as not to return empty-handed. Ross (1978) has recently demonstrated that among Amazonian groups for which fishing is the major focus, mammals may be acquired when they are encountered during fishing trips. In the interisland passes, large species such as albatrosses, yielding high return for handling costs, tend to congregate with smaller species, including both shearwaters and fulmars (*Fulmarus glacialis*). Exploitation of shearwaters and fulmars would then be advantageous because of low additional handling costs to items already being harvested. In fact, a similar argument may apply to all of the birds being hunted in the island passes. All of these species were probably important primarily as dietary supplements, rather than as objects of specialized hunts. They may have simply been obtained in the island passes from boats returning empty-handed from sea mammal hunts at nearby rookeries. Thus, all of these species could have been exploited as part of an optimal "coharvesting" strategy.

Perhaps the deviations from biomass rank correlations can best be depicted as a scattergram (figure 7.3) which plots the mean archeological site ranks against the biological biomass ranks.  A relationship obviously exists between the two sets of ranks, but the deviations from the regression line need to be explained in more detail.[5]

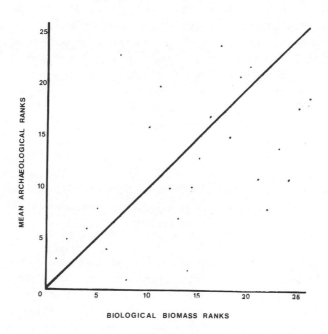

Figure 7.3.  Scattergram Showing Relationship between Archeological and Biological Biomass Ranks for Given Species.

### Explaining Food Preferences

The results of the above analysis mirror the problems that have confronted biologists in attempting to apply optimal foraging theory to the food preferences of other animals. In a recent survey, Maynard Smith (1978:52-53) notes:  "Tests of the quantitative predictions of optimization models in particular populations are beginning to be made.  It is commonly found that a model *correctly predicts qualitative features of the observations, but is contradicted in detail*" (italics mine).  Maynard Smith continues:

> In such cases, the Popperian view would be that the original model has been falsified.  This is correct, but it does not follow that the model should be abandoned.  In the analysis of complex systems it is most unlikely that any simple model, taking into account only a few factors, can give quantitatively exact predictions. Given that a simple model has been falsified by observations, the choice lies between abandoning it, and modifying it, usually by adding hypotheses.

The latter, apparently, is the solution that most investigators have opted for (see chapter 2, above).  The only other possibility, one might add, would be to throw out the baby with the bathwater.

---

5. Alternatively, biological biomass ranks could be compared with the biomass ranks from each site; this might be more informative about site-specific seasonal exploitation strategies, rather than regional harvesting patterns.  Still another possibility might be to use an archeological mean biomass rank weighted by the sample size (MNIs) at each archeological site.

Let me give a concrete example. I have assumed here that optimal solutions maximize energy inputs from the available resource biomass. However, this may not be the whole story. Optimal solutions really depend on maximizing energy capture over a set of energy expenditure variables--search, pursuit, immobilization, and retrieval of resources (Laughlin 1968). Several authors have developed optimal foraging models based upon energy consumption/expenditure ratios, in both humans (e.g., Perlman 1976 1978) and other animals (Caraco 1979; Norberg 1977; Kiester and Slatkin 1974; Paloheimo 1971; Emlen 1966). Some of these models are difficult to operationalize, because they compound more than one variable simultaneously. The approach that I have followed involves treating a single variable (energy) for the purpose of hypothesis testing and then developing a systematic set of alternative hypotheses to explain deviations. These deviations, however, are actually few-- the fact that a substantial degree of correlation exists between the two types of biomass ranks suggests that for the items harvested, energy yields alone (in the form of biomass) are a robust predictor of foraging behavior.

Nevertheless, the deviations that do exist require examination. For humans, the following six categories can be offered as explanations for food preferences apart from species size or density, which have been directly incorporated into the model in the form of biomass values and encounter rates, and apart from handling costs, which have been indirectly incorporated into the model in establishing the optimum diet itself.

## Resource Aggregation

The spatial concentration of certain resources may make them highly advantageous to exploit (Hassan 1975), even though small size may make them individually unattractive owing to high handling times. The major advantage is reduced mobility cost (Wilmsen 1973; Harpending and Davis 1977; Gamble 1978). Typically, the solution is to match the aggregation of resources with an ecologically corresponding degree of aggregation of the hunting band (Lewis 1978; Wilmsen 1973). More mobile hunter-gatherers tend toward dispersed settlement patterns, matching their own distributions to those of their resources (unless the resources are unpredictable; cf. Wilmsen 1973 and Heffley, chapter 6, above). By matching site location to the location of resources, mobility cost to each resource is reduced. For terrestrial hunter-gatherers species biomass again becomes the controlling variable for species represented within the aggregation (as in the Aleutian case of marine invertebrates). Therefore, archeological biomass data *from each site location* should accurately reflect the density of each species. Any species present but not harvested presumably has a very low energy return per unit pursuit or handling cost.

However, for more sedentary hunter-gatherers, living in large units, such as coastal (or, to some extent, riverine) populations, the foraging distance from the settlement becomes more important. A greater percentage of foods are returned directly to a home base (frequently with the use of boats), resulting in a greater degree of what has been termed "central place foraging" (Orians and Pearson 1979). Resource aggregation itself also tends to be greater in coastal or riverine areas.

There are two types of resource aggregation (Brown and Orians 1970). The first type involves the coalescence of more than one species in a "patch" or particular portion of the hunter-gatherer exploitational area. For example, a salt lick might be an excellent place to hunt a number of species simultaneously. Essentially, this type of resource aggregation is a by-product of characteristics of the habitat, particularly its "patchiness."

The second type of aggregation results from the behavioral adaptations of various species, i.e., the tendency toward herding rather than solitary dispersion among species such as caribou.  Other species may "yard" or aggregate during specific times of the year (e.g., deer or moose).  In either case, many individuals can be hunted simultaneously. This type of aggregation pattern is advantageous to the hunter, even if species mobility is high, since storage or caching of meat may enable many individuals to be consumed even if the species is present in the area only for brief periods during the year.

## Ease of Exploitation

By this term I do not mean direct time or energy costs involved in the pursuit, capture, immobilization, retrieval, or processing of resources.  Instead, I am including here non-energy-related factors that make the pursuit process easier or more difficult.  One example of this would be *danger* associated with the exploitation of certain species. Clearly, certain species must be avoided to the degree to which there is a potential cost to life or limb of the hunter.  This particularly applies to various carnivorous or predatory species (Laughlin 1968).  Perhaps this factor could be included in an optimization hypothesis, if one could incorporate likelihood estimates of morbidity or mortality per encounter with different species.

## Nonfood Yield

Certain species may be valued for nonfood yield.  Skin, hair, feathers, or internal organs may be useful for the manufacture of clothing; sinew may be obtained to sew these items; other items (bird bills, feathers, turtle carapaces, seashells, antlers, teeth) may be valued for decorative purposes.  Bones, antlers, and teeth may all be useful for tool making, an important subsistence-related task for hunter-gatherers.  These returns are not accounted for in an energy currency model.

## Social Value

The "social value" of a particular species is frequently held responsible for nonoptimizing behavior.  A hypothesis of "social value" for foraging behavior is difficult to verify or refute in the archeological case, and for that reason is not the most attractive secondary hypothesis.

Social value may be offered as an explanation for either the favoring or the tabooing of certain species.  Social value is sometimes offered as the reason why groups place emphasis on the hunting of animals that are low in density (Carneiro 1978).  However, optimal foraging theory predicts that if the net energy return on the pursuit of a species is high enough so that it comes within the optimal diet breadth, then it will be harvested whatever its density.  In this case, social value is an ecologically unnecessary secondary hypothesis.  Species difficult to exploit are a different matter, however; if net return on pursuit is quite low, then the need of a secondary hypothesis of social value is more apparent. Such species, for example, may be quite large in size, offering a larger gross (as opposed to net) energy yield.  If "prestige" value is attached to a large but difficult-to-exploit animal, high energy expenditure may be mobilized in order to ensure high absolute rates of energy return.  Social value is therefore not an explanation for nonoptimizing behavior, but for the level at which energy is both expended and returned.

A different analysis, however, must be applied to the other end of the scale--food taboos.  Food taboos are usually offered to explain why animals are *not* favored in spite of their size, abundance, density, or ease of exploitation.  Again, however, an optimal foraging interpretation may suffice.  Density or abundance alone is not sufficient to place a species within the diet of an optimal forager, and neither is size unless it correlates with efficient harvesting.

For example, food taboos may be seen as a mechanism of preventing overexploitation of resources by limiting the exploitation of species with lower net recruitment rates (Slobodkin 1968). Such species may well yield high net returns on energy expended, but if intensively hunted would be easily overexploited. Food taboos would then be seen as counterweights to the idea of social value, in the sense that they may prevent the over-hunting of large, low-density species that also have low recruitment rates (McDonald 1977; Cooke 1978). However, an optimal foraging approach would postulate that, as heavily ex-ploited animals become rare, they would be less frequently encountered, and hence less ex-ploited. Food taboos would be necessary, then, only to the extent that humans fail to for-age optimally.

## Taste

Of all the explanations as to why people select certain foods, taste is the one most difficult to quantify. Taste depends on learned behavior, and thus varies substantially in different human cultures. Yet its basis is biological (Moskowitz, et al. 1975). Other animal species have "tastes," but these cannot be determined except by food preferences and the degree to which such preferences deviate from abundance or nutritional value.

These comments apply to humans as well as other animals. For example, Jochim (1976) has recently argued that the subcutaneous fat content of a species is the most important and reasonably accessible factor underlying its taste. He uses animal fat content as a taste variable *"f"* in developing equations relating to hunter-gatherer subsistence strate-gies. As evidence, Jochim cites several cases from Arctic (Eskimo) and subarctic (Indian) groups.

Several authors have noted that only when all foods concerned are relatively abundant does taste become a factor in determining food preferences. Silberbauer (1972) has shown this to be true of central Kalahari San; Lippold (1966) has argued similarly that food abundance and diversity allowed the prehistoric Aleuts to be "selective" in this manner.

Finally, the converse--rejection of species because of poor taste--should also be noted. This may represent simply a lack of fat content, as Jochim has argued, or the meat itself may have a bad flavor caused by rut or animal feeding habits. For example, carni-vores or scavengers are frequently avoided as food. In some cases, they may harbor greater numbers of parasites or disease microorganisms.

## Nutrition

Nutrition is a more easily quantified and falsifiable alternative hypothesis. For an omnivorous predator certain species offer higher concentrations of various nutrients per unit weight of flesh. The nutrients may be essential amino acids, vitamins, or minerals. Species offering higher concentrations of such nutrients may be favored, at least at cer-tain times of year, in spite of size or density constraints which give them a low energy value (Pulliam 1975; Westoby 1974 1978; Sih 1979; Keene 1979a, chapter 8, below). Unques-tionably, insufficient attention has been given to nutritional factors (both by animal ecologists and by anthropologists) in developing models of optimal foraging (Yesner 1979; Reidhead 1977; Reidhead and Limp 1974).

## Other Explanations

In addition one may also consider aspects of resources that are primarily *time-dynamic* in nature (Harpending and Bertram 1975): their predictability (changing patterns of pres-ence or absence in an area, or changing biomass yields even if present); and their vulnera-bility to long-term human predation. This subject is far too extensive to be considered here. Finally, "cultural lag" is sometimes cited as an explanation for nonoptimal behavior, but hypotheses such as this can contribute little to the present discussion.

We can now return to the Aleutian Islands example to evaluate the deviations from optimal foraging as predicted by the model presented earlier. Previously, it has been argued that "food preferences" affected the frequency with which prehistoric Aleuts exploited certain species (Lippold 1966). Our task, then, is to examine the six factors listed above to determine whether we can explain foraging behavior which does not completely correspond to that predicted by the model.

## Evaluating the Model

### Aggregation

As noted above, two types of aggregation that affect encounter rates may be relevant to the analysis of food preferences as a part of human hunting strategies. Of these, social or herding aggregation appears not to have been a factor in the Aleutian case. The colonial birds, for example (cormorants, murres, puffins, harlequin ducks, kittiwakes, and so on), do seem to have been favored in proportion to their abundance in the environment. Environmental patchiness, however, does appear to have been a factor underlying discrepancies in the Aleutian data. An example is the relative representation of albatrosses in the archeological record. Albatrosses were the greatest contributors to the avian portion of the prehistoric Aleut diet. They have an archeological biomass rank of 1, in contrast to a modern biomass rank of only 8 (table 7.6).[6] Why was this the case? Albatrosses are summer-fall visitors to the Aleutians, wintering in the south Pacific. The correlation of albatross archeological frequencies with those of fulmars and shearwaters, which also migrate to the Aleutians from the south Pacific during the same summer-fall period, is higher than correlations between frequencies of any other avian groups (Yesner 1976).[7] Shearwaters and fulmars, like albatrosses, are planktonic feeders, and are found today in large numbers in upwelling zones between islands where plankton is abundant. It is likely, then, as argued previously, that all three species were hunted together in the same environmental "patch." Thus, in the Aleut case, patchiness encouraged the simultaneous exploitation of multiple species, a large one (the short-tailed albatross) along with two abundant ones (shearwaters and fulmars).

### Ease of Exploitation

A few examples of foraging behavior apparently unrelated to considerations of energy efficiency can be demonstrated for the prehistoric Aleuts. Some species were evidently hunted extensively even if relatively dangerous to exploit. Eagles, for example, appear to have been favored by the Aleuts, evidently because their "social value" outweighed other considerations. Conversely, certain species such as ptarmigans were not exploited at all by the Aleuts, evidently because they live in the island interiors, and to hunt them would

---

6. The modern biomass was tabulated by summing the abundance of both modern species of albatross, the Laysan and black-footed albatrosses. This was necessary since the short-tailed albatross, which constituted ninety-five per cent of the archeological remains, has become nearly extinct in the past one hundred years, and has been replaced to some extent by the other species (Yesner 1976). Even if this method of tabulating the former abundance of albatrosses results in an underestimation, the difference in biomass ranks (1 in the prehistoric biomass versus 8 in the modern biomass) does indicate a nonoptimal preference in the hunting of these birds.

7. The correlations, however, were not high enough to violate the data independence assumptions of the Spearman ranked correlation coefficient test.

require a complete retooling of the Aleuts' otherwise exclusively maritime-oriented subsistence strategy.  Similar arguments have been made for the failure of the Haida Indians of the Queen Charlotte Islands to hunt terrestrial mammals.

### Nonfood Yield

Nonfood yield does appear to have been an important consideration in the extensive exploitation of certain species by the prehistoric Aleuts.  The best explanation, for example, as to why two species of eider ducks had a significantly higher representation in archeological than modern biomass ranks is that, in addition to their food value, the down of these birds was important for clothing.  Cormorants were also used for the manufacture of feather parkas (Veniaminov 1840; Jochelson 1933), and cormorant bones were favored for the manufacture of bone tools such as awls and needles.  At first glance, the nonfood yield of cormorants appears not to have had measurable effect on their archeological representation.  However, when one considers that "shags" (cormorants) are not universally considered very tasty food, nonfood yields become more important in explaining why they were used.

### Social Value

As indicated above, certain species such as eagles were important in various Aleut ritual observances; similar patterns are found among many American Indian groups (Parmalee 1975).  The reason for this ritual importance may lie in the similar behavior of man and other predators; an analogous argument has been made for the origin of subarctic bear cults.

### Taste

Certain species appear to have been avoided, at least in relation to their available biomass, for reasons of taste.  Among the Aleuts, gulls, jaegers, and oystercatchers, being scavengers, were probably avoided on the basis of taste.  Gulls, for example, even though extremely abundant, of large size, and present on a year-round basis (resulting in a modern biomass rank of 2), are not comparably abundant in the middens.  Cormorants were mentioned above.  Certain other species were probably favored by the Aleuts for reasons of taste, a judgment coincident with their nutritional status.

### Nutrition

Certain species appear to have been disproportionately favored because of their body fat content.  In the Aleutians, for example, some waterfowl contain higher percentages of fats.  This may have something to do with the intensive exploitation of particular species such as emperor geese (table 7.6).  Denniston (1973) gives evidence of other nutritional factors in the prehistoric Aleut diet, and Ransom (1946) discusses them from an ethnographic viewpoint.

The six factors listed above may be seen as explanatory devices for flaws in the proportional hunting hypothesis.  However, they should be viewed as modifications of the hypothesis, not necessarily as causes for its rejection.  Unfortunately, it is impossible at present to rank these six factors in order of importance for various environments or hunting and gathering groups.

## Discussion

If the data on prehistoric Aleut harvesting strategies may be taken as representative of general hunter-gatherer foraging strategies, the following points emerge:

Archeological data, particularly faunal remains, can be a good source for testing hypotheses concerning optimal foraging strategies.  As long as either the paleoenvironment can be reconstructed in detail, or ecological congruence can be shown between past and present environments, and as long as some control can be exercised over changes in settlement patterns and various taphonomic factors, rigorous hypothesis testing is possible with archeological data. It is even possible to use qualitative rather than quantitative data on species abundance to test such hypotheses, as long as the data are adjusted for seasonal changes in species presence or absence.

Other things being equal, the size and abundance of animal species, as measured by biomass values--as well as harvesting costs--are important determinants of optimal foraging strategies. (In the Aleut case, biomass values alone are a robust predictor of dietary preferences.) Certain species are included as part of the optimal diet of hunter-gatherers, primarily for reasons of energy efficiency. Among the species that are exploited, individuals tend to be taken "as encountered," resulting in what I have termed "proportional" (as opposed to truly "random") hunting. These "fine-grained" foraging strategies are as characteristic of human hunter-gatherers as of any other large carnivore.

The following factors seem to be most important in explaining individual cases where optimal behavior is not proportional to biomass: species aggregation and environmental patchiness; ease of resource exploitation (unrelated to energy costs); nonfood yields; social value; taste factors; and nutritional value.

### Appendix 1: Common Names for Bird Species in Table 7.6

| Scientific Name | Common Name |
| --- | --- |
| *Phalacrocoras pelagicus* | Pelagic cormorant |
| *Larus glaucescens* | Glaucous-winged gull |
| *Uria* spp. | Murres |
| *Lunda cirrhata* | Tufted puffin |
| *Fulmarus glacialis* | Northern fulmar |
| *Anas crecca* | Green-winged teal |
| *Diomedea albatrus* | Short-tailed albatross |
| *Haliaeetus leucocephalus* | Bald eagle |
| *Histrionicus histrionicus* | Harlequin duck |
| *Rissa tridactyla* | Black-legged kittiwake |
| *Gavia immer* | Common loon |
| *Somateria mollissima* | Common eider |
| *Phalacrocorax urile* | Red-faced cormorant |
| *Gavia stellata* | Red-throated loon |
| *Anas platyrhynchos* | Common mallard |
| *Corvus corax* | Common raven |
| *Falco peregrinus* | Peregrine falcon |
| *Haematopus bachmani* | Oystercatcher |
| *Olor* spp. | Swans |
| *Philacte canagica* | Emperor goose |
| *Phalacrocorax auritus* | Double-crested cormorant |
| *Somateria spectabilis* | King eider |
| *Mergus merganser* | Common merganser |
| *Branta nigricans* | Black brant |

Appendix 2: Method Adopted for Estimating Biomass
from Qualitative Data on Bird Species Abundance

The five qualitative codes used by the U. S. Fish and Wildlife Service to estimate seasonal bird abundance ("abundant," "common," "occasional," "unusual," and "rare") were converted into numbers by substituting the constants "1," "2," "3," "4," and "5," respectively.

The numbers for each species were then averaged over the four seasons and the result rounded to the nearest whole number.

The figure obtained for each species was then transformed into a relative order of magnitude, substituting "$10^2$," "$10^1$," "$10^0$," "$10^{-1}$," and "$10^{-2}$," respectively, for the "1," "2," "3," "4," and "5" designations.

For each species the relative order of magnitude of species abundance was multiplied by the mean weight for a single individual of that species, yielding the species archeobiomass. Seasonal weight changes were averaged wherever possible. If the species was present only during part of the year, and seasonal weights were available, only weights applicable to the time of residence were used.

A total avian biomass estimate was obtained by summing over all species, so that the biomass for each could be expressed as a percentage of the total.

This method tends to underestimate biomass for seasonal species. Therefore, a second method was developed that transforms each of the "1" to "5" codes into a relative order of magnitude *before* averaging over the four seasons of the year. In other words, the orders of magnitude themselves were averaged over the four seasons. Following this, the "average" orders of magnitude were again multiplied by mean species weights to yield the species archeobiomass. This method tends to *over*estimate slightly the biomass of seasonal species. As applied, the methods produce roughly equivalent results.

# 8

# Optimal Foraging in a Nonmarginal Environment: A Model of Prehistoric Subsistence Strategies in Michigan

Arthur S. Keene

## Objectives

Current theories of hunter-gatherer behavior rely heavily on ethnographic description of extant foragers inhabiting marginal or extreme environments, that is, those environments which are the least productive in terms of resources necessary for human subsistence. In building models of human foraging adaptations, anthropologists frequently invoke data on the Inuit, the Cree, or the Kalahari San. Our knowledge of hunter-gatherers in more benevolent environments is severely limited. Yet, if we hope to build realistic, general models, we must base our assumptions and theories on knowledge of a broad spectrum of human foraging adaptations, including those associated with a variety of nonmarginal settings. Unfortunately, a large segment of this behavior is no longer accessible ethnographically or ethnohistorically. In the temperate forests of North America, for example, food production largely replaced foraging in the prehistoric period. Therefore, if we hope to work from a representative data base, the problem must be approached archeologically (see also Wobst 1978).

An archeological approach, however, is not without problems. Archeologists studying prehistoric foragers have traditionally relied on a limited number of sites with unusually rich archeological assemblages and well-preserved faunal and floral remains. There has been a tendency to focus on those sites with the highest visibility, the greatest accessibility, and the largest material inventories. Such a strategy does not provide an unbiased sample. Our current knowledge of prehistoric foraging adaptations may thus be based on a sample skewed by biases introduced through the processes which form the archeological record (i.e., the natural and cultural processes which select for what is preserved archeologically [Schiffer 1976; Binford 1976 1978]), as well as biases in previous research designs. In attempting to transcend the limitations of the archeological record, paleoanthropologists have developed behavioral models that generate predictions about behavior which may not be clearly manifest in material remains (e.g., Jochim 1976; Keene 1979a; Wobst 1974).

Anthropology has often benefited from models initially developed in other disciplines. Recent work (Keene 1979ab; Perlman 1976; E. A. Smith 1978; Winterhalder 1977) suggests that our understanding of hunting and gathering adaptations can be enhanced by examining previous

I am grateful to Van Reidhead, John Speth, R. Brooke Thomas, and H. Martin Wobst for comments and criticisms on previous drafts of this paper.

empirical and theoretical research on the behavior of nonhuman foragers (e.g., Emlen 1968; MacArthur and Pianka 1966; Norberg 1977; Pyke, et al. 1977; Schoener 1971). Such research raises important questions about the nature of foraging which are significant to the study of human foragers as well. For example, in our studies we will want to consider which factors govern the processes of food selection among human foragers. Which resources will be exploited at specific times of the year and under specific environmental conditions? Where will these resources be acquired and in what quantities? What is the optimum foraging group size for a given environment or a given prey? What territory size can be exploited with maximum security and efficiency? In sum, what are optimal subsistence strategies? To what extent do observed patterns differ from the optimum and why? If we hope to understand the reasons for stability and change in human subsistence strategies, and especially the shift from foraging to food production, we must consider these questions in detail.

Optimal foraging theory (Pyke, et al. 1977; Krebs 1978; Maynard Smith 1978) has been effectively used by evolutionary ecologists to develop models which deal with the aforementioned questions with respect to nonhuman foragers. Such theory attempts to explicate strategies of predation or adaptation which are optimal with respect to specific criteria (generally those strategies which maximize the fitness or survival potential of the individual or population). Winterhalder (1977) and E. A. Smith (1978) have shown that optimal foraging theory can be equally enlightening for the study of contemporary hunter-gatherers. Keene (1979ab), Perlman (1976), Yesner (chapter 7, above) and Moore (chapter 9, below) have also relied on optimal foraging theory in the study of historic and prehistoric foraging patterns.

Previous chapters in this volume have examined the problems of optimal diet composition, optimal group size, and optimal foraging space. These models have relied primarily on energy as a "currency" (Maynard Smith 1978) to be optimized. In this chapter, I will concentrate solely on the problem of food selection (optimal diet) among hunter-gatherers and will utilize a currency which considers, in addition to energy, an array of critical nutrients as well as risk. The primary questions to be considered here are: What factors influence the food procurement decisions of hunter-gatherers? How do hunter-gatherers schedule their utilization of resources, and how may this scheduling change in response to specific perturbations to the natural and human ecosystem? How do these theoretically optimal patterns compare with observed behavior? In an attempt to deal with these questions, I have developed a model which predicts the optimal food procurement schedule among hunter-gatherers under specific conditions of resource distribution, availability, and abundance. The model is theoretically grounded in evolutionary ecology and uses a method known as linear programming, an optimization technique frequently employed by economists and ecologists in problems of resource allocation.

In the following pages, I will first present some background on the method and theory on which the model is based. The model incorporates an unconventional measure of cost and utility (currency), and therefore a major portion of the chapter elaborates on the development of this measure. This model has been applied elsewhere (Keene 1979b) to the study of hunting and gathering adaptations in a nonmarginal environment, specifically the deciduous forest of southern Michigan during the Late Archaic period (4000-1000 B.C.); and the results of this application will be briefly reviewed. The implications of these results will then be discussed, and the value of such models to the study of hunter-gatherers and more specifically to archeological problems will be evaluated.

## Method and Theory

### Assumptions

The model of optimal food procurement is based on six assumptions. While these assumptions are simplistic, they are necessary for the operation of these particular models. By starting with the simplest of assumptions, it is easy to identify the complicating variables. These assumptions are outlined briefly below and are discussed at length in Keene (1979b:16-25).

Assumption 1:  Economic activities among hunter-gatherers are patterned.

Human groups make decisions with respect to the specific needs and means of members of the population. These decisions are manifest in patterned activities or strategies.

Assumption 2:  Economic activity among hunter-gatherers is directed toward providing the basic nutritive and other raw materials necessary for the survival of members of the population.

This model deals solely with the biological needs of members of populations. The full set of these needs may not be consciously recognized by the population. The human organism requires an array of critical nutrients: energy, vitamins, minerals, and amino acids in order to remain viable. In addition to satisfying dietary needs, the organism must cope with certain stresses to ensure its vitality (for example, protecting the body from excessive temperature changes). Such needs may be satisfied through the acquisition of both food resources (e.g., for maintaining proper body temperature) and nonfood resources (e.g., for clothing, fuel, and shelter). For a population to remain viable, individuals must be maintained at a healthy level. It is assumed that the primary goal of hunter-gatherers will be to satisfy their basic life requirements. In this respect, nonhuman models apply well to human foragers. It is assumed that there is selection across time in favor of behaviors which satisfy these requirements, and that this satisfaction is facilitated through cultural mechanisms which govern food preferences and choices.

Assumption 3:  When faced with a choice between two resources of equal utility, the one of lowest cost will be chosen.

*Utility* refers to the value or payoff associated with a decision. Typically, in predator-prey studies, utility is a measure of the gross energy yield of a prey. In this model, utility is a measure of the combined nutritional and nonfood value of a given resource. Here, utility is quantified in terms of ten critical nutrients and one nonfood value (see below).

*Cost* may be defined in terms of what the decision maker must give up as a result of a decision. It is the "price paid" in order to receive the payoff. Cost is often measured in terms of time invested or energy expended in capturing a prey. Here, cost is regarded as a complex function of time invested, energy expended, and risk incurred. Thus, the assumption states that, with all other things being equal, hunter-gatherers will adopt the strategy which requires the least effort and involves the least risk. However, all other things are rarely equal.

Assumption 4:  Faced with an array of resources of varying costs and varying utilities, hunter-gatherers will attempt to select the combination of resources which can satisfy their basic needs at the lowest possible cost.

In this model, hunter-gatherers are faced with the problem of allocating time, energy, and risk among alternative ends--satisfaction of a variety of food and nonfood needs with resources of varying utility.  This is in contrast to most predator-prey models, in which the predator typically has a single task, satisfying a daily energy ration with the least possible effort (Schoener 1971).

Assumption 5:  Resources are finite.

There are limits to the amount of any given resource that can be acquired in a given amount of time using a given technology.  The effects of any perturbation to a subsistence system, either internal or external (e.g., population increase, technological change, resource depletion, or shifting resource distribution) can be modeled in terms of changes in costs and/or limits of resource exploitation.

The model incorporates only one cultural variable explicitly--technology.  Yet it can be seen that any of the parameters which define the model can be extended through cultural means.  For example, risk, an important factor in calculating costs, can be ameliorated through a number of cultural means such as reciprocity, redistribution, food storage, and information sharing.  Exploitation limits can be increased through changes in technology, pursuit strategies, or territory size.  It is assumed that any change in subsistence patterns can be modeled in terms of changes in the parameters which define the model (see Winterhalder, chapter 2, above, for a similar argument).

Assumption 6:  In this model, population is treated as an independent variable in a closed system.

An initial population size is established a priori by the modeler, and the consequences of specific conditions and decisions are examined given that population size.  In this case, the population size was arbitrarily set at twenty-five and held constant.  The time span of this model is one year; however, both population size and time span can easily be varied.  The basic food procurement model assumes that there is no interaction with other populations (e.g., trade, competition, or information flow).  It is not within the scope of this model to investigate specific demographic problems, though the implications of certain population trends can be examined using the model results.

## Linear Programming Models

### Currency

Economic models in anthropology have often measured cost and benefit solely in terms of efficiency of energy capture (e.g., Lee 1968; Perlman 1976; Rappaport 1968; Smith 1979b; Thomas 1973; Winterhalder 1977).  It is assumed in evolutionary ecology that fitness varies directly with the efficiency of energy capture.  It is argued that the time freed from activities devoted to energy capture can be devoted to activities which ensure reproductive success or increase fitness, such as the search for mates, or predator avoidance (Krebs 1978; Maynard Smith 1978; Pianka 1978:257-60).  The merits of using net energy efficiency have been demonstrated in a number of chapters in this volume (see also Smith 1979b; Winterhalder 1977); therefore, I will not review them here.  One problem associated with using energy as a currency, however, is that cost and utility are measured in terms of a single variable, net energy efficiency (i.e., energy gained over energy expended).  Hence, other critical requirements may be ignored.  This may result in misleading conclusions, particularly in situations where energy is not limiting and utility is thus largely a function of other variables (see below; Keene 1979a; Vayda and McCay 1975).

To avoid this problem, I have attempted to develop an alternative currency and a

measure of utility which consider a number of variables (Keene 1979a).  These measures
offer a more realistic and perhaps more precise currency than energy efficiency, but the
precision is achieved at the expense of some generality (Levins 1966:422; see also below).

Consideration of multiple variables requires multivariate methods.  Linear programming
is a well-established multivariate technique designed to deal with problems of resource
allocation (Hillier and Lieberman 1974; Wagner 1975; Walters and Hilborn 1978).  Recently,
it has found increasing use in the field of anthropology (see Reidhead 1979 for a review).
Programming is the mathematics of allocating limited resources among competing activities
in an optimal manner.  A program is simply a plan or schedule of activities which best satisfies a specified goal among all feasible alternatives.  The goal is defined in terms of
maximizing or minimizing a function of several variables subject to certain constraints,
for example, maximizing production or minimizing cost subject to the availability of capital, labor, or raw materials.

The use of linear programming necessitates the construction of a mathematical model
to describe the problem of concern.  With linear programming, all mathematical functions
contained in the model must be linear.  The model is phrased as a series of linear equali-
ties and inequalities which are solved simultaneously, usually with the assistance of a
computer algorithm.  It is not the purpose of this chapter to provide an introduction to
the construction and mechanics of linear programming models, as this has been done elsewhere (Reidhead 1976 1979; Keene 1979ab).  Therefore, I will just briefly summarize how
such a problem is set up.

A linear programming problem may be visualized as a matrix, such as the one presented
in figure 8.1.  In this case, the problem is to calculate the optimum resource use schedule
which satisfies the biological needs of the population at the lowest possible cost.  The

|  |  | Resources | | | Requirements | |
|---|---|---|---|---|---|---|
|  |  | Bear | Beaver | ... | n | B |
| Nutrients and Nonfood | Energy 1 | $a_{11}$ | $a_{12}$ | ... | $a_{1n}$ | $b_1$ |
|  | Protein 2 | $a_{21}$ | $a_{22}$ | ... | $a_2$ | $b_2$ |
|  | Calcium 3 | $a_{31}$ | $a_{32}$ | ... | $a_{3n}$ | $b_3$ |
|  | $m$ | $a_{m1}$ | $a_{m2}$ | ... | $a_{mn}$ | $b_m$ |
| Costs | $c$ | $c_1$ | $c_2$ | ... | $c_n$ |  |

Figure 8.1.  Sample Matrix.

column vectors of the matrix represent available resources, and the rows, the nutritional
and nonfood values of the resources.  Thus, item $a_{32}$ represents the value of the third
nutrient, calcium, for the second resource, beaver.  Item $a_{ij}$ represents the value of the
$i$th element for the $j$th resource, and so on.  Two additional vectors are considered.  The
far right-hand column, or $\vec{b}$ vector, represents the constraints of the model, or the minimum
requirements which must be satisfied.  The bottom row, or cost vector, represents the cost

of each individual resource, i.e., the cost associated with each column. The problem, then, is to minimize:

$$z = \sum_{j=1}^{n} c_j x_j \qquad j = (1, 2, 3, \ldots, n) \tag{1}$$

subject to

$$b_i = \sum_{j=1}^{n} a_{ij} x_j \qquad i = (1, 2, 3, \ldots, m) \tag{2}$$

where $z$ = the total cost of production, $c_j$ = the cost of resource $j$, $x_j$ = the amount of resource $j$ acquired, and $b_i$ = the minimum requirement for constraint $i$. The result of this calculation is the optimal solution, that is, the set of resources in appropriate quantities which satisfies the right-hand side at the lowest possible cost (for elaboration see Cooper and Steinberg 1974; Keene 1979ab; Reidhead 1979; Wagner 1975).

In addition to providing an optimal solution, most linear programming algorithms provide supplemental data, known as *postoptimal* information, which can contribute to more meaningful interpretations of results. Two kinds of postoptimal information are generally provided: (1) indication of the *binding constraints* of the model; and (2) measures of sensitivity.

*Binding constraints*. A binding constraint is simply the constraint in the model which has not been satisfied when all other constraints have been satisfied at the lowest possible cost. It represents the critical element of those being considered which is in shortest supply (Pianka 1978:90-91). This does not mean that these elements are lacking or deficient in the diet, but does indicate that, of all elements considered, these are present in the least amount. In other words, they are the requirements most difficult to satisfy. In satisfying all other requirements at lowest possible cost, the binding constraints will remain unfulfilled. Satisfying these requirements as well will further increase the cost of production. Therefore, it is the binding constraints which have the greatest effect on the composition of the optimal solution, since the model will "key" on those resources which can most efficiently satisfy these constraints.

*Sensitivity measures*. Typically, in formulating an optimization problem, we have to estimate some of the quantitative input. Thus, it would be useful to know over what range these input values can vary without altering the optimal solution. If the range is large, and the current value is at the center of the range, we can assume that the model is stable and not sensitive to changes in that particular value or errors in its estimation. However, if the range is small, then the model is sensitive to this particular value, and this sensitivity must be considered in interpreting the results. An indication of the sensitivity of model variables is *shadow prices*. Shadow prices are statements of marginal cost or value. For resources, shadow prices indicate the change in cost necessary before the composition of the optimal solution will change. For resources which are not included in the optimal resource schedule, shadow prices tell us the cost reduction necessary before these resources would be used. For resources which have been expended (used to their maximum available limits), shadow prices indicate how much of an increase in cost would be tolerable before these resources would no longer be used to their maximum. For constraints (in this case nutrients or raw materials), shadow prices indicate the cost of increasing or decreasing the requirement by a single unit (e.g., increasing protein requirements by a single gram). Shadow prices thus indicate the range over which input values may vary without altering the composition of the optimal solution. They provide, in effect, a confidence interval for costs or other quantitative input, a range over which we need not worry about changes in values or errors in estimation.

To summarize, the model consists of a body of quantified variables. The resources available to the foraging population are identified, and associated with each is a cost and a utility. Associated with each cost and utility is a shadow price indicating the variation in these quantitative values that is possible without altering the optimal solution.

## Cost

Clearly, the key to building such a model lies in the development of a reliable currency, in this case a measure of cost. I have previously attempted to develop a cost measure which would express relative differences in acquisition cost based on the distributional characteristics of resources (Keene 1979a). A similar approach was used by Jochim (1976) in attempting to build a general measure of resource utility. The measure I used was theoretically grounded in previous models of optimal feeding strategies among nonhuman foragers. The same measure was modified slightly for use in this study.

Ecological studies on animal feeding strategies have generally divided the food acquisition process into two stages, search and pursuit (Norberg 1977; Pyke, et al. 1977; Schoener 1971). Search time ($T_s$) can be regarded as the time invested in locating a resource. Pursuit time ($T_p$) refers to the time from detection of prey until the time that capture and consumption is completed. While it does not appear that actual consumption time should be a critical consideration in this model, the costs of making food consumable are a significant and important consideration. In the following discussion, the cost of pursuit and the cost of processing for consumption will be considered separately.

Search time is often calculated as an inverse function of the density of food available (Norberg 1977:514; Schoener 1971:377), or

$$T_s \propto d^{-1} \tag{3}$$

Search time would be expected to decrease as overall resource density increases, since higher resource density would increase the probability of encounter. It can be suggested that random search is not really applicable to human foragers, primarily because of the advantages of shared and culturally stored information. Since hunters know the habitat types preferred by a species, we can assume that they have evolved reasonably efficient search strategies which tend to maximize hunter-prey contacts (Marks 1976:217). Thus there is a systematic element to search time which should permit the hunter to narrow his range. Marks (1977b:25) supports this idea of systematic foraging, noting that "hunters do not indiscriminately stalk every animal or group they encounter but orient themselves toward certain species," specifically those which appear the most vulnerable.

When search is not random, and when predator and prey are mobile, mobility must also be taken into consideration. Mobility is actually a multicomponent attribute (Jochim 1976: 27). One component relates to absolute mobility or the distance covered by a prey species in a given time (i.e., speed); another refers to the regularity of spatial behavior, or locatability, of a resource. If the location of a resource can be predicted, search time will be reduced. Animals which move in a systematic or predictable pattern would be less costly to exploit than those with random patterns of movement. Likewise, among populations with equivalent densities, search time should be less for more sedentary resources than for those which undergo large-scale regional movements. It is assumed that search time will increase as resource mobility increases and resource density decreases (see also Jochim

1976:77). In this study mobility is measured as the seasonal range of prey species and is considered as an indicator of resource predictability.

In his work among the Cree, Winterhalder (1977) observed that among resources with low predictability, mobility may actually decrease search time. In such cases hunters look for tracks or other directive signs rather than for the animal itself. A highly mobile animal would produce more directive signs and thus have a lower search cost (assuming the tracks could be followed and an encounter would ultimately result). Thus, it is possible that under conditions of random search, resource mobility may decrease search costs. However, in this model, as noted above, it is assumed that search and encounter are not totally random.

Pursuit time often is estimated as the amount of time necessary to run down a prey after the prey is located. Tracking would thus be regarded as an aspect of search rather than pursuit. Pursuit success is a function of the ability of the prey to detect and escape the forager and is often calculated as a function of predator speed, prey speed, predator field of vision, and prey field of vision (Schoener 1971:378). Human predators generally rely on technology rather than speed to capture prey (see Laughlin 1968:117). The major component of pursuit time thus lies in the stalk, that is, the interval of time between the sighting of the prey and initiation of capture. Marks (1976:233) notes that as the initial distance between hunters and prey increases, the odds of failure also increase (see also Marshall 1978:135). I suggest that the critical component of stalking time may be approximated in terms of a critical distance ($q$) as follows:

$$q = (D_1 - D_2) \tag{4}$$

where $D_1$ is the distance at which a predator is perceived by a given prey species and $D_2$ is the distance from which the predator can strike.

We would expect pursuit time to increase as critical distance increases. We would also expect the probability of success to increase as critical distance decreases. Pursuit time would additionally decrease as resource aggregation size increases, since higher aggregations increase the probability of successful pursuit and also the probable yield per hunt. Some animals such as caribou become much less wary in the presence of a large herd (Banfield 1974:385); however, others, such as bison, become more wary in large groups (Wheat 1972:87). Yet Wheat (1972:87-89) points out that the tendency of large bison herds to stampede when frightened made them particularly easy prey for mass slaughter. In general, we would expect the probability of successful pursuit to be higher for large aggregations of prey than for individuals. Pursuit time obviously is not a major consideration in the exploitation of plant resources: pursuit in these cases amounts to the time it takes to walk to the plant after it has been sighted. However, we would expect total pursuit time to be less for plants exhibiting clumped or aggregated rather than dispersed distribution patterns.

Consumption and processing time is difficult to estimate. As was noted above, the critical cost factor to the hunter would not be in actual consumption of a resource but in making the food consumable. Thus, butchering and food-processing costs are the major components of consumption time ($T_c$). In a previous study (Keene 1979a) I assumed that consumption and processing time could be roughly approximated as a function of animal weight; that is, as animal size goes up, processing time increases proportionately. This simplifying assumption cannot be used, however, when plant resources enter into the analysis, for with plant resources there appears to be little relationship between weight and processing time. For example, the cost of processing nuts involves search, collection, hulling,

cracking, pounding, and sometimes leaching or boiling (Keene 1979b:117-24; Reidhead 1976).
The labor associated with producing grapes includes search, collection, and sometimes dry-
ing.  The effort which goes into producing a kilogram of edible food from nuts far exceeds
that required for grapes.  For lack of a better measure, the plant and animal resources in
the study were rank ordered according to estimated total processing time (see Keene 1979b:
44, 227).  The rank ($y$) serves as a coefficient of processing cost.  Since there appeared
to be little difference in the processing time between certain resources, some were given
the same rank.

In summary, search time decreases as prey mobility decreases and as density increases
or:

$$T_s \; \alpha \; m/d \tag{5}$$

However, this approximation produces a rather small value in relation to the estimates for
pursuit and consumption time.  Since empirically, search time is a major component in the
cost of acquisition of animal resources, the coefficient has been corrected by a constant
($k$) (in this case arbitrarily set at 100) to make the estimate of search time more compat-
ible with the other estimates.  Thus:

$$T_s \; \alpha \; k(m/d) \tag{6}$$

Pursuit time decreases as critical distance decreases and aggregation size increases or:

$$T_p \; \alpha \; q/a \tag{7}$$

A final factor to consider in the construction of a cost measure is the concept of
risk.  Risk can be defined as the probability of a loss or the possibility of an unfortu-
nate outcome (Wiessner 1977:5).  Inherent in risk in predation are two separate components.
The first involves risk to the personal well-being of the decision maker.  The pursuit of
certain species of animals, such as bear, or the utilization of certain hunting areas, such
as thin ice, may entail specific hazards for the hunter which can figure into the decision
process.  Nelson (1969:377) notes: "The Eskimos seem to have an unspoken concept of 'percentage risk.'  Thus a certain activity might be done without danger eight out of ten times,
but because of this twenty per cent risk, the Eskimo seldom carries on the activity as long
as it can be avoided."

Another important, and perhaps more significant, aspect of risk concerns the security
of a resource, or the risk of coming home empty-handed.  Lee (1968) demonstrates that the
!Kung emphasize gathered vegetable foods in their diet because these items are so readily
accessible and so reliable.  Among the !Kung, hunting is a relatively high-risk, low-return
activity in terms of energy production, whereas gathering is a relatively low-risk activity
and provides a high return.  Wiessner (1977) has recorded the importance of risk in influencing modes of exchange among the !Kung.  Johnson (1971), Ortiz (1967), and Nietschmann
(1973) have demonstrated the significance of the risk of "crop failure" or failure of a production strategy on decision making in nonforaging subsistence economies.  And Jochim (1976:
50-53) and Wilmsen (1973:6-10) have shown that resource security is a primary factor in the
determination of site location and group composition among hunter-gatherers.  This aspect of
risk is to some extent subsumed in the calculation of search and pursuit costs; however, it
is also important to make the distinction between long-term and short-term risks.  It may be
more risky to focus on stable but poor producers than to focus on less secure resources which
will ultimately return high yields (E. A. Smith, pers. comm.).  In other words, in the long
run, a more risky resource might be the most effective for satisfying requirements.

Risk will vary in importance depending on the presence of food storage, food-sharing

practices, and the degree of information sharing. Group size and relative food abundance
will also effect risk. There is always a risk associated with any procurement strategy
(i.e., a risk of failure), but this risk can be ameliorated through cultural means such as
those mentioned above. Let us assume that this basic risk, exclusive of cultural ameliora-
tion, can be evaluated with reference to resource predictability. Predictability can be
partially approximated in terms of resource stability. Highly stable resources whose numbers, movements, and location change little from year to year may be regarded as relatively
secure. Less secure would be resources susceptible to regular or periodic fluctuations in
population size or that undertake mass migrations. These resources would not be consistently available, but the decision maker would at least have some idea of when a shortage
was imminent. Even less secure would be those resources subject to erratic fluctuations
in numbers, range, and location. We would thus expect cost of acquisition ($c$) to decrease
as total risk decreases. Resources in this model were classified as low, moderate, and
high risk based on predictability and were assigned risk coefficients ($r$) of 1, 1.25, and
1.5, respectively. Admittedly, this is not a particularly satisfying way to accommodate
the problem. The coefficients are arbitrary and can be manipulated to alter results; however, given the level of generality of the data used in this study and the lack of a better
measure, the risk coefficients appear to be a tolerable option for the present. Cases
where the risk coefficient may have significantly affected the final solution may be isolated in the final analysis and dealt with on an individual basis.

The cost measure used in this study, taking into consideration search, pursuit, and
processing expenditures, and risk, is represented by the following formula:

$$c = (T_s + T_p + T_c)r \tag{8}$$

or

$$c = [(m/d)k + (q/a) + y]r \tag{9}$$

This cost coefficient is an artificial measure. It cannot be converted into hourly labor
input, caloric expenditure, or any other absolute value. However, it should approximate
relative differences in acquisition cost. Naturally, a coefficient such as this one, which
is based partially on manufactured parameters such as risk, contains a significant potential for error. The reader is cautioned that the numbers themselves are of limited value
unless considered within the broader context of the postoptimal analysis. Ideally, we
would like to use empirically verifiable curves to represent cost functions; however, for
archeological applications this is rarely possible. Appropriate ethnographic analogs are
often not available for certain archeological contexts. Until a means of generating a
more accurate measure is developed, the approach advocated here seems to be a viable alternative.

### Linearity and Costs

The discussion has been based on the premise that cost bears a linear relationship to
production when, in fact, cost is usually a curvilinear function of production (Keene 1979b:
56-65).[1] In the case of foraging within a circumscribed area, the cost of acquiring a
given prey should increase with each successive individual taken (as a result of the relationship between decreasing density and increasing search time). If foraging continues,
cost should eventually increase to the point where it is no longer profitable to forage

---

1. Linear programming models can accommodate nonlinear functions through a method
known as separable programming, in which a curvilinear function is broken up into several
small linear segments. The problem is then solved with a standard linear programming algorithm (Hillier and Lieberman 1974).

within that area.  This is essentially a simplified extension of Charnov's (1976) marginal
value theorem, which predicts when a forager should abandon an environmental patch in favor
of a new patch.  Charnov (1976:131) maintains that a predator possessing prior knowledge
of expected yields across all patches should leave a patch when capture rate in the patch
drops to the average capture rate for the entire habitat.  In other words, the average
yield in a given territory will eventually decline to the point where it is lower than the
average yield across all territories.  In modeling predation, the rate at which cost increases at the margin is largely dependent on the size of the circumscribed area.  I have
argued elsewhere (Keene 1979b:67-69) that because of the relative abundance of food resources in the temperate forest of southern Michigan during the Late Archaic period, increasing marginal cost owing to decreasing resource density should not be a significant
consideration in these models.  Therefore, I have employed an *average cost* measure, a common practice in optimization problems (Driebeek 1961:61), though not without drawbacks.

The use of an average cost value may mask the effects of temporal variability in costs.
The validity of the average cost value can be considered, however, in a sensitivity analysis
of the model results.  Cost was calculated for each resource in the model using equation
(9) above.  Since the cost of utilizing a resource varies according to mode of preparation,
stored and fresh resources were treated as separate variables in the model.

## Utility

Resource utility was measured in terms of ten nutrients critical to the human diet:
energy, protein, calcium, iron, phosphorous, vitamin A, thiamine, riboflavin, ascorbic
acid (vitamin C), and niacin.  These obviously do not encompass all nutrients essential to
human nutrition but represent a sample of those nutrients most frequently quantified in the
literature.  Nonfood needs were also considered.  The ethnographic literature suggests that
among populations in northern woodlands and boreal and Arctic environments, a primary nonfood requirement is raw material for the manufacture of clothing (Foote 1965; Gramly 1977;
Rasmussen 1931; Rogers 1967).  Nonfood value is measured here in terms of hides which are
suitable for producing clothing.  While it is recognized that human populations have a wide
variety of nonfood needs, it is assumed that fulfilling minimum clothing requirements is
the most essential of these needs.  Each resource in this model was assigned a hide value,
with deer used as the reference standard (Keene 1979b:253).

Resource utility will vary seasonally and with the mode of preparation.  In some mammals, seasonal depletion of subcutaneous fat reserves may result in a loss of sixty per
cent of the fall maximum weight (a 77% decrease in the energy content of the animal) (Mech,
et al. 1968; Keene 1979b:71, 241).  All resource values in this study have been adjusted for
seasonal changes in body composition.  Different modes of food processing can significantly
alter the nutritional composition of a food resource.  All resource values were adjusted
to account for losses in cooking or preparation.  Again, stored and fresh foods were
treated as separate variables (Keene 1979b:242-46).  All requirements were calculated
relative to specific standards for age and sex.  Age-sex composition of the model population was established based on Weiss's (1973:119) model table MT 15-50.

## Net Productivity

A final consideration in building the model is the net productivity of a resource.
Assumption 5 states that the amount of any resource available for procurement is limited.
Usually, among human foragers, these limits are far below the gross productivity of the
environment.  What then limits procurement among human foragers?  I have argued elsewhere
(Keene 1979ab) that, among human foragers using a rudimentary technology, exploitation

limits are not generally density dependent (cf. Paine 1973; Laughlin 1968), but rather that
exploitation is limited by technology (and, in the case of migratory prey, access time and
mobility). In building a linear programming model, it is possible to establish a priori
limitations on the exploitation or production of a given variable. Previous models of
human foraging have often established limits of production in terms of safe sustainable
yields, usually the recruitment rate of a given species (Smith 1975:21-26; Reidhead 1976).
Yet, for most aboriginal hunters, the limits of exploitation will be far below the maximum
sustainable yield. Thus, net productivity is a difficult variable to estimate. I have
cautioned that one can easily manipulate the results of a model such as this, simply by altering the maximum limits of exploitation (contrast Keene 1979a and Reidhead 1976 with
Keene 1979b). Therefore, in the model discussed below, no a priori limits were placed on
the exploitation of resources. Note that this places no control on potential overexploitation of resources in the model solution. Overexploitation is possible; however, it was not
predicted in the model solutions. The implications of using an unbounded model are discussed more extensively in Keene (1979b).

## Overview of Structure

To reiterate, the problem is to calculate the optimum schedule of resource utilization
for a group of Late Archaic hunter-gatherers under specified conditions of resource availability, distribution, and abundance, and given a set of one nonfood and ten dietary needs
which must be satisfied. Since cost of acquisition and resource utility vary seasonally,
a number of separate models were constructed, one for each month of the year for an average
year. Model input represents a substantial body of data which cannot possibly be summarized
here. These data and the methods used in their collection are documented fully in Keene
(1979b:74-252).

## Model of Late Archaic Subsistence

The model is used to analyze hunter-gatherer adaptation within the deciduous forest
of southern Michigan during the Late Archaic period. The Saginaw Valley (figure 8.2), the
focus of this study, has been intensively investigated since the turn of the century
(Smith 1901; Hinsdale 1931; Dustin 1968; Fitting 1972; Taggart 1967; Ozker 1977). During
the Late Archaic period, Saginaw Bay extended inland into the low-lying areas of the
Saginaw Basin to form a large shallow lake or embayment. The embayment, also known as
Shiawassee Bay, offered a highly productive environment for human foragers, and Late Archaic sites are abundant on the fossil beaches demarcating its margins (Fitting 1975;
Keene 1979b). While the area has been well studied, many questions regarding prehistoric
subsistence in the area remain unanswered (Taggart 1967; Peebles 1978). The Saginaw Valley
is representative of a "typical" archeological data set. Preservation of organic remains
in the area is poor as a result of highly acid soil conditions. Site survey has not been
systematic. It has focused on the most visible and accessible sites and has been largely
limited to the area that constituted the fossil shoreline of Shiawassee Bay. River valley
and upland areas have been for the most part ignored.

The model of optimal foraging in the valley was constructed without reference to the
archeological data in order to generate predictions of the type of subsistence patterns we
might expect under optimal conditions. The differences between model predictions and empirical case have important implications for the way in which we use models and archeological data. These will be discussed later in the chapter.

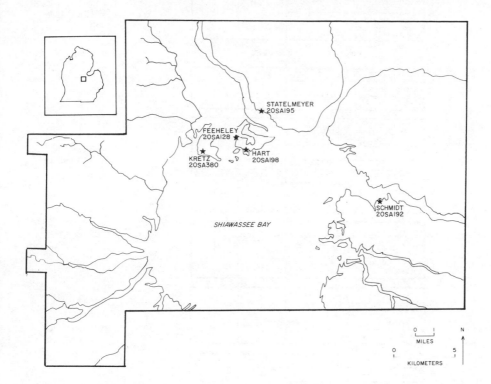

Figure 8.2.  Map of Study Area Showing Principal Sites.

## Model Results:  Summary

The results of the model are represented graphically in figure 8.3 which summarizes optimal monthly procurement schedules for a population of twenty-five.  Specific quantitative results along with postoptimal data may be found in Keene (1979b:497-529).  Primary resources, as indicated in figure 8.3, are those resources which were predicted for utilization in an optimal food procurement schedule for a given month.  Secondary resources represent the most likely alternatives to the resources used in the optimal solution. Secondary resources are those resources within the set of nonoptimal resources which have the lowest marginal cost (shadow prices).  These resources would enter the optimal solution if their cost were reduced slightly.  Marginal resources are those resources which would require drastic reductions in cost (e.g., 50% or more) before they would be included in the optimal solution.  All resources which are not listed as primary or secondary resources in the figure are regarded as marginal.

## Limiting Factors/Binding Constraints

The minimum requirements for various nutrients and the amount actually acquired in the optimal solution are summarized for select months in table 8.1.  Those constraints which were not satisfied in surplus represent the binding constraints of the model.  The binding constraints in various months were:  hides (October),[2] energy (April-September,

2.  Monthly requirements were established for all constraints except hides, for which an annual requirement was established.  In successive programs it was determined that the

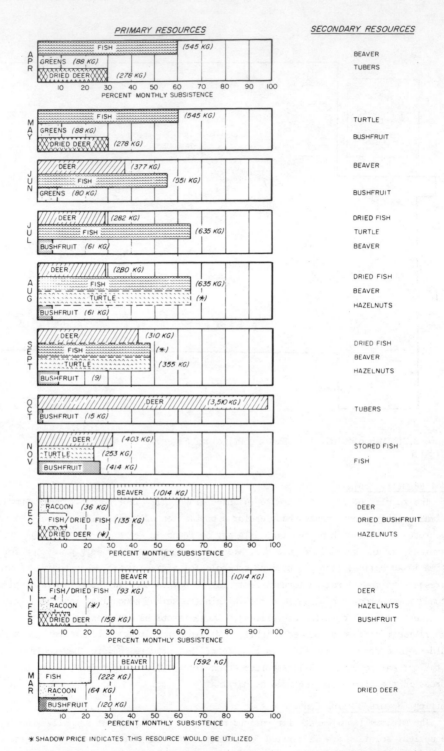

Figure 8.3.  Graphic Representation of Optimal Solution to Linear Programming Problem.

*Table 8.1*

*Percent of Minimum Monthly Requirements of a Population of 25 Individuals Fulfilled in the Optimal Solution of the Models during Selected Months*

|               | Jan | Apr | Jul | Oct   |
|---------------|-----|-----|-----|-------|
| Hides         | 0   | 0   | 0   | 100   |
| Energy        | 262 | 100 | 100 | 874   |
| Protein       | 727 | 577 | 654 | 1,868 |
| Calcium       | 100 | 100 | 100 | 108   |
| Phosphorus    | 288 | 188 | 231 | 707   |
| Iron          | 457 | 135 | 135 | 842   |
| Vitamin A     | 472 | 355 | 131 | 858   |
| Thiamine      | 100 | 147 | 105 | 459   |
| Riboflavin    | 615 | 187 | 201 | 828   |
| Ascorbic acid | 100 | 100 | 100 | 100   |
| Niacin        | 848 | 192 | 296 | 1,422 |

November, March), calcium (November-September), thiamine (January), and ascorbic acid (January-December). The models for individual months will thus key on those resources which can satisfy the respective binding constraints at the lowest possible cost. Further insight into the sensitivity of the models to various limiting factors may be gained from a study of shadow prices. In order to assess the relative differences in marginal costs of limiting variables and in the demand for these elements, I have graphed the cost of increasing the requirement for each constraint by one per cent. This information is summarized in figure 8.4.

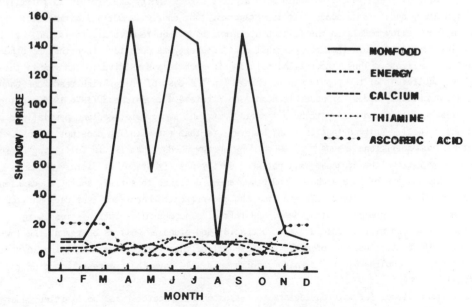

Figure 8.4. Cost of Increasing the Requirement of Select Constraints by 1%.

---

majority of the hide requirement should be fulfilled in October. See Keene (1979b:281) for details.

It is clear that the model is more sensitive to nonfood needs than to any of the other limiting variables. By extension, the importance of clothing requirements in Late Archaic foraging adaptations in southern Michigan is emphasized. Deer, the mainstay of the Eastern Archaic economy, enters the optimal solution in quantity because of the nonfood needs of the population.

Postoptimal data for the models suggest that there is a good deal of room for flexibility and variation in optimal food procurement patterns of Late Archaic foragers in the Saginaw Valley. Shadow prices indicate that, among a number of resources, there are only slight differences in cost-benefit ratios, and hence one resource may be substituted for another without significantly altering the overall cost of production. A high degree of variation in subsistence patterns is thus possible and expected. One exception to this expected flexibility, however, comes during the months in which raw materials for clothing must be obtained (i.e., fall). During these months there are few alternatives. Aside from deer, all resources which yield usable hides have high marginal costs (Keene 1979b: 305). Hence deer is a critical resource in the Saginaw Valley economy, not as a source of quality protein, but as the only resource available which provides raw materials for the production of quality clothing. It is interesting to note that the season of greatest food abundance, fall, is the most sensitive and most limiting season of the year in terms of the overall economy.

Energy is also a limiting factor in the Late Archaic diet. This is significant because in a previous paper (Keene 1979a), I suggested that energy should be a surplus nutrient in optimal diets of most human foragers. This assertion was based on the observation that, in diets of Arctic hunters, satisfaction of hide, calcium, and ascorbic acid requirements from an exclusively meat and fish diet inevitably produced a substantial surplus of energy and protein. It was assumed that other hunter-gatherers subsisting on a diet of primarily meat and fish would also acquire excess energy and protein in fulfilling other dietary and nonfood needs. It is noteworthy that energy is not a limiting factor in the Saginaw Valley models in the fall when minimum hide requirements are satisfied. It is also interesting to note that the marginal cost of energy is much less than that of other limiting nutrients. Thus, the optimal solution is much less sensitive to changes in the energy requirement of the population or changes in the cost of energy-rich resources than it is for calcium, hides, or ascorbic acid (see figure 8.4). Reidhead (1976 1980), using a similar model, found energy to be a limiting nutrient among Late Woodland populations of Indiana as well. An important caution, however, is that this finding does not suggest that minimum nutritional needs are subsumed by energy needs; that is, in fulfilling a minimum energy ration, the organism will not necessarily satisfy its other dietary needs as well. Simulations of Late Archaic food procurement designed to satisfy energy needs alone will provide a far different solution from the one presented here--one that deemphasizes the importance of greens, fruits, deer, and turtle. The optimal solution stresses resources which can provide calcium, ascorbic acid, and hides as well as energy at the lowest possible cost. And, as noted above, while all of these elements are limiting in terms of resource-scheduling decisions, hide requirements will have the greatest impact on the optimal strategy.

It is critical for anthropologists to evaluate which factors will be limiting under given conditions. Limiting factors will vary temporally and spatially. A shift in the resource base or a change in the mode of production or in the biological requirements of the population may also change those factors which are limiting in the diet. Reidhead

(1980) notes that a shift to corn agriculture results in a shift from energy to protein as a limiting factor in the diet of prehistoric populations of southeastern Indiana. In addition, the limiting factors in a given habitat may not always be intuitively obvious.

The appearance of thiamine as a binding constraint in the winter model is surprising, since thiamine is found in sufficient quantity in most food resources of the Saginaw Valley so that a short supply is highly unlikely. It appears that the limiting status of thiamine may be at least partially attributed to the fact that, in calculating the nutrient content of foods, I decreased thiamine values by fifty per cent in all foods prepared by cooking, in order to compensate for cooking losses (Keene 1979b:243). In retrospect, I believe that this adjustment may have been too severe.

It should not be surprising, however, that calcium is isolated as a limiting nutrient in the model, as others have made similar observations for the eastern United States (Reidhead 1980; Heidenreich 1971:165, 167). Because calcium is limiting, the models place strong emphasis on calcium-rich resources, and this partially explains the importance ascribed to fish, turtle, and greens (potherbs) in the model. Similarly, ascorbic acid, a limiting factor in all months, is responsible for the emphasis placed on fruits and berries.

The question has been raised as to whether calcium or ascorbic acid can truly be regarded as limiting factors in a human diet (J. V. Neel, pers. comm.; A. A. Yengoyan, pers. comm.). Can calcium deprivation over the course of a single month diminish the fitness of the organism? Will long-term deprivation diminish fitness? Calcium requirements and the pathologies allegedly associated with calcium deficiency are not well understood (Keene 1979b:486; Garn, et al. 1967; Hegsted 1967). In the case of ascorbic acid, however, it appears that body stores may be sufficient to sustain the body for up to four months in the absence of dietary ascorbic acid before clinical evidence of deprivation will be manifest (Robson 1972:260). On the other hand, the relationship of short-term deprivation to such factors as greater susceptibility to disease or infection is not well understood, and could be potentially significant. It is possible that, at least for some nutrients, a month is too short an interval of analysis. On the other hand, some nutrient requirements must be satisfied on a daily basis or the deficiency will be manifest clinically and possibly contribute to a decrease in fitness (increased morbidity or mortality or decreased fertility). In attempting to assess the implications of short-term deprivation on resource decisions, I lowered calcium requirements and ascorbic acid requirements to twenty-five per cent of the base minimum daily intake necessary to maintain good health. Even under these conditions, these two nutrients continued to be limiting constraints in the model, suggesting to me that they should figure significantly in determining the composition of the optimal diet within the Saginaw Valley if the assumptions of this model are accepted.

## Subsistence Patterns

The model essentially predicts four basic economic seasons for Late Archaic foragers in the Saginaw Valley: intensive fishing in the spring, intensive deer hunting in the fall, and a broad spectrum of subsistence activities in the summer and winter. The pattern of spring fishing and fall deer hunting appears quite stable. Shadow prices suggest that drastic perturbations in the availability of deer and fish would be necessary to alter the basic predicted subsistence patterns for spring and fall. However, food procurement patterns for summer and winter are not at all clear-cut. A good deal of variation is possible and may be expected without much deviation from the minimum cost.

A subtle contrast with previous characterizations of Late Archaic economy in the Great Lakes is the significance the model accords to gathered food. According to the model, gathered foods make a critical contribution to the diet, fulfilling two of three binding constraints in all months except October.  Although frequently regarded as a supplemental activity, particularly in the Great Lakes, gathering in the deciduous forest of Michigan is the primary means by which scarce nutrients are introduced to the diet.  Hunting should provide the bulk of the diet, but gathered foods are accorded the highest marginal value.  The by-products of hunting (i.e., skeletal refuse) dominate the organic materials preserved and hence recovered from archeological sites in the area.  Thus, hunting has received the greatest attention of archeologists attempting to study prehistoric subsistence.  It is gathering activities, however, which are responsible for maintaining the quality of the diet.  Gathering activities facilitate a lower cost adaptation than would be possible from hunting alone.  Thus, it is critical that we not underestimate the significance of gathered foods in Late Archaic subsistence in the Great Lakes and the reasons for their significance.

The quantitative results of the model (Keene 1979b) offer innumerable opportunities to explore the relationship between dietary requirements and roles of resources in the economy.  One example will now be reviewed.

### The Role of Nuts

Eastern Archaic adaptations have been characterized as showing an increasing dependence on nut products (Ford 1974 1977).  Nut foods were abundant in the Saginaw Valley during this time (Keene 1979b:95-112), yet the model not only excludes nuts from the optimal solution, but indicates that nuts have a relatively low marginal value in the Saginaw Valley.  Nuts represent a compact package of energy (approximately 600 kcal per 100 g vs. approximately 125 kcal per 100 g for lean meat), but are not unusually rich in other nutrients.  For example, walnuts and hickory nuts are lacking in a critical nutrient, calcium (Watt and Merrill 1963).  The low value of nuts in the model may be partially due to low calcium content.  However, even when calcium requirements of the population are drastically reduced (see Keene 1979b:524), the importance of nuts does not increase significantly.  A more critical reason for the absence of nuts in the optimal solution is their high processing costs (Reidhead 1976; Keene 1979b) relative to other resources.  The model suggests that a cost reduction or an error in estimation of over ninety five per cent would be necessary before nuts would be equivalent in cost/benefit to other resources.  This should not be difficult to accept intuitively, since it is well documented empirically that plant processing is a labor-intensive activity (see Reidhead 1976 or Keene 1979b for a review).  The model suggests that some plant foods, particularly greens and fruit, are incorporated into the diet because they represent the least costly sources of calcium and ascorbic acid.  Nuts, however, while excellent sources of energy and protein, are not exclusive sources of these nutrients.  Alternatives are available in all seasons which can supply these nutrients at a lower cost.

Under the conditions of the model, we would expect nuts to be important only when their cost is greatly reduced relative to other resources.  This might result from an increase in the cost of other less costly resources or a decrease in the cost of nut production as a result of improved nut-processing technology, as has been suggested by Ozker (1977).  This is not to say that nuts should have been excluded from the diet of Saginaw Valley foragers or that nuts were not important elsewhere in the eastern United States; however it does argue that intensive or systematic exploitation of nut crops would be far from an optimal strategy in the Saginaw Valley.

A final comment on nuts is that shadow prices suggest that the value of stored nuts is greater than the value of fresh nuts (Keene 1979b:305). The season of most intense hunting activity according to model predictions is also the season of maximum nut yield. Nuts are most abundant at a time when fresh game is also most abundant. At this time, game can fulfill a wider range of needs than nuts and at a lower cost. Nuts take on greater importance as a food resource which can be easily stored for use during the lean seasons. Ozker (1977) has suggested that, in southern Michigan, nut foods would be stored most efficiently when reduced to oil and that this could be accomplished most effectively with the aid of ceramic containers for boiling and storage. She posits that nuts should become an important element in the subsistence base only after the advent of ceramics, that is, in the Early Woodland period. However, whether ceramics would significantly alter storage and processing costs of prepared foods is not yet clear.

What are the implications of the above discussion? Nuts, according to the stated conditions of the model, have a high marginal cost in the Saginaw Valley. We would expect them to increase in importance as other, less expensive sources of protein and energy become limited, or as processing costs decrease. However, if other resources were depressed to the point that nuts became a critical source of protein and energy, this would raise serious questions about the stability of the adaptation given the high expected *variability* in nut production (Keene 1979b:95-116). Moreover, if a population in the Saginaw Valley had to rely on nuts at the stated costs as a critical source of protein, it is likely that the population would have difficulty in meeting its nonfood needs. This reiterates the argument on limiting factors. The Saginaw Valley is capable of feeding a much larger population than it can clothe. Nuts are not particularly rich in scarce nutrients, nor are they inexpensive to utilize. Thus, they do not fit into an optimal foraging strategy in this area. One may ask whether the model would predict the same result in an area where nut utilization was known to have been important, and this remains to be investigated. But the results do caution against the careless extension of models outside the region for which they were developed.

## Archeological Application

The model of optimal food procurement in the Late Archaic of the Saginaw Valley was compared with the available archeological data base for the area (see Taggart 1967; Fitting 1975; Keene 1979b). The aim of this comparison was to isolate areas of congruence and disparity between expectations of optimal behavior and observed behavior. Model predictions were viewed not as a means of verifying optimality in prehistoric subsistence behavior, but as a means of augmenting an incomplete data base, and of generating predictions about behaviors which might not have been obvious had we relied on the archeological record alone.

The archeological manifestations of predicted optimal patterns in the Saginaw Valley were reconstructed and are described at length in Keene (1979b:320-45). These expectations were generated after careful consideration of the cultural and natural processes which may affect the formation of the archeological record. Expectations were formulated primarily in terms of expected tool inventory, faunal inventory, floral inventory and site location. Because of poor preservation in the area, most fauna recovered from these sites could be identified only to the level of vertebrate class (Cleland 1966; Fairchild 1977; K. H. Moore 1979). Expectations were therefore formulated in terms of between-class ratios. This obviously produces a highly generalized comparison.

Predictions were compared with the available Late Archaic data from the Saginaw Valley (this being information from five excavated sites) and site location data from another thirty sites on the margins of Shiawassee Bay. Because of the relatively small sample of excavated sites, we would not expect the data to encompass the full range of variability that might be anticipated in this area; yet the model and data did exhibit a surprising degree of congruence for certain seasonal manifestations. Again, these comparisons are described fully in Keene (1979b), and I will only briefly summarize them here.

Four of the five excavated sites exhibited a very close fit with the expected manifestation of a spring fishing camp. This is of interest because one of these sites was previously interpreted as a winter habitation (Taggart, n.d.). The other excavated site fit the expected manifestation of a summer camp as predicted by the model. This site has been previously interpreted as a winter campsite (Taggart 1967) and as a base camp occupied year round (Fairchild 1977). The model suggests that two seasonal manifestations (fall and winter) are not represented in the current archeological data base of the Saginaw Valley. This should not be surprising, as decades of archeological reconnaissance in the area have focused almost exclusively on the fossil beach ridges surrounding Shiawassee Bay while ignoring the uplands and river valleys. I believe that further investigations in these areas should reveal the entire spectrum of Late Archaic subsistence activities (see also Carmichael 1977; Peebles 1978).

There were of course areas of disparity between model and data, but the significance of these disparities is not at all clear. For example, nut fragments were recovered from numerous proveniences at all of the sites. The model predicts that nuts should not be significant in the diet. Does the presence of nuts indicate a significant disparity from the optimal pattern of behavior? The nuts may represent the product of incidental collection, such as for snack food. They may represent food that was stored through the winter. They may represent a significant subsistence item. Or, since the total sample from any given site weighs less than two grams, they may even represent items which have accidentally entered the archeological record--for example, nuts which were buried by rodents or accidentally kicked into a hearth.

At present, we have little basis for assessing the quantitative significance of these nut remains (Cowan and Smart 1979). Previous interpretations of subsistence patterns in this area have suggested that nuts were probably important in the diet because they are present at these sites (Peebles 1978:119; Yarnell 1964:142). The model suggests otherwise. The issue here is not so much the role of nuts in Late Archaic subsistence, but our ability to make inferences from an archeological data base. The archeological record alone tells us that these resources were available in the area and little else. The models suggest their potential role in the diet. The current data base is not sufficient to test the reasonableness of these inferences; however, the model has clearly pointed out where additional data and more precise analyses are necessary and has thus indicated the direction for future research in the area.

Winterhalder (1977:556) and Earle (1980) note that additional variance between the optimum and the observed may be attributed to competing culturally determined goals which are unspecified in the model. It might also be suggested that in benevolent environments, when resources are abundant and when risk is minimal, there is greater leeway to deviate from the optimal pattern of behavior without risk to security or fitness. Such might be the case in the prehistoric Saginaw Valley where, in most months, minimum needs can be satisfied cheaply and efficiently from a variety of alternative resources of relatively equivalent cost and utility.

It is important to note that the comparison is not offered as a "test" of the model or model propositions. Typically, in archeology we tend to accept or reject our models based on the accuracy of model predictions. We expect a tight fit between our predictions and our observations, and models are frequently evaluated on the basis of goodness of fit (Jochim 1976; Reidhead 1976). A poor fit is generally regarded as falsification of the model or the propositions on which the model is based. I suggest that, in archeology, there is a tendency to reject our models prematurely when a poor fit between model and empirical case is encountered, without consideration of the reasons for the poor fit. Similarly, a good fit between model and empirical case is often readily accepted as validation of a model without consideration of the possibility that a good fit may be spurious. If our evaluations are to be meaningful, we must first account for the sources of variance between models and data.

Winterhalder (1977) notes that a model can make a prediction, and even though the assumptions and parameters may be accurate, it may still account for only part of the variance in observed behavior. Models are simplifications of real world phenomena and may not allow for the influences of factors which have been ignored or omitted (Maynard Smith 1978; Winterhalder 1977). Similarly, when dealing with the archeological record, we must remember that we are dealing with an incomplete account of real world behavior, and we cannot therefore read the record as a literal transcription of past events. We must first account for the processes which have transformed archeological data into their current state. I believe that archeologists too often attempt to fit models to data or validate models without considerations of the above problems. In attempting to be scientific, in attempting to validate and falsify, we neglect critical issues.

The comparison in this paper has revealed a high degree of congruence between model and data. Does this congruence verify the model? Does it validate the model assumptions? A convincing argument could be made for either case; however, I do not believe that verification (or falsification) can be supported on the basis of such a comparison. The implications of this particular comparison are ambiguous. Expectations are generalized, data are poor, sample size is small, and variability has been treated in a very basic manner. The comparison offers an inconclusive "test" of the model, but does generate some interesting questions. The comparison between model and data is useful because, in examining the variance that is observed between the two, we are forced to consider what disparities are products of site formation processes and what disparities are products of model-building processes. The result, it is hoped, leads to a more meaningful analysis of the problem at hand.

Levins (1966), in a cogent analysis of the strategy of modeling, stresses that models are not tested. The validation of a model comes in its ability to generate good, testable hypotheses. I have suggested (Keene 1979a:400) that models such as the one described in this chapter are most useful as heuristic devices, as mechanisms which structure our investigations. Such models are valuable, not because they make predictions to a specific degree of accuracy, not because they replicate the archeological record, but because they enable us to see the actual complexities of our problems (even if we cannot presently accommodate those complexities) and to trace the potential relationships between variables. The models are useful because they force us to ask relevant questions and to consider the implications of the relationships we have postulated.

## Currency Revisited

An alternative currency (i.e., measure of cost and benefit) has been introduced in this chapter. The model results illustrate some additional insights which can be achieved when additional variables are added to the analysis. This can also be accomplished for other optimal foraging models discussed in this volume. Let us take one example, the MacArthur-Pianka diet breadth model (MacArthur and Pianka 1966; see Winterhalder, chapter 2, above). The implications for this model of a multinutrient model should be clear. In situations where dietary complements are necessary (i.e., where a single resource cannot fulfill the full array of needs of the organism), a far broader diet would be necessary than would be predicted by the MacArthur-Pianka model, which considers only a single need.

As noted previously, the added precision and realism in the cost-benefit measure used here are achieved at the expense of some generality. Energy models, on the other hand, must sacrifice some precision to achieve a high level of generality and realism. Both approaches lend valuable insights into the problems at hand. Levins (1966) has noted that it is not possible to maximize all three characteristics (realism, generality, and precision). Thus, we must often sacrifice at least one characteristic to achieve the others. A more thorough or productive approach to any problem will come from the combined use of interrelated models, both general and specific, with overlapping objectives (see below).

## Assessment

Outlining the problems and necessary cautions inherent in the use of these particular linear programming models could fill a chapter in itself. However, I would like to point out two broad areas which require careful consideration.

The first deals with *assessment interval*. These models are essentially static models. They use average values designed to represent mean environmental characteristics of the Late Archaic period. In reality, of course, the values are not static, but may vary considerably around the mean or within a range. The model offers no explicit treatment of this variability. One benefit of a linear programming approach is that we can assess the effects of variability in certain variables after the fact, through a postoptimal analysis. It is important, however, that we define the time scale our analysis is meant to cover. Behavior which is optimal over the short run may be suboptimal in the long run. Similarly, behavior which appears suboptimal over a short time span may be optimal in a long-term adaptation. If our assessment interval is long, then we must consider the effects of long-term variability. In dealing with variability, we must consider whether we want to deal with the full range of variability or merely a portion. For example, some events may occur so infrequently (such as a hundred-year flood) that the value of modeling a response to them would be questionable. The ability of a population to deal with environmental variability is largely a function of its ability to collect, process, and store information regarding this variability. The appropriate interval over which optimal behavior is assessed should probably correspond to the effective lifespan of information collected about environmental variability. This problem requires an entirely separate set of models to be handled effectively.

The second area which is critical to the study of human subsistence, but which has been largely ignored here, is population as a variable. In order to assess the relationship between resource pressure, group size, group interaction, social organization, settlement pattern, and population mobility (see Keene 1979b), demographic processes must be treated as more than a static parameter. The nature of population growth, stability, and competitive interactions must be specified. The interactions of these considerations with locational and food procurement parameters and nutritional factors must be considered. This is beyond the scope of the present model and will, in fact, require the development of a separate family of biological and sociocultural models to accommodate the population problem.

This chapter has not offered a definitive statement of foraging adaptations in the deciduous forest, nor can the model in its current state realistically examine many of the behavioral generalities which are commonly attributed to human foragers, aside from those which relate specifically to diet.  Rather, the study has been of limited scope, focusing primarily on food procurement among hunter-gatherers.  Food procurement is of course but one component of hunter-gatherer subsistence and optimal foraging patterns.

In thinking about models of foraging adaptations, we tend consciously to recognize the systemic relationship among components of hunter-gatherer subsistence settlement systems (Jochim 1976:11-13).  Yet, in developing models, we tend to treat these systemic components as theoretical isolates, by examining, for example, food procurement exclusive of many of the constraints imposed by demographic and locational variables.  We do this not from oversight, but from the technical constraints which limit the number of variables and the number of systemic interactions we are capable of perceiving or operationalizing in any given model.  We tend to build simple, focal models which serve as valuable analytical and heuristic tools.  Our goal need not be in the direction of building more complex, comprehensive models which can simultaneously accommodate *all* of the interrelationships we should be considering.  As Levins (1966) and others have noted, the most fruitful results will come from the use of families of overlapping, complementary models which permit us to cope with different aspects of the same problem and hence increase the scope of our investigations (see also Winterhalder, chapter 2, above; Moore, chapter 9, below).

At the outset of this chapter, I argued that in order to make our studies of human foragers representative, we would have to bring an archeological perspective to our analysis.  I have argued that in order to do this, we must expand the scope of archeological investigations, and that this can be done only by augmenting the archeological data base with behavioral models.  The linear programming models offer a number of insights which we might otherwise lack were we to rely solely on the archeological or ethnographic record.  The models, of course, are accompanied by numerous problems; but the problems too have heuristic value.  The use of models such as these in conjunction with a set of interrelated models yet to be developed should ultimately yield more comprehensive and more meaningful analysis of human foraging adaptations.

# 9

# The Effects of Information Networks in Hunter-Gatherer Societies

James A. Moore

## Introduction

This chapter is about information flows at a regional level. Both the scale and the topic make somewhat odd bedfellows with optimization theories. The expansion of scale, and the divorce from the concept of the "economic man," are responses to critiques of optimization theory. One of the heftiest criticisms cast against optimization studies is the charge of reductionism. There are two aspects to this charge. Energy is a convenient concept, and calories are a convenient unit, but survival involves additional dimensions of existence. Secondly, on the issue of scale, the critiques are possibly even more disturbing. The local-level analysis of diet selection, foraging patterns, task group composition, and settlement location reveals a pattern to the opportunism long noted to exist among hunter-gatherer societies, but these parts are noticeably less than the whole. It seems unlikely that strictly local-level interactions of man and landscape can be put together to build regional or supraregional interactions. Does local-level optimization fully determine the patterns of low-energy societies? Or are the major patterns of hunter-gatherer behavior determined by other factors?

The response presented here to these criticisms revolves around a single issue--a misunderstanding about the use of models shown by both advocates and critics of optimization studies. Different uses of models will be presented and explained, as the relationships among local-level optimization, information processing, and regional-scale settlement processes are explored.

## Information and Regional Settlement

Cultural systems function through flows of matter, energy, and information (Miller 1965; Flannery 1972; Adams 1975). Energy flows can be traced through detailed recording of diet and subsistence activities, and the flows of matter can be followed to document the social and economic aspects of exchange networks. The ephemeral quality of information flows, however, has limited their study. Most theories have no explicit role for information sharing and processing as a variable. Whether one looks to geography, ecology, or economics, the role of information sharing as a dynamic social process is hidden behind the familiar visage of the rational "economic man." As an all-knowing, computationally perfect

I would like to thank the University of Massachusetts Computing Center for its generous grants. This paper has profited greatly from discussion with Art Keene, Bob Paynter, Kate Pfordresher, Dolores Root, and Martin Wobst. Any demonstration of ignorance which remains is, of course, of my own doing.

decision maker, the "economic man" serves the useful modeling function of holding the informational capabilities and capacities constant while the dynamic created by variations in the flows of matter and energy is investigated. This assumption is justified, not by its reasonableness, but by the powerful and elegant models of human behavior which have been based on the simplification.

Successful as these models have been, we should not be limited to the questions which they can answer. Such models tell us only how individuals should behave if computationally perfect with free access to all the information relevant to each decision. It is not surprising, then, that real human behavior deviates from the predictions of the models. However, the interpretation of these deviations is problematic. There have been few systemic studies exploring the patterns of deviations arising from the very real human characteristics of ignorance and error (Salop 1978). At a minimum, we should develop ideas about how imperfect individuals acting with imperfect knowledge attempt to adapt, and how the patterns of information sharing and processing affect the degree to which optimal behavior is attainable.

Information processing has effects at different scales. At the local level, information about the abundance and distribution of resources will affect the selection of diet items and the formation of foraging groups (cf. Winterhalder and Smith, chapter 1, above). The methods of collecting information about resources can also influence deviations from the behaviors predicted using optimization models. Preliminary investigations of these topics have begun: models of within-group information sharing (Reynolds 1978), of within-group decision making (Reynolds and Ziegler 1979), and foraging-area reconnaissance (Moore, in preparation) offer insights into how patterns of information processing may create systematic deviations from the predictions of optimization models.

Further, some local-level optimization analyses usually assume that the task group or individual acts in an isolated setting. As applied to anthropological cases, it is assumed that benefits are not reduced nor are costs increased by the presence of other groups or settlements. Given this simplifying assumption, the determinants of optimal behavior naturally enough are identified as the distribution and abundance of resources, and the relative costs of foraging activities. This simplification has led to insights into the local-level processes, and has aided in the discovery of patterns in the seemingly opportunistic behavior of hunter-gatherers. The results have buttressed and elaborated ideas stressing the covariation of hunter-gatherer economic and social organization and ecology.

In the present chapter the simplifying assumption of an isolated settlement will be abandoned in order to investigate (1) the effects of information processing; and (2) the interaction of settlements on a regional scale. The recent development of optimal foraging models for centrally based foragers provides the foundation for the development of regionally oriented settlement models (Hamilton and Watt 1970; Horn 1968; Orians and Pearson 1979). This expansion of scale has implications for the analysis of the limitations on the regional settlement process. Assuming that hunter-gatherers must attempt to organize their subsistence and settlement behavior on the basis of incomplete knowledge of the regional social and natural environment, several interesting problems develop. Under these conditions, active search and information sharing are the only means available for gaining information about the distribution of resources, and the seasonal dispersal plans of other groups (Moore 1977 1978). Thus the regional pattern of information sharing has an important influence in organizing the subsistence and settlement activities which occur.

Locational criteria provided by central place foraging models will be used in computer simulation experiments designed to study the impact of changing patterns of information sharing on the regional hunter-gatherer settlement. The results suggest that differences in the information networks can account for varying responses of hunting and gathering populations. In particular, the problems of hunter-gatherer seasonal settlement locations and of agricultural expansion on this locational behavior will be investigated. With respect to the latter, the decline of hunting and gathering is not simply a process of group by group (or settlement by settlement) replacement of one mode of subsistence with another. Analyses focusing on comparisons of single hunter-gatherer camps with isolated agricultural settlements are likely to be incomplete. Studies of regional locational processes surmount this limitation by focusing on how locational behavior is influenced by both the distribution and abundance of resources, and the distribution of other human groups.

## A Model of Models

Models are simplifications of reality which keep intact the essential features of a problem and its proposed solution. The distinction between simplification and oversimplification is a difficult one; it depends on both the nature of the problem and the state of the discipline (Levins 1966). As complex models become better understood, it becomes desirable to release simplifying assumptions to explore the dynamics created by incorporating additional types of variability.

But even less well understood are the uses to which models are put. In spite of the large literature discussing the nature and features of models, there is very little discussion concerning how an individual is to go about using models. The common statement that one uses models to replicate (predict, retrodict) important aspects of reality is more a symbol of the naïveté brought to the problem than a solution. All researchers have the desire to maximize the realism, precision, and generality of their findings, but this must remain an ultimate, perhaps unattainable goal. In his discussion of the major dimensions of variation among models, Levins (1966) points out that all modeling efforts are constrained by the complexity of the real world. "Naive, brute force modelling" rapidly leads to a system of relations which is beyond analytic solution or the computational powers of even a larger computer. Even when these brute force solutions are successful, the results tend to be without intuitive meaning--an intellectually paralyzing phenomenon referred to as Bonini's paradox (Bonini 1963). To avoid this dilemma, Levins suggests that more attainable proximate goals be set for the modeling effort. The modeler can effectively approach these more limited aspirations by maximizing two of the three dimensions of models. Thus, in Levins's typology, models can be classified as either (1) realistic and precise; (2) general and precise; or (3) realistic and general. It is for the modeler to specify which of the dimensions is least important to the problem at hand.

In addition, each type of model has its application (Levins 1966; Moore 1979). Real/ precise models lend themselves most readily to a rigorous hypothesis-testing approach. It is rightfully expected that the real and precise predictions of the models should match the behavior of the phenomena being modeled. As long as the requisite model parameters are known, attempts at falsification will indicate whether the modeled relations faithfully replicate the aspects of reality deemed important. It should be noted that among ethnologists and archeologists there is a tendency to believe that this is *the* use of modeling.

General/precise models have a different methodological orientation. By the very fact that general relations and processes are involved, an exact fit between the implications of the general model and the conditions of reality is no longer expected. In fact, it is expected that the behavior of the general model will deviate from the patterns of the data set. The model stands as an ideal construct, a research instrument against which the complexity of the world is gauged. The patterning of the deviations from the model becomes the focus of research; hypothesis testing is no longer the major concern of this approach to research. Variability not explained by the model is analyzed to locate the existence of factors which identify how the specific case at hand differs from what are thought to be the general features of the problem. The task then comes to be to determine whether the deviations are due to the lack of realism, or to some general relationship previously overlooked. Within this orientation, scientific investigation proceeds through a series of approximations as if it were a stepwise multiple regression. Hypothesis testing, to the extent to which it exists, deals with predictions of the expected patterns of deviations away from the model.

Finally, precision may be sacrificed to gain additional realism and generality. When choosing this approach, qualitative rather than quantitative results are sought. General/ real model predictions are expressed as trends between polar states of the controlled variable. Thus this sort of model homes in on the trends which exist, for example, between predictable and unpredictable resources, heterogeneous and homogeneous habitats, or, as in this study, locational choice with perfect knowledge and without it.

Optimization theories highlight the relations of certain clearly specified variables, using a set of tightly controlled assumptions. The strength of the optimization approach rests on predictions about the processes of diet selection, foraging patterns, task group formation, and settlement location. Because of the clarity and logical robustness of the optimization models, the present study makes little effort to test their implications. Rather, it will attempt to uncover likely patterns of deviations, and to explain these patterns by using information flow variables not normally considered in the model framework. Models of hexagonal packing of multiple settlement systems and optimal locations for single settlements serve as the baseline for investigating patterned deviations.

## The Hexagonal Landscape

Equilibrium models of settlement systems demonstrate hexagonal spacing; this shape maximizes the use of space while minimizing transport, administration, and market costs. Squares and equilateral triangles, while also packing efficiently, have longer perimeters and a greater average distance to all interior points for unit-area figures. Circles have the smallest perimeter and the lowest transport costs, but when packed into a region leave areas unutilized. As long as one recognizes efficient packing as a constraint, hexagonal lattices offer the best solution to space-filling problems. The clarity and simplicity of this argument have made hexagonal lattices attractive to modelers concerned with spatial problems. As a result, the use of hexagonal lattices in the study of spatial processes has become so widespread that it borders on convention. Krzywicki (1934) is generally recognized as the first to comment on the cellular pattern of hunter-gatherer spacing, while describing the distribution of Australian bands. Later Birdsell (1958 1968 1973) used counts of contact neighbors as empirical justification for the hexagonal framework adopted in his models of inter- and intragroup interaction and the emergence of dialectical tribes. In efforts to integrate Horn's (1968) ecological optimal location model with geographic theories of the effect of distance on interaction, Wilmsen (1973) found a useful convergence in assumption on the part of both model and theories of regular spacing created

by hexagonal lattices. Johnson (1978), Williams (1974), and Wobst (1974) use hexagonal
lattices to link the operation of nonspatial processes to spatial implications. Yet, there
are several assumptions underlying the use of hexagonal models which can make them inappropriate for the investigation of hunter-gatherer locational problems.

In proposing an alternative to deterministic locational theory, Curry (1964:139)
analyzes the widespread use of uniform, hexagonal landscapes in geographic theory: "The
reason that the regular or uniform distribution has been so popular [is] because it greatly
facilitates the study of spatial processes. . . . However, any useful statements made from
the models constructed are not tied to absolute space, since, being general, they refer to
relative position only." The hexagonal lattice is not a universal property of the spatial
processes themselves; it is a logical entailment of the simplifying assumptions. Curry
proposes that the salient theoretical relationships concern the interaction of competition,
least effort, and optimizing principles. The appearance of regular, space-filling hexagonal lattices on a uniform landscape is a side issue.

Given Curry's reservations, what are we to make of the empirical observation of regular spacing among hunter-gatherer groups? It is well documented that the mean number of
contact neighbors--groups sharing boundaries--consistently approaches six. Birdsell (1958:
196-99) reports a mean of 5.5 contact neighbors for a sample of 100 Australian Aborigine
bands. Wilmsen (1973:11) calculates a mean of 5.4 for a sample of 22 Northern Paiute bands
and 5.5 for a sample of 15 Southern Paiute bands. Working from Rogers's (1969) map of
eastern subarctic groups, Wobst (1974) found a mean of 5.67 for 31 bands. My own counts,
based on Tindale's (1964) map of all Aboriginal groups, resulted in a mean of 5.97 for 398
noncoastal groups. These figures are usually interpreted by comparing them to the features
of regular hexagonal lattices. For as Haggett (1966:51) points out: "A second characteristic associated with the regular hexagonal tesselation is the number of contacts between any
one territory and adjacent territories. In a regular hexagonal system, the contact number
would clearly be six as one area would be contiguous with its six neighbors, each of which
would in turn have six neighbors." This observation is the basis for identifying six contact neighbors as a characteristic of regularly spaced distributions (Smith 1974). However,
there is a difficulty with this line of argument. The mean number of contact neighbors
for the network of polygons constructed around a *randomly* spaced set of points was not determined. In other words, it was not shown that six contact neighbors is uniquely characteristic of regular hexagonal lattices.

Fortunately, Woldenburg (1972) provides a thorough investigation of the characteristics of systems of polygons. Working from a justification of the universality of three-
edged corners, Woldenburg proceeds to prove that all networks of three-edged corners will
approach a mean of six contact neighbors, and that the deviations from six have systematic
properties. In any network which has only three-edged corners, the deviation of the mean
number of contact neighbors from the value of six, characteristic of regular hexagons, depends solely on the number of exterior edges, the number of exterior corners which belong
to only a single polygon, and the number of polygons in the network. The mean number of
contact neighbors can be less than, equal to, or greater than six depending on these factors. However, the results will consistently approach six with or without regularity of
spacing generated by competition, least effort principles, or any other behavioral assumption. Furthermore, the deviations depend largely on the characteristics of the exterior
edge of the polygonal network.

Anthropologically, the mean number of contact neighbors for hunter-gatherer groups

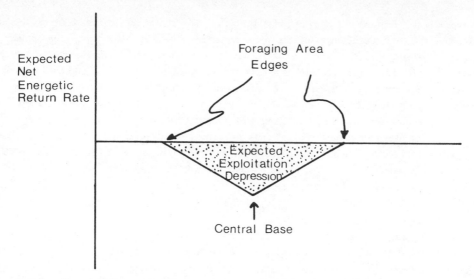

Figure 9.1. Expected Pattern of Resource Depression Created around the Base of a Centrally Based Forager. The expected depression of the net return rate can lead to avoidance of the area by competing foragers.

will consistently approach six even if spacing is random. The standard interpretation that six contact neighbors invariably implies regular spacing and full and efficient use of space is unfounded. This also leads to questions about adaptive interpretations of uninhabited and underutilized "buffer zones" surrounding hunter-gatherer groups (Ross 1978; Hickerson 1965). Hunting-gathering may not be the close-packed and spatially efficient adaptation that is commonly assumed. Rather than careful ecological management strategies, the buffer zones may indicate an inability to coordinate seasonal locational activities among the groups of the region (Moore 1977).

The spatial inefficiency of hunter-gatherers is ethnographically supported. The Peel River Kutchin showed little concern about the limits of their range (Slobodin 1962). Helm (1972:76) observed of the Dogrib: "The region and the regional band are defined in terms of the 'road' of winter and summer movement. The regional band's territory thus has an axis rather than boundaries or edges." The Mistassini have a similar pattern: "The boundaries of each group's territory are known only within a limit of several miles. Several informants could not locate boundaries to some sections of their territories except in a vague manner" (Rogers 1963:69). This lack of "boundary consciousness" is incongruous with the idea of packing efficiency, and would tend to imply that spatial packing of band territories is not a consistently important aspect of hunting and gathering adaptations, but rather a dynamic variable in its own right.

Beyond efficient packing, there are other assumptions which may make the use of standard settlement and locational theories inappropriate. In his explorations of random spatial economies, Curry (1964:138) provides an important insight into the assumptions of locational models:

Locational theory . . . has been phrased as a static equilibrium problem with a maximum efficiency postulate based on optimizing behavior and competition. . . . The complex of physical capital appearing as settlement and communication networks are 'going concerns' with a locational stability greater than the individual units composing them.

In other words, geographic models of settlement take as a given the initial cost of settlement and the developmental costs of the very communication system which makes the optimizing behavior possible. The individual decision makers do not bear the cost of establishing the settlement infrastructure. Locational models are designed to predict the ongoing patterns of optimal behavior in a *fully developed* settlement system. The processes and costs involved in the development of such equilibrium systems are not within the problem framework of most settlement models. In particular, the informational costs are ignored. Without any cost to the decision maker, conventional locational models make available information about the locations which minimize competition, and the waste and costs generated through nonoptimal decisions (Pred 1967). These assumptions are inappropriate for the study of hunting and gathering settlement systems where the locational stability of institutions is not a given, and where the costs of establishing and maintaining the settlement infrastructure are an integral part of the location decision process.

   The two points raised here--the spatial inefficiency of hunter-gatherer adaptations, and the developmental costs of settlement infrastructure--will be combined with ecological optimization models to explore the regional implications of settlement processes based on the behavior of decision makers acting with incomplete knowledge of the settlement system. The relative spatial efficiencies of the settlement processes will thus be generated without assuming optimization to be the goal of some regional superorganic entity. The hexagonal lattice model will be referred to as a standard, and in this manner the effects of imperfect information of the regional settlement system can be gauged.

## The Optimal Location Model

   A major problem in expanding ecological optimization theories to the regional level is linking changes in the regional settlement system to the costs and benefits experienced by individuals. It is insufficient to argue for cost-benefit changes for the region itself; it is not the region which is optimizing but the individual. Thus it is important to consider how changes observable at the regional scale are related to the net energy return rate associated with individual behaviors. Without such mechanisms the evaluation of the optimizing behavior--within an evolutionary ecology framework--is impossible (Maynard Smith 1978). To this end, the mechanism of locational choice and seasonal settlement movement will operate in the framework of the local-level optimal location model. Regional optimization refers then not to the net return rate for the region, but to the number of settlements which leads to the maximum expected net return rate for the individual settlements.

   The general principle of foraging optimization studies is that the net energy return rate will be maximized (Smith 1979b). In models that deal with a heterogeneous environment, the optimization strategy maximizes the net energy return by feeding in dense resource patches, while minimizing the risk and/or the time spent traveling between resource patches (Cody 1974; MacArthur and Pianka 1966; Pianka 1978; Schoener 1971; Wiens 1977). Thus optimal behavior is strongly affected by the distribution of resources in time and space. For centrally based foragers, the location of the base as well as the foraging route is open to optimization (Horn 1968). If optimization is the criterion influencing the selection of a central base, the optimal location is one which minimizes travel time and energy, that is, the site which lies at the center of gravity of the weighted resource distribution (Andersson 1978; Orians and Pearson 1979; Schoener 1979). The resource locations are weighted by both resource abundance and the probability of foraging success. It is conventional to use the expected net return as the weighted resource value (Horn 1968). The term "expected return" is used in the statistical sense--as the best estimate of the mean return rate. As a result, the locational rule for the individual settlement is clear and simple, but the costs of locating and establishing the base at the optimal location are ignored.

Besides considerations of optimal location, ecologists have developed models of optimal foraging for centrally based foragers. Andersson's (1978) investigation of the optimal allocation of search effort contains an interesting implication for regional locational problems. In a uniform habitat, search effort is optimally allocated if and only if the marginal food acquisition cost is equalized throughout the foraging area. On this basis, the models predict that the optimal search time per unit area should decrease roughly linearly as the distance from the central point increases. Also, resource depletion in the foraging area will be proportional to the amount of time spent in the area. Using these arguments, it is possible to derive the *expected* resource distribution for the foraging area at the end of the foraging period. This resource depletion curve drops off linearly with the distance from the home base (figure 9.1). The degree of expected depletion can influence the potential foraging success of intruders. Andersson (1978:405) states: "Even in the absence of territorial defense, it might profit a competitor little to hunt near the central place of the forager after a substantial proportion of the foraging period has elapsed." If the forager operates on the expected depletion of the resource rather than on the actual state of depletion, Andersson's statement suggests that it would benefit a competitor to establish its base camp so that its foraging area does not overlap with areas of other centrally based foragers.

The spatial implications of resource depression for centrally based foragers are further developed by Charnov, Orians, and Hyatt (1976). If a resource patch is subject to visitation by resource competitors, the return time (the time between profitable patch visits) may be difficult for the forager to estimate. An important aspect of holding exclusive space may be the improvement of estimates of return times for the various patches of an area. This would permit the user to schedule visits so that the net energy return is increased (Charnov, et al. 1976:256). Furthermore, if the "owner" of the foraging area has information about the schedule of return times, its expected benefits are greater than those of the interloper which must forage without this information. In this situation a sort of mutualism may exist. The potential intruder can use the information about boundaries to avoid depleted areas; both the owner and the invader benefit. This does, however, require that the invader gain by the avoidance decision. This model thus assumes that space exists for the invader to establish its own centrally based foraging area, and that the costs of finding this area are less than the reduction of expected benefits due to foraging in the depressed area.

Defense of resources is often taken as the defining characteristic of territoriality. Andersson's and Charnov's models make it clear that actual defense of resources may appear only if other mechanisms for regulating spacing have broken down. Boundaries should be recognized, not because of the threat of force, but because in a wide range of circumstances it is more energy efficient to avoid areas of high probability of resource depletion.

Several ethnographic examples suggest boundary behavior which can be attributed to resource depression. Holmberg's (1950:132) report of the Siriono hunting behavior mentions this:

Bands possess no prescribed territory. If one band runs across hunting trails of another, however, they do not hunt in that area. When I was travelling with Indians of one band in the neighborhood of a house of another, they were reluctant to do any hunting. Informants told me that where trails of another band existed, the animals of that area belonged to the people who made the trails.

Apparently the Siriono recognized energy gains to be made by avoiding areas which *may* have their resources depressed by the use of other groups. Marshall (1959:337) notes similar limitations on locational behavior: "!Kung of the Nyae-Nyae region almost never went outside their region because in strange places they cannot depend upon food reciprocity and either *do not know where wild foods grow* or might not be allowed to gather them" (emphasis added). Note that food reciprocity and information sharing about the distribution of food resources are implied to be coterminous, and that withholding information about the distribution of resources can be an effective mechanism for controlling the use of resources. These two brief examples indicate that hunter-gatherers avoid areas where they are at a competitive disadvantage owing to the lack of information about resource location and harvesting schedules.

The model of regional location for centrally based foragers will incorporate features of the models discussed above. For an individual settlement and its inhabitants, a location is optimal when it provides the greatest net return to the central base. This condition is met when: (a) the base is located in the center of gravity of the weighted resource distribution; and (b) the foragers show avoidance of other foraging areas because of the expected resource depression of those areas. These principles form the local-level rules for all of the regional location simulations. The characteristics of regional-level settlement patterns will emerge from the operation of these local-level decision criteria in specific habitats.

## The Nonhexagonal Landscape

Simulation experiments which use these optimization rules to control the seasonal movement of human foraging groups on a regional scale will now be presented. The nonhexagonal landscape of the simulations is standardized to permit controlled comparisons of the effects of changing the amounts of information available about (1) the distribution of resources, and (2) the seasonal movement plans of other groups. The simulation habitat has two resource types--stationary resource clusters and uniformly distributed resources. The predictable clustered resources determine the locations of the seasonal camps. The number of these clusters remains constant throughout the series of simulations. These resource clusters have a *rectangular random* distribution over the simulation landscape, meaning that cluster locations are independent of each other with each point of the simulation landscape having an equal probability of being the location of a resource cluster. Each resource cluster, in conjunction with a standardized foraging area of the homogeneously distributed resources, supports a seasonal camp for the duration of the economic season. Since there is an equal resource potential for each of the optimal locations, each camp has the same population size, is centered on a single resource cluster, and has a catchment area with the same radius containing uniformly distributed resources.

In addition, the location model sets up constraints on acceptable locational moves. Each seasonal camp must have full access to a resource cluster; only one camp is permitted at any cluster. Similarly, the catchment areas for the homogeneous resources are not permitted to overlap because of the expected depression of resources which would result:

twice the radius of the catchment area is the minimal permissible distance between seasonal camps.

The specifics of the simulation follow from these general features. The size of the region is large in relation to the catchment requirements of the individual camps. The region measures 100 by 100 units, while the radius of the foraging areas is 4 units. The spatial requirements of each camp are only 0.502 per cent of the total region. Placing the foraging areas into the region with the closest, nonoverlapping arrangement results in occupation by 168 settlements. Because of the space wasted between circular catchment areas and the effect of the linear edge of the region, this maximum packing occupies only 84 per cent of the total area. The resource clusters are abundant with 500 clusters spread with a rectangular random distribution over the region. On the average, each circular catchment area will have 2.5 clusters. Since the distribution of clusters per catchment area follows a Poisson distribution, the variance will also be 2.5. This relatively high density of resource clusters will be constant throughout the series of simulations. The variability in the simulation outcomes will not depend on changing these resource parameters, or on the local-level optimization rules, but on changes in the information available to the locational decision makers.

## The Simulation Experiments

The simulations are divided into two sets. In the first set, the decision makers have full knowledge of resource distributions in the region, but operate with the limiting condition of no information about the seasonal movement plans of the other groups. In the second set of simulations, the decision makers have perfect knowledge of the seasonal movement plans of the other groups but move through the region with varying degrees of information about the distribution of food resources.

The results are presented in graphic form. Rather than presenting a single curve of the net resource return rate, the expected costs of gathering information are separated from the expected benefits of the seasonal settlement location. In this way it is possible to isolate the behavior of the cost curve as the number of settlements in the region increases. These curves represent the expected costs and benefits for the individual camps, and not the cumulative results for the region. Their interpretation is straightforward. The optimal number of settlements in the region is identified when the net return rate for individual settlements is maximized. Graphically this is recognized when the vertical distance between the cost curves and the benefit curves is greatest. This condition occurs when the increase of benefits due to the addition of a settlement equals the increase in costs due to its addition; in other words, when the slopes of the lines are equal. It should be noted that the graphs represent qualitative relationships. The benefits per settlement are arbitrarily established, while the costs are measured in terms of the number of moves required to find a location which meets the local-level optimal settlement rules, or by the number of moves required to gather information about the abundance and distribution of resource clusters. For convenience, I assume that the benefits are measured in move-equivalent units.

### Simulation 1:  Location with Constant Costs and Perfect Knowledge

As noted, most models of optimal location operate with the assumption that either there is only one group in the region or that locational costs are constant. This latter situation is implied in the use of the hexagonal model. Horn's (1968) optimal location model and much geographic settlement theory contain such assumptions.

Simulation 1 uses a nonhexagonal landscape in which the expected benefits of each location are equal. The assumption of a constant locational cost for all settlements means
that the locational costs of search and seasonal movement are independent of the number of
settlements (equivalent to saying that there is only one group in the region). With these
simple locational rules there is no need to use the computer. The slope of both the expected
cost and the expected benefit curve is zero (figure 9.2). The interpretation of this graph
is simple although unexpected from an optimization viewpoint. Quite simply, any number of
settlements is optimal. The number of settlements in the region does not affect the costs
or benefits of individual settlements. From the perspective of regional optimization, these
results are not very interesting, but they are the regional implications of most local-level
optimal settlement models. Removing the assumption of constant locational costs leads to
a more interesting situation.

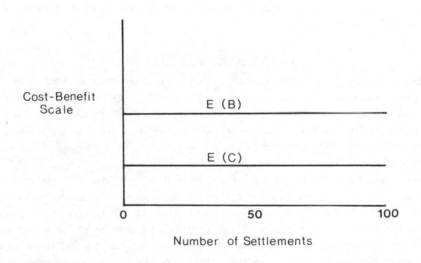

Figure 9.2. Cost-Benefit Analysis of a Typical Site-Centered Locational Model. With costs
and benefits independent of the number of settlements, the regionally optimum number of
settlements is indeterminate.


## Simulation 2:  The Costs of Random Search

In the previous simulation, the cost of information was zero. Simulation 2 begins with
the assumption that there is *no information* shared among the groups involved in the seasonal
settlement dispersal. The only means for acquiring information about the distribution of
the other settlements is through active search of the region. The groups begin dispersing
from a uniform hexagonal lattice of locations, and move to the nearest known resource cluster to find out if it is already occupied or if the foraging area around this cluster overlaps with an already established camp. If there is an overlap, the group randomly selects
a new resource cluster and continues to search until an acceptable location is encountered.
The expected locational costs are calculated by dividing the total number of unsuccessful
searches by the number of settlements. Although the costs are not evenly distributed
among the groups, the mean is the appropriate index of cost. Individual settlements

cannot anticipate how many seasonal camps are already established and so must operate on the long-term expectation provided by the calculation of the mean.

This simulation runs until there are no resource clusters remaining which meet the local-level optimization criterion of nonoverlapping foraging areas. We can now compare the maximum packing generated by a hexagonally gridded region with the maximum packing resulting from uncoordinated random search in the nonhexagonal landscape. The differences are caused by a regionally uncoordinated packing strategy. As shown in figure 9.3, it is possible for three groups to close out a rather large area from further settlement.

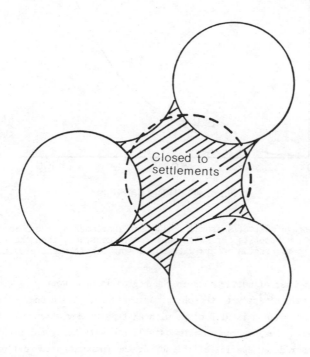

Figure 9.3.   Uncoordinated settlement strategies can lead to the creation of unintentional buffer zones and increased settlement costs, because of the inefficient use of space.

The expected costs per settlement grow at a nearly exponential rate as the number of settlements in the region increases (figure 9.4). This is because the probability that a resource cluster will have a foraging area overlapping with that of already-established settlements increases with the number of established camps. As a result, the expected movement cost per settlement increases as a geometric probability distribution based on the probability of overlap. Combining this cost curve with the condition of constant expected benefits per settlement leads again to an unexpected result. The maximum net rate of resource return occurs with one settlement in the region. As long as the assumption is maintained that there is no gain in benefits owing to settlement interaction in the region, the optimal number remains one. Anthropologically, this is again a rather uninteresting model. Settlements do not commonly exist in isolation. Yet mutual benefits created by the interaction of settlements have been only infrequently included in settlement optimization models. The effects of the domestic and political economy clearly influence settlement optimization.

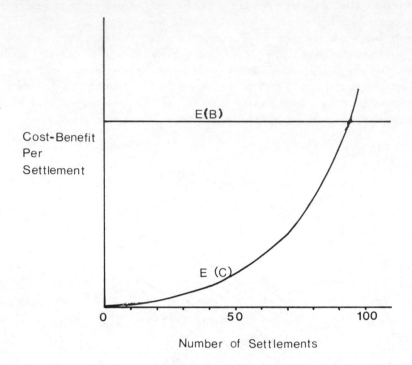

Figure 9.4. If the average cost of seasonal settlement increases as the number of settlements increases, while the benefits per settlement remain constant, then the greatest net
return per settlement in the region occurs with but a single settlement present.

The mean maximum number of settlements in the region is also worthy of comment, although it does not pertain directly to the optimization issue. Based on twenty-two runs of
the simulation, the mean maximum is 91.0 camps with a standard deviation of 3.18 (see figure
9.4). When compared with the 168-camp maximum established with hexagonal packing of circular foraging areas, the reduced spatial efficiency of the uncoordinated settlement process
is readily apparent. The uncoordinated packing is only 54 per cent as efficient as the
hexagonal packing in terms of utilization of space. But optimization is based on the net
resource return rate to individual settlements in the region and not simply on the efficient
utilization of regional space.

Mechanisms for mutual interactions among settlements which result in increases in the
net return rate are explored in the third simulation.

### Simulation 3: The Benefits Derived from Other Settlements

The previous two experiments have located a major problem in extending local-level optimization rules to the regional scale. Without better grasp of the benefits derived from
the interaction of the regional settlements, the settlement pattern ends with trivial solutions: the number of settlements in a region is either indeterminate or one. These results
are consistent with the biases of the ecological literature. May (1976) points out that
processes of competition and predation have been widely explored but that there is a lack
of theoretical concern for the processes and mechanisms of mutualism. An exception is the
development of optimal task group formation (Caraco and Wolf 1975; Smith, chapter 3, above),
but this development holds little immediate promise for regional settlement questions.

A reformulation of the problem provides one solution to the difficulty. Optimal location models generally assume that the regional environment is static. In simulation 3, this
assumption will be modified to include a limited component of environmental variation. The
assumption that the long-term expected net resource return rate is equivalent for all resource clusters and foraging areas is maintained. However, the model now recognizes fluctuations in the resource abundance *following* the period of seasonal dispersal. Given this
condition of environmental uncertainty, risk aversion becomes part of the optimal settlement
problem (Vayda and McCay 1975).

The environmental uncertainty can be attributed to variability in temperature, in rainfall, in task group formation, or in foraging efficiency. Furthermore, it is assumed that
deviations for each potential foraging area have a normal distribution with a known standard
deviation over the region and through time. With this knowledge, confidence limits around
the expected benefits per settlement can be established. It is thus possible to calculate
the expected benefits at the lower confidence limit once a level of risk aversion is set.
For example, we can decide that it is reasonable to expect that groups may operate with a
level of risk aversion which means that the expected net return rate will be met or exceeded
at an arbitrarily established 84 per cent of the time. For a single settlement this means
that the confidence limit will be set at one standard deviation below the long-term expected
benefit level.

The importance of this modification lies in the well-known manner in which hunting and
gathering groups cope with environmental variation. Variability and risk are shared over
an entire region through the mechanism of inter- and intraband visiting. This visiting
permits rapid and effective redistribution of the population as a response to fluctuations
in resource availability (Lee and DeVore 1968 1976; Bicchieri 1972; Damas 1969c). Lee
(1972b:350) provides a particularly apt description of the extent of the visiting and residential fluidity:

> The composition of these camps changes from month to month and from day to day. . . .
> Intercamp visiting is the main source of fluctuation, but about 15 percent of the pop-
> ulation makes a permanent residential shift from one camp to another. Another 35 per-
> cent divide their time equally between periods of residence at two or three different
> camps both in and out of the Dobe area.

The effects of this flexibility can be brought into the regional settlement model by considering settlements as providing samples of the habitat's net resource return rate. In
effect, the settlement process is a sampling problem; the addition of settlements increases
the sample size.

The effects of increasing the sample size can best be described in terms of the standard error of the estimate of the mean. The standard error describes the variability of
the distribution of all possible sample means around the population mean. Increases in
sample size lessen the variability in the distribution of sample means. In the case considered here, increases in the number of risk-and-resource-sharing groups in the region
will reduce the variability in the expected benefits ("the sample mean"). This reduction
in the "shared" variability in turn affects the confidence limits. Consider each settlement as randomly selecting a foraging area from the regional set of foraging areas. If
there is but a single seasonal camp in the region, the standard error is equal to the standard deviation of the population of foraging areas. There is an 84 per cent probability
that the single settlement will realize benefits greater than one standard deviation
below the mean. But increases in the number of settlements in the region and the

sharing of risks among the regional population by visiting and reciprocal exchange change the value of the standard error. The standard error is:

$$S.E. = \frac{\sigma}{\sqrt{n}}$$

where $\sigma$ = the standard deviation of the benefits of the foraging areas and n = the number of settlements in the region. For any set confidence level, this means that the expected benefits at the lower confidence limit increase with the number of settlements in the region. With twenty-five settlements, the confidence limit is only one-fifth of a standard deviation below the mean expected benefits. This effect is illustrated in figure 9.5. The slope of the "expected benefits at the lower confidence limit" curve, E(B-SE), is dependent on both the sample size and the value of the regional standard deviation.

These results represent a nontrivial case of settlement optimization. While the long-term expected benefits (the mean return) for each settlement are constant and independent of the number of settlements in the region, the benefits expected at a specified level of risk aversion increase with the addition of seasonal camps to the region. As long as the level of risk aversion is held constant, increasing the number of settlements in the region has the effect of increasing the expected benefits of each individual settlement. At the same time, the costs of finding a suitable foraging area increase for every additional settlement. The slopes of the cost curve and the benefit curve are equal when there are about thirty interacting groups in the region (see figure 9.5). It should be remembered that this value is dependent on the arbitrarily established standard deviation and cost per move values. The figure of thirty is of no general value, but it will provide a basis of comparison in later simulations which use the same standard deviation and cost curves.

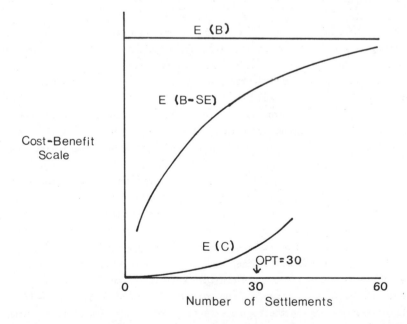

Figure 9.5. If risk reduction due to increases in the number of settlements in the region is considered, then there is a nontrivial solution to the regional optimization problem. The greatest average net return per settlement occurs with thirty settlements in the region. This is the regional optimum.

The calculation of the standard error assumed that the deviations for each foraging area are independent. For the following simulations this assumption is maintained. However, its reasonableness depends on the spatial correlation in resource fluctuations over the region. It is possible to derive the equation which will include the effects of correlation on the value of the standard error, but a qualitative understanding is sufficient for present purposes. Where fluctuations are independent over space the standard error will decrease as indicated above; but when there is a correlation of the fluctuations over the region, deviations from the expected benefits will not "balance themselves out." As the correlation increases, the reduction in the standard error will not be as marked. In the most extreme case, if there is a perfect correlation of the deviations over the region, increasing the number of settlements sharing the risk will have no effect on reducing the standard error. Visiting will not increase the expected benefits at the confidence limit, because quite simply there is nothing to share and no place to run.

An example will clarify the anthropological importance of this correlation factor. Consider two regions which have identical means and standard deviations of the benefits expected from the foraging areas. The first has a low degree of spatial correlation while the second has a moderate degree of correlation. The area with the low correlation will have a greater reduction in the value of the standard error as the number of settlements increases than will that with moderate correlation. In the second area, a greater number of settlements must be integrated if the same level of benefits/settlement (at the same level of risk) is to be maintained. This difference exists even though the long-term expected benefits for settlements in both regions are equal. Whether or not the same level of benefits is reached depends in large part on the costs of locating the camps in the region, and the costs of integrating these groups. Leaving aside for a moment the issue of social integration, the effect of a moderate spatial correlation on the confidence limit curve has clear implications. The reduction of the standard error will be less and the curve will be flatter than curves for regions with low correlation among the foraging areas. The slope of the locational cost curve will be equal to the slope of the confidence limit curve when there are fewer settlements in the region. As a result, the optimal number of settlements will be lower for the moderately correlated region.

Among well-reported contemporary hunting and gathering groups, the degree of correlation among the foraging areas appears to be low. The San (Lee 1976), Australian Aborigines (Meggitt 1962; Tindale 1974; Yengoyan 1968; Birdsell 1968), Eskimo (Damas 1972: 9-11; Nelson 1969), and Shoshone (Steward 1938; Thomas 1973) live in habitats with highly localized weather patterns which influence the abundance or availability of food resources. Given the benefits of distributing the risk, it is understandable that visiting and residential flexibility are common characteristics. But the question remains if these "typical band features" will be found to the same extent in habitats which show a higher level of spatial correlation. Given the costs of social integration, and the low level of benefits returned through risk sharing, such habitats might show a hunting and gathering organization with less-developed patterns of residential flexibility. In effect, do some habitats show more spatial correlation, and does this mean that hunter-gatherers in those habitats will show a different social adaptation?

## Simulation 4: The Effects of Agricultural Expansion

With the model of hunter-gatherer regional settlement optimization now developed, it is possible to return to the question of the effects of agricultural expansion on the hunter-gatherer settlement system. The expansion of agriculture is often explained in terms of its ecologic or economic superiority, presented as an increase in net yield, a reduction of risk, or an increase in marginal value for subsistence effort. The role of labor intensification and the greater marginal value of labor in agricultural subsistence (as a response to population growth) are well documented (Boserup 1965; Spooner 1972), but there is little support for the hypothesized increase in net return rate or risk reduction. In fact, most evidence points to a decrease in the net return rate, with an increase in yield attributable only to increased amounts of time spent in subsistence activities (Limp and Black 1977; Harris 1979). Agriculture appears to be superior to hunting and gathering only after population increases press the marginal return rate of foraging to a point below the marginal return of agriculture. For this reason most explanations of agricultural expansion are heavily dependent on the concept of population pressure (Cohen 1977).

The assumptions about agriculture's economic superiority may ultimately be proven true, but simulation 4 requires only that agriculture be energy equivalent at the local settlement level. The remaining assumptions are fairly straightforward. Sedentary agricultural groups move into the region, locate themselves randomly, and establish use areas which are the same size as the foraging areas of the hunter-gatherer groups. The hunter-gatherers then begin their seasonal settlement dispersion. The conditions of local-level optimization remain unchanged. The hunter-gatherer foraging areas cannot overlap with the agricultural use areas. Since the hunter-gatherers "know" the locations of the agricultural settlements, no attempts are made to search the agricultural use areas for foraging areas. Even though these areas are avoided, the loss of potential foraging areas increases the probability of unsuccessful searches for foraging areas. This increases the expected locational costs per settlement. These increased costs result in a lowering of the optimal number of hunter-gatherer seasonal camps in the region.

A comparison with simulation 3 reveals the trend. With no agriculturist present, the optimal number of hunter-gatherer seasonal camps is thirty (figure 9.5), as previously established. When ten agricultural settlements are added to the region the optimal number of hunter-gatherer camps drops to twenty-three (figure 9.6). The optimal number of hunter-gatherer settlements is further reduced to seventeen once the presence of twenty

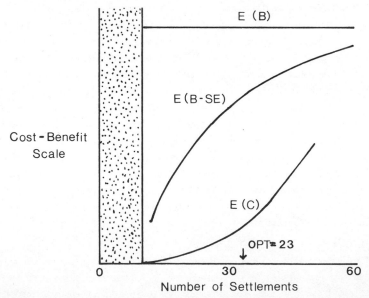

Figure 9.6. The addition of ten sedentary settlements to the region (the speckled region of the graph) increases the seasonal movement costs for mobile groups. These increased costs change the regionally optimal number of settlements. The maximum net return rate for each settlement is now achieved with 23 hunter-gatherer groups in the region.

agricultural groups complicates the seasonal settlement process (figure 9.7). In interpreting the results, the trend and not the absolute values are important. The optimal number of settlements depends on several parameters which have been set arbitrarily. The trend is clear, however. The expansion of agriculturalists into the region reduces the optimal number of hunter-gatherer seasonal camps. This, of course, does not necessarily mean that the number of hunter-gatherer seasonal camps will be reduced. Rather, it implies that the thirty hunter-gatherer groups will find the expected net benefit return rate reduced, and, furthermore, there will exist a selective advantage for any adaptation which

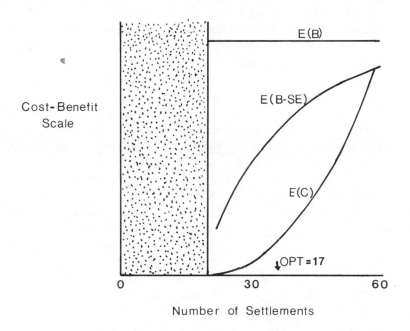

Figure 9.7. With twenty sedentary settlements in the region, the locational costs are further increased. The net return rate for each hunter-gatherer settlement is now maximized with seventeen hunter-gatherer groups in the region.

(1) reduces the number of hunter-gatherer settlements, (2) reduces the seasonal mobility requirement and hence lowers the locational costs, or (3) increases the information-sharing capacity of the hunter-gatherers. All this occurs while the combined hunter-gatherer and agriculturalist settlement density remains low. With the twenty simulated agricultural settlements and seventeen hunter-gatherer camps, only 19 per cent of the region is exploited for subsistence. It is difficult to argue for the direct displacement of hunter-gatherers by agriculturists given that 81 per cent of the region is not utilized. Nor does the argument for resource competition seem to be compelling. The immediate factors influencing the impact of agricultural expansion on hunter-gatherer settlement optimization are the information-processing abilities of the hunter-gatherers, the cost of the information, and the gains in risk aversion attributable to intercamp visiting. The implications of these points will be developed in the discussion.

Simulation 5:  Aggregation and Dispersal

In simulation 5, the impacts of seasonal movement patterns and level of information sharing are explored from a different set of assumptions. Rather than assuming perfect knowledge of the distribution of resources and no knowledge of the seasonal movement plans of other groups, we assume the opposite. All groups have complete information about the seasonal settlement plans of all the other groups. There are no unsuccessful locational attempts since planning avoids overlap of the foraging areas. As a result, movement costs are minimal. What is varied in simulation 5 is the amount of information available about the location of clustered resources. The seasonal dispersal plans of the groups are made on the basis of incomplete knowledge of the distribution of resources. The locational costs of this simulation are then the costs of locating clustered resources which meet the conditions of local-level settlement optimization.

The search for the resource clusters proceeds so that the knowledge of their location is added randomly. The knowledge of the location of known resource clusters does not af-fact the location of the next resource cluster found. As with other assumptions involved with these locational cost models, this may seem highly arbitrary. Knowledge of the envi-ronment is most likely spatially biased, so that knowledge of resource clusters is most likely to be gained near areas which already have known resource clusters. However, the assumption of a random process permits controlled conditions against which the effects of improved efficiency of information sharing and the patterns of seasonal movement can be compared.

The cost of randomly collected information is not a linear relationship. When the amount of information is low, additional information can be collected at low costs. How-ever, as the amount of information collected is increased, the marginal cost for useful in-formation grows rapidly. This can be attributed to the increasing density of known clus-tered resources, which also increases the probability that any new cluster will lie within the foraging area of an already-known cluster. It is the redundancy of the information concerning the foraging areas which increases the costs of adding an additional camp to the region. In other words, the addition of knowledge concerning resource cluster locations opens access to new foraging areas only to the extent that these areas could not be ex-ploited from previously known clusters.

Depending on whether we assume aggregated or dispersed camps to begin with, we get different responses to the addition of information about seasonal resource distributions. The previous simulation experiments have all begun with the hunter-gatherer groups dispers-ing from a uniform hexagonal distribution; the results represent a dispersed to dispersed-seasonal movement pattern. To explore the impact of aggregation on the regional settlement pattern, only one change is required. Simulation 5 includes an experiment that starts with all the groups gathered into a single aggregation. The movement rules remain the same as before; each group moves to the nearest available resource cluster which does not overlap foraging areas of previously settled groups.

These two seasonal movement patterns result in differences in the optimal number of settlements in the region (figure 9.8). When there is little sharing of information about the distribution of resource clusters, as might be expected in regions where the patterns of resource distribution and abundance are highly unpredictable, there is no significant difference between the two seasonal movement patterns. However, as the amount of shared information increases, the aggregated to dispersed-seasonal pattern becomes increasingly more effective in placing the seasonal camps in the region. With both seasonal movement patterns operating with complete knowledge of the distribution of resources, the mean num-ber of settlements was 100 for the simulation of the aggregated to dispersed-seasonal pattern, while the dispersed to dispersed-seasonal settlement simulations have a mean of 91. As a comparison, hexagonal packing results in 168 foraging areas in the simulation landscape. The aggregated to dispersed-seasonal movement plan has an optimum of 73 settlements under the conditions simulated, while the dispersed to dispersed-seasonal pattern has only 60 camps as the optimal. This difference is due to the combination of the common dispersal point of the initially aggregated groups and the minimum movement rule. Together these factors lead to closer spacing between the foraging areas, less wasted space between the foraging areas, lower probabilities that the resource clusters will be located in this wasted space, and hence a greater number of regionally optimal settlements for the initially aggregated groups than for the initially dispersed groups. Seasonal aggregation provides

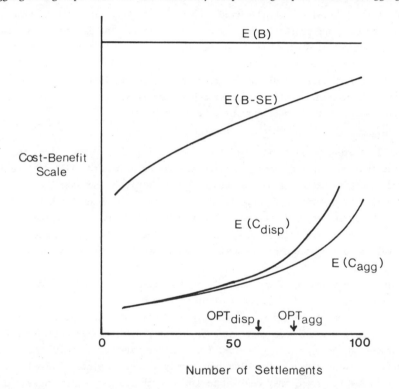

Figure 9.8. The pattern of seasonal movement affects the regional settlement optimization. Settlement systems with aggregation achieve greater maximum net return rates than seasonal movement patterns characterized by dispersed to dispersed movement.

a spatial structuring of the settlement system which extends the value of the information; the difference in the optimal number of settlements exists even though it was assumed that the cost of information, bit for bit, was the same for both seasonal movement patterns. Yet, it is very likely that the groups which begin aggregated would have lower information-processing costs, and so have even higher optimal settlement numbers.

The benefits derived from seasonal aggregations are delayed until the following economic season. As a result, aggregation strategies need not always give the greatest immediate return. It may be advantageous to use an aggregation strategy which, while failing to give optimal returns during the period of aggregation, more than repays the shortfall through the greater access to resources during the period of dispersal.

## Discussion

The goal of this paper has been to use simulation modeling as a tool to point out patterns of variability not usually explored in local-level models of hunter-gatherer settlement processes. The models have grown in complexity as the variables required for the regional settlement model have been identified and incorporated, but rigorous control of assumptions has been maintained. The results have been examined not as precise implications, but as trends in regional patterns discovered by manipulating the important system variables. These discoveries can be used to inform our explanations of regional settlement behavior.

A test of the model goes well beyond the scope of this chapter. Basic modifications transforming many of the general and standardized aspects of the model into the hypothesis-testing format of a precise and realistic model would be required. The gains provided in the general simulations presented here have been the identification of variables important to the process of regional settlement and the recognition of trends in regional settlement systems caused by these variables. A discussion of each of these variables will reveal what has been gained through this qualitative approach to modeling, and will identify specific problems which serve as challenges for future research.

### Seasonal Movement Plans

Ethnographically there appears to be a great deal of variability in the extent to which resource locations and seasonal movement plans are shared. Steward (1938:247) reports an organized information-sharing system among the Owen's Valley Shoshone:

> Many larger villages, however, had a single headman. His title means 'talker'. His task was principally to keep informed about the ripening of plant foods in the different localities, to impart this information to the villagers and, if all the families travelled to the same pine nut area, to manage the trip and help arrange where each was to harvest.

Helm provides a similar observation of the Dogrib's organization of seasonal movement. But evidence exists for a lack of coordinated information sharing as well:

> Neither the composition of the group Le Jeune wintered with nor their ultimate destination was definitely known when they set out. Shortly after his party of 19 left Quebec in canoes and *chaloupes*, they learned from another party of 16 that 'there were a great many Montagnais near the place where they wished to winter,' and together with this second group, they decided to 'turn Northward lest...(they) starve each other.' However, they met ten Indians in four canoes 'which turned them back to the South, saying that the hunting was not good to the North'. The three tent groups decided to winter on the south shore of the St. Lawrence. Leaving their canoes and *chaloupes* at the coast, they went inland, shifting camp twenty-three times in the period of November 12 to April 22. [Leacock 1954:14, translating Le Jeune's account in *The Jesuit Relations*]

There is presently little understanding about how variations in social organization affect the flow of information. Until the information-processing characteristics of various social forms are better understood, much of the variability in settlement behavior will be only poorly explained (Johnson 1978).

### Risk Avoidance

Risk avoidance is another variable which affects the optimal number of settlements in the region. While presently this variable is difficult to measure, it strongly affects

the shape and slope of the confidence limit curve. The entire issue of risk aversion deserves serious anthropological and ecological attention. The fact that risk aversion is
generally studied as a psychological variable should not bar its reformulation for incorporation into a more ecological framework. Some preliminary studies have explored this
problem, but there is much theoretical work to be done. It is likely that a relationship
exists among level of risk aversion, cost of risk aversion, and cost of "losing the bet."
If the decision maker is unable to withstand a large loss, or a series of losses, he may
prefer to bear a moderate risk aversion fee in order to avoid the penalties of the loss.
In this regard, it should be pointed out that the rules of decision making should reflect
the ability of the decision maker to withstand losses; the frequently used optimality es-
timator--the expected net return rate--is justified only as long as the decision maker has
the capacity to endure the short-term fluctuations which occur en route to the long-term
gains (Bradley 1976). The inability of individuals to absorb stochastic fluctuations often
makes the expected net return rate a poor decision-making criterion. Thus risk aversion
may be found to be a function of environmental variability, the ability of the decision-
making unit to survive losses, the response of the risk reduction mechanism when brought
to its limit, and the information-processing powers of the decision makers (Simon 1956).

In particular, the *mechanisms* of risk aversion require investigation. There are two
areas of immediate concern which can be briefly mentioned. First, when and how can an individual optimize the net resource return rate and still manage to leave buffers for the
uncertainty of the future?

Secondly, and of greater anthropological interest, how is risk shifted from individuals to groups, and perhaps back again to individuals, and how does this depend on the
nature of the risk (Vayda and McCay 1975)? Many anthropological phenomena are assumed to
be risk reduction mechanisms, but until the issue of risk reduction is integrated into optimization theory the evaluation of these arguments will remain inconclusive.

## Differential Interactions

In the simulations the mechanism of risk avoidance was the visiting and residential
flux which continuously redistributed the population among the resources. This interaction
of the regional groups was considered as an unweighted factor--each additional group participated fully and equally with every other group. The rate of visiting and residential
shifts was independent of the number of settlements or the relative location of the settlements. These features need to be expanded to incorporate additional complexity before precise predictions can be made. Specifically, the decline of interaction over distance and
the effects of the relative spatial positions in the visiting network need to be considered.
In addition, the patterns of visiting, residence rules, and trading partner formation could
all affect the interactions. The inclusion of distance and social network factors change
the impact of the increased number of regional settlements. The limited ability of hunter-
gatherer band organizations to integrate risk sharing over large numbers of individuals may
be a limiting feature of band organization.

## Resource Abundance

The characteristics of the habitat also play a role in the determination of the number
of settlements. Increases in the abundance of food resources would decrease the size of
the foraging area. As the radius of the foraging areas decreases, there is an accompanying
decrease in the probability that foraging areas will overlap for a given number of settlements. The exact nature of this change, however, depends also on the density of the

resource clusters, which determines the probable distance between foraging area circumferences, and hence the size of the deviation from the condition of closest packing.

## Resource Variability

Besides these static conditions of the habitat, the variability of the environment was also considered. Variability was conceptualized as the standard deviation of the expected benefits, and it thus, in turn, defined the shape of the confidence limit curve. With a specific number of settlements in the region, highly variable habitats without correlation have greater standard errors, and, for each additional settlement, a greater rate of increase in benefits at the lower confidence limit. These more variable habitats need to integrate a greater number of settlements to achieve the regional optimum.

This returns us once more to the difficult issue of the cost of social integration. Given certain assumptions about the form of communication networks and the costs of information processing, it can be shown that the costs of integrating information flows over a region increase sharply as the size of the communication network grows (Johnson 1978). These costs have not been considered in this modeling, but it should be apparent that the costs of nonhierarchial information integration could be great enough to limit the number of settlements to a figure well under the regional optimum identified in the simulation experiments. Under such conditions, however, one might wonder why hunter-gatherers maintain an egalitarian organization, at least with respect to information. Indeed, there is a growing recognition of the nonegalitarian features of many hunting and gathering societies, ranging from Paleolithic Europe to precontact California.

## Spatial Correlation

The degree of spatial correlation among the resource fluctuations was found to affect the benefits expected from group interaction. Correlations among the fluctuations of the foraging areas reduced the benefits of residential flexibility. As the degree of correlation increases, there is a greater likelihood that fluctuations in the expected return will not be canceled out by the mechanisms of visiting or changing residence. There is, as a result, a shallower confidence limit curve, and a generally lower number of optimal settlements. This variable is interesting because there is relatively little attention paid to spatial correlation in discussions of settlement behavior. Yet this may be one of the more important variables for understanding residential flexibility among hunter-gatherers. Additionally, there are few examples of ethnographically described hunter-gatherers from habitats showing high levels of correlation. If temperate forest zones show a greater tendency toward correlation of resource fluctuations, the analogies based on the hunter-gatherers of regions without strong correlation may be misleading. Less residential flexibility and less informal visiting may characterize these groups than present models of hunter-gatherer behavior predict.

## Conclusion

Realism is not a concern of this series of models. The results of the simulations are general and they are precise, but they are noticeably less complex than reality. Resource clusters are not randomly distributed over the landscape, hunter-gatherers do not walk around the environment in a state of total ignorance, and few resource clusters are discovered by hunter-gatherers by using a random walk search pattern. Why, then, should there be all this effort devoted to something which is little more than fantasy?

The answer is simply that it is our theories and models which inform the data. Models which treat settlement as a process which does not necessarily operate with the goal of filling space provide new solutions for old paradoxes, and raise new questions. If hexagonal packing provides for the most efficient use of space and resources, then how is it that overexploitation is avoided? The answer is that it is not the goal of the settlement strategies to fill space, but to maximize the net return rate for each settlement. The models go further by pointing out that optimization for the single settlement has a regional component--the interactions among settlements influence the net return rates. Finally, regional interaction of settlements is more than just the flow of goods, services, and energy; it is the flow of information about the social and ecological environment. The models developed for the interaction of space, information, and resources are less than real, but at least the research does not begin by assuming that social organization (the carrier of information) does not exist.

Ignorance and error are part of everyday life. They are as much a part of the context of human behavior as the distribution of resources or kinship. Yet the limitations of imperfect information and the mechanisms which generate these limitations have been given scant attention by theoreticians. As a result we have an abundance of theory which reveals to us how people should behave rather than how they actually do behave. But the realism or lack of realism of these theories is not the problem. Attempts to confirm that the world meets the assumptions of normative ideal models and, thus, that the implications of these models are directly applicable are misplaced. The generalizations and simplifications which serve as assumptions are, after all, falsified daily by our own experience. The advantage of normative models is that they create yardsticks--standards for measuring the characteristics of the world against a set of firmly anchored concepts. It is through this process that we can identify the cleavage planes in the lattice of our theories, assumptions, and observations. With the identification of these cleavage planes, of the disjunctures created by opposing assumptions and unarticulated variables, we become aware of our theoretical blindspots.

This chapter has identified some of the blind spots of optimal foraging theory by locating the disjuncture which occurs when one moves beyond the opportunistic locational behavior shown at the local level to the settlement optimization behavior shown at the regional level. At the local level, all behavior and the implications of that behavior are observable by the group. For the participants, there is no need to negotiate "understandings" or limitations on the range of behavior. Behavior is negotiated freely and continuously. However, as the effects of distance are felt in the frequency of interaction and communication, the limits imposed by ignorance and error begin to become noticeable. Above the local level, behavioral flexibility can create difficulties as opportunistic behavior by one individual can create disaster for the unknowing. Under these conditions, limits on the range of behavior may be negotiated and "expected" ranges of behavior develop. This limitation on behavioral flexibility contradicts the assumption of full behavioral flexibility which is basic to local-level optimization models.

The simulation experiments have identified some of the factors affecting the size of information-sharing systems and some of the trends in regional settlement systems created by variability in these factors. Within this formulation it is the information-sharing system which carries much of the interplay between local-level flexibility and the development of expected ranges of behavior at larger scales. The capacities of the information-sharing system then can begin to explain some of the variability between opportunistic and "expected" behavior.

# 10

## Overview:
## Optimal Foraging Analysis in Human Ecology

William H. Durham

The various subfields of anthropology have long been united by the common goal of interpreting and explaining the diversity of human attributes in time and space. The studies in this volume contribute directly to this goal through analyses of the diversity of foraging behaviors and settlement patterns among hunter-gatherers, past and present. They show plainly that ecological principles can be called upon to explain an important though surely nonexhaustive proportion of the diversity in these attributes.

The major explanatory principle of this book is adaptation. The authors show that differences in the sizes of human foraging groups, for example, or differences in strategies of resource procurement can often be explained as adaptations to local and regional environmental features. Although the thesis itself is not particularly new in anthropology (see, for example, Hardesty 1977; Moran 1979; and Netting 1977), this book features an explicit definition of adaptation and an accompanying body of theory that are important innovations.

The concept of adaptation embraced here is both rigorous and testable. That concept is the cornerstone of current evolutionary ecology, modified as appropriate for the human context (see Durham 1976a and Richerson 1977), but retaining the basic notion of comparison among "character states" (i.e., alternative forms of an attribute, also called the phenotype set) according to the criterion of reproductive fitness. For human populations, an attribute is adaptive when it can be shown in comparison with alternative character states to confer the likelihood of maximum survival and reproduction for its carriers. Conceived in these terms, the concept of adaptation does not itself prescribe or require any particular evolutionary pathway, biological and/or cultural. Indeed both genetic and cultural modes of inheritance are likely to contribute to many traits in interacting and compounding ways. In the analyses of diversity presented in this volume, the emphasis is on assessing adaptation however evolved. No attempt is made to apply the specifically genetic theories of natural selection to human behaviors. The result, then, is not sociobiology but good and solid human ecology.

It is reasonable to ask of these studies, and indeed of any attempt at ecological anthropology, why a priori one would expect "adaptive explanations" to apply to cultural attributes and life-styles as diverse as those described here for Athapaskans and Inuit. Why, in short, should an ecological approach apply in richly cultural contexts and to peoples who often express concerns far removed from ecological exigencies and the problems of survival and reproduction? A complete answer to such questions is beyond the scope of this volume, but the implicit argument deserves to be aired.

The cultural creations of humanity, including the most richly imaginative of symbols and values, all owe their existence to the biological evolution of unique neurophysiological structures lumped loosely under the term "capacity for culture." Scholars have realized for years that this capacity was itself a product of biological adaptation, but only recently have we begun to explore the full implications of that conclusion. By far the most spectacular of the biological adaptations involved in the emergence of culture was encephalization--the increase through time of cranial capacity far beyond that expected by body size enlargements alone. Harry Jerison (1975:52) summarized the appropriate deduction most succinctly: "The evolution of encephalization in the hominids was the evolution of very large amounts of neuronal tissue beyond the amounts evolved in any other species of primates. This could have occurred *only if* the additional tissue were required to govern selectively advantageous behavior" (emphasis added). The implication is important: as the neuronal tissue evolved and grew, its product, culture, played an increasingly important role in hominid survival and reproduction. One may conclude that adaptation has been a major concern, though certainly not the only concern, of culture and cultures for more than three million years. Against this background, a culture whose attributes reflect little concern for human survival and reproduction must surely be seen as some kind of exception, not the rule. Of course, this does not mean that any society's full set of cultural attributes are uniquely explained by adaptation (see discussion in Durham 1976a). Rather, it means that ecological analysis will have a major, if limited, interpretive power for understanding cultural diversity. This volume represents an important effort in that direction.

Its second feature is the use of optimization models. Drawing upon the work of animal ecologists and economists, the authors attempt to explain hunter-gatherer subsistence activities as part of general "strategies" for optimal resource procurement. This approach assumes that hunter-gatherer survival and reproduction are maximized when the techniques of resource harvest optimize the returns per unit of time and/or energy expended. If this is true, then much of the variability in hunter-gatherer food preferences, settlement patterns, spatial and temporal organization of foraging, and social organization of subsistence should be interpretable as the product of ecological adaptation to different environments and different resources.

In a first attempt to test these expectations, these authors address four questions either implicitly or explicitly: (1) What are the theoretically optimal patterns of resource procurement for hunter-gatherers in a given environment or set of environments? (2) To what extent do hunter-gatherer activities conform to the expected, optimal patterns? (3) How and why did they come to be that way? And finally, (4) to what extent do optimization models help us understand hunter-gatherer diversity? Each of these questions is discussed in turn below.

## What Are the Optimal Strategies?

For most of these authors, answers to question 1 are based on the theoretical arguments of optimal foraging theory. As discussed in chapters 1 and 2, optimal foraging theory is particularly attractive to ecological anthropology because it provides relatively robust and testable predictions on the basis of relatively few assumptions. The authors have taken full advantage of the theory, using it imaginatively and well to characterize energy optimizing diets, group sizes, and hunting techniques in a variety of habitats. Nevertheless, they also make it clear that there is much more to be done. Despite the editors' emphasis on *adapting* the optimal foraging theory models to the human context, the models still have some serious shortcomings that future work must rectify. Let me simply mention two of them.

First, there is a problem in that many optimal foraging theories were developed for studying *solitary* foragers (e.g., the models of diet breadth, patch use, and marginal value). Hunter-gatherer activity is, of course, often collective, and within that collective it is often specialized with respect to resources sought and the direction of the search. Of course, one can argue that the goals of the enterprise are still congruent with the interests of each individual forager in most band-level societies, but this may well be the case only where foraging costs and benefits (and therefore skills) are very evenly distributed. Interesting and largely unexplored variations on the optimality theme are possible when even a small degree of "skewing" is permitted (see discussion in Vehrencamp 1979). For example, when other things are equal, optimal group size will be larger with an even as opposed to uneven distribution of resource returns. Alternatively, a foraging strategy might be skewed by an influential elder or headman in such a way that routine costs and benefits become suboptimal for the *average* forager of a group, or even for the majority of foragers in a group. While again this may not be commonplace in egalitarian bands, it does suggest a need to study the distribution within the group of energies spent and gained. New insights may be forthcoming when we include the systems of distribution and exchange of calories in the analysis in addition to aggregate returns per foray.

A second difficulty with optimal foraging theory is that many of the original arguments involve assumptions unrealistic or overgeneralized for the human context. For one example, the MacArthur-Pianka patch use model (see chapter 2) assumes that foragers search at random through the patches of their habitat, effectively requiring either no familiarity with or no memory of good locations. For another example, the marginal value theorem assumes that foragers have a low probability of return in short intervals to any patch, a condition that is difficult to meet if they depend on a permanent water hole or a circumscribed hunting grounds. To be sure, many assumptions like these are made in the name of simplicity or convenience in order to make a model tractable. In some cases, the predictions are robust and still valid when the assumptions are relaxed. This is true, for example, in the case of Horn's model of colonial nesting which assumes that no information is exchanged among group-living foragers. Allowing such exchange does not alter the major qualitative predictions of the model concerning dispersed versus aggregate settlement, although it could easily affect the size and packing of aggregations. In chapter 5, Heffley is therefore able to draw on Horn's model to interpret relative aggregation/disaggregation cycles in Athapaskan settlement patterns, and the success of her analysis is testimony to the validity of the approach. In general, however, things are not always that nice. For the most part the authors here are cautious, pointing out many of the assumptions violated by human foragers and discussing some of the implications for hunter-gatherer research. However, their new discoveries (such as the "interstice foraging" of chapter 4) and surprisingly ambiguous results (e.g., the discussion of breathing hole hunting in chapter 3) point to the need for building whole new models specifically tailored to the special properties of human foragers. This may prove to be an ambitious goal, but it is also the best way forward.

Moore, in chapter 9 takes a step in the right direction. He begins with a critique of the "all-knowing, computationally perfect decision maker" that is assumed by most optimal foraging theories. Moore's point is that information is itself a resource not freely and uniformly available. In reality, even optimal foragers must organize their activities

on the basis of an incomplete understanding of the environment.  Through a computer simulation of regional hunter-gatherer settlement patterns, we get some idea of just how this
more realistic, limited knowledge assumption may affect hunter-gatherer activity.  If information were perfect, Moore's simulation would allow space for up to 168 optimally foraging "camps" in a hypothetical region.  The number drops to a mean maximum of only 91
camps when groups lacking information attempt an "uncoordinated random search."  Moreover,
location and settlement costs per group grow exponentially with the number of camps already
established.  Obviously, most real situations would fall somewhere between the perfect information and no information models, and, sure enough, a simulation with some information
sharing (simulation 5) produced a mean of 100 settlements (about 60% of the maximum) and a
more gradual increase of location costs.  The implication, of course, is that sparse settlement and "no man's lands" are a ready result of even an optimal foraging strategy.  But the
study has a second important implication deriving from the mechanism of information sharing
in simulation 5.  Part of an optimal foraging strategy may be a seasonal aggregation of
camps into a regional band for the mutual sharing of information that can reduce movement
costs.  As Moore notes, such aggregation may be advantageous even if it fails to give optimal resource returns at the time, so long as it more than compensates during dispersal
through greater (or less costly) access to resources.  These contributions, though relatively modest in themselves, give some idea of the kinds of insights and elaborations we
can expect from more human-centered optimal foraging theories.

Chapter 8 is notable for its relatively novel approach to optimization.  Instead of
drawing on optimal foraging theories from evolutionary ecology, Keene uses linear programming analysis as developed in economics.  The technique, reviewed in Reidhead (1979),
specifies that one combination of available resources that both satisfies the subsistence
needs of a group and does so at the lowest possible cost of time and risk.  Its major advantage over standard optimal foraging theory approaches lies in taking more than the
caloric needs and time constraints of a population into account.  For example, in Keene's
analysis of optimal foraging in the Saginaw Valley in the Late Archaic period, energy was
effectively the "binding constraint" for only four of the calendar months studied (the
relatively low sunlight months of March, April, September, and November).  Constraints
during other months included hides, calcium, and ascorbic acid.  Needless to say, this
technique greatly improves the specificity of optimization research, allowing in Keene's
case for the conclusion that gathering, as opposed to hunting, provided two out of three
key resources in all months except October.  This kind of detail, however, comes at a cost
to the researcher--that of specifying both the foraging costs of each resource included in
the model and the minimum requirement levels for each vitamin, mineral, amino acid, etc.,
included as a criterion.  To make matters worse, the resource costs should be calculated
in a way that does not assume a completely separate foray for each resource, particularly
those that can be hunted or collected as part of mixed or multipurpose strategies.  This
problem can be partially alleviated, although it is not clear that Keene has done so, by
averaging the calculated costs per resource over all the kinds of forays in which it can
be (or has been) obtained.  Provided that one has these kinds of data and patience, however, the technique of linear programming is certain to prove useful for predicting optimal
patterns of resource procurement.  It takes little imagination to predict a bright future
for this approach.

## Do Hunter-Gatherers Conform?

The second major question posed by this volume asks to what extent hunter-gatherers conform to the expectations of optimization theories.  Even the quickest glance at Smith's
table 3.7 on the Inuit or at Yesner's 0.55 rank order correlation for Aleut bird hunting
(chapter 7) is convincing that the results are, in a word, mixed.  The studies assemble
enough positive evidence to be provocative and tantalizing, but the evidence is too scattered and tentative to permit a firm conclusion one way or the other.  Still, there are
reasons to remain optimistic.  As a number of the authors point out, the mixed success is
largely attributable to small sample sizes and weaknesses in optimization models as currently conceived, rather than to an unequivocal test of hypotheses.  A look at a few cases
is instructive.  Consider, for example, Smith's analysis of variability in the size of
foraging groups among the Arctic Inuit.

The central hypothesis of Smith's analysis, that modal group sizes maximize rates of
per capita energy return, is based on a simple graphical model (see figure 3.2) that incorporates two underlying trends.  First, the model allows for what may be called "social
facilitation."  It assumes that the net energy capture rate per individual often increases
with group size over some interval (as shown in figure 10.1 by curve $A$), presumably because
additional foragers allow larger game to be taken or because they help in reducing search
and pursuit times.  The other factor implied by the model is a resource ceiling (see discussion in Durham 1976b).  Let us assume that a foraging group habitually exploits a
bounded foraging area (that it may or may not share with other foraging groups) with a
constant technology.  Under these conditions, we may hypothesize that there exists some
potential upper limit to the rate of total free energy capture from the environment, a
limit set in part by the growth rates and population dynamics of game animals.  If we assume that this maximum "energy potential" is not greatly affected by foraging group size,
it generates a second curve of hyperbolic decrease in the maximum rate of energy capture
per individual as group size increases (curve $B$ in figure 10.1).  If hunter-gatherers are
efficient foragers, the model then predicts a modal foraging group size near the point of
intersection between the two curves.

If I am correct in unraveling the model's assumptions this way, there are a number of
additional predictions worth exploring.  First, one would expect more skilled (more efficient) hunters or gatherers within a population to forage in smaller units than less
skilled (reflecting a steeper slope of curve $A$ in figure 10.1).  Moreover, one would also
expect a smaller variance (or mean/variance ratio) in group sizes among them.  Second,
this form of model calls attention to the way in which individuals are added to or excluded
from the foraging group.  Even in the ideal, energy-conscious population, a close fit between model and behavior can be expected only where foraging group size may vary in a
smooth and continuous fashion.  When harpooning whales, to take a fictitious example, it
may be theoretically most efficient to work as a team of five.  On a calm sea that may
well be possible.  But in bad or unpredictable weather, if the boats can hold only a crew
of four, foraging groups of four or eight may be more common.  If bad weather is more frequent than good, modal group size may well violate the energy optimum.

A similar kind of problem can complicate the analysis of optimally sized residence
units.  Suppose that, in principle, a camp is energy optimal with fifty members.  Provided
the energy does enhance human survival and reproduction (a basic assumption of optimal
foraging theory), group size will eventually swell above fifty, reducing the per capita
energy returns.  But even if such a reduction were noticed right away, one could hardly

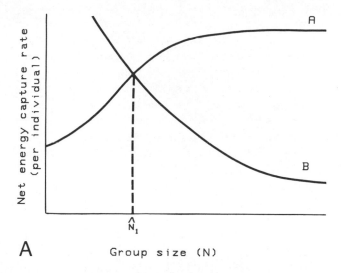

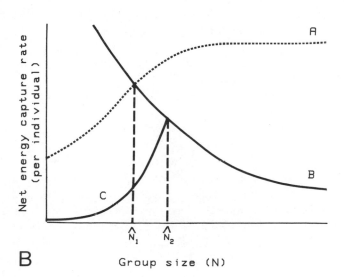

Figure 10.1. Net Energy Capture Rate as a Function of Group Size for a Hypothetical Human Foraging Group. The foragers are assumed to exploit a bounded foraging area with a constant technology. (A) The optimal group size for foraging efficiency ($\hat{N}_1$) occurs at the intersection of curves A and B. Curve A represents "social facilitation," the increased potential efficiency of collective foraging. Curve B depicts a resource ceiling caused by an upper limit to the total energy available from a particular foraging area resource base and technology. (B) The optimal group size for risk avoidance ($\hat{N}_2$) occurs at the intersection of curves C and B. $\hat{N}_2$ will often be greater than $\hat{N}_1$ as shown. The curves labeled A and B are as described above. C represents a hypothetical "reliable rate of energy capture" as a function of group size. It can be measured as the average per capita rate of energy acquisition in the least successful X percent of all hunts.

expect immediate group size adjustment.  First, kinship and lineage affiliations, for
example, or political considerations could hold individuals to the group.  Second, there
is always the issue of just who and how many should go.  Third, even individuals who would
consider leaving may realize that they are better off in a group too large than in a
splinter group with even less efficient foraging.  The point, then, is that the mechanics
of recruitment and fission may mean that the group sizes of efficient foragers only approximately or temporarily correspond with model predictions.

Other factors can cause a more continuous and systematic deflection of group size
from the optimum defined by rates of energy acquisition alone.  First, hunting may commonly
serve *social* functions above and beyond resource procurement, including the education of
future hunters and their socialization into traditional subsistence-related sex roles.
Hunts that regularly assume an additional function of this kind will typically have an optimal foraging group size slightly larger than that expected for energy efficiency, particularly when the apprentice hunters are not yet capable of full participation.  Balikci
(1970:105) provides an example from the Netsilik where boys begin at age ten or eleven to
accompany their fathers on hunting and fishing trips, "performing various light but useful
tasks."  A similar social function may complicate the energy efficiency of the Inuit hunt
types described by Smith.  However, this is unlikely to explain the observed discrepancy
of breathing hole hunting (Smith, figure 3.5) since only able-bodied adults were observed
to take part in those hunts.

A second possible source of systematic bias in group size is perhaps a more important
factor in seal hunting by the Inuit and in other cases as well.  As Smith points out,
*average* per capita rates of energy harvest may be less important than the *variance* in those
rates when a vital resource is both scarce and relatively unpredictable.  Instead of maximizing the overall rate of energy return per se, the optimal strategy may be to maximize
the chances of at least *some* net energy gain with each foraging effort.  In other words,
reliability may be more important than efficiency in an environment where these are to
some extent conflicting goals.

The hypothetical influence of reliability on optimal group size is shown schematically
in figure 10.1B.  Reliability (represented by curve $C$) is shown as an increasing function
of group size.  (Reliability can be operationally defined as the average rate of energy
acquisition in the least successful $X$% of all hunts.  Appropriate values of $X$ are influenced by foraging frequency, storage capacity, nutritional status, and other factors.)
Each value of group size ($N$) is associated with an *average* per capita rate of energy acquisition (defined by curves $A$ and $B$) and a *reliable* per capita rate of energy acquisition
that can be much lower than the average.  As shown in the figure, for example, reliable
energy returns are only one-third of the average.  According to the criterion of reliability, optimal group size will therefore generally be larger than $\hat{N}_1$ by an amount that depends on the density and unpredictability of limiting resources.  In a "harsh" environment
of low density and high unpredictability like winter for the Inuit, human survival and reproduction may depend heavily on reliability with an optimal group size $\hat{N}_2$ considerably
above $\hat{N}_1$ as shown.  Less efficient foraging units may thus be part of a "risk aversion"
strategy of resource procurement.

Smith's data on breathing hole hunting are consistent with these arguments.  As shown
in his figure 3.5, the modal frequency is shifted right from 3 hunters (the size of
greatest efficiency) to 4.  The sample is small (19 hunts), however, and it is not clear
how scarce, unpredictable, or important the seals were during his season of fieldwork.

Nevertheless, it is possible that the observed hunting pattern reflects a traditional emphasis on reliability rather than efficiency.

Additional, descriptive support for the reliability factor is provided at the coresident group level by Balikci's (1970:58) discussion of winter sealing camps among the Netsilik:

Numerous factors influenced settlement dimensions. One was seal availability. Under decreased ecological pressure, the necessity for large groups of people to hunt and stay together decreased and sections of the big community might break away. As soon as the seal hunting returns became less regular, the tendency toward larger group formation reasserted itself.

Unfortunately, Balikci's account does not specify whether the component foraging groups themselves grew larger or were simply more numerous in the larger group formation. Even so, his description does imply that an increase in coresident unit size was a response to irregularities in seal supply.

O'Connell and Hawkes (see chapter 5, above) raise similar questions concerning diet and patch choice by a group of Alyawara foragers in central Australia. They focus on gathering rather than on hunting, and examine a subsistence pattern that contributes less than 5 per cent of today's welfare-subsidized diet. Nevertheless, the data suggest that risk avoidance is again a factor in foraging decisions.

O'Connell and Hawkes present data on nineteen Alyawara forays to three different kinds of patches (mulga woodland, sandhills, and riverine floodplain). One of their conclusions relates directly to efficiency--despite the abundance of seeds in all three patches, seeds have been deleted from the Alyawara diet owing to high collecting and processing costs and the availability of higher-ranked resources. This inference is also consistent with some anecdotal evidence regarding regional variation in Aboriginal diet (seeds are still consumed in other, more arid areas) and the longer-term history of seed and cycad consumption (seeds may have been added to the diet during a dry period 17,000 to 18,000 years ago, and cycads still more recently).

Their second conclusion, however, points to the importance of risk aversion in the choice of foraging patches by contemporary Alyawara. Out of nine forays where low-cost transportation was available (the ethnographer's vehicle) and where the foragers determined their own patch choice, five trips were made to the high-return sandhill sites. But once the known, first-choice sites were exploited, the search for new patches at long distance became "a chancy business." The patch preference of the Alyawara then shifted in three instances to the mulga woodland where they were "more assured of a good [if not maximal] return." The remaining vehicle foray is explained as a "reconnaissance visit" for information more than efficient energy. The risk of failure thus emerges as a factor in one-third of the relevant cases, and this in a society where at least today this kind of risk taking does not have life-and-death consequences.

Admittedly in both Smith's study and that by O'Connell and Hawkes, sample sizes are small and the data are largely inconclusive. Still, the studies do suggest a need to work factors other than energy efficiency per se into models of human foraging. The mechanisms of fission and recruitment, and the social functions of hunting, underscore the need for ecological analyses to be tailored carefully to the cultural as well as the natural environment. The problem of reliability, moreover, emphasizes the need for explicit models of risk aversion in addition to those of optimal efficiency. In the meantime, we run the risk of "false negative" hypothesis testing in terms of optimization.

Smith raises another point requiring serious consideration in future research.  In the discussion of Inuit lake ice jigging he reports that a wide range of group sizes occurs with no clear energy benefit and suggests that in many instances recreational rather than foraging goals may be primary.  The idea here is that recreational foraging may represent a *deliberate* departure from norms of efficiency in a society.  If the foragers consciously seek vacation from normal constraints, then one has a priori grounds for treating the activity as a special exception.  But while there is a certain intuitive appeal to the principle, there is also a danger that we will uncritically label as "recreation" any activity that does not conform to predictions!  In future research we are likely to need some kind of foolproof methodology for recognizing and separating out recreational foraging.

Some similar difficulties were encountered by Yesner (chapter 7) in his analysis of prehistoric food preferences among the Aleuts.  Using optimal foraging theory, Yesner predicts that within the diet breadth of the Aleut, food items should have been harvested in proportion to their natural biomasses.  When testing this prediction against remains in the midden, however, he reports evidence for additional, non-biomass-related selectivity in the harvest of marine invertebrates and birds.  In the ensuing discussion, Yesner lists no fewer than seven additional factors that are ignored by the optimization model in its simplest form but that could help in a fuller explanation of food preferences (species aggregation, ease of exploitation, nonfood yield, social value, taste, nutritional content, and vulnerability to long-term predation).  In this case, as in chapter 3 and elsewhere, the lack of congruence between models and observation is a measure not so much of the theory's failure as of the incompleteness of our models.

My comments to this point imply that hunter-gatherer activity may well be optimized to a great extent, but optimized in ways that we simply do not understand with present models.  That said, however, there is also a reverse problem.  It is always possible that the consistencies we do get between optimal foraging theory and observed foraging behaviors will occur for reasons other than those assumed in the theory.  In the spirit of constructive criticism, let me briefly discuss one possible "alternative explanation" that occurs to me in the exemplary analysis of Cree foraging by Winterhalder (chapter 4).

One of several important contributions here is the finding that Cree abandon even their preferred patches well before the supply of game is exhausted.  As Winterhalder discusses, this is a foraging pattern consistent with the marginal value theorem.  The problem, however, is that this pattern is not a unique prediction of that theory.  Figure 10.2A is a representation of the marginal value theorem showing the time $(T_A)$ that an optimal forager will remain in patches of type $A$ in a mosaic environment.  Figure 10.2B is an alternative scheme based on the idea of "resource management" for the same resource from patches of type $A$.  It shows the hypothetical "total stock" of the resource in a particular patch measured along the left $Y$-axis, a hypothetical renewal rate for the resource on the right $Y$-axis (with a maximum at $K/2$ assuming logistic regrowth), and time in the patch along the $X$-axis as in the Charnov model.  As shown in figure 10.2B, a forager enters the patch and begins harvesting from the resource, causing a decrease in total stock $(S)$ over time (a smooth curve is assumed for simplicity).  Corresponding to each value of total stock is a population growth rate or renewal potential $(R)$ for the resource, measured at right.  A forager that can be expected (1) to return to this patch, (2) to depend upon repeated harvest of the resource there, and (3) to restrict the access of foreign foragers by some form of home range protection (an assumption that avoids the "prudent predator" problem) is predicted to remain in the patch for a roughly equivalent amount of time, $T_A$.

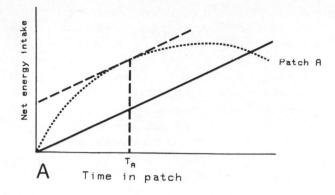

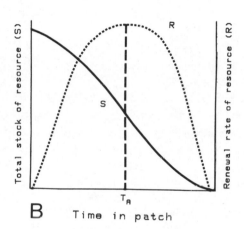

Figure 10.2. Two Models to Explain Forager Abandonment before Depletion. (A) The "marginal value theorem" as explained further in chapter 4. At time $T_A$, when the net rate of energy intake in a given foraging patch (shown as a small dotted curve) drops to the average over all patches (solid line), a forager or group of foragers is expected to abandon the patch. (B) A "resource management theorem" for the same phenomenon. The forager is expected to harvest from the total stock S of the resource or resources in a patch (solid curve) until the time $T_A$, when the remaining stock will have a maximum or near-maximum regrowth rate (shown by dotted curve). Foraging in accordance with this model can provide the maximum sustainable yield from a fixed set of patches.

The forager will thereby maximize the sustainable yield of resources from the patch.

Of course, model 10.2B has its own restrictive assumptions. It is appropriate where there are not infinite numbers of resource patches available, either because of social circumscription or because of time and energy limits on a home range. My point is simply that both models predict the same behavior: both A and B style foragers will leave patches before they are depleted of a resource. In addition, any increase in the rates of harvest by the foragers will, in both cases, cause earlier abandonment. Of course, I cannot claim any expertise on the subject of Cree foraging, but the idea of their resource management is not an idle one. In a film by Ianzelo (National Film Board of Canada, 1975), some Cree hunters discuss their deliberate practice of allowing hunting grounds to lie essentially "fallow" when successive years of hunting cause game to become scarce.

It may be that we simply cannot tell from current knowledge just what causes the Cree to abandon patches before depletion, or it may be both of these reasons and possibly others. My point, however, is that we must consider alternative explanations whenever possible. Alternatives like 10.2A and 10.2B will commonly have important, if subtle, differences in their predictions, and these differences can be compared with empirical data. Such efforts will be rewarded by increasing our sense both of the value and of the limitations of optimal foraging theory.

## Why Do Hunter-Gatherers Optimize (If They Do)?

Of the four questions posed at the outset of this chapter, "why do they optimize?" remains, in my opinion, the least successfully analyzed. Unfortunately, it is also extremely important if only to assess the generality of findings reported here. We need to know both what the specific pressures are for optimal foraging (for example, calorie or protein shortages, heat conservation or stress, cf. Blurton-Jones and Sibly 1978), and when and how those pressures influence changes in behavior. Sadly, few of the authors and little of the data shed new light on the subject.

In chapter 4, Winterhalder perhaps comes the closest to answering such questions in his study of the Cree. He argues that food shortages, even starvation, were recurrent problems during the fur trade period in Canada and presumably even earlier. Attempts to solve these problems would have led to efficient foraging, we suppose, but we do not know the details or even if it was a conscious strategy. It would clearly be useful, given the neo-Darwinian "flavor" of optimization analysis, to understand more of the mechanics of such an adaptation. Ultimately, we would want to know how an optimal solution was struck-- whether by the trial-and-error perseverance of individuals, for example, or by some process of intuition and "rational pre-selection" (after Boehm 1978), or by a group-level mechanism. Other authors here, notably Keene and Yesner, imply or assume that "there is selection across time in favor of groups whose members satisfy [their] requirements, and that this satisfaction is facilitated through cultural mechanisms which govern food preferences and choices" (see chapter 8, above). Group-level selection processes like these are popular in anthropology, and there is no doubt but that they can be and are efficacious. In the context of optimization theory, though, an assumption of group selection raises two additional questions.

First, unless the process is everywhere total and complete, there should remain considerable variability in the levels of optimization achieved by foraging groups. This, of course, implies a very different conception of the world from the alternative view predicting that foragers everywhere optimize as best they can given the constraints of history, chance, and competing goals, and one of its implications is that optimal foraging theory will itself have reduced utility as a general explanatory tool. Second, group selection notions beg the question of how intergroup variability in foraging efficiency would arise in the first place. Some lower-level (individual?) process would still be necessary to explain the emergence and spread of optimal activities within a group. Group selection can therefore not be assumed to be the only process behind optimization, or even the most important of several processes. But the fact remains that we do not fully understand what the other processes are or how they operate. We simply do not know enough about the levels and mechanisms of cultural evolution, either in theory or in practice. More attention to these questions, and to the historical evolution of cultural practices, will greatly help us assess both the validity and the limitations of optimal foraging theory.

To return to chapter 4, Winterhalder clearly favors an individual-level process (see also chapter 2), but again we know next to nothing of the history of Cree foraging practices. He clearly implies that optimization arose in the past as a response to food scarcity, and suggests that the patterns have persisted to the present, even though food shortages are no longer imminent. As he (p. 67, above) says, "The desire to have leisure time within the village and to be with a family, to appear a competent and effective hunter and trapper, and to consume 'healthy' bush food all contribute to the pressure to forage optimally, even though food may be available at a local store." The argument is plausible, and I am certainly sympathetic to the approach. But in the absence of historical data, I find myself wondering about an almost opposite logic. Can we be sure that optimization among the Cree (and elsewhere) occurs simply *despite* the penetration of the outside economy and not to a large extent *because* of that economy? Could it be that outside links since the fur trade, together with the introduction of cash, wristwatches, and internal combustion, have provided many of the problems or at least the priorities behind the optimization we observe? It is difficult to tell from the information available, and to me this only emphasizes the importance of studying the "why" question. In this endeavor, we will need more information on both the history of foraging practices and the reasons people give for doing what they do.

## Does Optimization Theory Help Explain Diversity?

Happily, this review of successes and failures of optimization theory in human ecology can conclude on a positive note in answering the final question, Does it help to explain human diversity? However preliminary these analyses, however crude and rough our models, and however scanty and thin the evidence at present, the work of these authors shows that optimal foraging theory and the linear programming technique can be of significant value in understanding human foragers. The signs all point to an active role for optimization analysis in the development of a true human ecology.

I have two principal reasons to offer for this optimism, one empirical and one philosophical. First, the implication of these studies is that at least in some cases, efficiency models do give empirically verifiable explanations for differences in group foraging activity. The analyses here have helped us to understand the great flexibility in the settlement patterns of the Chipewyans, for example, as they moved through an annual cycle and lived, as they said, like the caribou. They have also helped us account for variability in food preferences among foragers, both over the long haul as in Winterhalder's analysis of reduced diet breadth among the Cree, and over the course of a calendar year as in Keene's description of binding constraints in the Saginaw Valley. In these cases and others, optimization principles have given us at least part of the answers we need, and they have generated further hypotheses and research goals. Continued work will no doubt help us to understand why some subsistence patterns are stable and others changing, why some hunter-gatherers persist in foraging and others shift to agriculture, why some diets are specialized and others more diverse, why some groups aggregate seasonally and others remain dispersed, and why some groups deliberately conserve resources and others exploit and move on, to name a few areas. The models will probably get both more specifically human oriented and more sophisticated, but an important start has here been made.

A second reason for optimism about optimal foraging analysis is that the subject is a good microcosm for studying the patterns and processes of human adaptation. As we have seen, optimization models deal with the same cost-benefit tradeoffs and simultaneous solutions to multiple demands that adaptation itself engenders, at least according to current theory. Moreover, whatever else human societies may do in an environment, they must always establish behavior patterns appropriate to the acquisition and control of sufficient free energy. In some cases, these patterns are only a very small part of total behavior, to be sure, but even then energy relations are a sort of "bottom line" on human adaptation. Studying that bottom line is an appropriate and urgent prerequisite to understanding the other facets of society and culture.

Ultimately, of course, adaptation is believed to work in units of reproduction--not in time, energy, or nutrients--and the resulting attributes are thought by most scholars to be reproduction optimizers rather than energy optimizers per se. Still, there is a place for energy-based analysis (or combined energy-nutrient analysis). First, there are practical concerns. Energy is frankly a convenient proxy for survival and reproduction as a measure of adaptation. It is measurable, additive, and of equivalent meaning across time periods and habitats. As Moore (chapter 9) points out, it is certainly not a perfect measure; but it correlates. Moreover, the state of energy-based theory is reasonably well advanced, offering both optimal foraging theories and linear programming techniques as research tools, as we have seen. As unsatisfying as these procedures may sometimes be, they are certainly better than starting out cold. One may predict an increased use of demographic measures and nutritional status in future studies of forager adaptation, but, in the meantime, energy analysis may be the best we can do.

Second, apart from convenience, energy and nutrients are probably very good proxies for the study of foraging adaptations in many of the world's environments and social systems. As discussed by Smith (1979b), there is reason to expect a relatively close correlation between rates of energy acquisition (and/or nutrient acquisition) and foragers' survival and reproduction both in diverse ecological settings and over much of the existing range in acquisition rates. Where energy is itself a limiting resource, increased efficiency or reliability of procurement will contribute directly to human reproductive success. This leads one to predict a very useful application of optimal foraging analysis in habitats of low biological productivity (e.g., at high latitudes, high altitudes, or areas with low precipitation). Many of the world's foraging peoples presently inhabit these so-called "marginal" habitats, and, indeed, many of the best examples of optimal foraging assembled in this volume come from such environments.

The correlation, however, is certainly not restricted to low-productivity environments. Again, Smith (1979b) has argued that acquisition rates will correlate with adaptive success wherever time is a direct or indirect constraint for foragers. In these situations, optimal foraging is expected because it will help to free time for other pursuits. Its benefits are therefore not limited by the theory to marginal environments. Of course, there may always be exceptional cases in which human foragers are limited by social or environmental factors that time and energy cannot supply. Any such "original affluent society" will organize its activities and pursue subsistence tasks without regard to efficiency, reliability, or waste. Although these cases are probably rare, their existence in no sense undermines the utility of optimal foraging analysis in other places. The assumptions of optimization theorems define their appropriate if not universal realm of application among hunter-gatherer populations. Within this realm, optimal foraging analysis can and does provide new insights and explanations of human diversity, as we have seen. It is a safe bet that the lessons learned in this realm will be useful as we expand and work toward a more general understanding of patterns and processes of human adaptation.

# References

Adams, R. H. 1975. *Energy and structure: a theory of social power*. Austin: University of Texas Press.

_____. 1978. Man, energy and anthropology: I can feel the heat, but where's the light? *Am. Anthrop.* 80:297-309.

Ahti, T., and Hepburn, R. L. 1967. *Preliminary studies on woodland caribou range, especially on lichen stands, in Ontario*. Ontario Department of Lands and Forests Research Report (Wildlife) No. 74.

Aigner, J. S. 1974. Studies in the early prehistory of Nikolski Bay: 1937-1971. *Anthrop. Pap. University of Alaska* 16:9-25.

_____. 1976. Early Holocene evidence for the Aleut maritime adaptation. *Arctic Anthrop.* 13:32-45.

Alcock, J. 1975. *Animal behavior: an evolutionary approach*. Cambridge, MA: Sinauer.

Alexander, R. D. 1974. The evolution of social behavior. *Ann. Rev. Ecol. Syst.* 5:325-83.

Alland, A., Jr. 1975. Adaptation. *Ann. Rev. Anthrop.* 4:59-73.

Alland, A., Jr., and McCay, B. J. 1973. The concept of adaptation in biological and cultural evolution. In *Handbook of social and cultural anthropology*, ed. J. Honigmann, pp. 143-78. Chicago: Rand McNally.

Allen, H. R. 1972. Where the crow flies backwards: man and land in the Darling Basin. Ph.D. dissertation, Australian National University.

_____. 1974. The Bagundji of the Darling Basin: cereal gatherers in an uncertain environment. *World Archaeol.* 5:309-22.

Allen, W. T. R., and Cudbird, B. S. V. 1971. *Freeze-up and break-up dates of water bodies in Canada*. Canadian Meteorological Service (CLI-1-71), Toronto.

Altman, S. A., and Wagner, S. S. 1978. A general model of optimal diet. In *Recent advances in primatology*, Vol. 1, ed. D. J. Chivers and J. Herbert, pp. 407-14. London: Academic Press.

Anders, G., ed. 1967. *The east coast of Baffin Island: an area economic survey*. Ottawa: Department of Native Affairs and Northern Research, Industrial Division.

Anderson, D. R. 1975. Optimal exploitation strategies for an animal population in a Markovian environment: a theory and an example. *Ecology* 56:1281-97.

Anderson, J. N. 1973. Ecological anthropology and anthropological ecology. In *Handbook of social and cultural anthropology*, ed. J. Honigmann, pp. 179-239. Chicago: Rand McNally.

Andersson, M. 1978.  Optimal foraging area: size and allocation of search effort.  *Theor. Pop. Biol.* 13:397-409.

Andrews, J. T. 1973.  The Wisconsin Laurentide ice sheet: dispersal centers, problems of rates of retreat, and climatic implications.  *Arctic and Alpine Res.* 5:185-99.

Baker, P. T. 1962.  The application of ecological theory to anthropology.  *Am. Anthrop.* 64:15-22.

Balikci, A. 1964.  Development of basic socio-economic units in two Eskimo communities.  National Museums of Canada Bulletin 202.  Ottawa.

_____. 1970.  *The Netsilik Eskimo.*  Garden City, NY: Natural History Press.

Banfield, A. W. F. 1954a.  Preliminary investigation of the barren-ground caribou, Part 1.  *Canadian Wildl. Mgmt. Bull.*  Series 1, No. 10A.

_____. 1954b.  Preliminary investigation of the barren-ground caribou, Part 2.  *Canadian Wildl. Mgmt. Bull.* Series 1, No. 10A.

_____. 1974.  *The mammals of Canada.*  Toronto: University of Toronto Press.

Bartholomew, G. A., Jr. 1942.  The fishing activities of double-crested cormorants on San Francisco Bay.  *Condor* 44:13-21.

Bartholomew, G. A., Jr., and Birdsell, J. B. 1953.  Ecology and the protohominids.  *Am. Anthrop.* 55:481-98.

Beardsley, R. K. 1956.  Functional and evolutionary implications of community patterning.  In *Seminars in archaeology: 1955,* ed. R. Wauchope, pp. 129-57.  Society for American Archaeology Memoir No. 11.

Beaton, J. M. 1977.  Dangerous harvest: investigations in the late prehistoric occupation of upland south-east central Queensland.  Ph.D. dissertation, Australian National University.

Bellrose, F. C. 1976.  *Ducks, geese and swans of North America.*  Harrisburg, PA: Stackpole Books.

Belovsky, G. E. 1978.  Diet optimization in a generalist herbivore: the moose.  *Theor. Pop. Biol.* 14:105-34.

Bennett, J. W. 1969.  *Northern plainsmen: adaptive strategy and agrarian life.*  Chicago: Aldine-Atherton.

Berkes, F. 1977.  Fishery resource use in a subarctic Indian community.  *Human Ecol.* 5:289-308.

Berkes, F., and Farkas, C. S. 1978.  Eastern James Bay Cree Indians: changing patterns of wild food use and nutrition.  *Ecology of Food and Nutrition* 7:155-72.

Bertram, B. C. R. 1976.  Kin selection in lions and in evolution.  In *Growing points in ethology,* ed. P. P. G. Bateson and R. A. Hinde, pp. 281-301.  Cambridge:  Cambridge University Press.

_____. 1978.  Living in groups: predators and prey.  In *Behavioral ecology: an evolutionary approach,* ed. J. R. Krebs and N. B. Davies, pp. 64-96.  Oxford: Blackwell Scientific Publications.

Bicchieri, M. G., ed. 1972.  *Hunters and gatherers today.*  New York: Holt, Rinehart and Winston.

Binford, L. R. 1976.  Forty-seven trips.  In *Contributions to the anthropology of the interior peoples of north Alaska,* ed. E. S. Hall.  *Archeol. Survey of Canada* 49:299-351.

_____. 1978.  *Nunamiut ethnoarchaeology.*  New York: Academic Press.

_____. 1980.  Willow smoke and dogs' tails: hunter-gatherer settlement systems and archeological site formation.  *Am. Antiq.* 45:4-20.

Birdsell, J. B. 1957. Some population problems involving Pleistocene man. *Cold Spring Harbor Symp. Quant. Biol.* 22:47-69.

_____. 1958. On population structure in generalized hunting and collecting populations. *Evolution* 12:189-205.

_____. 1968. Some predictions for the Pleistocene based on equilibrium systems among recent hunter-gatherers. In *Man the hunter*, ed. R. B. Lee and I. DeVore, pp. 229-40. Chicago: Aldine.

_____. 1973. A basic demographic unit. *Curr. Anthrop.* 14:337-56.

Bishop, C. A. 1974. *The northern Ojibwa and the fur trade: an historical and ecological study*. Toronto: Holt, Rinehart and Winston of Canada.

Bishop, R. H., and Rausch, R. A. 1974. Moose population fluctuations in Alaska. *Naturaliste Canadien* 101:559-93.

Black, M. 1970. The Round Lake Ojibwa: 1968-1970. In *The Round Lake Ojibwa: the people, the land, the resources, 1968-1970*, pp. 154-378. Indian Development Study in North-western Ontario. Ontario: Department of Lands and Forests.

Black, R. F. 1974. Late Quaternary sea-level changes, Umnak Island, Aleutians: their effects on ancient Aleuts and their causes. *Quaternary Res.* 4:267-84.

_____. 1975. Late Quaternary geomorphic processes: effects on the ancient Aleuts of Umnak Island in the Aleutians. *Arctic* 28:159-69.

_____. 1976. Geology of Umnak Island, eastern Aleutian Islands, as related to the Aleuts. *Arctic and Alpine Res.* 8:73-75.

Blurton Jones, N. G. 1976. Growing points in human ethology: another link between ethology and the social sciences? In *Growing points in ethology*, ed. P. P. G. Bateson and R. A. Hinde, pp. 427-50. Cambridge: Cambridge University Press.

Blurton Jones, N. G., and Sibly, R. M. 1978. Testing adaptiveness of culturally determined behavior: do Bushmen women maximize their reproductive success by spacing births widely and foraging seldom? In *Human behaviour and adaptation*, ed. N. G. Blurton Jones and V. Reynolds, pp. 135-57. Society for the Study of Human Biology Symposium No. 18. London: Taylor and Francis.

Boas, F. 1888. *The central Eskimo*. Sixth Annual Report, Bureau of American Ethnology. Washington, D. C.: Smithsonian Institution. (Repr. 1964. Lincoln: University of Nebraska Press.)

Boehm, C. 1978. Rational preselection from *Hamadryas* to *Homo sapiens*: the place of deci-sions in the adaptive process. *Am. Anthrop.* 80(2):265-96.

Bonini, C. P. 1963. *Simulation of information and decisions systems in the firm*. Englewood Cliffs: Prentice-Hall.

Boserup, E. 1965. *The conditions of agricultural growth*. Chicago: Aldine.

Bowdler, S. 1977. The coastal colonization of Australia. In *Sunda and Sahul: prehistoric studies in Southeast Asia, Melanesia and Australia*, ed. J. Allen, J. Golson, and R. Jones, pp. 204-46. New York: Academic Press.

Bowler, J.; Hope, G.; Jennings, J.; Singh, G.; and Walker, D. 1976. Late Quaternary climates of Australia and New Guinea. *Quaternary Res.* 6:359-94.

Bradley, J. V. 1976. *Probability, decision, statistics*. Englewood Cliffs: Prentice-Hall.

Brand, C. J.; Keith, L. B.; and Fischer, C. A. 1976. Lynx responses to changing snowshoe hare densities in central Alberta. *J. Wildl. Mgmt.* 40:416-28.

Brokensha, P. 1975. *The Pitjantjatjara and their crafts*. Sydney: Aboriginal Arts Board.

Brown, J. L. 1963. Social organization and behavior of the Mexican Jay. *Condor* 65:126-53.

_____. 1964. The evolution of diversity in avian territorial systems. *Wilson Bull.* 76:160-69.

Brown, J. L. 1975. *The evolution of behavior*. New York: W. W. Norton.

Brown, J. L., and Orians, G. H. 1970. Spacing patterns in mobile animals. *Ann. Rev. Ecol. Syst.* 1:239-62.

Bryson, R. A. 1966. Air masses, streamlines and the boreal forest. *Geog. Bull.* 8:228-69.

Bryson, R. A., and Hare, F. K. 1974. The climates of North America. In *World Survey of Climatology*, Vol. 11: Climates of North America, ed. R. A. Bryson and F. K. Hare, pp. 1-47. Amsterdam: Elsevier.

Bryson, R. A.; Wendland, W. M.; Ives, J. D.; and Andrews, J. T. 1969. Radiocarbon iso-chrones on the disintegration of the Laurentide Ice Sheet. *Arctic and Alpine Res.* 1-14.

Bulmer, M. G. 1974. A statistical analysis of the 10-year cycle in Canada. *J. Animal Ecol.* 43:701-18.

Burch, E. S., Jr. 1972. The caribou/wild reindeer as a human resource. *Am. Antiq.* 37: 339-68.

Burling, R. 1962. Maximization theories and the study of economic anthropology. *Am. Anthrop.* 64:802-21.

Busse, C. D. 1978. Do chimpanzees hunt cooperatively? *Am. Nat.* 53:767-70.

Butzer, K. W. 1975. The ecological approach to archaeology: are we really trying? *Am. Antiq.* 40:106-11.

_____. 1977. Environment, culture and human evolution. *Am. Sci.* 65:572-84.

_____. 1978a. Toward an integrated, contextual approach in archaeology: a personal view. *J. Archeol. Sci.* 5:191-93.

_____. 1978b. Climate patterns in an un-glaciated continent. *Geographical Magazine* 51(3):201-8.

Callan, H. 1970. *Ethology and society: towards an anthropological view*. Oxford: Clarendon Press.

Campbell, D. T. 1965. Variation and selective retention in sociocultural evolution. In *Social change in developing areas*, ed. H. R. Barringer, G. I. Blanksten, and R. W. Mack, pp. 19-49. Cambridge, MA: Schenkman.

Caraco, T. 1979. Time budgeting and group size. *Ecology* 60:611-27.

Caraco, T.; Martindale, S.; and Whittam, T. S. n.d. An empirical demonstration of risk-sensitive foraging preferences. *An. Behav.* (in press).

Caraco, T., and Wolf, L. 1975. Ecological determinants of group sizes of foraging lions. *Am. Nat.* 109:343-52.

Carbyn, L. N. 1971. Densities and biomass relationships of birds nesting in boreal forest habitats. *Arctic* 24:51-61.

Carmichael, D. L. 1977. Preliminary archeological survey of Illinois uplands and some be-havioral implications. *Midcontinental J. of Archaeol.* 2:219-52.

Carneiro, R. L. 1978. Comment on "Food taboos, diet, and hunting strategy," by E. B. Ross. *Curr. Anthrop.* 19:19-20.

_____. 1979. Tree felling with the stone ax: an experiment carried out among the Yanomamo Indians of southern Venezuela. In *Ethnoarchaeology*, ed. C. Kramer. New York: Columbia University Press.

Cashdan, Elizabeth. 1980. Egalitarianism among hunters and gatherers. *Am. Anthrop.* 82: 116-20.

Chang, Kwang-Shih. 1962. A typology of settlement and community patterns in some circumpolar societies. *Arctic Anthrop.* 1:28-41.

Charnov, E. L. 1976a. Optimal foraging, the marginal value theorem. *Theor. Pop. Biol.* 9:129-36.

_____. 1976b. Optimal foraging: attack strategy of a mantid. *Am. Nat.* 110:141-51.

Charnov, E. L., and Orians, G. H. 1973. Optimal foraging: some theoretical explanations. Department of Biology, University of Utah.

Charnov, E. L.; Orians, G. H.; and Hyatt, K. 1976. Ecological implications of resource depression. *Am. Nat.* 110:247-59.

Chesson, J. 1978. Measuring preference in selective predation. *Ecology* 59:211-15.

Chippendale, G. M. 1971. Check list of Northern Territory plants. *Proc. Linnaean Soc. New South Wales* 96(4):209-67.

Clark, J. G. B. 1975. *The Earlier Stone Age of Scandinavia*. Cambridge: Cambridge University Press.

Cleland, C. E. 1966. The prehistoric animal ecology and ethnozoology of the upper Great Lakes region. *Anthropological Paper* No. 29. Museum of Anthropology, University of Michigan, Ann Arbor.

_____. 1976. The focal-diffuse model: an evolutionary perspective on the pre-historic cultural adaptations of the eastern United States. *Midcontinental J. of Archaeol.* 1:59-76.

Cleland, J. B. 1932. Botanical notes of anthropological interest from MacDonald Downs, central Australia. *Trans. Royal Soc. of South Australia* 56:36-38.

Clutton-Brock, T. H. 1974. Primate social organisation and ecology. *Nature* 250:539-42.

Clutton-Brock, T. H., and Harvey, P. H. 1977. Primate ecology and social organisation. *J. Zool.* (London) 183:1-39.

_____, eds. 1978a. *Readings in sociobiology*. San Francisco: W. H. Freeman.

_____. 1978b. Mammals, resources and reproductive strategies. *Nature* 273:191-95.

Coady, J. W. 1974. Influence of snow on behavior of moose. *Naturaliste Canadian* 101:417-36.

Cody, M. L. 1971. Finch flocks in the Mohave Desert. *Theor. Pop. Biol.* 2:142-58.

_____. 1974. Optimization in ecology. *Science* 183:1156-64.

Cody, M. L., and Diamond, J. M., eds. 1975. *Ecology and the evolution of communities*. Cambridge, MA: Harvard University Press.

Cohen, M. 1977. *The food crisis in prehistory: overpopulation and the origins of agriculture*. New Haven: Yale University Press.

Colwell, R. K., and Futuyama, D. J. 1971. On the measurement of niche breadth and overlap. *Ecology* 52:567-76.

Comins, H. N., and Hassell, M. P. 1979. The dynamics of optimally foraging predators and parasitoids. *J. An. Ecol.* 48:335-51.

Cooke, R. G. 1978. Maximizing a valuable resource: the white-tailed deer in prehistoric central Panama. Paper presented to the Society for American Archaeology, Tucson.

Cooper, L., and Steinberg, D. 1974. *Methods and applications of linear programming*. Philadelphia: Saunders.

Cowan, C. W., and Smart, T. 1979. Plant remains from 20SA198 and 20SA380. In A. S. Keene, Prehistoric hunter-gatherers of the deciduous forest: a linear programming approach to Late Archaic subsistence in the Saginaw Valley (Michigan), pp. 435-65. Ph.D. dissertation, University of Michigan.

Cowie, R. J. 1977. Optimal foraging in great tits (*Parus major*). *Nature* 268:137-39.

Crook, J. H. 1965. The adaptive significance of avian social organization. *Symp. Zool. Society of London* 14:181-218.

_____. 1970a. Introduction -- social behaviour and ethology. In *Social behaviour in birds and mammals*, ed. J. H. Crook, pp. xxi-xl. London: Academic Press.

_____. 1970b. Social organization and the environment: aspects of contemporary social ethology. *An. Behav.* 18:197-209.

_____. 1972. Sexual selection, dimorphism, and social organization in the primates. In *Sexual selection and the descent of man, 1871-1971*, ed. B. G. Campbell, pp. 231-81. Chicago: Aldine.

Crook, J. H.; Ellis, J. E.; and Goss-Custard, J. D. 1976. Mammalian social systems: structure and function. *An. Behav.* 24:261-74.

Cummins, K. W., and Wychuck, J. C. 1971. Caloric equivalents for investigations in ecological energetics. Internationale Vereinigung fuer Theoretische und Angewandte Limnologie Mitteilung No. 18.

Curry, L. 1964. The random spatial economy: an exploration in settlement theory. *Ann. Assoc. Am. Geog.* 54:138-46.

Dacey, M. F. 1963. Certain properties of edges on a polygon in a two dimensional aggregate having randomly distributed nuclei. University of Pennsylvania, Wharton School. Mimeo.

Dadswell, I. W. 1934. The chemical composition of some plants used by Australian Aborigines as food. *Australian J. Experi. Biol. Medical Sci.* 12:13-18.

Dall, W. H. 1877. On succession in the shell-heaps of the Aleutian Islands. In *Tribes of the extreme Northwest*, ed. W. H. Dall. Washington, D.C.: Government Printing Office.

Damas, D. 1969a. The study of cultural ecology and the ecology conference. In *Contributions to anthropology: ecological essays*, ed. D. Damas, pp. 1-12. National Museums of Canada Bulletin 230. Ottawa.

_____, ed. 1969b. *Contributions to anthropology: ecological essays*. National Museums of Canada Bulletin 230. Ottawa.

_____, ed. 1969c. *Contributions to anthropology: band societies*. National Museums of Canada Bulletin 228. Ottawa.

_____. 1972. The Copper Eskimo. In *Hunters and gatherers today*, ed. M. Bicchieri, pp. 3-50. New York: Holt, Rinehart and Winston.

_____. 1973. Environment, history, and central Eskimo society. In *Cultural ecology*, ed. B. Cox, pp. 269-300. Toronto: McClelland and Stewart. (Orig. pub. 1969 in *Ecological essays*, ed. D. Damas, National Museums of Canada Bulletin 230. Ottawa.)

Davies, N. B. 1977. Prey selection and the search strategy of the spotted flycatcher (*Muscicapa striata*): a field study on optimal foraging. *An. Behav.* 25:1016-33.

Denham, W. W. 1972. The detection of patterns in Alyawara nonverbal behavior. Ph.D. dissertation, University of Washington.

_____. 1974a. Infant transport among the Alyawara tribe, central Australia. *Oceania* 44:253-77.

_____. 1974b. Population structure, infant transport, and infanticide among modern and Pleistocene hunter-gatherers. *J. Anthrop. Res.* 30:191-98.

_____. 1975. Population properties of physical groups among the Alyawara tribe of central Australia. *Archaeol. and Phys. Anthrop. Oceania* 10:114-51.

_____. 1977. Alyawara ethnographic project: a status report. *Newsletter of the Australian Inst. of Aboriginal Studies* 7:45-47.

_____. 1978. Alyawara ethnographic data base. HRAFlex Book 015-001. New Haven: Human Relations Area Files.

_____. n.d. Unpublished field notes. Australian Institute of Aboriginal Studies.

Denham, W. W.; McDaniel, C. K.; and Atkins, J. R. 1979. Aranda and Alyawara kinship: a quantitative argument for a double helix model. *Am. Ethnol.* 6:1-23.

Denniston, G. B. 1973. Ashishik Point: An economic analysis of a prehistoric Aleutian community. Ann Arbor: University Microfilms.

Dortch, C. 1976. Two engraved stone plaques of late Pleistocene age from Devil's Lair, Western Australia. *Archaeol. and Phys. Anthrop. Oceania* 11:32-44.

Draper, H. H. 1977. The Aboriginal Eskimo diet in modern perspective. *Am. Anthrop.* 79: 309-16.

Driebeek, N. J. 1969. *Applied linear programming.* Reading: Addison-Wesley.

Dunning, R. W. 1959. *Social and economic change among the northern Ojibwa.* Toronto: University of Toronto Press.

Durham, W. H. 1976a. The adaptive significance of cultural behavior. *Human Ecol.* 4:89-121.

_____. 1976b. Resource competition and human aggression, part I: a review of primitive war. *Q. Rev. Biol.* 51:385-415.

_____. 1978. Toward a coevolutionary theory of human biology and culture. In *The sociobiology debate*, ed. A. L. Caplan, pp. 428-48. New York: Harper and Row.

Durnin, J. V. G. A., and Passmore, R. 1967. *Energy, work and leisure.* London: Heinemann.

Dustin, F. 1968. Saginaw Valley archaeology. *Mich. Archaeol.* 14:1-130.

Dyson-Hudson, R., and Smith, E. A. 1978. Human territoriality: an ecological reassessment. *Am. Anthrop.* 80:21-41.

Earle, T. K. 1980. A model of subsistence change. In *Modeling of prehistoric subsistence economics*, ed. T. K. Earle and A. L. Christensen, pp. 1-29. New York: Academic Press.

Eisenberg, J. F.; Muckenhirn, N. A.; and Rudran, R. 1972. The relation between ecology and social structure in primates. *Science* 176:863-74.

Elton, C. 1942. *Voles, mice and lemmings.* Oxford: Clarendon Press.

Ember, C. R. 1978. Myths about hunter-gatherers. *Ethnology* 17:439-48.

Emlen, J. M. 1966. The role of time and energy in food preference. *Am. Nat.* 100:611-17.

_____. 1968. Optimal choice in animals. *Am. Nat.* 102:385-89.

_____. 1973. *Ecology: an evolutionary approach.* Reading, MA: Addison-Wesley.

Emlen, S. T. 1978. Co-operative breeding. In *Behavioral ecology*, ed. J. R. Krebs and N. B. Davies, pp. 245-81. Oxford: Blackwell Scientific Publications.

_____. 1980. Ecological determinism and sociobiology. In *Sociobiology: beyond nature/ nuture?* ed. G. W. Barlow and J. Silverberg, pp. 125-50. Boulder, CO: Westview Press.

Emlen, S. T., and Oring, L. 1977. Ecology, sexual dimorphism, and the evolution of mating systems. *Science* 197:215-23.

Environment Canada 1963-1975. *Canadian Weather Review.* 13 Vols. Downsview, Ontario: Environment Canada, Atmospheric Environment.

Estabrook, G. F., and Dunham, A. E. 1976. Optimal diet as a function of absolute abundance, relative abundance, and relative value of available prey. *Am. Nat.* 110:401-13.

Fairchild, J. D. 1977. The Schmidt site: a pre-Nipissing village in the Saginaw Valley, Michigan. M.A. thesis, Western Michigan University, Kalamazoo.

Farmer, F. A.; Ho, M. L.; and Neilson, H. R. 1971. Analyses of meats eaten by humans or fed to dogs in the Arctic. *J. Canadian Diet. Assoc.* 32:137-41.

Farmer, F. A., and Neilson, H. R. 1967. The caloric value of meats and fish of northern Canada. *J. Canadian Diet. Assoc.* 28:174-78.

Fay, F., and Cade, T. J. 1959. An ecological analysis of the avifauna of St. Lawrence Island, Alaska. *University of California Publications in Zoology* 63:73-150.

Feit, H. A. 1973. The ethno-ecology of the Waswanipi Cree; or How hunters can manage their resources. In *Cultural ecology*, ed. B. Cox, pp. 115-25. Toronto: Stewart and McClelland.

Fiscus, C. H. 1961. Growth in the steller sea-lion. *J. Mammal.* 42:218-23.

Fitting, J. E., ed. 1972. The Schultz site at Green Point. University of Michigan Museum of Anthropology Memoir No. 4.

_____. 1975. *The archaeology of Michigan*. Bloomfield Hills, MI: Cranbrooke Institute of Science.

Flannery, K. V. 1972. The cultural evolution of civilizations. *Ann. Rev. Ecol. Syst.* 3: 399-426.

Foley, R. 1977. Space and energy: a method for analyzing habitat value and utilization in relation to archaeological sites. In *Spatial archaeology*, ed. D. L. Clarke. New York: Academic Press.

Foote, D. C. 1965. Exploration and resource utilization in northwestern Arctic Alaska before 1855. Ph.D. Thesis, McGill University.

_____. 1967. Nutrient values of selected animals. In *The east coast of Baffin Island: an area economic survey*, ed. G. Anders, Appendix A. Ottawa: Department of Indian and Northern Affairs.

_____. 1968. An Eskimo sea-mammal and caribou hunting economy: human ecology in terms of energy. Eighth International Congress of Anthropological and Ethnological Sciences, Tokyo, pp. 262-67.

Foote, D. C., and Williamson, H. A. 1966. A human geographical study. In *Environment of the Cape Thompson region, Alaska,* ed. N. J. Wilimovsky and J. N. Wolfe, pp. 1041-1107. Washington, D.C.: U.S. Atomic Energy Commission, Division of Technical Information, PNE - 481.

Ford, R. J. 1974. Northeastern archeology: past and future directions. *Ann. Rev. Anthrop.* 3:385-413.

_____. 1977. Evolutionary ecology and the evolution of human ecosystems: a case study from the midwestern U.S.A. In *Explanation of prehistoric change*, ed. J. N. Hill, pp. 153-84. Albuquerque, NM: University of New Mexico Press.

Formozov, A. N. 1973. Snow cover as an integral factor of the environment and its importance in the ecology of mammals and birds. Occasional Publ. of the Boreal Institute of the University of Alberta No. 1, Trans. W. Prychodko and W. O. Pruitt, Jr. (Orig. pub. 1946.)

Francis, G. R., and Stephenson, A. B. 1972. *Marten ranges and food habitats in Algonquin Provincial Park, Ontario*. Ontario Ministry of Natural Resources Research Report (Wildlife) No. 91.

Freeman, M. M. R. 1970. Studies in maritime hunting I. Ecologic and technologic restraints on walrus hunting, Southampton Island, N.W.T. *Folk* 11/12:155-71.

_____, ed. 1976. *Inuit land use and occupancy report*. Ottawa: Queen's Printer.

Fretwell, S. D. 1975. The impact of Robert MacArthur on ecology. *Ann. Rev. Ecol. Syst.* 6:1-13.

Fretwell, S. D., and Lucas, H. L. 1969. On territorial behavior and other factors influencing habitat distribution in birds. I. Theoretical development. *Acta Biotheoretica* 19:16-36.

Friedman, J. 1974. Marxism, structuralism, and vulgar materialism. *Man* 9:444-69.

Gamble, C. 1978. Resource exploitation and the spatial patterning of hunter-gatherers: a case study. In *Problems in social and economic archaeology,* ed. G. Sieveking, et al. London: Duckworth.

Gardner, P. M. 1972. The Paliyans. In *Hunters and gatherers today*, ed. M. G. Bicchieri, pp. 404-50. New York: Holt, Rinehart and Winston.

Garn, S. M. 1967. Bone loss as a general phenomenon in man. *Fed. Proc.* 26:17-29.

Geertz, C. 1973. *The interpretation of cultures*. New York: Basic Books.

Geist, V., and Walther, F., eds. 1974. *Behavior of ungulates*. International Union for the Conservation of Nature Publication. Morges, Switzerland: IUCN.

Glander, K. E. 1981. Feeding patterns in mantled howling monkeys. In *Foraging behavior*, ed. A. C. Kamil and T. D. Sargent, pp. 231-58. New York: Garland STPM Press.

Godin, G. J. 1972. A study of the energy expenditure of a small Eskimo population. In *International biological program--Igloolok HA study Physiology Section Report*, ed. R. J. Shephard, A. Rode, and G. Godin. Department of Environmental Health, School of Hygiene, University of Toronto.

Godin, G. J., and Shephard, R. J. 1973. Activity patterns of the Canadian Eskimo. In *Polar human biology*, ed. O. G. Edholm and E. K. E. Gunderson, pp. 193-215. London: Heinemann.

Golson, J. 1971. Australian Aboriginal food plants: some ecological and culture-historical implications. In *Aboriginal man and environment in Australia*, ed. D. J. Mulvaney and J. Golson, pp. 196-238. Canberra: Australian National University Press.

Gordon, B. H. C. 1975. Of men and herds in barrenland prehistory. National Museum of Canada Ethnology Division Mercury Series, Archaeological Survey of Canada, Paper No. 28. Ottawa.

Gould, R. A. 1967. Notes on hunting, butchering, and sharing of game among the Ngatatjara and their neighbors in the west Australian desert. Kroeber Anthropological Society Paper No. 36.

_____. 1969. Subsistence behavior among the Western Desert Aborigines of Australia. *Oceania* 39:253-74.

_____. 1977. Puntutjarpa Rockshelter and the Australian desert culture. *Am. Mus. Natural History Anth. Paper* 54(1):1-187.

Gould, R. A., ed. 1978. *Explorations in ethnoarchaeology*. Albuquerque: University of New Mexico Press.

Gould, S. J. 1978. Sociobiology: the art of storytelling. *New Scientist* 80:530-533.

Graburn, N. H. 1969. *Eskimos without igloos: social and economic development in Sugluk*. Boston: Little, Brown.

Graburn, N. H., and Strong, B. S. 1974. *Circumpolar peoples: an anthropological perspective*. Pacific Palisades: Goodyear.

Gramly, R. M. 1977. Deerskins and hunting territory: competition for a scarce resource. *American Antiquity* 42:601-4.

Grayson, D. K. 1973. On the methodology of faunal analysis. *Am. Antiq.* 38:432-39.

_____. 1974. The Riverhaven No. 2 vertebrate fauna: comments on methods in faunal analysis and on aspects of the subsistence potential of prehistoric New York. *Man in the Northeast* 8:23-39.

Grodzinski, W. 1971. Energy flow through populations of small mammals in the Alaskan taiga forest. *Acta Theriol.* 16:231-75.

Guedon, M.-F. 1974. People of Tetlin, why are you singing? National Museum of Canada Ethnology Division Mercury Series, Paper No. 9. Ottawa.

Haggett, P. 1966. *Locational analysis in human geography*. New York: St. Martin's Press.

Haldane, J. B. S. 1936. Some principles of causal analysis in genetics. *Erkenntnis* 6:346-56.

_____. 1947. The interaction of nature and nurture. *Annals of eugenics (Journal of Human Genetics)* 13:197-205.

Hall, R. 1977. Paleobiology and systematics of canids and hominids. *J. Human Evol.* 6:519-31.

Hallpike, C. R. 1973. Functionalist interpretations of primitive warfare. *Man* 8:451-70.

Hames, R. B. 1979. A comparison of the efficiencies of the shotgun and the bow in neotropical forest hunting. *Human Ecol.* 7:21-52.

Hames, R. B., and Vickers, W. n.d. Optimal diet breadth and hunting image: examples from the Siona-Secoya, Ye'kwana, and Yanomamö. In prep.

Hamilton, A. 1971. Socio-cultural factors in health among the Pitjantjatjara: a preliminary report. MS, Macquarie University.

Hamilton, W. D. 1964. The genetical evolution of social behaviour. *J. Theor. Biol.* 7:1-52.

_____. 1971. Geometry for the selfish herd. *J. Theor. Biol.* 31:295-311.

Hamilton, W. J., III, and Watt, K. E. F. 1970. Refuging. *Ann. Rev. Ecol. Syst.* 1:263-86.

Hardesty, D. L. 1977. *Ecological anthropology*. New York: John Wiley.

_____. 1980. Ecological explanation in archaeology. In *Advances in archaeological method and theory*, Vol. 3, ed. M. B. Schiffer. New York: Academic Press.

Hare, F. K., and Hay, J. E. 1974. The climate of Canada and Alaska. In *World survey of climatology*, Vol. 11: *Climates of North America*, ed. R. A. Bryson and F. K. Hare, pp. 49-192. Amsterdam: Elsevier.

Hare, F. K., and Thomas, M. K. 1974. *Climate Canada*. Toronto: Wiley.

Harner, M. J. 1972. *The Jivaro*. Garden City, NY: Natural History Press.

Harpending, H. n.d. Perspectives on the theory of social evolution. MS, Department of Anthropology, University of New Mexico, Albuquerque, NM.

Harpending, H., and Bertram, J. 1975. Human population dynamics in archaeological time: some simple models. In *Population studies in archaeology and biological anthropology*, ed. A. C. Swedlund, pp. 82-91. Society for American Archaeology Memoir No. 30. Washington, D.C.

Harpending, H., and Davis, H. 1977. Some implications for hunter-gatherer ecology derived from the spatial structure of resources. *World Archaeology* 8:275-86.

Harris, M. 1968. *The rise of anthropological theory*. New York: Crowell.

_____. 1971. *Culture, man and nature*. New York: Crowell.

_____. 1979. *Cultural materialism: the struggle for a science of culture*. New York: Random House.

Hassan, F. A. 1975. Determination of the size, density and growth rate of hunting-gathering populations. In *Population, ecology, and social evolution*, ed. S. Polgar, pp. 27-52. The Hague: Mouton.

Hatch, E. 1973. The growth of economic, subsistence and ecological studies in American anthropology. *J. Anthrop. Res.* 29:221-43.

Hebb, D. O. 1953. Heredity and environment in mammalian behaviour. *Brit. J. Animal Behav.* 1:43-47.

Hegsted, D. M. 1967. Nutrition, bone and calcified tissue. *J. Am. Dietetics Assoc.*

Heidenreich, C. 1971. *Huronia: a history and geography of the Huron Indians, 1600-1650*. Toronto: McClelland and Stewart.

Heller, C. A., and Scott, E. M. 1967. *The Alaska dietary survey 1956-1961*. Public Health Service Publication No. 999-AH-2. Washington, D.C.: Government Printing Office.

Helm, J. 1962. The ecological approach in anthropology. *Am. J. Soc.* 17:630-39.

Helm, J. 1968. The nature of Dogrib socioterritorial groups. In *Man the hunter*, ed. R. B. Lee and I. DeVore, pp. 118-25. Chicago: Aldine.

_____. 1972. The Dogrib Indians. In *Hunters and gatherers today*, ed. M. G. Bicchieri, pp. 51-89. New York: Holt, Rinehart and Winston.

Helms, M. W. 1978. On Julian Steward and the nature of culture. *Am. Ethnol.* 5:170-83.

Heusser, C. J. 1973. Postglacial vegetation on Umnak Island, Aleutian Islands, Alaska. *Rev. Paleobotany and Palynology* 15:277-85.

Hewitt, D. F., and Freeman, E. B. 1972. *Rocks and minerals of Ontario*. Ontario Department of Mines and Northern Affairs, GC13.

Hickerson, H. 1965. The Virginia deer and inter-tribal buffer zones in the upper Mississippi Valley. In *Man, culture and animals: the role of animals in human ecological adjustments*, ed. A. Leeds and A. P. Vayda, pp. 43-66. Washington, D.C.: American Association for the Advancement of Science.

Hill, J. N. 1971. Research propositions for consideration (by the) Southwestern Anthropological Research Group. In *The distribution of prehistoric population aggregates*, ed. G. J. Gumerman. Prescott, AZ: Prescott College Press.

Hillier, F. S., and Lieberman, G. J. 1974. *Introduction to operations research*, 2d ed. San Francisco: Holden-Day.

Hinsdale, W. B. 1931. Archaeological atlas of Michigan. University of Michigan Museum, Handbook Series 4.

_____. 1932. Distribution of the aboriginal population of Michigan. University of Michigan Museum of Anthropology Occasional Contribution 2.

Hitchcock, R. K., and Ebert J.,1980. Foraging and food production among Kalahari hunter-gatherers. In *The causes and consequences of food production in Africa*, ed. J. D. Clark and S. A. Brandt. Berkeley: University of California Press.

Ho, M. L.; Farmer, F. A.; and Neilson, H. R. 1971. Amino acid content of birds, fish and mammals from northern Canada. *J. Canadian Dietetic Assoc.* 32:198-203.

Holmberg, A. R. 1950. Nomads of the long bow: the Siriono of eastern Bolivia. Smithsonian Institute of Social Anthropology No. 10. Washington, D.C.

Holmes, C. E. 1975. A northern Athapaskan environment in a diachronic perspective. *Western Canadian J. Anthrop.* 5:92-128.

Horn, H. S. 1968. The adaptive significance of colonial nesting in the Brewers blackbird (*Euphagus cyanocephalus*). *Ecology* 49:682-94.

Horne, G., and Aiston, G. 1924. *Savage life in central Australia*. London: Macmillan.

Hustich, I. 1957. Comparison of the flora and vegetation in the Fort Severn and Big Trout Lake area. Arctic Institute of North America, Montreal. Mimeo.

Hutchinson, G. E. 1959. Homage to Santa Rosalia, or why are there so many animals? *Am. Nat.* 93:145-59.

_____. 1965. *The ecological theater and the evolutionary play*. New Haven: Yale University Press.

_____. 1975. Variations on a theme by Robert MacArthur. In *Ecology and the evolution of communities*, ed. M. L. Cody and J. M. Diamond, pp. 492-521. Cambridge: Harvard University Press.

_____. 1978. *An introduction to population ecology*. New Haven: Yale University Press.

Isaac, G. L. 1976a. Early hominids in action: a commentary on the contribution of archeology to understanding the fossil record in East Africa. *Yearbook of Phys. Anthrop.* 19:19-35.

_____. 1976b. The activities of early African hominids: a review of archaeological evidence from the time span two and a half to one million years ago. In *Human origins: Louis Leakey and the East African evidence*, ed. G. L. Isaac and E. R. McCown, pp. 483-514. Menlo Park, CA: W. A. Benjamin.

Isaac, G. L. 1978. Food sharing and human evolution: archaeological evidence from the Plio-Pleistocene of East Africa. *J. Anthrop. Res.* 34:311-25.

Jamison, P. L., and Friedman, S. M., eds. 1974. Energy flow in human communities. Proceedings of a Workshop, 30 January 1974. University Park, PA: Human Adaptability Coordinating Office.

Jarvenpa, R. 1977. Subarctic Indian trappers and band society: the economics of male mobility. *Human Ecol.* 5:223-60.

Jay, P. C., ed. 1968. *Primates: studies in adaptation and variability*. New York: Holt, Rinehart and Winston.

Jerison, H. J. 1975. Fossil evidence of the evolution of the human brain. *Ann. Rev. Anthrop.* 4:27-58.

Jochelson, W. 1933. *History, ethnology and anthropology of the Aleut*. Washington, D.C.: Carnegie Institute of Washington.

Jochim, M. A. 1976. *Hunter-gatherer subsistence and settlement: a predictive model*. New York: Academic Press.

_____. 1979. Breaking down the system: recent ecological approaches in archaeology. In *Advances in archaeological method and theory*, Vol. 2, ed. M. B. Schiffer, pp. 77-117. New York: Academic Press.

Johnson, A. W. 1971. Security and risk taking among poor peasants: a Brazilian case. In *Studies in economic anthropology*, ed. G. Dalton, pp. 144-51. American Anthropological Association, Anthropological Studies Series 7.

_____. 1975. Time allocation in a Machiguenga community. *Ethnology* 14:301-10.

Johnson, E. A., and Rowe, J. S. 1975. Fire in the subarctic wintering ground of the Beverly caribou herd. *Am. Midland Nat.* 94:1-14.

Johnson, G. 1978. Information sources and the development of decision-making organizations. In *Social archaeology: beyond subsistence and dating*, ed. C. L. Redman, et al., pp. 87-112. New York: Acadmic Press.

Jolly, A. 1972. *The evolution of primate behavior*. New York: Macmillan.

Jolly, C. J. 1973. Changing views of hominid origins. *Yearbook Phys. Anthrop.* 16:1-17.

Jones, R. 1973. Emerging picture of Pleistocene Australians. *Nature* 246:275-81.

_____. 1978. Why did the Tasmanians stop eating fish? In *Explorations in ethnoarchaeology*, ed. R. A. Gould, pp. 11-48. Albuquerque: University of New Mexico Press.

_____. 1979. The fifth continent: problems concerning the human colonization of Australia. *Ann. Rev. Anthrop.* 8:445-66.

Jorgensen, J. G. 1972. A variation on traditional concerns: the neofunctional ecology of hunters, farmers and pastoralists. In *Biology and culture in modern perspective*, ed. J. G. Jorgensen, pp. 328-31. San Francisco: W. H. Freeman.

Kamminga, J., and Allen, H. 1973. Alligator Rivers environmental fact-finding study: report of the archaeological survey. Darwin: Department of the Northern Territory.

Katz, P. 1974. A long-term approach to foraging optimization. *Am. Nat.* 108:758-82.

Keene, A. S. 1979a. Economic optimization models and the study of hunter-gatherer subsistence settlement systems. In *Transformations: mathematical approaches to culture change*, ed. C. Renfrew and K. Cooke, pp. 369-404. New York: Academic Press.

_____. 1979b. Prehistoric hunter-gatherers of the deciduous forest: a linear programming approach to Late Archaic subsistence in the Saginaw Valley (Michigan). Ph.D. dissertation, University of Michigan.

_____. 1980. Nutrition and economy: models for the study of prehistoric diet. In *Techniques for the analysis of prehistoric diets*, ed. R. I. Gilbert and J. Mielke. New York: Academic Press (in press).

Keith, L. B. 1963. *Wildlife's ten-year cycle*. Madison: University of Wisconsin Press.

_____. 1974. Some features of population dynamics in mammals. *Proc. Int. Cong. Game Biol.* 11:17-58.

Kelsall, J. P. 1960. Co-operative studies of barren-ground caribou 1957-1958. *Canadian Wildl. Bull.*, Series 1, No. 15.

_____. 1970. The migration of the barren-ground caribou. *Natural History* 39:98-106.

Kemp, W. B. 1971. The flow of energy in a hunting society. *Sci. Am.* 224(3):104-15.

Kemp, W. B., and Smith, E. A. n.d. Time budgets and energetic expenditure of a group of Inuit hunters (in prep.).

Kemp, W. B.; Wenzel, G.; Jensen, N.; and Val, E. 1977. The communities of Resolute and Kuvinaluk: a social and economic baseline study. Appendix C: weights and percentages used for calculation of nutrition tables. Report presented to the Resolute Community Council and the Polar Gas Project. Montreal: McGill University, Office of Industrial Research.

Kenyon, K. W., and Scheffer, V. B. 1955. *The seals, sea-lions, and sea-otters of the Pacific coast*. Washington, D.C.: Government Printing Office.

Kiester, A. R., and Slatkin, M. 1974. A strategy of movement and resource utilization. *Theor. Pop. Biol.* 6:1-20.

King, G. E. 1975. Socioterritorial units among carnivores and early hominids. *J. Anthrop. Res.* 31:69-87.

_____. 1976. Society and territory in human evolution. *J. Human Evol.* 5:323-32.

_____. 1978. A cross-cultural model for sociospatial organization among hunter-gatherers. Paper presented at the 77th Annual Meeting, American Anthropological Association, Los Angeles.

Klopfer, P. H., and MacArthur, R. H. 1960. Niche size and faunal diversity. *Am. Nat.* 94:293-300.

Kranz, P. M. 1977. A model for estimating standing crop in ancient communities. *Paleobiology* 3:415-21.

Krebs, J. R. 1973. Behavioural aspects of predation. In *Perspectives in ethology*, ed. P. P. G. Bateson and P. H. Klopfer, pp. 73-111. New York: Plenum Press.

_____. 1974. Colonial nesting and social feeding as strategies for exploiting food resources in the great blue heron (*Ardea herodias*). *Behaviour* 51:99-134.

_____. 1977. Optimal foraging: theory and experiment. *Nature* 268:583-84.

_____. 1978. Optimal foraging: decision rules for predators. In *Behavioural ecology*, ed. J. R. Krebs and N. B. Davies, pp. 23-63. Oxford: Blackwell Scientific Publications.

Krebs, J. R., and Cowie, R. J. 1976. Foraging strategies in birds. *Ardea* 64:98-116.

Krebs, J. R., and Davies, N. B., eds. 1978. *Behavioural ecology: an evolutionary approach*. Oxford: Blackwell Scientific Publications.

Krebs, J. R.; MacRoberts, M. H.; and Cullen, J. M. 1972. Flocking and feeding in the great tit, *Parus major*: an experimental study. *Ibis* 114:507-30.

Krebs, J. R.; Ryan, J. C.; and Charnov, E. L. 1974. Hunting by expectation or optimal foraging? *Animal Behav.* 22:953-64.

Krebs, J. S., and Barry, R. G. 1970. The Arctic front and the tundra-taiga boundary in Eurasia. *Geog. Rev.* 60:548-54.

Kroeber, A. 1939. *Cultural and natural areas of native North America*. Berkeley: University of California Press.

Kruuk, H. 1975. Functional aspects of social hunting by carnivores. In *Function and evolution in behaviour*, ed. G. P. Baerends, D. Beer, and A. Manning, pp. 119-41. Oxford: Clarendon Press.

Kryzywicki, L. 1934. *Primitive society and its vital statistics*. London.

Kummer, H. 1971. *Primate societies: group techniques in ecological adaptation*. Chicago: Aldine-Atherton.

LaRoi, G. H. 1967. Ecological studies in the boreal spruce-fir forests of the North American taiga. I. Analysis of the vascular flora. *Ecol. Monog.* 37:229-53.

Larsen, J. A. 1962. Major vegetation types of western Ontario and Manitoba from aerial photographs. Department of Meteorology Technical Report No. 7. Madison: University of Wisconsin.

_____. 1972. Vegetation and terrain (environment): Canadian boreal forest and tundra. Final report of research conducted under grants from the U.S. Army Research Office (Durham).

Laughlin, W. S. 1968. Hunting: an integrating biobehavior system and its evolutionary importance. In *Man the hunter*, ed. R. B. Lee and I. DeVore, pp. 304-20. Chicago: Aldine.

_____. 1972. Ecology and population structure in the Arctic. In *The structure of human populations*, ed. G. A. Harrison and A. J. Boyce, pp. 379-92. Oxford: Clarendon Press.

_____. 1974/75. Holocene history of Nikolski Bay, Alaska, and Aleut evolution. *Folk* 16/17:95-115.

_____. 1980. *Survivors of the Bering Land Bridge*. New York: Holt, Rinehart and Winston.

Lawrence, R. 1968. Aboriginal habitat and economy. Occas. Paper No. 6, Department of Geography, School of General Studies, Australian National University.

Leacock, E. 1954. The Montagnais "hunting territory" and the fur trade. *American Anthropological Association Memoir* 78.

_____. 1973. The Montagnais-Naskapi band. In *Cultural ecology*, ed. B. Cox, pp. 81-100. Toronto: Stewart and McClelland.

Lee, R. B. 1965. Subsistence ecology of the !Kung Bushmen. Ann Arbor: University Microfilms.

_____. 1968. What hunters do for a living, or, How to make out on scarce resources. In *Man the hunter*, ed. R. B. Lee and I. DeVore, pp. 30-48. Chicago: Aldine.

_____. 1969. !Kung Bushmen subsistence: an input-output analysis. In *Environment and cultural behavior*, ed. A. P. Vayda, pp. 47-79. Garden City, NY: Natural History Press.

_____. 1972a. !Kung spatial organization: an ecological and historical perspective. *Human Ecol.* 1:125-47.

_____. 1972b. The !Kung Bushmen of Botswana. In *Hunters and gatherers today*, ed. M. G. Bicchieri, pp. 327-68. New York: Holt, Rinehart and Winston.

_____. 1979. *The !Kung San: Men, women and work in a foraging society*. Cambridge: Cambridge University Press.

Lee, R. B., and DeVore, I., eds. 1968. *Man the hunter*. Chicago: Aldine.

_____. 1976. *Kalahari hunter-gatherers*. Cambridge, MA: Harvard University Press.

Leith, H. 1973. Primary production: terrestrial ecosystems. *Human Ecol.* 1:303-32.

LeResche, R. E. 1974. Moose migrations in North America. *Naturaliste Canadien* 101:393-415.

LeResche, R. E.; Bishop, R. H.; and Cody, J. W. 1975. Distribution and habitats of moose in Alaska. In *Moose ecology: international symposium on moose ecology*, ed. J. Bedard, pp. 143-78. Quebec.

Levins, R. 1966. Strategy of model building in population biology. *Am. Sci.* 54:421-31.

_____. 1968. *Evolution in changing environments*. Princeton: Princeton University Press.

Lewis, R. B. 1978. Resource dispersion and hunter-gatherer band spacing. Paper presented to the Society for American Archaeology, Tucson.

Lewontin, R. C. 1970. The units of selection. *Ann. Rev. Ecol. Syst.* 1:1-18.

_____. 1974a. *The genetic basis of evolutionary change*. New York: Columbia University Press.

_____. 1974b. The analysis of variance and the analysis of causes. *Am. J. Human Genetics* 26:400-411.

_____. 1977. Sociobiology: a caricature of Darwinism. *Philosophy of Science Assoc.* 2:22-31.

_____. 1979a. Fitness, survival and optimality. In *Analysis of ecological systems*, ed. D. J. Horn, G. R. Stairs, and R. D. Mitchell, pp. 3-21. Columbus: Ohio State University Press.

_____. 1979b. Sociobiology as an adaptationist program. *Behav. Sci.* 24:5-14.

Limp, W. F., and Black, G. A. 1977. The economics of agricultural dispersal. Paper presented at the 1977 Annual Meeting of the Society for American Archaeology, New Orleans.

Lippold, L. K. 1966. Chaluka: the economic base. *Arctic Anthrop.* 3:125-31.

Little, M. A., and Morren, G. E. B., Jr. 1976. *Ecology, energetics and human variability*. Dubuque: W. C. Brown.

Livingstone, D. A. 1975. Late Quaternary climatic change in Africa. *Ann. Rev. Anthrop.* 4:249-80.

Lorenz, K. 1950. The comparative method in studying innate behaviour patterns. *Symposia of the Society for Experimental Biology* 4:221-68.

Love, F. G. 1977. The biota of the Nikolski strandflat. *Anthropological Papers of the University of Alaska* 18:43-49.

MacArthur, R. H. 1960. On the relation between reproductive value and optimal predation. *Proc. Nat. Acad. Sci.* 46:143-45.

_____. 1961. Population effects of natural selection. *Am. Natur.* 95:195-99.

_____. 1965. Ecological consequences of natural selection. In *Theoretical and mathematical biology*, ed. T. Waterman and H. Morowitz, pp. 388-97. New York: Blaisdell.

_____. 1972. *Geographical ecology*. New York: Harper and Row.

MacArthur, R. H., and Pianka, E. R. 1966. On optimal use of a patchy environment. *Am. Natur.* 100:603-9.

MacKay, H. H. 1963. *Fishes of Ontario*. Fish and Wildlife Branch, Department of Lands and Forests, Ontario.

Mann, G. V., et al. 1962. The health and nutritional status of Alaskan Eskimos. *Am. J. Clin. Nutri.* 11:31-76.

Marks, S. A. 1973. Prey selection and annual harvest of game in a rural Zambian community. *East African Wildlife J.* 11:113-28.

_____. 1976. *Large mammals and a brave people: subsistence hunters in Zambia*. Seattle: University of Washington Press.

_____. 1977a. Perception and selection of Cape buffalo by Valley Bisa hunters in Zambia. *Western Can. J. Anthrop.* 7:53-67.

_____. 1977b. Hunting behavior and strategies of the Valley Bisa of Zambia. *Hum. Ecol.* 5:1-36.

Marshall, L. 1959. Marriage among !Kung Bushmen. *Africa* 29:335-65.

_____. 1965. The !Kung Bushmen of the Kalahari Desert. In *Peoples of Africa*, ed. J. L. Gibbs. New York: Holt, Rinehart and Winston.

_____. 1976. *The !Kung of Nyae Nyae*. Cambridge, MA: Harvard University Press.

Martin, J. 1973. On the estimation of sizes of local groups in a hunting-gathering environment. *Am. Anthrop.* 75:1448-68.

Martin, M. K. 1974. The foraging adaptation -- uniformity or diversity? Addison-Wesley Module in Anthropology No. 56.

Martin, P. S. 1973. The discovery of America. *Science* 179:969-74.

Mason, O. T. 1905. Environment. In *Handbook of American Indians*, ed. F. W. Hodge, pp. 427-30. Washington, D.C.: Bureau of American Ethnology.

May, R. M. 1976. Models for two interacting populations. In *Theoretical ecology*, ed. R. M. May, pp. 49-70. Philadelphia: Sanders.

_____, ed. 1976. *Theoretical ecology: principles and applications*. Philadelphia: W. B. Saunders.

Maynard Smith, J. 1978. Optimization theory in evolution. *Ann. Rev. Ecol. Syst.* 9:31-56.

Mayr, E. 1974. Behavior programs and evolutionary strategies. *Am. Sci.* 62:650-59.

_____. 1976a. Basic concepts of evolutionary biology. In *Evolution and the diversity of life: selected essays*, ed. E. Mayr, pp. 9-16. Cambridge, MA: Belknap/Harvard University Press. (Orig. pub. 1969. Grundgedanken der Evolutionsbiologie. *Naturwissenschaften* 56:14-25.)

_____. 1976b. Cause and effect in biology. In *Evolution and the diversity of life: selected essays*, ed. E. Mayr, pp. 359-71. Cambridge, MA: Belknap/Harvard University Press. (Orig. pub. 1961. Cause and effect in biology. *Science* 134:1501-6.)

McClellan, C. 1970. Introduction to special issue on Athapaskan studies. *W. Can. J. Anthrop.* 2:vi-xix.

McCormack, P. 1975. A theoretical approach to Na Dene archaeology. *W. Can. J. Anthrop.* 5:187-230.

McCullough, D. R. 1970. Secondary production of birds and mammals. In *Analysis of temperate forest ecosystems*, ed. D. E. Reichle. New York: Springer-Verlag.

McDonald, D. R. 1977. Food taboos: a primitive Environmental Protection Agency. *Anthropos* 72:734-48.

McKennan, R. A. 1959. The Upper Tanana Indians. *Yale U. Publ. Anthrop.* No. 22.

_____. 1969. Athapaskan groupings and social organization in central Alaska. In *Band societies*, ed. David Damas, pp. 93-114. National Museums of Canada Bulletin No. 228. Ottawa.

McLaren, I. A. 1962. Population dynamics and exploitation of seals in the eastern Canadian Arctic. In *The exploitation of natural animal populations*, ed. E. D. LeCren and M. W. Holdgate, pp. 168-83. Oxford: Blackwell Scientific Publications.

McNab, B. K. 1963. Bioenergetics and the determination of home range size. *Am. Natur.* 97:133-40.

Mech, D. 1966. *The wolves of Isle Royale*. Fauna of the National Parks of the U.S., Fauna Series No. 7. Washington: Government Printing Office.

Mech, D., et al. 1968. Seasonal weight changes, mortality and population structure of racoons in Minnesota. *J. Mammal.* 49:63-73.

Meehan, B. 1977a. Man does not live by calories alone: the role of shellfish in a coastal cuisine. In *Sunda and Sahul: Prehistoric studies in Southeast Asia, Melanesia, and Australia*, ed. J. Allen, J. Golson, and R. Jones, pp. 493-531. New York: Academic Press.

_____. 1977b. Hunters by the seashore. *J. Human Evol.* 6:363-70.

Meggitt, M. J. 1957. Notes on the vegetable foods of the Walbiri of central Australia. *Oceania* 28:143-45.

_____. 1962. *Desert people: a study of the Walbiri Aborigines of central Australia.* Sydney: Angus and Robertson.

_____. 1964. Aboriginal food-gatherers of tropical Australia. In *The ecology of man in the tropical environment.* International Union for the Conservation of Nature and Natural Resources, Ninth Technical Meeting, Proc. and Pap., Publ. Series 4. Morges.

Merrill, A. L., and Watt, B. K. 1955. *Energy value of foods: basis and derivation.* U.S. Department of Agriculture Handbook 74. Washington, D.C.

Miller, J. G. 1965. Living systems: basic concepts. *Behavioral Science* 10:193-237.

Mohr, C. O. 1940. Comparative populations of game, fur, and other mammals. *American Midland Naturalist* 2:581-84.

Moir, D. R. 1958. A floristic survey of the Severn River drainage basin of northwestern Ontario. Ann Arbor: University Microfilms. (Ph.D. dissertation, University of Minnesota.)

Montgomery, E. 1978. Towards a representative energy data: the Machiguenga study. *Fed. Proc.* 37:61-64.

Montgomery, E., and Johnson, A. 1977. Machiguenga energy expenditure. *Ecol. Food and Nutrition* 6:97-105.

Moore, J. A. 1977. Hunter-gatherer settlement systems and information flow. Paper presented at the 1977 American Anthropological Meeting, November 1977, Houston.

_____. 1978. What you don't know . . . : information processing hunter-gatherer agricultural frontier. Paper presented at the Frontier Systems and Boundary Processes Symposium, 1978 Annual Meeting of the Society for American Archaeology, Tucson.

_____. 1979. Terminal archaeology: the use of computer simulation in theory building. Paper presented at the 1979 Annual Meeting of the Society for American Archaeology, Vancouver.

Moore, K. H. 1979. Faunal remains from 20SA198 and 20SA380. In A. S. Keene, Prehistoric hunter-gatherers of the deciduous forest, pp. 466-475. Ph.D. dissertation, University of Michigan, Ann Arbor.

Moran, E. F. 1979. *Human adaptability: an introduction to ecological anthropology.* North Scituate, MA: Duxbury Press.

Morrison, D. W. 1978. On the optimal searching strategy for refuging predators. *Am. Natur.* 112:925-34.

Moskowitz, H. W.; Kumaraiah, V.; Sharma, K. N.; Jacobs, H. L.; and Sharma, S. D. 1975. Cross-cultural differences in simple taste preferences. *Science* 190:1217-18.

Mulvaney, D. J. 1975. *The prehistory of Australia.* 2d ed. Melbourne: Penguin.

Mulvaney, D. J., and Joyce, E. B. 1965. Archaeological and geomorphological investigations on Mt. Moffet Station, Queensland. *Proc. Prehistoric Soc.* 31:147-212.

Murdock, G. P. 1967. Ethnographic atlas: a summary. *Ethnology* 6:109-236.

Murie, O. J. 1940. Notes on the sea-otter. *J. Mammal.* 21:119-23.

Murphy, R. F. 1977. Introduction: the anthropological theories of Julian H. Steward. In *Evolution and ecology: essays in social transformation,* ed. J. C. Steward and R. F. Murphy, pp. 1-39. Urbana, IL: University of Illinois Press.

Naroll, R. 1970. Galton's problem. In *A handbook of method in cultural anthropology,* ed. R. Naroll and R. Cohen, pp. 974-89. Garden City, NY: Natural History Press/Doubleday.

National Film Board of Canada. 1975. *Cree Hunters of Mistassini.* New York.

NHRC. 1976a. *Research to establish present levels of harvesting by native peoples of northern Quebec*. Part I: *A report on the harvests by the James Bay Cree*. Montreal: Native Harvesting Research Committee.

_____. 1976b. *Research to establish present levels of harvesting by native peoples of northern Quebec*. Part II: *A report on the harvests by the Inuit of northern Quebec*. Montreal: Native Harvesting Research Committee.

_____. 1978. Summary harvest statistics for northern Quebec Inuit, 1977 calendar year. Unpublished.

_____. 1979. Research to establish present levels of native harvesting. Harvests by the Inuit of northern Quebec. Phase II (Year 1976). Montreal: Native Harvesting Research Committee.

Nelson, R. K. 1969. *Hunters of the northern ice*. Chicago: University of Chicago Press.

_____. 1973. *Hunters of the northern forest*. Chicago: University of Chicago Press.

Netting, R. M. 1971. The ecological approach in cultural study. Addison-Wesley Module in Anthropology No. 6.

_____. 1977. *Cultural ecology*. Menlo Park, CA: Cummings.

Nietschmann, B. 1973. *Between land and water: the subsistence ecology of the Miskito Indians, eastern Nicaragua*. New York: Seminar Press.

Norberg, R. A. 1977. An ecological theory on foraging time and energetics and choice of optimal food-searching method. *J. Animal Ecol*. 46:511-29.

Nunley, P. 1970. Toward a generalized model of hunting and gathering societies. *Texas Archaeological Society Bulletin* 42:13-31

Nybakken, B. H. 1966. The paleoecology of southwest Umnak Island and southwest Kodiak Island, Alaska. Ann Arbor: University Microfilms.

Oaten, A. 1977. Optimal foraging in patches: a case for stochasticity. *Theor. Pop. Biol*. 12:263-85.

O'Connell, J. F. 1977a. Aspects of variation in central Australian lithic assemblages. In *Stone tools as cultural markers: change, evolution and complexity*, ed. R. V. S. Wright, pp. 269-81. Canberra: Australian Institute of Aboriginal Studies.

_____. 1977b. Ethnoarchaeology of the Alyawara: a report. *Newsletter Australian Inst. Aboriginal Studies* 7:47-49.

_____. 1977c. Room to move: contemporary Alyawara settlement patterns and their implications for Aboriginal housing policy. *Mankind* 11:119-31.

O'Connell, J. F.; Latz, P. K.; and Barnett, P. n.d. Traditional and modern plant use among the Alyawara of central Australia. MS, Department of Anthropology, University of Utah.

Odum, E. P. 1971. *Fundamentals of ecology*. Philadelphia: W. B. Saunders.

Ontario Department of Lands and Forests. 1971. *The Round Lake Ojibwa: the people, the land, the resources, 1968-1970*. Toronto: Ontario Department of Lands and Forests.

Orans, M. 1975. Domesticating the functional dragon: an analysis of Piddocke's potlatch. *Am. Anthrop*. 77:312-28.

Orians, G. H. 1961. The ecology of blackbird (*Agelaius*) social systems. *Ecol. Monog*. 31:285-312.

_____. 1969. On the evolution of mating systems in birds and mammals. *Am. Natur*. 103:589-603.

_____. 1971. Ecological aspects of behavior. In *Avian biology*, Vol. 1, ed. Donald S. Farner, James R. King, and K. C. Parkes, pp. 513-46. New York: Academic Press.

_____. 1975. Diversity, stability and maturity in natural ecosystems. In *Unifying concepts in ecology*, ed. W. H. van Dobben and R. H. Lowe-McConnell, pp. 139-50. The Hague: Dr. W. Junk B. V.

Orians, G. H., and Pearson, N. E. 1979. On the theory of central place foraging. In *Analysis of ecological systems*, ed. D. J. Horn, G. R. Stairs, and R. D. Mitchell, pp. 155-77. Columbus: Ohio State University Press.

Ortiz, S. 1967. The structure of decision making among Indians of Colombia. In *Themes in economic anthropology*, ed. R. Firth, pp. 191-228. London: Tavistock.

Osgood, C. B. 1936. The distribution of northern Athapaskan Indians. Yale U. Publ. in Anthrop. No. 14.

_____. 1940. Ingalik material culture. *Yale U. Publ. Anthrop.* No. 22.

_____. 1958. Ingalik social culture. *Yale U. Publ. Anthrop.* No. 53.

_____. 1959. Ingalik mental culture. *Yale U. Publ. Anthrop.* No. 56.

Ozker, D. B. V. 1977. The nature of the Early Woodland adaptation in the Great Lakes region. Ann Arbor: University Microfilms. (Ph.D. dissertation, University of Michigan.)

Paine, R. T. 1971. The measurement and application of the calorie to ecological problems. *Ann. Rev. Ecol. Syst.* 2:145-64.

_____. 1973. Animals as capital: comparisons among northern nomadic herders and hunters. In *Cultural ecology*, ed. B. Cox, pp. 301-14. Toronto: McClelland and Stewart.

Paloheimo, J. E. 1971. On a theory of search. *Biometrika* 58:61-75.

Papadakis, J. 1969. *Soils of the world*. Amsterdam: Elsevier.

Parker, G. A., and Stuart, R. A. 1976. Animal behavior as a strategy optimizer: evolution of resource assessment strategies and optimal emigration thresholds. *Am. Natur.* 110: 1055-76.

Parmalee, P. W. 1975. Archaeologically derived bird remains: identification, analysis, interpretation. MS, University of Tennessee, Knoxville.

Peebles, C. S. 1978. Of archaeology and archaeologists in Saginaw County, Michigan. *Mich. Archaeol.* 24:83-129.

Pelto, P. J., and Pelto, G. H. 1975. Intra-cultural diversity: some theoretical issues. *Am. Ethnol.* 2:1-18.

Perlman, S. M. 1976. Optimum diet models and prehistoric hunter-gatherers: a test on Martha's Vineyard. Ann Arbor: University Microfilms.

_____. 1978. Mobility costs and hunter-gatherer group sizes. Paper presented to the 1978 Annual Meeting of the Society for American Archaeology, Tucson.

Perry, R. A., compiler. 1962. *General report on lands of the Alice Springs area, Northern Territory, 1956-57*. Melbourne: Commonwealth Scientific and Industrial Research Organization.

Peterson, J. T. 1978. Hunter-gatherer/farmer exchange. *Am. Anthrop.* 80:335-51.

Peterson, N. 1978. The traditional pattern of subsistence to 1975. In *The nutrition of Aborigines in relation to the ecosystem of central Australia*, ed. B. S. Hetzel and H. J. Frith, pp. 25-35. Melbourne: Commonwealth Scientific and Industrial Research Organization.

Pianka, E. R. 1976. Natural selection of optimal reproductive tactics. *Am. Zool.* 16:775-84.

_____. 1978. *Evolutionary ecology*. 2d ed. New York: Harper and Row.

Plog, F. T. 1975. Systems theory in archeological research. *Ann. Rev. Anthrop.* 4:207-24.

Prattis, J. E. 1973. Strategising man. *Man* 8:46-58.

Pred, A. 1967. *Behavior and location*. Part I: *Lund studies in geography*. Series B. Human Geography No. 27. Lund: Gleerup.

Prest, V. K. 1965. Geology of the soils of Canada. In *Soils in Canada: Geological, pedological and engineering studies*, ed. R. F. Leggett, pp. 6-21. Royal Society of Canada Special Publication No. 3. Toronto: University of Toronto Press.

Pruitt, W. O., Jr. 1958. Qali, a taiga snow formation of ecological importance. *Ecology* 39:169-72.

_____. 1960. Behavior of the barren-ground caribou. University of Alaska Papers 3.

_____. 1970. Some ecological aspects of snow. In *Ecology of the subarctic regions*, pp. 83-99. Paris: UNESCO.

Prus, T. 1970. Calorific value of animals as an element of bioenergetical investigations. *Polish Arch. of Hydrobiology* 17:183-99.

Pulliam, H. R. 1973. On the advantages of flocking. *J. Theor. Biol*. 38:419-22.

_____. 1974. On the theory of optimal diets. *Am. Natur*. 108:59-74.

_____. 1975. Diet optimization with nutrient constraints. *Am. Natur*. 109:765-68.

_____. 1978. On predicting human diets. In *Ethnobiology today*, ed. Marsha Gallagher. Museum of Northern Arizona Press (forthcoming).

_____. 1981. Learning to forage optimally. In *Foraging behavior*, ed. A. C. Kamil and T. D. Sargent, pp. 379-88. New York: Garland STPM Press.

Pulliam, H. R., and Millikan, G. C. n.d. Social organization in the non-reproductive season. In *Avian biology*, Vol. 6 (forthcoming).

Pyke, G. H.; Pulliam, H. R.; and Charnov, E. L. 1977. Optimal foraging: a selective review of theory and tests. *Quart. Rev. Biol*. 52:137-54.

Radcliffe-Brown, A. R. 1930. The social organization of Australian tribes. *Oceania* 1:34-63.

_____. 1935. On the concept of function in social science. *Am. Anthrop*. 37:394-402.

_____. 1956. *Structure and function in primitive society*. Glencoe, 1L: Free Press.

Rainey, F. G. 1947. The whale hunters of Tigara. Anthropological Paper 41, pt. 2. American Museum of Natural History.

Ransom, J. E. 1946. The Aleut natural food economy. *Am. Anthrop*. 48:607-23.

Rappaport, R. A. 1968. *Pigs for the ancestors: ritual in the ecology of a New Guinea people*. New Haven: Yale University Press.

_____. 1971a. Nature, culture and ecological anthropology. In *Man, culture and society*, ed. Harry L. Shapiro, pp. 237-67. New York: Oxford University Press.

_____. 1971b. The flow of energy in an agricultural society. *Sci. Am*. 224(3):117-32.

_____. 1977. Ecology, adaptation and the ills of functionalism (being among other things, a response to Jonathan Friedman). *Mich. Disc. Anthrop*. 2:138-90.

Rapport, D. J. 1971. An optimization model of food selection. *Am. Natur*. 105:575-87.

Rapport, D. J., and Turner, J. E. 1970. Determination of predator food preferences. *J. Theor. Biol*. 26:365-72.

_____. 1977. Economic models in ecology. *Science* 195:367-73.

Rasmussen, K. 1931. The Netsilik Eskimos. Report of the 5th Thule Expedition 8(1-2). Copenhagen: Glydendal.

Ray, A. J. 1974. *Indians in the fur trade: their role as trappers, hunters, and middlemen in the lands southwest of Hudson Bay*. Toronto: University of Toronto Press.

Reidhead, V. A. 1976. Optimization and food procurement at the prehistoric Leonard Haag Site, southeast Indiana: a linear programming approach. Ph.D. dissertation, Indiana University. Ann Arbor: University Microfilms.

Reidhead, V. A. 1977.  Labor and nutrition in food procurement: did prehistoric people optimize?  Paper presented to the Society for American Archaeology, New Orleans.

_____. 1979.  Linear programming models in archaeology.  *Ann. Rev. Anthrop.* 8:543-78.

_____. 1980.  The economics of subsistence change.  In *Modeling of prehistoric subsistence economies,* ed. T. K. Earle and A. L. Christensen, pp. 141-86.  New York: Academic Press.

Reidhead, V. A., and Limp, W. F. 1974.  Nutritional maximization: a multifaceted nutritional model for archaeological research.  Paper presented to the American Anthropological Association, Mexico City.

Reynolds, R. G. 1978.  On modelling the evolution of hunter-gatherer decision making systems. *Geographical Analysis* 10:31-46.

Reynolds, R. G., and Ziegler, B. F. 1979.  A formal mathematical model for the operation of consensus-based hunting and gathering bands.  In *Transformations: mathematical approaches to culture change,* ed. A. C. Renfrew, pp. 405-18.  New York: Academic Press.

Reynolds, V. 1965.  Some behavioral comparisons between the chimpanzee and the mountain gorilla in the wild.  *Am. Anthrop.* 67:691-706.

_____. 1966.  Open groups in Hominid evolution.  *Man* 1:441-52.

_____. 1968.  Kinship and the family in monkeys, apes and man.  *Man* 3:209-23.

Richerson, P. J. 1977.  Ecology and human ecology: a comparison of theories in the biological and social sciences.  *Am. Ethnol.* 4:1-26.

Ritchie, J. C. 1956.  The vegetation of northern Manitoba. I.  Studies in the southern spruce forest zone.  *Can. J. Bot.* 34:523-61.

_____. 1958.  A vegetation map from the southern spruce zone of Manitoba.  *Geog. Bull.* 12:39-46.

_____. 1960.  The vegetation of northern Manitoba. IV.  The Caribou Lake region.  *Can. J. Bot.* 38:185-99.

Robbins, L. 1932.  *An essay on the nature and significance of economic science.*  London: Macmillan.

Robson, J. R. K. 1972.  *Malnutrition: its causation and control.*  New York: Gordon and Breach.

Rogers, E. S. 1962.  *Round Lake Ojibwa.*  Occasional Paper No. 5, Art and Archaeology Division, Royal Ontario Museum, Toronto.  Toronto: Ontario Department of Lands and Forests.

_____. 1963.  *The hunting group -- hunting territory complex among the Mistassini Indians.*  National Museums of Canada Bulletin No. 195, Anthropological Series, No. 63.  Ottawa: Department of Northern Affairs and National Resources.

_____. 1967.  *The material culture of the Mistassini.*  National Museums of Canada Bulletin 218.

_____. 1969.  Band organization among the Indians of eastern subarctic Canada.  In *Contributions to anthropology: band societies,* ed. David Damas, pp. 21-50.  National Museums of Canada Bulletin 228.  Ottawa.

_____. 1972.  The Mistassini Cree.  In *Hunters and gatherers today,* ed. M. G. Bicchieri, pp. 90-137.  New York: Holt, Rinehart and Winston.

_____. 1973.  *The quest for food and furs: the Mistassini Cree, 1953-1954.*  Publications in Ethnology No. 5.  Ottawa: National Museums of Canada.

Rogers, E. S., and Black, M. B. 1976.  Subsistence strategy in the fish and hare period, northern Ontario: the Weagamow Ojibwa, 1880-1920.  *J. Anthrop. Res.* 32:1-43.

Ross, E. B. 1978.  Food taboos, diet, and hunting strategy: the adaptation to animals in Amazonian cultural ecology.  *Curr. Anthrop.* 19:1-36.

Rowe, J. S. 1972. *Forest regions of Canada*. Department of the Environment, Canadian Forestry Service Publication No. 1300.

Rowe, J. S., and Scotter, G. W. 1973. Fire in the boreal forest. *Quat. Res.* 3:444-64.

Royama, T. 1970. Factors governing the hunting behavior and selection of food by the great tit (*Parus major L.*). *J. Animal Ecol.* 39:619-68.

Sahlins, M. 1968. Notes on the original affluent society. In *Man the hunter*, ed. R. B. Lee and I. DeVore, pp. 85-89. Chicago: Aldine.

———. 1972. *Stone Age economics*. Chicago: Aldine.

———. 1976. *The use and abuse of biology*. Ann Arbor: University of Michigan Press.

Salop, S. 1978. Parables of information transmission in markets. In *The effects of information on consumer and market behavior*, ed. A. A. Mitchell, pp. 5-12. Washington, D.C.: American Marketing Association.

Sanger, G. A. 1972. Preliminary standing stock and biomass estimates of seabirds in the subarctic Pacific region. In *Biological oceanography of the north Pacific Ocean*, ed. A. Y. Takenouti, et al. Tokyo: Idemitsu Shoten.

Saraydar, S., and Shimada, I. 1971. A quantitative comparison of efficiency between a stone axe and a steel axe. *Am. Antiq.* 36:216-17.

———. 1973. Experimental archaeology: a new outlook. *Am. Antiq.* 38:344-50.

Schaffer, W. M. 1978. A note on the theory of reciprocal altruism. *Am. Natur.* 112:250-53.

Schaller, G. B., and Lowther, G. R. 1969. The relevance of carnivore behavior to the study of early hominids. *Southwestern J. Anthrop.* 25:307-41.

Schiffer, M. B. 1975. Archaeology as behavioral science. *Am. Anthrop.* 77:836-48.

———. 1976. *Behavioral archaeology*. New York: Academic Press.

Schoener, T. W. 1971. Theory of feeding strategies. *Ann. Rev. Ecol. Syst.* 2:369-404.

———. 1972. Mathematical ecology and its place among the sciences. *Science* 178:389-91.

———. n.d. Generality of the size-distance relation in models of optimal feeding. *Am. Natur.* (in press).

Seger, J. 1976. Models of gene action and the problem of behavior. Paper presented at the annual meeting of the American Anthropological Association, Washington, D.C.

Sekora, P. 1973. *Aleutian Islands National Wildlife Refuge wilderness study report*. Washington, D.C.: Government Printing Office.

Service, E. R. 1962. *Primitive social organization: an evolutionary perspective*. New York: Random House.

Shafi, M. I., and Yarranton, G. A. 1973a. Vegetational heterogeneity during a secondary (post-fire) succession. *Can. J. Bot.* 51:73-90.

———. 1973b. Diversity, floristic richness, and species evenness during a secondary (post-fire) succession. *Ecology* 54:897-902.

Sharp, Henry S. 1977. The Caribou-Eater Chipewyan: bilaterality, strategies in caribou hunting, and the fur trade. *Arctic Anthrop.* 14:35-40.

Shawcross, W. F. 1967. An evaluation of the theoretical capacity of a New Zealand harbor to carry a human population. *Tane* 13:3-11.

———. 1972. Energy and ecology: thermodynamic models in archaeology. In *Models in Archaeology*, ed. D. L. Clarke, pp. 577-618. London: Methuen.

Sih, A. 1979. Optimal diet: the relative importance of the parameters. *Am. Natur.* 113:460-63.

Silberbauer, G. S. 1972. The G/wi Bushmen. In *Hunters and gatherers today*, ed. M. G. Bicchieri, pp. 271-325. New York: Holt, Rinehart and Winston.

Simenstad, C. A., Estes, J. A., and Kenyon, K. W. 1978. Aleuts, sea otters, and alternate stable-state communities. *Science* 200:403-11.

Simon, H. A. 1956. Rational choice and the structure of the environment. *Psychol. Rev.* 65:129-38.

Siskind, J. 1973. Tropical forest hunters and the economy of sex. In *Peoples and cultures of native South America*, ed. D. R. Gross, pp. 226-41. Garden City, NY: Natural History Press.

Skoog, R. O. 1968. Ecology of the caribou (Rangifer tarandus granti) in Alaska. Ph.D. dissertation, University of California, Berkeley.

Slatyer, R. O. 1962. Climate of the Alice Springs area. In *General report on lands of the Alice Springs area, Northern Territory, 1956-57*, comp. R. A. Perry, pp. 109-28. Melbourne: Commonwealth Scientific and Industrial Research Organization.

Slobodin, R. 1962. Band organization of the Peel River Kutchin. National Museums of Canada Bulletin No. 197. Ottawa.

Slobodkin, L. B. 1962. Energy in animal ecology. *Adv. Ecol. Res.* 1:69-101.

————. 1968. How to be a predator. *Am. Zool.* 8:43-51.

————. 1973. On the inconstancy of ecological efficiency and the form of ecological theories. In *Growth by intussusception*, ed. E. S. Deevey, pp. 291-305. Trans. Conn. Acad. Arts and Sciences 44. Hamden, Conn.: Archon Books.

————. 1977. Evolution is no help. *World Archaeol.* 8:332-43.

Slobodkin, L. B., and Richman, S. 1961. Calories/gm. in species of animals. *Nature* 191:299.

Smith, B. D. 1975. Middle Mississippian exploitation of animal populations. University of Michigan Museum of Anthropology Anthropological Papers 57.

————. 1979. Measuring the selective utilization of animal species by prehistoric human populations. *Am. Antiq.* 44:155-60.

Smith, C. A. 1974. Economics of marketing systems: models from economic geography. *Annual Review of Anthropology* 3:167-201.

Smith, C. C. 1968. The adaptive nature of social organization in the genus of tree squirrels *Tamiascirius*. *Ecol. Monog.* 40:349-71.

Smith, E. A. 1978. Optimal foraging theory and the study of human hunter-gatherers. Paper presented at the 77th American Anthropological Association Meeting, Los Angeles, 1978.

————. 1979a. Data and theory in sociobiological explanation: a critique of van den Berghe and Barash. *Am. Anthrop.* 81:360-63.

————. 1979b. Human adaptation and energetic efficiency. *Hum. Ecol.* 7:53-74.

————. 1980. Evolutionary ecology and the analysis of human foraging behavior: an Inuit example from the east coast of Hudson Bay. Ph.D. dissertation, Cornell University.

Smith, H. I. 1901. The Saginaw Valley collection. *Am. Mus. J. (Suppl.)* 11:1-24.

Smith, J. G. E. 1970. The Chipewyan hunting group in a village context. *W. Can. J. Anthrop.* 1:60-66.

————. 1975. The ecological basis of Chipewyan socioterritorial organization. In *Proceedings: The Northern Athapaskan Conference*, pp. 12-24. National Museums of Canada Mercury Series, Canadian Ethnology Paper No. 27.

————. 1976. Local band organization of the Caribou-Eater Chipewyan. In *Chipewyan adaptations*. Special Issue, *Arctic Anthrop.* 13:12-24.

Smith, J. G. E. 1978. Economic uncertainty in an "original affluent society": caribou and Caribou-Eater adaptive strategies. *Arctic Anthrop*. 15:68-88.

Smith, J. N. M., and Sweatman, H. P. A. 1974. Food-searching behavior of titmice in patchy environments. *Ecology* 55:1216-32.

Southwood, T. R. E. 1976. Continuing the MacArthur tradition. *Science* 192:670-72.

Spaulding, D. J. 1964. Age and growth of female sea-lions in British Columbia. *J. Fish. Res. Brd. Can.* 21:415-17.

Spector, W. S., ed. 1956. *Handbook of biological data*. Philadelphia: W. B. Saunders.

Spencer, W. B. 1928. *Wanderings in wild Australia*. London: Macmillan.

Spencer, W. B., and Gillen, F. J. 1899. *Native tribes of central Australia*. London: Macmillan.

_____. 1927. *The Arunta*. London: Macmillan.

Spooner, B., ed. 1972. *Population growth: anthropological implications*. Cambridge, MA: Massachusetts Institute of Technology Press.

Stanley, O. 1976. Aboriginal communities on cattle stations in central Australia. *Australian Economic Papers* 15:158-70.

Stearns, Stephen C. 1976. Life-history tactics: a review of the ideas. *Q. Rev. Biol.* 51: 3-47.

Stenseth, N. C., and Hansson, L. 1979. Optimal food selection: a graphic model. *Am. Natur.* 113:373-89.

Stevens, F. 1974. *Aborigines in the Northern Territory cattle industry*. Canberra: Australian National University Press.

Steward, J. C., and Murphy, R. F., eds. 1977. *Evolution and ecology: essays on social transformation by Julian Steward*. Urbana: University of Illinois Press.

Steward, J. H. 1936. The economic and social basis of primitive bands. In *Essays in anthropology presented to A. L. Kroeber*, ed. R. H. Lowie, pp. 331-45. Berkeley: University of California Press.

_____. 1938. *Basin-plateau Aboriginal sociopolitical groups*. Bureau of American Ethnology Bulletin 120. Washington, D.C. (repr. 1970, University of Utah Press.)

_____. 1955. *Theory of culture change*. Urbana: University of Illinois Press.

_____. 1977. The concept and method of cultural ecology. In *Evolution and ecology: essays in social transformation by Julian H. Steward*, ed. Jane C. Steward and Robert F. Murphy, pp. 43-57. Urbana: University of Illinois Press. (Orig. pub. 1968.)

Stewart, F. L., and Stahl, P. W. 1977. Cautionary note on edible meat poundage figures. *Am. Antiq.* 42:267-70.

Strehlow, T. G. H. 1965. Culture, social structure, and environment in Aboriginal central Australia. In *Aboriginal man in Australia: essays in honour of Emeritus Professor A. P. Elkin*, ed. R. M. Brendt and C. M. Brendt, pp. 121-45. Sydney: Angus and Robertson.

Taggart, D. W. 1967. Seasonal patterns in settlement, subsistence and industries in the Saginaw Late Archaic. *Mich. Archaeol.* 13:153-70.

_____. n.d. Field summary of the Kretz Site (20SA380). Report on file, Great Lakes Range, University of Michigan Museum of Anthropology.

Tedrow, J. C. F. 1970. Soils of the subarctic regions. In *Ecology of the subarctic regions*, pp. 189-205. Paris: UNESCO.

Teleki, G. 1975. Primate subsistence patterns: collector-predators and gatherer-hunters. *J. Hum. Evol.* 4:125-84.

Terasmae, J. 1961.  Notes on late-Quaternary climatic changes in Canada.  *Annals N.Y. Acad. Sci.* 95:658-75.

_____. 1970.  Post-glacial muskeg development in northern Canada.  In *Proceedings of the 13th Muskeg Research Conference, 7 and 8 May 1970*, pp. 73-90.  National Research Council of Canada Associate Committee on Geotechnical Research Technical Memorandum 99.

Terrell, J., and Fagan, J. 1975.  The savage and the innocent: sophisticated techniques and naive theory in the study of human population genetics in Melanesia.  *Yearbook Phys. Anthrop.* 19:2-17.

Thomas, D. H. 1972.  A computer simulation model of Great Basin Shoshonean settlement patterns.  In *Models in archaeology*, ed. D. L. Clarke, pp. 671-704.  London: Methuen.

_____. 1973.  An empirical test for Steward's model of Great Basin settlement patterns.  *Am. Antiq.* 38:155-76.

_____. 1976.  *Figuring anthropology: first principles of probability and statistics.*  New York: Holt, Rinehart and Winston.

Thomas, R. B. 1973.  Human adaptation to a high Andean energy flow system.  Occasional Papers in Anthropology, No. 7.  University Park, Pennsylvania: Pennsylvania State University.

Thomas, R. B.; Winterhalder, B.; and McRae, S. 1979.  An anthropological approach to human ecology and adaptive dynamics.  *Yearbook Phys. Anthrop.* 22:1-46.

Thompson, P. R. 1975.  A cross-species analysis of carnivore, primate, and hominid behaviour.  *J. Hum. Evol.* 4:113-24.

Thompson, W. A.; Vertinsky, I.; and Krebs, J. R. 1974.  The survival value of flocking in birds: a simulation model.  *J. Anim. Ecol.* 43:785-820.

Tindale, N. B. 1931.  Geological notes on the Iliaura country north-east of the Macdonnell Range, central Australia.  *Trans. Royal Soc. South Australia* 55:32-38.

_____. 1953.  On some Australian Cossidae including the moth of the witjuiti (witchety) grub.  *Trans. Royal Soc. South Australia* 76:56-65.

_____. 1974.  *Aboriginal tribes of Australia.*  Canberra: Australian National University Press.

_____. 1977.  Adaptive significance of the Panara or grass seed culture of Australia.  In *Stone tools as cultural markers: change, evolution and complexity*, ed. R. V. S. Wright, pp. 340-49.  Canberra: Australian Institute of Aboriginal Studies.

_____. n.d.  Film of University of Adelaide Anthropological Expedition to MacDonald Downs, September, 1930.  South Australian Museum.

Tringham, R. 1978.  Experimentation, ethnoarchaeology, and the leapfrogs in archaeological methodology.  In *Explorations in ethnoarchaeology*, ed. R. A. Gould, pp. 169-99.  Albuquerque: University of New Mexico Press.

Turnbull, C. M. 1968.  The importance of flux in two hunting societies.  In *Man the hunter*, ed. R. B. Lee and I. DeVore, pp. 132-37.  Chicago: Aldine.

Turner, C. G., II; Turner, J. A.; and Richards, L. R. 1975.  The relation of Aleut population size to seasonality of marine fauna.  Paper presented at the 41st International Congress of Americanists, Mexico City.

Tuttle, R. H., ed. 1975.  *Socio-ecology and psychology of primates.*  The Hague: Mouton.

Usher, P. J. 1971.  *The Bankslanders: economy and ecology of a frontier trapping community.*  Vol. 2: *Economy and ecology.*  Northern Science Research Group Report NRSG 71-2.  Ottawa: Department of Indian Affairs and Northern Development.

Usher, P. J., and Church, M. 1969.  On the relationship of weight, length, and girth of the ringed seal (*Pusa hispida*) of the Canadian Arctic.  *Arctic* 22:120-29.

VanStone, J. W. 1963.  *The Snowdrift Chipewyan.*  Co-ordination and Research Center, Department of Northern Affairs and National Resources, Ottawa.

VanStone, J. W. 1974. *Athapaskan adaptations*. Chicago: Aldine.

Vayda, A. P., and McCay, B. J. 1975. New directions in ecology and ecological anthropology. *Ann. Rev. Anthrop.* 4:293-306.

Vayda, A. P., and Rappaport, R. A. 1968. Ecology, cultural and noncultural. In *Introduction to Cultural Anthropology*, ed. J. A. Clifton, pp. 477-97. New York: McGraw-Hill.

Vehrencamp, S. 1979. The roles of individual, kin, and group selection in the evolution of sociality. In *Handbook of behavioral neurobiology*. Vol. 3: *Social behavior and communication*, ed. P. Marler and J. G. Vandenbergh, pp. 351-94. New York: Plenum Press.

Veniaminov, I. 1840. *Notes on the islands of the Unalaska District*. St. Petersburg: Russian-American Co.

Verner, J. 1977. On the adaptive significance of territoriality. *Am. Natur.* 111:769-75.

Vickers, W. 1976. Cultural adaptations to Amazonian habitats: the Siona-Secoya of eastern Ecuador. Ph.D. dissertation, University of Florida, Gainesville.

Viereck, L. A. 1973. Wildfire in the taiga of Alaska. *Quat. Res.* 3:465-95.

Wagner, H. M. 1975. *Principles of operations research*, 2d ed. Englewood Cliffs, NJ: Prentice-Hall.

Walker, A., Hoeck, H. H., and Perez, L. 1978. Microwear of mammalian teeth as an indicator of diet. *Science* 201:908-10.

Walters, C. J., and Hilborn, R. 1978. Ecological optimization and adaptive management. *Ann. Rev. Ecol. Syst.* 9:157-88.

Ward, P., and Zahavi, A. 1973. The importance of certain assemblages of birds as "information centres" for food-finding. *Ibis* 115:517-34.

Washburn, S. L. 1976. Foreword. In *Kalahari hunter-gatherers*, ed. R. B. Lee and I. DeVore, pp. xv-xvii. Cambridge: Harvard University Press.

————. 1978. Animal behavior and social anthropology. In *Sociobiology and human nature*, ed. M. Gregor, A. Silvers, and D. Sutch, pp. 53-74. San Francisco: Jossey-Bass.

Washburn, S. L., and DeVore, I. 1961. Social behavior of baboons and early man. In *Social life of early man*, ed. S. L. Washburn, pp. 91-105. Viking Fund Publ. in Anthrop. No. 31. New York: Werner Gren Foundation.

Washburn, S. L., and Lancaster, C. S. 1968. The evolution of hunting. In *Man the hunter*, ed. R. B. Lee and I. DeVore, pp. 293-303. Chicago: Aldine.

Watt, B. K., and Merrill, A. L. 1963. *Composition of foods*. Agricultural Handbook No. 8. Washington, D.C.: U.S. Department of Agriculture.

Weiss, K. M. 1973. *Demographic models for anthropology*. Society for American Archaeology Memoir 27.

Werner, E. E., and Hall, D. J. 1974. Optimal foraging and the size selection of prey by the bluegill sunfish (*Lepomis macrochirus*). *Ecology* 55:1042-52.

Westoby, M. 1974. An analysis of diet selection by large generalist herbivores. *Am. Natur.* 108:290-304.

————. 1978. What are the biological bases of varied diets? *Am. Natur.* 111:627-31.

Wheat, J. B. 1972. The Olsen-Chubbuck Site: A Paleo-Indian bison kill. Society for American Archaeology Memoir 26.

White, J. P.; Crook, K. A. W.; and Ruxton, B. P. 1970. Kosipe: A Late Pleistocene site in the Papuan Highlands. *Proc. Prehistoric Soc.* 36:152-70.

White, J. P., and O'Connell, J. F. 1979. Australian prehistory: new aspects of antiquity. *Science* 203:21-28.

White, L. A. 1959. *The evolution of culture*. New York: McGraw-Hill.

White, T. E. 1953. A method of calculating the dietary percentage of various food animals utilized by Aboriginal peoples. *Am. Antiq.* 18:396-98.

Wiens, J. A. 1976. Population responses to patchy environments. *Ann. Rev. Ecol. Syst.* 7:81-120.

_____. 1977. On competition and variable environments. *Am. Sci.* 65:590-97.

Wiessner, P. W. 1977. Hxaro: a regional system of reciprocity for reducing risk among the !Kung San. Ph.D. dissertation, University of Michigan. Ann Arbor: University Microfilms.

Wilkinson, P. F. 1976. "Random" hunting and the composition of faunal samples from archaeological excavations: a modern example from New Zealand. *J. Archaeol. Sci.* 3:321-28.

Williams, B. J. 1968. The Birhor of India and some comments on band organization. In *Man the hunter,* ed. R. B. Lee and I. DeVore, pp. 126-31. Chicago: Aldine.

_____. 1974. *A model of band society.* Memoir of the Society for American Archaeology No. 29.

Williams, G. C. 1966. *Adaptation and natural selection.* Princeton: Princeton University Press.

Wilmsen, E. N. 1973. Interaction, spacing behavior, and the organization of hunting bands. *J. Anthrop. Res.* 29:1-31.

Wilson, D. S. 1976. Deducing the energy available in the environment: an application of optimal foraging theory. *Biotropica* 8:96-103.

Wilson, E. O. 1975. *Sociobiology: the new synthesis.* Cambridge, MA: Harvard University Press.

Winterhalder, B. 1977. Foraging strategy adaptations of the boreal forest Cree: an evaluation of theory and models from evolutionary ecology. Ph.D. dissertation, Department of Anthropology, Cornell University.

_____. 1978. Evolutionary ecology hypotheses concerning group formation in foraging populations. Paper presented at SUNY/Binghamton, Symposium on Aggregation/Dispersion among Hunter-Gatherers. April, 1978.

_____. 1980a. Canadian fur bearer cycles and Cree-Ojibwa hunting and trapping practices. *Am. Natur.* 115:870-79.

_____. 1980b. Environmental analysis in human evolution and adaptation research. *Hum. Ecol.* 8:135-70.

_____. 1980c. Competitive exclusion and hominid paleoecology. I. The competitive exclusion principle and determinants of niche relationships. *Yearbook Phys. Anthrop.* 23: 43-63.

_____. n.d.a History and ecology of the boreal zone in Ontario. In *Boreal forest adaptations: Algonkians of northern Ontario,* ed. A. T. Steegmann, Jr. New York: Plenum (in press).

_____. n.d.b Boreal foraging strategies. In *Boreal forest adaptations: Algonkians of northern Ontario,* ed. A. T. Steegmann, Jr. New York: Plenum (in press).

_____. n.d.c Competitive exclusion and hominid paleoecology. II. Limiting similarity, niche differentiation and the effects of cultural behavior. *Yearbook Phys. Anthrop.* 24 (in press).

Wissler, C. 1926. *The relation of nature to man in Aboriginal North America.* New York: Oxford University Press.

Wittenberger, J. F. 1980. Group size and polygamy in social mammals. *American Naturalist* 115:197-222.

Wobst, H. M. 1974. Boundary conditions for Paleolithic social systems: a simulation approach. *Am. Antiq.* 39:147-78.

Wobst, H. M. 1978.  The archaeo-ethnology of hunter-gatherers, or the tyranny of the ethnographic record in archaeology. *Am. Antiq.* 43:303-9.

Woldenburg, M. J. 1972.  The average hexagon in spatial hierarchies.  In *Spatial analysis in geomorphology*, ed. R. J. Chorley, pp. 323-52.  New York: Harper and Row.

Wolpoff, M. H. 1971.  Competitive exclusion among Lower Pleistocene hominids: the single species hypothesis.  *Man* 6:601-14.

_____. 1976.  Data and theory in paleoanthropological controversies.  *Am. Anthrop.* 78: 94-98.

Woodburn, J. 1968.  An introduction to Hadza ecology.  In *Man the hunter*, ed. R. B. Lee and I. DeVore, pp. 49-55.  Chicago: Aldine.

_____. 1972.  Ecology, nomadic movement, and the composition of the local group among hunters and gatherers: an East African example and its implications.  In *Man, settlement and urbanism*, ed. P. J. Ucko, et al., pp. 193-206.  New York: Schenkman.

Wooster, H. A., Jr., and Blanck, F. C. 1950.  *Nutritional data*.  Pittsburgh: H. J. Heinz.

Wrangham, R. W. 1977.  Feeding behaviour of chimpanzees in Gombe National Park, Tanzania.  In *Primate ecology*, ed. T. H. Clutton-Brock, pp. 503-38.  New York: Academic Press.

Wright, H. E., Jr., and Heinselman, M. L. 1973.  Introduction: the ecological role of fire in natural conifer forests of western and northern North America.  *Quat. Res.* 3:319-28.

Wright, R. V. S., ed. 1971.  *Archaeology of the Gallus Site*.  Canberra: Australian Institute of Aboriginal Studies.

Worsnop, T. 1897.  *The prehistoric arts, manufactures, works, weapons, etc. of the Aborigines of Australia*.  Adelaide: Government Printer.

Yallop, C. 1969.  The Aljawara and their territory.  *Oceania* 39:187-97.

_____. 1977.  *Alyawarra: an Aboriginal language of central Australia*.  Canberra: Australian Institute of Aboriginal Studies.

Yarnell, R. A. 1964.  Aboriginal relationships between culture and plant life in the upper Great Lakes region.  University of Michigan Museum of Anthropology Anthropological Paper 23.

Yellen, J. E. 1976.  Settlement pattern of the !Kung: an archaeological perspective.  In *Kalahari hunter-gatherers*, ed. R. B. Lee and I. DeVore, pp. 47-72.  Cambridge, MA: Harvard University Press.

_____. 1977.  *Archaeological approaches to the present: models for reconstructing the past*.  New York: Academic Press.

Yellen, J. E., and Harpending, H. 1972.  Hunter-gatherer populations and archaeological inference.  *World Archaeol.* 4:244-53.

Yellen, J. E., and Lee, R. B. 1976.  The Dobe-/Du/da environment.  In *Kalahari hunter-gatherers*, ed. R. B. Lee and I. DeVore, pp. 27-46.  Cambridge, MA: Harvard University Press.

Yengoyan, A. A. 1968.  Demographic and ecological influences on Aboriginal Australian marriage sections.  In *Man the hunter*, ed. R. B. Lee and I. DeVore, pp. 185-99.  Chicago: Aldine.

Yesner, D. R. 1976.  Aleutian Island albatrosses: a population history.  *Auk* 93:263-80.

_____. 1977a.  Prehistoric subsistence and settlement in the Aleutian Islands.  Ph.D. dissertation.  Ann Arbor: University Microfilms.

_____. 1977b.  Avian exploitation, occupational seasonality, and paleoecology of the Chugachik Island site.  *Anthropological Papers of the University of Alaska* 18:23-30.

_____. 1977c.  Resource diversity and population stability among hunter-gatherers.  *W. Can. J. Anthrop.* 7:18-59.

Yesner, D. R. 1978.  Animal bones and human behavior.  *Rev. Anthrop.*  8:333-55.

_____. 1979.  Nutrition and cultural evolution: patterns in prehistory.  In *Nutritional anthropology: evolutionary perspectives*, ed. N. Jerome, et al.  Pleasantville, NY: Redgrave.

_____. 1980.  Maritime hunter-gatherers: ecology and prehistory.  *Curr. Anthrop.* 21:727-50.

Yesner, D. R., and Aigner, J. S. 1976.  Comparative biomass estimates and prehistoric cultural ecology of the southwest Umnak region, Aleutian Islands.  *Arctic Anthrop.* 13:91-112.

# List of Contributors

William H. Durham
Department of Anthropology
Stanford University
Stanford, California 94305

Kristen Hawkes
Department of Anthropology
University of Utah
Salt Lake City, Utah 84112

Sheri Heffley
Department of Anthropology
Stanford University
Stanford, California 94305

Arthur S. Keene
Department of Anthropology
University of Massachusetts
Amherst, Massachusetts 01003

James A. Moore
Department of Anthropology
Queens College of the City
  University of New York
Flushing, New York 11367

James F. O'Connell
Department of Anthropology
University of Utah
Salt Lake City, Utah 84112

Eric Alden Smith
Department of Anthropology
University of Washington
Seattle, Washington 98195

Bruce Winterhalder
Department of Anthropology
University of North Carolina
Chapel Hill, North Carolina 27514

David R. Yesner
Department of Geography-Anthropology
University of Southern Maine
Gorham, Maine 04038

# Index

Animal resources, 151, 166
  birds, 57-61, 86, 89, 117, 131, 140,
    152-70
    seabirds and shorebirds, 152-70
    waterfowl, 57-60, 73, 78-97
  fish, 57-60, 73, 78-97, 131-46, 152, 154
    marine invertebrates, 152-55
  insects and reptiles, 101, 109-10, 117-25
  mammals
    large game, 41, 96, 131-33, 140-43;
      caribou, 57-63, 79-90, 126-46,
      178; moose, 74-94, 126, 132-33,
      140-45
    marsupials, 101, 117
    sea mammals, 43, 56-64, 152-58,
      224-25
    small game, 40, 73-96, 126-45, 152,
      157-58; furbearers, 57, 86-87,
      90-91, 93, 137 (see also
      Technology: traps, snares)
Archeology, 4-6, 8, 12, 34, 126, 171, 182
  and gathering, 188
  and nonmarginal environment, 171-93
  and optimal foraging theory, 8-12, 14,
    34-35, 66, 95-98, 148-70, 171-93;
    colonization, 114-16
    diet breadth model, 10, 96, 115,
      150-70, 172-93
    group models, 150, 161, 164, 169
    linear programming, 10-11, 172-93
    marginal value theorem, 97, 115
    patch choice model, 96-97, 149-50,
      167, 169

Band societies, 3-5, 7, 19, 41. *See also*
  Group models
Biomass, as energy currency, 148, 151-64,
  226

Capture rate: energy. *See* Energy; Energy
  efficiency
Capture rate: prey, and group formation,
  39-40, 43, 50
Cash economy, 17, 54, 56 n.2, 60, 67, 70-71,
  86, 88-89, 101-2, 137, 229. *See also*
  Currency; Nonforaging constraints
Colonization
  Australia, 10, 113-16
  North America, 97

Computer simulation of optimal behavior,
  11, 195-96, 202-17, 221
Cost-benefit theory, and optimal foraging
  models, 17, 20, 22-35. *See also*
  Currency
Currency (cost-benefit measure), 9, 67
  model and theory, 20-22, 23-35 passim,
    37-38, 173-74
  refinements and constraints (linear
    programming model), 174-82, 191-92
  *See also individual models;* Biomass;
    Cash economy; Cost-benefit theory;
    Energy; Energy efficiency; Multi-
    variate currency; Nutrients, as
    currency; Time and energy costs

Decision-making. *See* Strategy analysis
Diet breadth model (MacArthur and Pianka),
  10, 13-14, 22, 25, 148-50, 226
  applied, 57, 92, 101-25, 152-63
  described, 27-35 passim, 68, 107-10,
    150, 173-74; graphic analysis,
    23-26
  and food sharing, 46
  and group size, 46-50
  and patch choice, 27
  and processing costs, 108-10
  refinements and constraints, 11, 26, 69,
    84-90, 92, 94, 96-97, 109-10, 151,
    160, 163-69, 226; graphic analysis,
    183-84; regional, long-term, 113-16;
    linear programming model, 171-93

Encounter rate, 39-40, 43, 50, 52, 150, 164,
  169; and high-ranked resources, 108,
  110, 113
Energy (caloric value), quantification
  for costs, 71, 109, 118-25
  for resource returns, 52, 71, 96, 109,
    118-25, 166, 168-69; in archeologi-
    cal contexts, 149-151; seasonal and
    intraspecies fluctuations, 52, 56,
    181
Energy efficiency
  described, 13, 15, 19, 20-22, 23-35
    passim, 52-53, 150-52, 164; seasonal,
    81-87
  as measure of adaptability, 3, 20, 67,
    230

Energy efficiency *(continued)*
    refinements and constraints to model,
        10-11, 92, 105, 107 n.3, 108-16,
        118-25, 164-68, 221, 224, 230; linear
        programming model, 171-93 passim;
        regional applications, 194, 200
    *See also* Currency; Energy; Time and
        energy costs; individual models;
        various constraints
Environment
    affected by foragers, 28-30
    change in, long-term, 17-18, 33, 192,
        207-9
    disturbed: by natural fires, 78, 103,
        108-9, 112-13; for game management,
        141; long-term, 174
    effects on foraging (season, climate,
        terrain), 66, 72-90, 94, 104-6, 133,
        138, 144
    energy shortages in, 21, 67, 228
    heterogeneous, 13, 23, 26-30, 66-98
        passim, 200; causes, 68; "interstice
        pattern," 90-91 (*see also* Marginal
        value theorem; Patch choice model)
    homogeneous, 23, 152-63
    nonmarginal, 171-93, 230-31
    "richness," 69, 127

Fluctuation of resources, 21, 25, 129, 134,
    146, 180
    long-term, 79-91, 140-41, 146
    regional, 207-9
    seasonal (migration), 151-52, 167, 169;
        environmental causes, 67, 74, 80,
        94; and group distribution, 131-45;
        observed, 156-60, 162-65
Food consumption efficiency, 56, 71, 137
Food preservation and storage, 40, 46, 50,
    63 n.4, 140, 142, 144
    and diet breadth, 165, 174
    and Horn's model, 146-47
    in linear programming model, 181
    nuts, 188-89
    and risk, 179-80
Food processing
    costs, 10, 55, 82 n.1, 108-25, 177-79,
        188-89, 191, 225
    defined, 105-8
    and diet breadth model, 108-10, 115
    and patch choice model, 115
    in prehistoric contexts, 150, 161
    technology, 101, 110, 115, 155, 189
Food sharing, 40-41, 45-47, 50, 52-53, 63,
    96, 146; risk, 179-80
Forager mobility, 13, 27-30, 41, 72, 88-89,
    127, 137-46, 164. *See also* Foraging
    strategy; Group models, group distribu-
    tion; Patch choice model; Transport
Foragers, human
    defined, 23
    effect on environment, 17-18, 28-30 (*see
        also* Resource conservation)
    population, 44, 47-48, 50, 97; and
        agricultural expansion, 209-11;
        contemporary, 34
    unique behaviors, 34, 147 (*see also*
        Information sharing)
Foraging, defined, 14, 16-17

Foraging area, 44, 50, 149, 151-52, 194-217
    passim
    models described and evaluated, 26-35;
        regional, 202
    *See also* Group models, central place
        theory
Foraging pathway, 26, 29, 69, 93. *See also*
    Marginal value theorem; Patch choice
    model
Foraging phases
    pursuit, 24-25, 68, 82 n.1, 178-80
    search, 24-25, 68, 82 n.1, 177-80
    search and pursuit, as combined function
        (*see* Marginal value theorem; Patch
        choice model)
    *See also* Nonrandom search; Time and
        energy costs
Foraging strategies, 24-29, 66-69, 95
    for caribou, 134-37
    gathering, 10, 99-125, 187-89, 221, 225
    generalization/specialization, 23-25,
        27, 29, 69, 81, 90-91, 93, 96-97
    "hunt type" model, 51-54, 64-65;
        applied, 54-65
    "interstice pattern" model, 90-91
    multispecies ("coharvesting"), 59-61,
        63, 84-86, 137, 162, 165, 167;
        gathering, 99-125
    regional, and information sharing,
        194-217, 220-21
    regional change in, long-term (coloniza-
        tion), 113-16
    seasonal, 56-63, 66-98 passim, 104-5,
        109 n.5, 111-13, 118-25, 131-47,
        172-93 passim, 221 (*see also*
        Fluctuation of resources)
    *See also* Foraging phases; Group models;
        Groups observed; Strategy analysis

Graphic analysis, 18-20. *See also individ-*
    *ual models*
Group models, 9, 30-35, 36-42, 97, 126, 149,
    192-96, 200-202
    central place theory (foraging area
        model), 46-47, 127, 140, 146, 150,
        164, 197-200; graphic analysis, 11,
        13, 31-32; nonhexagonal critique,
        201-17
    group distribution, 5, 13, 30-32, 38,
        47-48, 50; seasonal, 10, 62, 126-47,
        164, 169, 220
    group location, 18, 150; location costs,
        200-217; and risk, 179
    group size, 9, 13-14, 22, 30-32, 36-65,
        62, 126, 137-47, 220, 222-24;
        graphic analysis, 37, 42, 48-49,
        222-23; and risk, 179-80
    group social organization, 9, 40-65, 96,
        137-47, 194-217 passim
    Horn's model (group distribution), 47,
        126-47, 220; and clumped, predict-
        able resources, 146-47; graphic
        analysis, 10, 30-32
    regional group distribution and organi-
        zation, 11, 41, 113-16, 134-47;
        location costs, 200-217 passim;
        seasonal, 11, 150, 194-217, 220-21

Groups observed
  Aleuts, 152-70
  Alyawara, 99-125
  Chipewyan, 129-31, 134-40, 146
  computer-simulated regional group
    structure, 202-16
  Cree, 66, 70, 72-81
  Ingalik, 129, 131-32, 142, 144-46
  Inukjuamiut Inuit, 9, 30, 36, 51-65
  Late Archaic group, 182-91
  Upper Tanana, 129, 132-33, 140-43, 146

Historical constraints, 16, 33, 87-89, 228-
  29. See also Technology; Transport
Hunting, defined, 16. See also Foraging
  phases; Foraging strategies

Individuals, in group models, 30, 38, 44,
  50-51, 57-64, 220
Information sharing, 30, 43-44, 50, 194-96,
  200, 214-17
  costs, 200, 203-4
  and diet breadth model, 174
  and group models, 31-32, 39-41, 43-47,
    50, 64, 126, 138-39, 146-47
  in linear programming model, 177
  long-term, 17-18, 192
  and marginal value theorem, 29
  regional 11, 194-217, 220-21
  and risk, 180
  seasonal, 138-39, 146-47

Knowledge, 28, 90, 93, 194-217, 221. See
  also Information sharing; Nonrandom
  search; Reconnaissance

Linear programming, 10-11, 18, 172
  applied to diet breadth model, 174-81;
    empirical test, 182-91
  described 175-77
  refinements and constraints, 191-93, 221

Marginal value theorem (Charnov), 28-35, 69,
  111 n.8, 148-49; graphic analysis, 28-29
  applied, 66-98
  refinements and constraints, 66-89
    passim; graphic analysis, 226-28;
    long-term, 180-81; linear programming
    model, 180-81
Modeling theory, 1, 4-5, 7-8, 11, 18-20,
  51-52, 65, 67, 92, 191-97. See also
  Computer simulation; Graphic analysis;
  Optimal foraging models
Multivariate currency, 10, 11, 172-74, 221
  applied, 182-89
  model, 172-82
  refinements and constraints, 183-93, 221

Nonfood use of resources, 42, 51, 54, 137,
  140-41, 165-68
  in multivariate currency, 173, 181,
    183-86, 189, 196
  prehistoric, 158
  trapping for money, 70-71, 86, 88, 137
Nonforaging constraints, 137, 229
  agricultural expansion and production,
    171-72, 179, 187
  hunting laws, 71
  nonforaged resources, 67, 70, 99, 101-2,
    107, 110, 115-16, 225

Nonforaging constraints (continued)
  risk of foraging, compared with non-
    foraging activity, 51, 179-80,
    209-11
  See also Cash economy; Environment,
    effects on foraging
Nonhuman foragers, 45, 85, 116, 148, 172-
  73, 177
  birds, 7, 13, 21, 39, 44, 127
  carnivores/herbivores, 21
  fish, 13
  mammals, 7, 39, 65
    hominids, 34, 96-97
    primates, 7, 13, 26, 34, 39, 65, 97
    social carnivores, 30, 34, 38, 97
Nonrandom search, 27, 93, 177-78, 194-217
  passim, 220-21
Nutrients, 15, 67, 148
  as "binding constraints," 186-89
  as constraints in energy currency, 166,
    168-89
  as currency, 21-22, 42, 43, 51
  in multivariate currency, 10-11, 173,
    176, 181-89 passim
  quantification, for resource returns,
    96, 181

Optimal foraging models, 6-12, 13-35 passim,
  148-49
  assumptions, 13, 15-20, 22
  currency selection, 20-22, 33
  hypothesis testing, 15, 19-20, 32-33,
    97-98, 149-50
  recognition of constraints, 16, 22,
    32-33
  "sufficient parameters," 32-33, 37-40,
    42, 52
  time scales, 17-18, 32-33, 78, 80-81,
    93, 192, 229
  treatment of empirical evidence, 16,
    18, 32-35, 94, 96
  value as models, 11-12, 18-20, 32-35,
    42, 65, 67, 92, 95, 116, 126-28,
    148-50, 168-69, 173-74, 176, 190-
    97, 200-202, 217, 218-31
  See also Diet breadth model; Foraging
    strategies; Group models; Marginal
    value theorem; Modeling theory;
    Patch choice model; Socioecology

Patch choice model (MacArthur and Pianka),
  9, 22, 81, 148-49
  applied, 66-98
  described, 28-35 passim, 68-69, 110,
    113; graphic analysis, 26-27
  "hunt type" model, 56-57
  refinements and constraints, 90-93,
    96-97, 111-16; regional, long-term,
    113-16
Plant resources, 4, 10, 46, 121, 225
  and multivariate currency, 186-89
  nuts, 178-79, 188-90
  seeds, 99, 107-10, 113 n.9, 114-25
  as sessile prey, 43-44, 178
  varieties, Australian, 101-25 passim

Ranked resources
  by actual harvest, 86
  by biomass, 86; prehistoric, 150-52,
    152-63, 168-69, 226

Ranked resources *(continued)*
    by energy efficiency, 24-25, 68, 110,
       113, 115, 150-52, 160-68, 221-226
       *(see also* Diet breadth model; Patch
       choice model)
    in linear programming model, 175-77
    by pursuit and processing costs, 99, 108
    by pursuit costs, 84
    by risk, 86, 94
    by search and pursuit costs, 96
    by seasonal energy return, 81-87
Reconnaissance, 18, 93, 112-13, 195, 225.
    *See also* Information sharing; Knowledge
Recurrence (return time), 28-29, 44, 50,
    78-79, 94, 201
Resource conservation
    by "game management," 16, 93, 97, 141,
       201, 226-28
    by taboos, 166
Resource depletion. *See* Marginal value
    theorem; Patch choice model; Recurrence
Risk
    of foraging, compared with nonforaging
       activity, 51, 179-80, 209-11
    as physical hazard, 67, 165, 167-79, 179
    as possibility of foraging failure, 39,
       40, 42, 46, 50, 94, 179-80, 207-11,
       214-15, 223-25; as currency, 173-74,
       179-80, 190, 200-201; in regional
       models, 207-11, 214-15; quantifica-
       tion, as cost, 96

Settlement pattern. *See* Group models, *esp.*
    group distribution
Sociocultural constraints, 28, 40, 48-49,
    92, 225-26, 229
    "healthiness" of bush food, 67
    local food preferences, 114, 165-69, 228
    prestige of foraging expertise, 67, 89,
       165-69
    recreational goals, 59, 65, 67, 226
    taboos, of food, 165-69
    taboos, inimical spirits in foraging
       site, 112
    *See also* Group models, social organiza-
       tion; Historical constraints; Non-
       foraging constraints; Technology;
       Transport
Socioecology, 1-12, 13-35, 218-31
    applicability, 5-9
    defined, 1
    history and scope, 1-7, 148-49
    *See also* Optimal foraging models
Specialization. *See* Foraging strategies,
    generalization/specialization
Stalking, 178
Starvation, 21, 67, 144, 146, 228
Strategy analysis, 17-18, 22-35 passim, 94,
    173, 194-95, 220-21
    independence of decision sets, 22
    prehistoric contexts, 95-96
    tracking and pursuit decision, 86

Taste, 107, 166, 168-69. *See also* Sociocul-
    tural constraints
Technology, 21, 56, 87-89, 90-91, 94-95,
    113, 149-50, 165-68, 174, 181-82, 229
    cash costs, 56 n.2, 71, 96
    gathering tools, 101
    guns, 54, 58-60, 63, 85-89, 92, 102
    harpoons, 58-60, 63

Technology *(continued)*
    ice-hole foraging for fish and seals,
       43, 56-64 passim
    nets, 54, 57-60, 80, 82, 87, 138,
       141-42; weirs, fishtraps, 141-44
    and prey types pursued, 85
    and pursuit, 178
    toolmaking, 165-68
    traps, snares, 61, 70-71, 80-92 passim,
       137, 141, 142; search-pursuit
       costs, 82 n.1
    *See also* Nonfood use of resources;
       Transport
Time and energy costs
    and diet breadth model, 24-25
    "handling" as capture, retrieval, and
       processing, 150, 162, 169
    and marginal value theorem, 28-30
    processing, 10, 55, 82 n.1, 108-25,
       177-79, 191; nuts, 188-89
    pursuit, 24-25, 32, 68, 81-84; gathering
       as pursuit, 107-13, 118-25, 178
    pursuit and processing, 10, 108
    quantification, 52, 54-56, 70, 96, 149;
       fuel costs, 56 n.2, 71
    search, 24-25, 32, 68, 81, 93, 112,
       201; by mechanized transport, 70,
       87-90; nonrandom, 27, 93, 177-78,
       194-217 passim, 220-21
    search and pursuit, 26-27, 82 n.1, 92,
       94; and ranked resources, 96; in
       linear programming model, 177-80;
       of trapping, 82 n.1; seasonal, 81-84
    search/pursuit ratio: 25, 44, 50, 89-90;
       described, 68; in diet breadth model,
       9, 66-98; in patch choice model,
       27-29
    and time shortages, 67
    travel: between and within patches, 27,
       69, 93 *(see also* Marginal value
       theorem; Patch choice model); to
       and from foraging area, 31, 47, 50,
       56, 82 n.1, 108 n.4, 110, 112
Time scales, in optimal tests. *See* Optimal
    foraging models, time scales
Tracking: and optimal models, 90-92; and
    technology, 88-89; as pursuit, 68, 82
    n.1, 86; as search, 90-91; versus
    stalking, 178
Transport
    modern, mechanized, 87-89, 90, 93, 95,
       113, 229; fuel and depreciation
       costs, 56 n.2, 71; search time,
       87-89
    airplanes, 70
    automobiles, 102-7, 110-13
    outboard canoes, 54-56, 58-60, 63,
       70, 73-74, 84, 87-90
    snowmobiles, 54-56, 58-61, 70, 86-90
    modern, nonmechanized, 58-60, 72-73, 84,
       86-87, 89; preferred for search, 70
    prehistoric/premodern, 89-90, 95, 137,
       141, 144, 164